HARVARD HISTORICAL STUDIES ◆ 188

Published under the auspices
of the Department of History
from the income of the
Paul Revere Frothingham Bequest
Robert Louis Stroock Fund
Henry Warren Torrey Fund

A BUSINESS OF STATE

*Commerce, Politics, and the Birth
of the East India Company*

RUPALI MISHRA

Harvard University Press

*Cambridge, Massachusetts
London, England
2018*

First printing

Library of Congress Cataloging-in-Publication Data

Names: Mishra, Rupali Raj, 1981– author.
Title: A business of state : commerce, politics, and the birth of the
    East India Company / Rupali Mishra.
Other titles: Harvard historical studies.
Description: Cambridge, Massachusetts : Harvard University Press,
    2018. | Series: Harvard historical studies | Includes bibliographical
    references and index.
Identifiers: LCCN 2017041765 | ISBN 9780674984561 (hardcover :
    alk. paper)
Subjects: LCSH: East India Company—History—17th century. |
    Corporations, British—India—History—17th century. | Business
    and politics—England—History—17th century. | England—
    Economic conditions—17th century.
Classification: LCC HF486.E6 M57 2018 | DDC 382.0941/05—dc23
    LC record available at https://lccn.loc.gov/2017041765

Contents

Note on Spelling, Dates, and Sources

Spelling and punctuation in the sources have been modernized, and all abbreviations have been expanded. The dates are old style, though the year is taken to begin on 1 January.

Whenever possible when citing from contemporary correspondence, I have noted the letter-writer, the recipient, and the date. In those cases where the writer or recipient is understood, I have not explicitly identified them. For example, citations from *The Letters of John Chamberlain* are always to letters written by John Chamberlain.

In the interest of making my citations from the East India Company court books easier rather than harder to find, I have cited them by date instead of by page number. Even though most entries are more than one page long, the numbering system of the volumes is erratic, and some volumes are not numbered in entirety; the date is therefore a more reliable and consistent aid to finding the source than a page number.

Lastly, unless otherwise noted, all citations from the court books are citations from meetings of the court of committees; I have specified when the meeting was a general court or other meeting.

A BUSINESS OF STATE

Introduction

SOMETIME IN EARLY 1617, an unidentified author at court compiled "an estimate showing what benefit his Majesty may make by the trade to the East Indies." The document listed several suggestions for how King James might turn the East Indies trade into ready money beyond what it already afforded him in customs revenue. Anticipating possible concerns, the author specified that what he proposed would "neither touch the king's honor, decrease his customs, nor tax the [East India] Company with any charge or loss worth the speaking of, nor disturb or alter the course they are now in, which are the most material things that may be objected."[1]

The proposals enumerated in the memo were creative and only questionably legal. After downplaying the political clout of East India Company members—characterized as "for the most part . . . rich gentlemen, merchants, and usurers that adventure out of the superfluity of their estate," alongside a "few lords and others of the [Privy] Council" who had been granted membership primarily to make the regime more sympathetic to the Company—the author emphasized how dependent the entire East Indies venture was on the royal prerogative. He noted that the Company's patent allowed for the monarch to revoke it with three years' notice, and he suggested that the monarch ought to use the threat of dissolution to compel payments of loans.[2] Each of the schemes described in the memo involved the transfer of money from Company members to the monarch. For example, one involved requiring investors to "lend his Majesty ten pounds *gratis* for three years," for each hundred pounds they invested in the Company. Another stated that since the Company collected a fine before allowing someone to become a member and "adventure" their money, "there is no reason why any should not give willingly to his Majesty as much as to private men," and the king should simply require thousand-pound investors to also pay him a hundred pounds. These demands might drive away the "obstinate and foolish" who would rather lose the investment opportunity than pay their sovereign the hundred pounds, but the author asserted that most would pay. Other proposals involved loans at 10 percent interest, with the loaned money to be invested in the Company. Such monies, the memo promised, were guaranteed—at least, based on past Company performance—to double within three years.[3]

This stray document in the Jacobean state papers is strange, even a little mysterious. The corresponding volume of the Company's court minutes for 1617 has not survived, so it is difficult for the historian to gauge the immediate circumstances that led to the document's creation or to determine whether it led to any action, and if so, what. Whether Company leaders had any knowledge of the memo is similarly unknown.[4]

In other ways, though, it is a very typical document, reflecting James's well-known lack of funds and use of innovative financial schemes by outlining an unlikely proposal for how James might quickly and easily secure a huge and renewable source of funding from the East India Company. The author mentioned an immediate sum of some £120,000, with more within three years. He anticipated that the requisitioned money would at least double as long as the Company's trade continued to be as profitable as it had been thus far, and in 1617 there was no reason to doubt that the phenomenal returns would continue.

Regardless of its outcome, the memo pointed to the curious relationship between the Company and the crown. Note, for example, the author's easy recourse to threats of dissolution via revocation of the patent, even as he noted that his suggestions should not hinder the Company's trade. He purported to have quantitative knowledge of the Company's recent profitability and demonstrated familiarity with and knowledge of the membership and functioning of the Company, while at the same time slighting its composition. It is not impossible that the author himself was part of the Company. The author saw the East Indies trade as something that already benefited the monarch, but that could be used to further advantage via the same tool that enabled the Company's existence. The document therefore highlighted the function of the royal prerogative in the early history of the Company, and ultimately the thorny relationship of the Company to the state.

What is also notable about this document is what it did not mention: empire. The author wrote of the East Indies trade, the monarch's honor, and adventuring. The schemes he suggested were predicated on the profitability of England's overseas ventures. Yet neither "empire" nor "imperial" as descriptors applied to what he sought to harness for James. Instead he spoke of "trade," "stock," "customs," and "taxes." When he imagined amending the Company to further benefit the state, it had to be through means that would not "disturb or alter the course they are now in"—in other words, that would not change its commercial character.

At the heart of this book is the very complicated relationship between the East India Company and the state in early seventeenth-century England. The leaders of the Company in the early 1600s knew that the trade they carried out in Asia was a matter of interest and importance to the English state. One Company member and early economic theorist, Thomas Mun, declared that trade was "the very *touchstone* of a kingdom's prosperity." Another Company leader observed that the Company was "composed of the greatest part of the Privy Council, of the nobility, of the judges of the land, the gentry of the kingdom, and [was] furnished with an assured stock of sixteen hundred thousand pounds [that is, £1,600,000]."[5] The Company was more than a commercial venture, these men contended; it was the key to England's future, and recognized as such by the nation's leaders.

The confident tone of Company insiders was not mere boasting; the regime echoed their high appraisals of the Company's importance. Privy Councilors characterized the Company and its trade as a "business of state," and their concerns as "matter[s] of state."[6] They negotiated and interested themselves in Company affairs as a matter of course, and a number of them were Company members. The early Stuart regimes took a surprisingly active role in the conducting of England's overseas enterprises, working closely with the merchants who directly ran the trade.

Despite these contemporary evaluations of the worth and importance of the Company, the early history of the East India Company is almost a blank. It has little place in works that focus on the eighteenth- and nineteenth-century heyday of the Company's power, and it barely exists in either the political history of the early seventeenth century or the history of seventeenth-century English overseas expansion. It is sometimes gestured toward but rarely studied, which is curious, as it might be expected to have a natural home in any of these larger fields.[7] The relative paucity of work is especially striking given how the East India Company has long been a representative institution of British imperial activity in the popular imagination. Its eighteenth- and nineteenth-century iterations have become shorthand for both the successes and excesses of mercantilism and empire. The early history of the Company, however, remains opaque, from its activities in the East Indies to those in London.[8]

Yet documents like the 1617 memo mentioned above should prompt historians to rethink institutions like the East India Company, their role in the development of the English state, and the meaning and use of overseas expansion. Such documents point out the importance of focusing on the Company's actions and meanings in London, at the center of the political nation. Not only did bodies like the Company mediate England's overseas experiences, but it was through these bodies that people understood and revealed their understanding of the functioning of power and the state. Using the rich archives left by the Company, *A Business of State* reveals the continuous and involved negotiations—within the Company, involving the Company, and outside of the Company—that characterized its daily functioning in the early seventeenth century.

For while the Company certainly operated far from England—indeed, its raison d'être was to develop and run a trade in the East Indies—it was based in London and rooted in that time and place. *A Business of State* traces the extensive involvement that the state—be it king, Privy Council, or occasionally Parliament—had in the life and functioning of the Company, and the extensive involvement that the Company had in the life and functioning of the state. The wider political context of the early seventeenth century shaped the Company as an institution in meaningful ways. It is impossible to understand the Company divorced from the City and Whitehall, or from the growing print market and networks of news transmission. Understanding how the Company functioned in its early years therefore requires delving into its political life.

The East India Company

What made the East India Company so distinctive? Early modern Londoners were familiar with all manner of companies. From the livery companies that organized many professions to the corporation of London that governed and ran the city, companies and corporations were an ever-present part of daily life in the city. They organized public demonstrations and civic pageantry to show their importance and promote corporate identity.[9] They sometimes loaned money to the crown. They chose their own leaders and governed themselves.[10] The chartering of the East India Company in 1600 added one more corporate body to a city that already had its fair share, and indeed, many of the founders of the East India Company belonged to one or more other corporate institutions in London.

Yet while the East India Company had some functional similarities to the Grocers' Company or the Vintners' Company, or to Bristol or London (as incorporated towns), it also differed in key ways from those corporate bodies, and even from other overseas trading companies. The amount of money the Company could command, for example, far outstripped that of most other corporate bodies. Initially, Company members had invested in specific voyages, but by the 1610s the Company had instituted joint stocks, which ran over multiple years and funded multiple voyages. Before 1640, besides the early separate voyages, there were three joint stocks (from 1613 to 1623, from 1617 to 1632, and from 1631 to 1642). The first joint stock had a capitalization of £418,691, the second £1,629,040, and the third £420,700. In comparison, the entire yearly expenditure of the city of Leicester in the early seventeenth century was £400–600.[11] In short, the Company was capitalized on a scale with the government of the kingdom, rather than the government of a city.

The constitution of the Company's membership also set it apart from many other corporate bodies. Most of the Company's initial members were London merchants, but by 1620 a significant number of courtiers, nobles, and gentry had sworn their oaths and invested their money. These men sought out and were sought out by the leaders of the Company, and they brought with them not just their money but also their diverse expertise and connections. The Company's membership thus drew together merchants (a number of whom had their own personal or familial connections to members of the regime) as well as many courtiers and nobles. These men brought their influence and interests to bear on (and for) the Company.[12] Ultimately, the Company's membership spanned the social spectrum in a way that the members of few other corporate bodies did. The ties of membership were not the cause of the close relationship between Company leaders and the monarch and privy councilors, but they did amplify the connection between the regime and the "business of state."

Lastly, the particular logistical requirements of the East Indies trade made the Company distinct. The East Indies trade was arguably the most expensive and riskiest of the overseas trades. Few merchants had the individual wherewithal to fund a long-distance overseas venture, especially to the East Indies. Even a successful voyage might tie up an investor's money for months or years. A voyage to Virginia was one of the shortest overseas ventures, but it still took approximately nine weeks out and six weeks back.[13] From England to the coast of India took six months, and the voyage could be made only at certain times of the year. A round trip to the East Indies took at least a year and a half, but often three or four years if the ship had to make the rounds of the Company's trading posts in the East Indies. Weather and wind patterns in the Atlantic meant that year-round voyages could take place there. However, monsoon patterns in the Indian Ocean meant that a ship could depart from England only in the early part of the year. Missing the spring window meant missing the chance of a voyage for an entire year. Additionally, many ships that were sent out never returned. Between 1601 and 1640, the Company sent a total of 168 ships to the East Indies. In that same period, only 104 ships arrived from the East Indies.[14]

To manage the various risks and logistical difficulties of the East Indies trade, the Company's operation was completely centralized. There was one fleet each year, and no one owned individual parts of any ship. The joint stock not only minimized risk and expense, but it also ensured that all ventures were joint ventures.[15] East India Company investors subscribed money to a common fund that paid for the voyage, and when the ships returned profits were divided according to how much each person had subscribed. Company members profited or lost together. Not all overseas trading companies pooled money in this way or sent out shared ventures. The Levant Company did not, for example. Instead, merchants had to be members of the Levant Company to take part in the trade, but they sent out their own ships.[16]

The centralized structure of the East India Company meant that its elected leaders—the governor, deputy governor, treasurer, and twenty-four committees—had executive power over the East Indies trade and had the significant resources of the Company at their disposal.[17] They had more power over the running of the East Indies trade than their counterparts in the Levant Company did over that trade, and certainly more than the more numerous members of the Company's generality who elected them and invested money but had little say over the operation of the trade. East India Company leaders met frequently, and because so much of their planning was detailed and long-term—securing victuals for months-long voyages, employing people they would not be able to easily oversee or recall, and negotiating with members of the regime for specific privileges or policies—the records they kept of their meetings were especially detailed. The richness of the Company's archives lay bare the inner workings of the Company as the records of no other early modern institution do.[18]

These distinctive features of the Company made for an active and vibrant political life within the institution. The concerns and debates that shaped the Company were the same ones that played out in the early Stuart polity. The mixed membership of the Company, the organization of the trade into a joint stock, the sums of money at stake, even the disparate frequency of Company meetings (meetings of the full Company took place only several times a year, compared to the sometimes daily meetings of the elected leaders)—these features made meetings of the Company fertile grounds for debates and disagreements, often about proper governance of the Company and the trade. How authority did and should function, how representative government worked, how disputes should be managed, and when Company matters should be made public were some of the questions that members took up in the Company's early years.[19] The contested working out of these questions reveals how deeply invested Company members were in them and how much they saw as being at stake. The working out also reveals how often internal Company matters became the sites of external comment and involvement, sometimes by the regime and sometimes by the public.

The Company and the State

The political life of the Company encompassed not only actions and debates within the institution, but also involved the wider place of the East India Company in the early Stuart polity. Far from being simply a mercantile endeavor, members of the East India Company saw themselves, and were seen, as powerful state actors.[20] Company leaders understood themselves as actively pursuing state ends—the language of the "state" appears throughout Company archives, testifying to that perception—even as they learned to maneuver around the demands of England's European conflicts and alliances to secure what they saw as the requirements of England's presence in the East Indies.

What was the "state" that showed up so frequently in Company records? In recent years, historians have shifted their focus from state building to state formation. This shift reflects a change in emphasis from the purposeful actions and initiatives of individuals to the institutional changes that drew people in and tied them to the state. Part of that shift has been a reevaluation of the role and meaning of the state: indeed, one historian has argued that we should not be discussing the growth of the state at all, but rather speaking of forms of state power active in the period.[21] Michael Braddick and Steve Hindle, in their respective works on state formation in the early modern period, have examined the range of local office holding and political participation that connected people across England to a developing conception of the centralized state, and who, through that same office holding and political participation, drew the "state" into the arenas of their daily lives.[22] Office, Braddick argued, was what gave "form and purpose to the state" as individuals acted in its name.[23] Similarly, Mark Goldie has argued for the existence of an "unacknowledged republic," citing the numbers of people who held office of some type—mainly at the parish or county level.[24] As local government expanded and tackled a wider variety of social issues, it brought the state with it. These local officeholders employed the language of the state to legitimize their actions, and in so doing, they increased the ability of the state to legitimize those activities. The state was effectively "a network of offices exercising political power." That network of officeholders was at the forefront of the development of the "state" as an abstract conception that was not quite the regime.[25] Certainly by the late sixteenth century, this type of usage of the term "state," as concerning the interests of the realm that superseded the desires of a particular monarch, was readily understood. The "state" was what maintained the commonwealth, both an instrument of power and a claim to authority.[26] This was the "state" of the East India Company: an amorphous, malleable entity, often but not entirely coterminous with the regime, that one could draw on to challenge or resist the regime—which, effectively, it helped create.

The East India Company and the men who made it up were not far from the centers of power: they were in London, and in almost daily contact with the lords of the Privy Council and other courtiers. Many of them were important and wealthy men. Yet Company leaders were distant (or have seemed to be) from the centers of power in other ways. For one thing, though wealthy and important, many of them were wealthy and important merchants, and historians have rarely focused on men like them.[27] For another, despite the belief of revisionist and postrevisionist historians that most politics took place outside of Parliament, most scholarly work has centered on that institution, to the detriment of institutions like the Company and the opportunities their study offers.[28] Company leaders were agents of the state, both self-consciously and conceptually. They drew legitimacy from their claimed role as state agents, and used "the state" and its needs and interests as justification and defense for their actions.

As this book will show, what it meant to be a commercial body pursuing state interests was complex. The East India Company in the early seventeenth century demonstrates the interplay of public and private initiative in commercial bodies in the early modern period. This blending of public and private initiative highlights a wider conundrum about state formation: matters of state were often implemented, by necessity, via programs or schemes that united the public and the private.[29] The mingling of the public and private, and the difficulty of disentangling the two, was the "problem" of the state in this period, as one historian has put it.[30] The state delegated authority to private groups or individuals who carried out its aims, often in return for some sort of privilege or recompense.[31]

The Company's own identity as a public or private institution was ambiguous, and questions about private interest and public benefit were raised explicitly in debates within and about the Company. Depending on the lens through which one viewed it, the Company could be seen as an institution made up of private merchants and investors whose primary aim was profit and who ran the trade at the expense of the commonwealth, or as an institution that managed to harness private aims to secure public benefits—in this case, revenue for the king and cheaper commodities for the commonwealth.[32] One Company formulation posited that an overseas trade could be run "either by private adventurers or some public companies," thus making a direct claim that companies had a public character and distinguishing between what the East India Company did and what other individuals might do.[33] In a variety of contexts and for various audiences, Company men found themselves defending actions that their critics suggested benefited only themselves at the expense of the full Company or the commonwealth. The leaders of the Company, whose personal fortunes often benefited most and who had such extensive control over Company resources, received the most sustained criticism for allegedly pursuing their private interest.

The Company's balance between being a public and a private institution was on display in other ways, too. The Company was a subject of interest to many people outside the body, and their interest and the ways they talked about the Company testified both to its place on the national stage and to the ways it resisted easy categorization. Newsletters reported Company news alongside the latest news and rumors from the court and London, carrying it far afield to Cambridge, Amsterdam, and Venice; and to clergymen, ambassadors, and foreign officials. The writers did not just report the news but commented on it, sometimes asserting a stake in the Company even when they were not members. Writing from London, John Chamberlain wrote of "our East Indian ships" and "our merchants," and the Cambridge scholar Joseph Mead similarly wrote of "our" ships. The news was not always favorable, and writers could be quite critical of the Company. When Sir Thomas Smith's tenure as governor of the Company finally ended in 1621, for example, Chamberlain noted that he was "at last removed from his warm seat."[34] Venetian ambassadors in London and The Hague regularly reported East Indies matters, and they were especially aware of the way East Indies affairs shaped national politics. These writers were active consumers of Company news and invested in the Company's situation, which they saw as relevant beyond the Company itself. Some of the information they exchanged was highly speculative. They noted less concrete information, for example, like popular opinion of Company affairs and actions the regime might or might not take on the Company's behalf, as well as the outcome of elections and the return of ships. In sum, their attention to the activities of the Company demonstrated that Company affairs were never solely Company affairs, whether they involved the corporation's internal political life or its interactions with the state. The Company existed at the intersection of private and public.

The concepts of public and private were both implicitly and explicitly complicated within the Company's political discourse. The words "public," "private," "publicly," and "privately" made frequent appearances in the court minutes, but the minutes did not always use these terms consistently. There was no simple distinction between "public" and "private"; instead, each term could function as a positive or negative quality depending on the context.[35] Hence public benefit and public utility were good, but public knowledge could be bad, while private information was good, but private interest was bad. Thus, while Company leaders often employed terms that implied a clear distinction and antonymic relationship, they did so with terms whose definitions were unfixed and whose connotative values were entirely case-dependent.

Several contemporary governance models explained, or at least used, paradoxical meanings of "public" and "private." The view that private actions could benefit the public, for example, undergirded contemporary models of the royal prerogative, where the use of the monarch's will secured the good of the commonwealth. In other words, there was a recognizable example for how a private will could guarantee the public benefit. It was through the delegation of the power of the prerogative that private interests—the pursuit of private profit—were recruited to the business of government and claimed to be part of the pursuit of the public good. Yet the monarch's use of prerogative power—the granting of letters patent and the creation of monopolies, for example—was also sometimes subject to criticism as an abuse of power or for not properly balancing private benefit and public utility.[36]

Significantly, it was not the legislative king-in-parliament, but the executive king-in-council that was at the center of the Company's conception of the state. The particular reason for the close relationship between the king and Privy Council on one hand and the Company on the other hand was twofold: first, most of the trading companies existed because of letters patent from the king, whose authority granted and enforced their privileges; and second, the conduct of foreign relations definitively was under the purview of the royal prerogative. Since trading companies engaged in a number of state functions abroad, which involved them in diplomacy and martial activities, they necessarily worked in close contact with the king and Privy Council. The East India Company, therefore, was a body for which the state often meant the monarch, Privy Council, and prerogative. Parliament was a more distant, though not unthreatening, concern.[37]

The example of the East India Company underscores the fact that the early Stuart state was found in places unexpected by historians, though contemporaries had fewer difficulties with the complicated places where power resided and ways it functioned. The Company's story reveals to us how the realm was governed in practice, and the ways that a corporate body in London could be a key part of the early Stuart state—because the state *was* merchants meeting with privy councilors and negotiating policy. It was being the object of public scrutiny and comment, and reflecting on self-government. It was both more mundane and more remarkable than historians have realized.

The Company, Commerce, and Empire

Seeing the East India Company as an institution deeply embedded in the politics and political culture of the early seventeenth century has consequences for how we understand the meaning and place of English overseas ventures and empire. It complicates the narrative of the origins of imperialism in the seventeenth century. What the example of the Company highlights is how the categories we use to understand empire and expansion obscure the extent to which the experience of empire and expansion in the early modern period existed between those categories. For example, "empire" has emerged as the defining political, intellectual, and even legal category of English expansion. Both David Armitage and Anthony Pagden have examined the ideologies of empire, particularly based on the classical concepts of *imperium* (absolute sovereignty) and *dominium* (the right to possess territory) and their wide-spread application to the New World in the early modern period. Ken Mac-Millan has built on these ideas, arguing that the early Stuart state consistently and coherently constructed its overseas ventures in the Atlantic world as imperial in nature.[38] These authors, among others, have deepened our understanding of the genealogy of the constructions of imperial land control and their use in the early modern period, and even of the blurring of legal and geographical boundaries between imperial powers, almost exclusively in the Americas.[39] If we take the presence of land claims by the state as the basis for empire, then the origins of the English empire lie firmly in Ireland and the Atlantic world—that is, the places where the English claimed land. The non-Western overseas commercial ventures in this case were something else, categorically different from early experiments with empire.

There are two problems with leaving the origins of empire as a story of growing territorial sovereignty. The first is that the categories of commercial venture and imperial venture were not nearly so clear-cut in practice.[40] The commercial aims of the East India Company sat alongside the territorial aims of other bodies in the minds of the early modern English, and the separation between the two was often negligible or nonexistent. The same merchants who advocated imperial ambition and permanent settlement in one hemisphere spoke equally persuasively of commercial ties and treaties in the other. Alison Games has demonstrated the way that the personnel involved in expansion—the men who served in a variety of overseas settings and became the de facto agents of English empire—moved easily between trading companies and colonies. She highlights how they themselves did not recognize the Atlantic world boundaries that have often shaped historians' investigations.[41] Empire and commercial expansion existed alongside each other, overlapped, and fed on each other.

The second is that there were other ways to exert power than through land claims. The East India Company almost never deployed the language of "empire" (specifically, claims of *imperium* and *dominium*) in the early seventeenth century, but it used the language of the "state" almost constantly. The "business of state" represented the intermingling of Company and state objectives. Company members assumed that the state would play an active role in promoting economic endeavors. Debates in the Privy Council and the Company, in person and in print, were early examples of political economy, and the growth of early modern state power was inseparable from the successes of overseas commercial ventures.[42] The origins of empire has roots in this story, too.

A merchant-led company acting abroad with powers delegated to it by the state and with the active participation of members of the regime in their official capacity was a manifestation of English power abroad, regardless of whether the company controlled land overseas. The Company's activities in the East Indies, after all, were the first sustained contact between the English state and the non-Western world.[43] If the Company's actions were not "imperial" as traditionally understood, they were not far from it. Indeed, in the 1630s, the monarch explored schemes to convert the commercial venture into an explicitly imperial one involving territorial acquisition. Although this proved unsuccessful, it highlighted how a body like the East India Company might move between the categories of commercial and imperial.[44] Additionally, as Philip Stern has shown, "empire" was not exactly out of the question for a trading company, even without crown influence. His work on the late seventeenth-century East India Company is further testament to how tenuous the distinction between "commercial ventures" and "empire" was. The Company-state, in his formulation, was a sovereign body in the late 1600s—it was effectively an imperial power, exercising sovereignty over the territories and peoples it controlled in the East Indies.[45] The variety and types of English actions abroad, in other words, defy simple categorization.

Cases like the East India Company, therefore, prompt a deeper understanding of English activities abroad in the early modern period, and of the relationship between the Stuart state and overseas activities—some of which focused on settlement and conquest, and some of which did not. In the early seventeenth century, the Company was a determinedly nonimperial international actor, yet one that grappled on a daily basis with the question of what role the state could and should play in its overseas activities. The example of the East India Company reveals how Company and crown struggled with conceptual questions of the relationship between the state, empire, and overseas activities in the early seventeenth century and underscores the connection between overseas activities and state formation.

Part One

GOVERNING
THE COMPANY

This part of the book investigates the internal life of the East India Company by examining topics that reveal the institution's political culture. Ranging from issues that took place wholly within the Company to ones that involved people unconnected to the body, the Company's political life involved not only its full membership but also the regime and members of the public.

Every opportunity, complication, and power in the East India Company's experience had roots in the Company's patent. Both the Company's internal government and its place in the wider Stuart state drew upon and tested the powers and privileges granted in the Company's patent. Chapter 1 explores the Company's patent, the privileges conferred in it, and the negotiations involved in securing that patent.

The Company's patent granted the right of self-government but gave limited direction for how it should work. Chapter 2 examines how the elected leaders of the Company constituted and exercised their authority over the Company's general membership. Establishing and maintaining authority required constant effort, and members excluded from leadership positions sometimes resented that authority. Chapter 3 traces how the membership of the Company changed during the early seventeenth century, as Company leaders sought to recruit influential figures as members. The result was that the Company's membership came to overlap extensively with those of the royal court and other prominent state institutions. Courtiers and aristocrats brought special skills and connections to the Company, and Company leaders purposefully cultivated these men for membership.

Chapters 4 and 5 look at the form and meaning of challenges to the Company's leadership and style of government. Company members debated at length their own government as a representative body, and how power should be organized within it. Chapter 4 follows the types of opposition by members to the elected leaders of the Company, focusing on election-day disputes and proposals for procedural changes. Some Company leaders traced opposition in the Company, which they often labeled faction, to the increased presence of courtiers and gentlemen in the membership and the outsize demands they made, though the challengers frequently cited the lack of transparency and infrequent turnover of leadership as the cause of their concerns. Chapter 5 investigates the debates about the Company and its government that took place in print. The Company became the target of public suspicion as printed pamphlets appeared that alleged the Company had mismanaged the trade and harmed the commonwealth. Critics charged that the East Indies trade benefited the private interests of Company members rather than serving the public good. To defend against these accusations, Company writers reconceptualized private interest, developing new arguments about how the pursuit of private interest actually served the commonwealth. Answering the external critics led Company leaders to grapple with questions of public appeal and to begin experimenting with new tools as they entered the public arena to defend themselves and their trade.

This part of the book shows how central these questions of power and authority were to the East India Company, and how the Company became the site of contests about the proper use of power not only within the corporation but also in the wider commonwealth. These chapters demonstrate how the business of state prompted debate and new answers to questions about the nature and purpose of self-government, private interest and public benefit, and the aim of overseas ventures.

I

The Patent and the Formation
of the Company

IN THE EARLY seventeenth century, trading with the East Indies was a significant challenge—and not solely because of distance. That a body such as the East India Company should exist and develop a trade such as the East India trade, in a place such as the East Indies, was the fruit of concerted work by a varied group of people. The prospective adventurers had to answer a number of possible objections to show that the trade was viable, would not infringe on Spanish or Portuguese claims in the East Indies, and would provide a real benefit to the commonwealth—all with the object of securing a letter patent from Elizabeth I for the trade. Only through a letter patent could a group of merchants be transformed into an incorporated body with powerful privileges. The trade they sought to develop would have enforceable legal protections, and they would have authority to govern themselves in both London and the East Indies.

Without a patent, merchants could still have organized a trade, but they would have had no guarantees or special legal powers. They could still have banded together to send a ship, but they would have had no way of preventing anyone else from also sending ships. Competition might mean infighting, which would have prevented a strong English presence in the East Indies. The death or disinterest of a particular merchant active in the trade might mean the end of the trade altogether. They would have no authority to govern themselves or, arguably, even to assemble. At the other extreme and most important, without the imprimatur of the state, a group of merchants in the East Indies might be at the mercy of the power of rival European powers in the East Indies, unable to rely on official support for their venture.

An early modern patent, therefore, was a powerful thing. It was powerful symbolically and politically. A patent represented the moment when the private interest of individuals and the interest of the commonwealth were bound together. It signified how the monarch, through an act of the royal prerogative, could harness the endeavors of a group of individuals for the benefit for the whole nation. It transformed what could be a problem—the exercise of self-interest—into a method of growing the power and reach of the state. In the case of the East India Company, the patent gave a group of merchants the means of developing a new trade through the delegation of powers and privileges that they saw as necessary for that trade to succeed.

Yet a patent represented not only the moment of creation, but also the ongoing relationship between the parties named in it. The connection between the monarch and the individuals named in the patent did not end with the granting of powers. As with any relationship, the meaning of the patent changed over time—both in formal terms, as new powers or privileges were delegated, and in informal terms, with changes in the named parties' interpretation of the powers and privileges granted. For the East India Company, that meant that the patent was and continued to be a guide for both the regime and Company members for how the Company should function within the state, even as the grantor and grantee of a patent could and often did have very different understandings of what the patent promised.

The early years of the Company's existence (and the years before its existence) witnessed frequent and sometimes tense negotiations between crown and Company (or its future members) over the meaning of the patent and the privileges it granted. The patent was the cornerstone of the Company's relationship with the crown. How faithfully the monarch respected the patent provided a gauge of the state of the relationship between the Company and crown. Without the patent (or charter, as it was sometimes called), the East India Company would not exist, and Company leaders generally sought to protect and enlarge its existing privileges. Meanwhile the crown sought to compel Company leaders to use those privileges granted by the monarch in ways that were most useful or convenient to the regime. Despite the appearance of permanence and transparent meaning that a written patent gave, the patent and exactly what its grant encompassed were always fluid, with different parties' understandings shaped by changing circumstances.

Patents and Trading Companies

When the East India Company was founded in 1600, as an incorporated company engaging in a long-distance trade, it was an institution at the cutting edge of both the English state and private enterprise. The world of English trade in the early seventeenth century was much more regional than global. In 1600, England's biggest export crop was wool, which was exported primarily to the Low Countries. That commodity accounted for the vast majority of English trade and had been traded since at least the fourteenth century.[1] However, English overseas horizons were expanding. Since the mid-1500s, English merchants had engaged in trades in the Baltic and to Muscovy. Since 1581, England had had a formal trade in the Mediterranean, through the Turkey or Levant Company. By 1600, there had been a few unsustained ventures to North America, and the Virginia Company was founded a few years later, in 1606. Other companies, such as the Somers Island Company and the Royal Africa Company (founded in 1615 and 1618, respectively), were formed in the following years. In addition to these formal trades—meaning organized trades run by merchants—English privateers operated in the Atlantic and Indian Oceans and the Mediterranean Sea. The East India Company was part of this flowering of English overseas endeavors and was responsible for English activities east of the Cape of Good Hope.

The legal mechanism that undergirded English overseas expansion—that helped make the risks and expense bearable—was the letter patent. Increasingly in the sixteenth and seventeenth centuries, groups of investors, often merchants, turned to patents to establish new overseas trades. Crown-chartered trading companies were a relatively new feature of the economic landscape, compared to the much older trading guilds of the Merchant Adventurers (founded in 1407) and the Merchant Staplers (founded sometime in the fourteenth century), which together ran much of England's cloth trade. In comparison, the first joint-stock trading company, the Russia or Muscovy Company, was created by letter patent in 1555. The overseas trading companies of the late sixteenth and early seventeenth centuries were almost all constituted by letters patent.[2]

Prospective adventurers were open about the value and use of a letter patent and the privileges it conferred. A proposal for a trade to "lands beyond the equinoctial" presented to Lord Burghley in 1573 directly requested a letter patent. It asked that the queen give a patent "to the authors and fellowship of this voyage in nature of a corporation." The patent should "add such franchise and privilege as in this case is requisite." The proposal explicitly noted the need for the patent to grant the company the ability to form a government for itself: "to stablish some form of governance and authority in some persons of the company of this adventure, so as by some regiment obedience, quiet unity, and order may be preserved."[3] A separate proposal in 1580 for a company (also to trade "beyond the equinoctial line") directly asked Elizabeth to "grant like privileges as have been granted by her and her progenitors unto her subjects trading into the dominions of the emperor of Russia."[4] Neither of these patents was granted, but they testify to the perceived value of a patent and what prospective adventurers wanted from one.

The letters patent that groups of adventurers sought and were granted shared several key features: they granted exclusive rights to something (an activity, a trade, or presence in a particular geographic area); they incorporated the prospective adventurers; and they granted that incorporated body the right of self-government.[5] The specifics of each of those grants could vary considerably, but the essence of the grants was the same. There were other types of early modern letters patent, granting other types of powers and privileges. Patents could grant land and powers related to land, office, and commissions and had a variety of other functions. They could even grant the power to claim and possess new lands, as did the patents given to individuals (and companies) in the Americas.[6] However, the letters patent that created trading companies formed an unofficial subset, defined by their shared and distinctive powers that granted exclusivity, incorporation, and self-government.

The grant of exclusivity made patents essentially grants of monopoly. The scope of the exclusivity thus granted could range from the importation or manufacture of a specific commodity (like soap, playing cards, or particular types of woven goods) to the development and conduct of a trade to a particular place. The exclusivity ceded to the trading companies usually reflected geographical locations. This could mean a specific place, like Spain, or more general regions, like Muscovy, the Eastlands, the Levant, and the East Indies. Sometimes the grant of a particular place effectively meant a grant of exclusive access to particular commodities. The Levant Company brought in the nation's supply of currants, for example, just as the East India Company was the source of indigo.[7] The fundamental characteristic of the patent was that it gave the sole right to something, though that "something" varied considerably.

The grants of incorporation and self-government were no more standard in their meaning than the exclusivity grant. What exactly incorporation meant was not always clear. Though corporate institutions had existed for centuries, the idea that merchant trading bodies should be incorporated was not standard before Elizabeth's reign. Grants of privileges to the Merchant Adventurers residing in Calais in 1505 by Henry VII and to the merchants trading to Andalusia in 1530 by Henry VIII did not explicitly grant incorporation, though they granted the right of self-government.[8] The Muscovy Company was directly incorporated in its letter patent in 1555, however, and subsequent patents for other companies generally followed suit. The 1606 patent for the Virginia Company did not explicitly mention incorporation, but that omission was remedied in the 1609 patent. By the late sixteenth century, groups of adventurers regularly sought and were granted incorporation.

Yet the legal rights and privileges associated with incorporation were very much in flux. Where the meaning of incorporation was mentioned or alluded to in patents, it generally referred to the legal perpetuity of the body and its ability to buy land, resort to law, and conduct other business as a unit.[9] However, the first book on corporate law, for example, was not published until 1659, and Sir Edward Coke's famous assertion that corporations had no souls, could own land, and had rights that extended beyond the lifetime of their founders was given as a commentary on a case that took place in 1612 (the Case of Sutton's Hospital). In sum, the legal certainties that the patents suggested were not actually certainties. Thus, though corporate bodies were common, and the corporate structure something adventurers desired, the rights attendant on them were not standard.[10] Indeed, a number of companies—not solely the East India Company—struggled to demarcate the powers that incorporation granted them in the early seventeenth century.

The mechanisms for self-government laid out in letters patent varied significantly from body to body. The crucial shared feature was that a body's leadership was elected and supposed to be either changed or reelected at regular intervals. In other ways, the form and function of one corporation's leadership could differ dramatically from another's. The 1555 Muscovy Company patent set up an initial governor for life (Sebastian Cabot), who would be succeeded at his death by a governor elected yearly. The company's governor was aided by a slate of other elected officials: four consuls and twenty-four assistants. In contrast, the 1600 Levant Company patent set up an elected governor with twelve assistants, and the 1610 patent of the Newfoundland Company had an elected council of twelve members plus an elected treasurer.[11] The 1606 patent for the Virginia Company specified an elected treasurer and a council of thirteen, while the 1609 patent named a council of some fifty people, to be changed and replaced as necessary.[12] Other companies had other structures.

If letters patent rarely explained why incorporation was granted, they did often note the reason for self-government. The 1573 proposal for a corporation mentioned above summed things up nicely: the point of government was so that "obedience, quiet unity, and order may be preserved."[13] The 1609 Virginia patent noted that the "provident and good direction of the whole enterprise" required a "careful and understanding council."[14] The Muscovy Company patent explained that the governing body had the authority "to rule and govern all and singular [*sic*] the merchants of the said fellowship and communality, and to execute and do full and speedy justice to them, and every of them, in all their causes, differences, variances, controversies, quarrels, and complaints."[15] Government within the trading companies, in other words, should essentially do what government of the commonwealth did: preserve order and enable prosperity.

Thus, the corporations and patents that enabled the expansion of English overseas activities were both homogenous and heterogenous. They shared essential aims and powers but differed in the particulars of how those aims and powers were expressed. There was one other characteristic that united the group, however, and with far less variation from patent to patent: the exercise of royal prerogative power that created them.

Patents and the Prerogative

It was no coincidence that trading companies relying on patents multiplied in the late sixteenth and early seventeenth centuries and not earlier. The use of patents as a mode of economic licensing and delegation of power by the state to spur economic growth was a sixteenth-century development. The first patents of invention—patents granting exclusive privileges in return for introducing a new commodity or trade into the commonwealth—were granted in the mid-sixteenth century. The Muscovy Company's patent was given in 1555, and the first patents for new processes (for making white soap and saltpeter) were granted in 1561.[16] By the end of Elizabeth's reign, dozens of patents of monopoly existed, including twenty-three issued in 1601 alone—which made this use of prerogative powers both novel and increasingly common.[17] The licensing of monopolies and granting of patents that arose in and characterized the late sixteenth and early seventeenth centuries were part of an overarching state policy to extend the crown's influence in economic development. Monopolies in the early modern period, as one historian has put it, were "emblem[s] of the state," in that they created new enterprises that could not have existed without them. In the process, they created state clients of the monopoly holders—they drew people into a version of the state that was predicated on the exercise of royal power and the prerogative.[18]

Such was the tie between prerogative and patent that the monarch could (and did) easily interpret criticism of monopolies, which commonly identified them as a negative outcome of licenses and patents, as an attack on the prerogative. At the close of the 1597 parliament, for example, after listening to considerable criticism of monopolies, Elizabeth I commented that she hoped members of Parliament would temper their anger at monopolies and "not take away her prerogative . . . but that they will rather leave that to her disposition."[19] Francis Bacon, defending the monarch's power to grant patents, argued in 1601 that it was encompassed in the "enlarging and restraining liberty of her prerogative."[20] When Parliament took up the case of monopolies again in 1624 (ultimately passing the Statute of Monopolies, which repealed earlier monopolies and limited future ones to patents of invention), James I reiterated that patents were not a matter for Parliament's consideration, stating explicitly that "patents are not to be judged unlawful by you."[21] The Statute of Monopolies was not the first time that James and Parliaments had wrangled over either the issue of monopolies or the limits of the prerogative, which had arisen in several sessions of his first Parliament (which sat from 1604 to 1610) and were major concerns in the 1621 parliament.[22]

Even some of the harshest critics of monopolies, however, acknowledged that the monarch's exclusive grants were sometimes appropriate. The reports on the Case of Monopolies (*Darcy v. Allen*), a common law case decided in 1603 in which the court had found most restrictions on trade by the monarch to be unlawful, made one exception. "Where any man by his own charge and industry," jurist William Noy's commentary on the case explained, "or by his own wit or invention doth bring any new trade into the realm or any engine tending to the furtherance of a trade that never was used before; and that for the good of the realm; that in such cases the king may grant to him a monopoly-patent for some reasonable time."[23] The justification for the imposed limitation was that new trades benefited the commonwealth more than the temporary restriction of the trades harmed it.

Noy's reference to the furtherance of trade was a recognition of the special needs of the development of a new trade and the role of the monarch in granting restrictions to promote economic endeavors.

The letters patent that the East India Company received made the relationship between royal prerogative power and patents explicitly clear. The 1600 patent, for example, specified that it was "granted by her Majesty," and that its power extended to all people "within this our realm of England as elsewhere under our obedience and jurisdiction." The patent's wording continually referred to the specific and personal power of the monarch who had created it, repeating the formulation of the monarch's "special grace, certain knowledge and mere motion" that instituted each provision of the patent. Repetitions of the phrases "we will, ordain and grant," "we will and grant" and "our will and pleasure is" appeared throughout the 1600 patent, and all of these formulations directly referred to the role of the prerogative power ("we will" as an active verb) in constituting the Company's privileges. The patent that James granted the East India Company in 1609 used the same phrases, as did the patent that Charles I gave to the rival Courten Association in 1637.[24] These patents were essentially speech acts, granting the powers they described to the bodies they created through their utterance and recording. They were actions of the royal will that brought companies into being, and these formulations made the link between the companies and the monarch via the patent and prerogative power readily evident to contemporaries.

Prerogative power was the constitutive power underlying all letters patent. Though not all patents used the exact same formulation—the 1606 patent of the Virginia Company, for example, did not use the "special grace and mere motion" formulation, instead employing the terms "grant and agree," "grant and give," and "our will and pleasure" to refer to the actions of the monarch—all referred to the prerogative power of the monarch and the act of will that created the body described in the patent.[25] Indeed, most used the same formula of "special grace, certain knowledge and mere motion," in addition to the commands "will" and "grant."[26] The 1555 Muscovy Company patent referred to the "especial grace, certain knowledge and mere motion" of the monarch and directly spoke of the prerogative.[27] The 1568 patent for the Mines Royal Company used this language, as did the 1600 patent given to the Levant Company, the 1612 patent for the Newfoundland Company, and many others.[28]

Thus, the foundation of trading companies by letters patent could not be separated from the power of the state and the exercise of the royal prerogative. From the legal formulas used in patents to the critiques of the granting of patents, patents were tied to the prerogative.

The Formation of the East India Company

Elizabeth I was the first monarch to authorize and then deal with a formal and official East Indies trade in the form of the East India Company. The few English ventures to the East Indies over the last decades of the sixteenth century had enjoyed only limited success and pointed to the need for a unified and organized trade to reap maximum benefits. For example, John Newbery and Ralph Fitch had arrived in India in 1583 to explore the possibilities of a sea trade to the East. They represented two well-known and wealthy London merchants already active in the Levant trade but had almost no official support from the regime.[29] Voyages by James Lancaster and Benjamin Wood in 1591 and 1596, respectively, demonstrated to English merchants the physical dangers and financial risk involved in the East Indies trade. Both commanders lost multiple ships and many men in the course of their ventures, though they brought back tantalizing tales of Eastern riches.

Making the poor outcomes of these English voyages even worse was the fact that Dutch merchants were faring better: in 1599, a Dutch fleet returned richly laden from the East Indies, demonstrating both the feasibility of the trip and the possible profits to these other newcomers to the trade. The Dutch success also showed that rivals were already profiting, and English merchants could not wait if they wanted part of the trade. Developing a sea trade while lowering the financial risk led interested English merchants to band together and approach the monarch and Privy Council for a patent to form a company, as the Indies were "so far remote from hence [that they] cannot be traded but in a joint and united stock."[30]

Few documents about the English East Indies trade survive from before the official formation of the East India Company, though those that do testify to the negotiation between merchants and regime and the balancing of different interests in the process. By late September 1599, at least 140 people were ready to join together as adventurers for an East Indies voyage. They met formally, electing a government and keeping a record of the meeting. They seem to have already had some promise of royal support at that point.[31] However, they did not have a formal grant of privilege or incorporation, and they still needed to secure one. The merchants agreed to send a petition to Elizabeth and the Privy Council providing reasons—which emphasized competition and the national interest—for the East Indies trade. This type of petition had become part of the normal process of securing a patent.[32] The London merchants were "induced by the success of the voyage performed by the Dutch nation" and "were stirred up with no less affection to advance the trade of their native country than the Dutch merchants were to benefit their commonwealth."[33] In light of these goals, they asked for incorporation and other privileges. The preliminary response was positive and confirmed the promise they had already received: the Privy Council agreed to support the merchants in their request.[34]

For Elizabeth, the East Indies trade was good in that it would enrich the nation and emulate (and challenge) the Dutch. However, it was not so valuable that it was worth championing at the expense of a possible peace treaty with Spain. In other words, she and the Privy Council weighed the benefits of this extra-European trade against the possible consequences for England's more immediate international concerns. Only a few weeks after the Privy Council gave the merchants its approval, it changed its mind. A peace treaty with Spain would do more good for the English commonwealth than the East Indies trade, no matter how profitable. The merchants attending the Council meeting reported that the Council members thought it "more beneficial for the general state of merchandise to entertain a peace than that the same should be hindered by the standing with the Spanish commissioners for the maintaining of this trade to forgo the opportunity of the concluding of the peace." Afraid that they might commit money and time to a voyage that would not take place, the merchants decided to table the prospect of an East Indies voyage.[35]

The merchants did not meet officially for over a year, but they did not abandon the idea of the East Indies trade and continued to cultivate the Privy Council. They recruited Richard Hakluyt to prepare a memo defending their entry into the East Indies, and in early 1600, approximately when the proposed voyage would have departed, they presented to the queen and Privy Council a list of reasons why the English might trade in those regions that were not subject to Spain or Portugal. The list included the sources consulted to learn about the East Indies, including Portuguese, Spanish, and Dutch authors and Englishmen "yet living" who had been to the East Indies.[36] It established the merchants as authorities well able to launch the trade, and it laid the conceptual foundation for refusing to allow Spain and Portugal to restrict English access to the region.

The hopeful adventurers tried to address the concerns of the regime about antagonizing Spain or Portugal. The memo suggested that the Privy Council "urge" the commissioners sent from Spain to set down in writing "all such islands, towns, places, castles, and fortresses as they are actually at this present possessed of" past the Cape of Good Hope. If the adventurers had no information disputing those claims, they would neither "disturb nor molest" the Spanish or Portuguese in the places where they enjoyed authority. Beyond that list, however, the memo argued that English adventurers would be completely within their rights to venture to points east: "all the rest rich kingdoms and islands of the East, which are in number very many, are out of their power and jurisdiction, and free for any other princes and people of the world to repair unto." Indeed, the memo concluded, the Spanish had no "just or lawful reasons" to stop English ventures into the East Indies. Using arguments later made famous in Hugo Grotius's 1609 *Mare Liberum*, the memo claimed that the Spanish could not stop "her Majesty and all other Christian princes and states of the use of the vast, wide, and infinitely open Ocean Sea, and of access to the territories and dominions of so many free princes, kings, and potentates in the East, in whose dominions they have no more sovereign command or authority, than we, or any Christians whosoever."[37]

The memo prompted additional inquiry. Elizabeth, via Sir Francis Walsingham, charged Fulke Greville—a man whose posts included treasurer of the Navy and who had interests in English expansion—with investigating further. He did so, writing a memo on 10 March that confirmed the merchants' claims about the East Indies, though he focused on the specifics of places and commodities rather than the ideological arguments for or against the trade.[38] Another petition from 1600 from the merchants to the Privy Council showed them laying the groundwork for the practical considerations needed to run the trade, asking that they be given permission to export bullion and that their ships, when sent, would not be stopped in case they lost that year's voyage through the delay.[39]

These petitions succeeded, and by September 1600 the merchants had received permission to proceed with a voyage. Elizabeth had agreed to allow the East Indies venture to go forward and would give them privileges. Indeed, in September the merchants began meeting formally, with elected officials and records of their minutes—slightly anticipating their patent and the powers granted in it. No one mentioned Spain this time, and on the last day of December 1600, the merchants received a patent creating the East India Company, officially known as the "Company of Merchants of London Trading into the East Indies." Weeks later, they also had in hand Elizabeth's commission to their chosen commander, James Lancaster, granting him the powers necessary to govern the fleet soon to be sent.[40]

The merchants' patent incorporated them and detailed procedures for the new body's self-government. The central event of the Company's corporate life was the annual election, which took place in the first week of July each year as specified in the patent. At the election, the generality—the whole body of the Company's members—elected a governor, deputy governor, treasurer, and twenty-four committees (so named because responsibility was committed to them).[41] These were positions of great power within the Company, as these people would govern the Company and oversee the extensive resources at its disposal.

The Company's patent specified these offices and their responsibilities. According to the patent, these men collectively had the authority to run the trade, including directing the voyages, ordering the merchandise that went on the ships, and selling the merchandise that they imported.[42] They would be bound by their oaths and could govern the corporation as long as their rules did not contradict the laws of England.[43] The patent outlined the many powers they had in conducting activities in London as well as in the East Indies, but it gave few directives—beyond detailed rules concerning the Company's elections and the procedures for both removing a governor from power and transferring power mid-year due to a death—about the day-to-day governance of the Company. Notably, the government that the merchants had created upon the promise of the patent did not actually match the provisions for government laid down in the patent. This suggests that the adventurers did not have perfect knowledge of the patent they would be granted and that negotiations involved in the drafting of the patent could change key provisions, as the adventurers would have little reason to implement a government they would immediately have to change. Though the merchants had begun meeting, had elected leaders, and taken minutes, they had to bring their newly incorporated body's government into conformity with the patent.

The Company's letter patent granted these and other privileges to the merchants for a period of fifteen years. For that period they had the exclusive rights to "directly or indirectly visit, haunt, frequent, or trade, traffic or adventure" into the East Indies, to any lands held by non-Christian rulers not already in league or amity with her Majesty. This meant that the East India Company merchants were, according to the patent, the only English who could legally go to or trade in the East.[44]

Less than a year later, however, the matter of the exclusivity grant and how the good of the traders and the good of the commonwealth could be kept in harmony was at issue again. Elizabeth grew annoyed with the East India Company for not preparing for a second voyage, and the question arose of what exactly the patent privileges required of the Company. On her behalf, in late 1601 Robert Cecil, Earl of Salisbury and secretary of state, and Charles Howard, Earl of Nottingham and lord admiral, inquired why the Company was "so slack in seconding their former voyage." The Dutch, they noted, had successfully managed it, and it seemed to them that "this Company were not so respective of her Majesty's honor and the honor of their own country as were fit they should be."[45] The Privy Council followed up this gentle hint with a letter to the effect that the queen, having graciously given the Company a patent allowing it to send six ships and six pinnaces a year, expected it to send six ships and six pinnaces a year. To rumors that the Company, like the Dutch, was preparing for a second expedition before the return of the first, she had a "very good liking."[46]

The privileges granted in the patent were always negotiable. Elizabeth's praise for the possible second voyage was followed with a lightly veiled threat: she had also heard that the Company's leaders were hesitating, hoping to wait for the return of the first fleet, and she did not like this rumor nearly so much. Instead she essentially commanded the leaders to prepare and send the second fleet because their actions reflected on the honor of the nation, telling them that:

> We have thought fit to move you, to be better advised in the carriage of such an action as this, where the world hath had so great expectation, because you shall thereby lay an imputation upon the State as if there were either such inconstancy in these purposes or such necessity amongst you that where other States (after such beginning) go on contently and orderly you are either so changeable or so unable as you do not ensure those courses which yourselves have propounded and concluded.[47]

She warned Company leaders that if they did not feel able to send the second fleet, there were "divers ready (in your default) to enter [the trade]."

Privileges unused would not be regarded as sacrosanct: "you cannot justly hinder under where [on account] of the privileges, when you do not use the benefit of one."[48] Not only was the granting of privileges tied to the honor of the monarch and state, therefore, but so was the use of those privileges.

Company leaders were well aware of the malleability of the meaning of what the patent granted. They used this flexibility to their benefit when possible and took steps to circumvent it at other times. For example, at the same time that they were delaying using their own patent privileges in 1601 and being warned by Elizabeth as a result, they were exploring the logistics of infringing on other companies' privileges. They saw the potential of doing so, as long as they could make an argument for why their infringement would benefit the commonwealth and therefore was more important than the sanctity of someone else's privilege. This logic that the needs of the commonwealth trumped all other concerns mirrored the crown's warning to them about their nonuse of privileges for the East Indies.

The second voyage the East India Company wished most strongly to undertake in 1601 was not an expedition to the East Indies, but rather an exploratory voyage for the northwest passage. The problem for Company leaders was that such a voyage would pass through seas and lands that fell, geographically, in the purview of the Muscovy Company. Should the East India Company adventurers proceed in their intention, they would be violating another company's privileges. The court minutes noted that concern when the court of committees considered the issue: "there is some question made or doubt conceived that the Muscovy Company may by virtue of their privileges claim the interest of the northwest passage."[49] It was not the infringement of another company's privileges per se that gave the East India Company leaders pause, but rather the concern that the East India Company expedition would pay for the voyage and find the passage, only to have exclusive rights to it then claimed by the Muscovy Company on the basis of its own patent. In some ways this was a strange distinction to make, as a number of East India adventurers were also Muscovy merchants, and vice versa. Yet Company leaders consistently acted for the Company without acknowledging the interests of other bodies they might be members of, and in ways that benefited the Company but could do so at the expense of those other bodies.

With regard to the Muscovy Company's possible right to the northwest passage, Company leaders consulted legal authorities, who assured them that the East India Company had a legal right to the northwest passage.[50]

The Privy Council supported their actions in spite of any Muscovy Company concerns, "since the same is intended for the common benefit and honor of the realm."[51] Therefore in this case, East India Company leaders were able to employ the same principle against the Muscovy Company that had made them vulnerable to Elizabeth when they considered delaying their second voyage: a privilege was not to have but to use, and neglecting to use a privilege was tantamount to forfeiting it to someone else who would use it for the common good.

This early maneuvering between Elizabeth and the Privy Council on one side, and the East India Company on the other, thus demonstrated the ways in which patents and privileges existed in particular political contexts. The negotiation both before and after the granting of the patent highlighted the fact that the patent was a living document, subject to interpretation, as well as alterable in its essence. What it granted changed as circumstances did. The founding of the East India Company had depended on England's wider geopolitical situation. While the example of the Dutch showed the possible profits of East Indies voyages managed through joint stocks, diplomatic negotiations with Spain revealed the potential cost of an English East Indies trade.[52] The granting of the East India Company patent thus reflected not only mercantile interests but also other geopolitical requirements of the state. Perhaps because of those considerations, once the crown had made commitments to the trade and the merchants, it expected them to use the privileges they had been granted—with Dutch merchant ventures once again providing the example that English merchants should emulate.

Implicit in the early maneuvering over the meaning and use of the patent was how it shaped the relationship of Company leaders to the rest of the Company's members. With the patent as a goal, interested merchants had begun to meet formally, adopting structures of government that could legitimately exist only once the monarch actually granted the patent. They adopted a corporate structure before it was theirs in truth, and then they had to change their government to match what the patent prescribed. The adventurers wanted the extra powers a patent gave them, even as it reduced the power individual adventurers would have over the new trade. It introduced division among the adventurers, creating those who governed and those who were governed.

The language of the honor of the monarch and the state that was rooted in the meaning and purpose of the patent could be deployed to very different ends. It could be used by the regime to compel Company leaders to perform particular actions. However, it could also be used by Company leaders to mobilize the Privy Council on their behalf against the rest of the Company's members—those who were governed. For example, when some of the newly pledged adventurers proved slow to pay in their adventures (in other words, their investment) in that first year, Company leaders argued that though the East Indies trade was secured in private hands, it was also a matter of state. Company leaders had little hesitation in asking the Privy Council to put a little muscle behind their requests to compel defaulting adventurers to pay up. They demanded that investors who wanted to permanently or temporarily delay their payment explain why to the Privy Council, since they understood that some people had withheld their money on the basis of "some rumors or doubts" that a voyage would actually take place. The court of committees informed them that "the action undertaken by them [the Company] was a public action and not to be dallied withal," and that therefore the names of the unwilling would be sent to the Privy Council and possibly called up for further examination.[53] The Privy Council eventually sent an order to compel, or at least encourage, payment, as the nonpayment and possible jeopardizing of the voyage "importeth the honor of the state, that so public an action should not receive scandal or shameful imputation."[54] Both Council and Company were willing to make use of the link between Company actions and state affairs to prosecute the trade, or at least get it established. To do so, however, they essentially used the patent against the people bound by it, raising the possibility of contestations about the meaning and use of the patent within the Company.

The early years of the Company, culminating in the granting and first use of the patent, forged the relationship between Company leaders and the regime. Monarch and privy councilors worked closely with Company leaders. The queen could and did directly shape the East Indies venture, even beyond the granting of the patent. Privy councilors met with Company leaders to negotiate between the monarch and the Company. Company leaders could and did mobilize the Privy Council to act on their behalf, even on what were ostensibly matters of internal governance. Both sides— Company and regime—shared the understanding that the good of the Company was compatible with the good of the commonwealth, even if their aims did not fully overlap in particular instances.

The Company's relationship with the crown did not end with the exercise of the royal prerogative that constituted it. Even the most basic questions about the relationship between Company and monarch had to be asked and answered anew in each reign. For example, James's death years later prompted Company leaders to ask if they needed to renew the patent, before deciding that it was not necessary as their most recent patent had been granted on behalf of James and his heirs.[55] Company leaders worked closely with monarch and Privy Council even on day-to-day Company affairs. In light of the lack of institutional traditions governing the relationship between Company and monarch in the early years of the Company's existence, the particular set of expectations that each monarch had of the Company played a major role—alongside the expectations Company leaders had of their venture—in shaping what the Company was and did, as well as what the practical relationship between Company and crown should be.

The most fundamental question for Company leaders was whether or not the monarch considered the granting of privileges sacrosanct, and if so, to what extent. Company leaders throughout the early seventeenth century argued that in granting trading privileges to a company, the monarch also granted sole rights for bringing certain goods into the country—and therefore that the company also had sole access to the regions where those goods were to be found (at least for the duration of the patent). They held to the argument that the East Indies trade existed only in relation to their actions and thus was inseparable from the East India Company. The monarch's view on these matters was not nearly so clear-cut, and it shifted not only with the tides of succession but also with numerous and variable economic, political, and geopolitical factors. The way the monarch answered this question depended upon how the crown perceived the relationship between a company and the trade it conducted. For example, was the English East Indies trade dependent on the activity of the East India Company, or could the trade exist without the Company? If the Company was necessary for the conduct of the trade, then the regime needed to maintain the Company to keep the trade. This was the logic of granting a patent to develop a new trade, yet at some point a new trade became an established trade and could be argued to exist without the company that had established it.

The seeds of all of the questions and themes that shaped the Company's activities throughout the early seventeenth century were present in the patent and the early negotiations that concerned it. The patent and the prerogative were at the heart of both the Company's internal government and the relationship between Company and state. The patent determined the relationship between members of the Company and the structures of power within the corporate body. The political life of the Company derived from the privileges granted in the patent, but exactly what the patent granted was contestable. Because the patent was not static, it played an ongoing role in debates about governing the Company. The patent was also central to the relationship between Company and state, with crown and Company drawing upon it to press particular interpretations of how the Company fit into the wider English polity. In this context, too, the exact meaning of the patent and its grants was a recurring feature in negotiations between Company leaders and the regime, and in the background of every interaction between the two groups. Patent and prerogative created the Company and bound it and the crown together in valuable, imprecise, and negotiable ways.

2

Constituting Authority

The Court of Committees and the Generality

I N 1619, the court of committees found itself debating what to do with a copy of the newly agreed-upon articles of a trade accord between the English and Dutch East India Companies. The information was sensitive and the agreement hard won—it had taken years for the companies to negotiate an acceptable arrangement—and it was important for Company leaders to be familiar with the terms of the agreement. Yet they were not sure how familiar Company members besides themselves should be with the agreement. After some discussion, they decided "not to have [the copy of the articles] left in the counting house, for any of the generality to see at their pleasure, to take notes to publish them abroad."[1]

This decision reflected many of the overarching concerns of Company leaders that shaped how they managed the relationship between the government of the Company and its wider membership. The debate about who should have access to sensitive information, the decision to restrict access to the trade articles, and the consequences the court of committees stated that it hoped to prevent through that measure—the publishing abroad of the articles—were in keeping with a number of other decisions Company leaders made to control information related to the East Indies trade. They had ambivalent feelings about the interest their own generality might take in Company affairs and placed high importance on keeping certain information secret. The leaders of the Company saw the public circulation of information about the East Indies trade as a liability and treated information shared with the generality as part of that public circulation. Among themselves, they openly discussed methods for controlling information as a means of asserting power.

Corporate institutions like the East India Company were political spaces in addition to fulfilling whatever other purpose the institutions had. Ranging from incorporated cities, to guilds like the London livery companies, and to joint stock ventures like the East India Company, corporate institutions peppered the early modern political landscape. Indeed, corporate citizenship was one of the primary and even defining political experiences in the lives of a wide range of (often, though not exclusively, non-elite) people.[2] In these corporate institutions, participants governed themselves and wrestled with many of the same political issues that exercised the wider political nation. These institutions were the spaces where people practiced political engagement, held offices, learned to govern and be governed, and helped construct or critique institutional structures of power. They were, in many ways, microcosms of the early Stuart polity.[3]

How people acted in these spaces revealed their wider political concerns and ideas about power. Though historians have thus far not treated these corporate bodies as obvious arenas for examining political culture, they provide good examples for its study because political activity in these corporate spaces was often so self-conscious. East India Company leaders knew they were wrestling with political questions: they saw wider political resonances and meanings in questions about their own internal governance and structure. Most important for historians, the institutional records they kept revealed the problems of government and power they grappled with—the most pressing of which was how to manage the relationship between those who governed and those who were governed, or between the elected officials and the generality.

The court of committees had a complicated relationship with the wider Company membership. Company leaders saw themselves as a separate group within the Company, with different responsibilities than the generality. In many ways, the groups were separate, as high incumbency rates helped consolidate executive power in the hands of selected men. Certainly stylistic conventions in the Company's records suggested clear divisions between the groups. Despite the ways Company leaders tried to manage the general membership, because the generality was ostensibly the deciding body on a number of major issues—funding the joint stock and organizing the trade, for example—the court of committees had to reveal much information about the workings of the Company to them. This necessity to reveal was at odds with the desire to control and restrict information. Additionally, members of the generality often pushed back against decisions to limit their access to information. These circumstances led to an ongoing assessment by Company leaders of what to reveal, when, to whom, and under what circumstances. It also led Company leaders to monitor their own reputations, as they sought to shape what was known and what was alleged about them. Information, public criticism, reputation—these were the tools Company leaders had to construct and maintain authority over the generality and the East Indies trade, but they were also tools that others could wield against the leaders.

Company Leaders and the Generality

Members of the East India Company rarely applied the various widely known contemporary metaphors for the political nation to themselves. Yet they were a body politic, with the Company leaders (the governor, deputy, treasurer, and twenty-four committees) as the head, and the generality (the rest of the adventurers) as the body. Each had assigned roles and tasks in the functioning of the Company, though the proper relationship between the parts of the body politic—like that of the political nation as a whole—was at times bitterly contested.[4]

To regularize the Company's government, and for the better governing of the body, the members of the full Company put together bylaws that they published as the *Laws or Standing Orders* of the Company in 1621. The bylaws detailed all the officers of the Company and their duties.[5] This elaboration of the Company's government fell under the patent provision that the Company could govern itself as it saw fit, provided that the government was not contrary to the laws of England.[6]

The biggest division within the Company was between its leaders and the generality. This division was reinforced in numerous ways. Most prominently, the responsibilities of Company leaders differed greatly from those of the generality. The 1621 *Laws or Standing Orders* specified the responsibilities of the governor, deputy, treasurer, and committees and gave wide-ranging power over the East Indies trade to the Company's elected officials. Company leaders were responsible for almost all aspects of the Company's business. The governor called and presided over meetings, met with the monarch and lords of the Privy Council, managed information to and from the East Indies, and the like. The treasurer controlled the Company's money, accounts, debts, and written documents. The committees oversaw every aspect of the Company's running, from shipbuilding to bills of exchange.[7] The elected officials met together frequently, with each meeting called a "court of committees." That term could refer to individual meetings—a minute might refer to something that happened at a previous court of committees—and also served as a shorthand for the body of elected officials that met—for example, the court of committees could decide something. Most of the surviving Company records are minutes of these closed meetings, and indeed, this was where most of the day-to-day business of the Company was conducted, for the "speedy dispatch, and ordering of the Company's affairs."[8]

There were some checks on the court of committees to ensure proper government. A quorum of thirteen committees besides the governor or deputy was required for a meeting. A meeting could not be held without the governor or deputy. Orders made in a court of committees were binding on Company leaders unless an equal or greater number of committees decided to change them in another court (an order decided upon in a court with sixteen committees present could be changed only by a subsequent court where at least sixteen committees were present, for example). No one but committees and the governor and deputy could speak in a court of committees, and questions in a meeting were decided by majority vote. Additionally, once a committee was charged with performing a particular task, another committee was not allowed to meddle in his performance.[9] Detailed rules, in short, guided the actions of Company leaders as they handled the majority of the Company's affairs.

In contrast, the primary exercise of power that the *Laws or Standing Orders* specified for the generality was the annual election of the governor, deputy, treasurer, and committees. Beyond this duty, the main responsibility of the generality was to pay their adventures promptly. There were also general courts, which the whole body of the Company's members—both elected leaders and the generality—were supposed to attend and at which new members were sworn in, announcements made, and some of the Company's major decisions debated. The sale of goods also took place in these meetings. Company officers checked attendance against a book with the names of all the members, and everyone listed was expected to attend or be fined for being absent.[10] Minutes of the previous general court (though not minutes of any of the recent courts of committees) were often read at the start of these meetings.[11] The *Laws or Standing Orders* did acknowledge

that "matters which concern the Company" were subject to consideration in
a general court, so members of the generality might have a greater role at
those meetings than they did in the day-to-day running of the Company.
Indeed, the *Laws or Standing Orders* directed how a member of the generality might properly take part in a general court. Correct conduct for such a
person included standing up and speaking bareheaded, speaking no more
than three times on any particular topic, and addressing all speech during a
general court to the governor (not to other "particular persons").[12] Only a
few general courts were held each year; though there was no limit on how
many there could be, only two were mandated.[13] In short, Company rules
limited the responsibilities of most members and the avenues for their active participation.

There were fundamental differences between courts of committees and
general courts. The court of committees met far more frequently than the
general court. In October 1609, for example, there were eleven courts of
committees, one mixed meeting including some committees and selected
members of the generality, and two general courts. In November, there
were twelve courts of committees, and in December there were fifteen.
There were no general courts in either month.[14] Usually there were a few
general courts each year, and a court of committees every few days or weeks.

Neither of these types of meetings was open to the general public, but the
meetings of the court of committees were closed even to the Company's
generality. Most of the debate and decisions that structured the Company's
business took place in the closed court of committees, and this fact could
lead to occasional and recurrent tension between the court of committees
and members of the generality. In fact, the court of committees often discussed and strategized about how to manage general courts, sometimes
planning events and debates in advance.

The Company minutes give the impression that the Company leaders were
a coherent unit. Decisions and actions came from the whole court of committees. Discussion within the court of committees took place between one
committee and another, with individual names rarely appearing. The actions and opinions of particular committees are almost impossible to trace
across a given year, though the committees assigned to specific tasks might
be named sometimes. Even in the case of the governor, deputy, and treasurer,
where only one person held each office, names rarely appeared to modify the
elected title. "Mr. Governor" was more likely to speak than "Mr. Governor
Abbot" or "Mr. Governor Smith." Contentious debates within the court of

committees almost always took place between unnamed committees—the minutes certainly recorded debates and differences of opinion but made them anonymous. To a member of the generality (or a historian) who might have access to the Company records, the court of committees was remarkably unrevealing of individuals' contributions or views.

The lack of identifiers and names also meant that the Company leadership appeared to be a coherent unit over time. There was little sense in the records of how the makeup of the committees changed from year to year, or what effect the change of the leadership's makeup might have. By the early 1620s, Company members as a whole had decided that a certain proportion of the court of committees should change each year—the number settled on by 1623 was six out of the twenty-four—but that change was almost invisible in the Company minutes, beyond the changes in the names listed as present at the beginning of each meeting's record.[15] An unnamed committee in 1613 was indistinguishable on paper from an unnamed committee in 1635.

Based on election results, the Company's leadership was indeed a relatively closed group. The positions of governor, deputy governor, and treasurer did not change hands often. In the period from 1601 to 1635, six men served as governor, six as deputy governor, and five as treasurer. The leadership changed hands less frequently than those numbers suggest, as a few people held office for the majority of those years. For example, together Governors Sir Thomas Smith and Sir Morris Abbot led the Company for at least twenty-three years, and Abbot had been deputy governor for almost ten years before becoming governor. Christopher Clitherow was deputy governor from 1624 to 1635 and became governor in 1638, succeeding Abbot. Robert Bateman was treasurer for all of the years from 1621 to 1635 for which records survive.[16]

These men were part of the merchant elite of London, with connections to many companies and City institutions, as well as official roles in government. For example, Smith was also a governor of the Muscovy Company, Levant Company, and Virginia Company, and an alderman and sheriff of London. He went as ambassador to Muscovy in 1604, sat in several parliaments, and served as a commissioner in Anglo-Dutch negotiations on several occasions. He had been implicated in the Essex rebellion, but emerged largely unscathed by the association. His house served as the East India Company's meeting place for years, and one could see there objects (and sometimes people) sent from all over the world. Abbot was a leading member of the Levant Company, serving in some capacity in that company's leadership for a number of years. He also participated in the Muscovy Company, Virginia Company, and several other overseas ventures. Like Smith, he served as a commissioner in Anglo-Dutch negotiations and was a member of several parliaments and an alderman of London. He was also the brother of George Abbot, archbishop of Canterbury. Other elected Company leaders were similarly well-connected, powerful, and deeply involved with England's overseas expansion.[17]

The yearly elections for these positions followed an unofficial script. Several men would be nominated for the position (often the same men year after year). These were usually prominent men in the City, and the nomination itself seems to have been a mark of respect. The incumbent would assert his intention to quit the position, asking the generality not to reelect him and giving some reasons before leaving the room. For example, in 1615 Smith asked the generality not to reelect him as governor, claiming that he had already served them long, needed to recoup his strength, and would be happy to assist the Company as a regular member. Despite the pleas to be released from service, the generality frequently reelected the sitting officer, with the voting almost always conducted by a show of hands. There were a few occasions where the sitting officer was not reelected. For instance, Deputy Governor William Greenwell was not reelected in 1615 after asking not to be and stating that he had become so old and decrepit that "his members and sense fail him, both sight, hearing, and his teeth (whereby his speech is hindered)." Possibly because his complaints were so specific (or so evident), the generality instead elected Morris Abbot for his first term as deputy governor.[18] Once elected or reelected, the officer would take an oath of office. This was the overall pattern for the election of the governor, deputy governor, and treasurer in the early seventeenth century.

In contrast to the election of the officers, the elections of the twenty-four committees were handled as a group. No individuals gave speeches or asked to be excused from reelection. The names of all men nominated for the open seats were listed, then the names of those chosen. The elections of committees as well as officers seem to have taken place via some sort of single transferable vote—though since no description of the actual voting system survives, that is a guess based on how members could vote by raising hands to narrow a large pool. Newly elected or reelected committees took their oath of office at the election meeting, though occasionally committees not present took their oaths at a later date.

Like the Company's officers, the elected committees were a group with limited turnover. Incumbency was common. For the elections for which a comparison with the previous year is possible, the rate of incumbency was never lower than 62.5 percent (fifteen of the twenty-four elected committees were reelected) and at times as high as 79.1 percent (nineteen of the twenty-four) were reelected.[19] After the passage of rules requiring at least six of the twenty-four committees to change each year, no more than 75 percent were incumbent, and in the majority of years, seventeen or eighteen committees were reelected.[20] The incomplete nature of the records means that all calculations are necessarily limited, but based on the surviving records (which cover twenty-one elections), of the 139 men who were elected as committees in the period from 1601 to 1635, almost 60 percent served more than once as committees, and almost 47 percent served more than twice. Many men served for much longer. At least 39 men (almost 30 percent) served as committees five or more times, and at least 14 (10 percent) served for over ten years in the period.[21] Only a little over 36 percent served just once, and if the missing records could be examined that number might be lower.

Therefore, there was a core group whose members held power in the Company year after year. The elected leadership was an exclusive club, and positions in it did not turn over frequently. Over a quarter (26.8 percent) of the men nominated to serve as committees were never elected, while a majority of men served as committees more than once. It is possible that nomination as a committee was an honor in the way that nomination for governor or deputy governor was. Yet some of the men nominated for governor, deputy governor, or treasurer were then elected as committees later in the same meeting. Someone nominated as a committee and not elected had no other position open to him. At least a few men were nominated as committees year after year and never chosen. They remained part of the generality, without access to the power and information that Company leaders had. It is possible that some of those men resented being kept out of the hallowed circle.

Just as the Company leaders were not treated as individuals in the court minutes, neither were members of the generality. The names of individual members rarely appeared. Instead, in a general court meeting, "some" might raise an issue, and "others" might respond. On rare occasions, in especially contentious debates, a few participants' names might be noted, and when that happened, their presence in the minutes is striking. On occasion, the presence of different groups within the generality became evident. For example, in debates in 1629 the wishes of a group of "old adventurers" were set against the wishes of "new adventurers," meaning adventurers in the second and third joint stocks, respectively. In this case, distinctions that actually existed in the aggregate whole of "the generality" were evident, but it was only on rare occasions that the minutes reflected this.[22] It was more usual for Company leaders in courts of committees to refer to "the generality" or "some among the generality," again eschewing individual names or distinctions between groups.

Indeed, so oblique were references to individual members that in the absence of the roll books and detailed records of adventures (which have not survived), it is impossible to determine with any precision how many people composed the generality. A comment in a debate in 1635 noted that 300–400 members of the generality had voted on a particular question at an earlier date, but how that number related to the total number of adventurers is uncertain.[23] Even the imprecise range mentioned—300 to 400—suggested that this number was not an accurate assessment of total numbers of general members. It seems almost certain that there were at least 400 members of the generality (and that number could be a drastic underestimate), but given the missing ledgers of adventurers, a precise number of total members is impossible to provide—much less how many members attended the average meeting or stayed through entire meetings.[24] For example, a vote recorded from another election meeting of the general court listed a total number of votes as ninety-six, but with no comment on whether that was an especially poor or average turnout.[25] These few instances were the exceptions, however, and stood in sharp contrast to the imprecise and generic references to the general members elsewhere in the minutes, where the generality remained an amorphous group.

The effect of these stylistic characteristics—which did not change in the early decades of the seventeenth century—was to establish the court of committees and the generality as two coherent and distinct groups. Though differences of opinion within the two cohorts did make it into the record, the omission of names meant that the groups effectively remained monolithic. The written minutes did not support the notion that someone might take part in a debate as a member of the generality in a given week, then stand for election and become a committee, and after a year not be reelected and rejoin the generality—in short, that there might be fluidity between the groups, and that the gulf between the court of committees and the generality might not always be wide. Instead the minutes encouraged the sense of a separation, and specific policies enacted by the court of committees reinforced the division. However, the distinction between the court of committees and the generality was not as sharply drawn as the records made it appear.

In addition, a few people stood outside the sharp division between the two groups. The Company's secretary, for example, and any assistants he employed, were members neither of the generality nor of the court of committees. Their exclusion from either body was not solely a function of the positions: these men were not required to be adventurers in the Company and were Company employees rather than members. Yet they attended court of committee meetings and took an active role in the Company's business, keeping the minutes, controlling communication into and out of the Company, and keeping track of a host of unspecified "particular affairs."[26] The secretary was, essentially, the living and breathing archive of the Company, responsible for reminding the court of committees of its obligations and keeping comprehensive membership lists, as well as books of the letters and memos of the Company. The secretary even kept the keys to the Company's house at night after the porter locked up.[27] Effectively, the secretary acted at times in a capacity similar to that of a committee—as when, in July 1625, Company secretary Edward Sherburne was charged with attending the lord keeper (the bishop of London) on a matter involving customs.[28] The secretary held an elected position and was bound by an oath to the Company—bound "by oath not to discover any of the secrets of this Company" and not to "draw up any part of the said courts, by the persuasions or directions of any particular men whosoever"—but the position was not one of honor in the way that those of governor, treasurer, and committee were.[29] Additionally, there was no official mechanism for picking a secretary's assistant, and as a committee pointed out in 1632, given that the secretary's assistant was neither elected nor oathbound, yet had access to many Company secrets, the position represented a possible liability.[30]

It was not unusual for the Company's secretary to have extensive powers. Livery companies, similar in some organizational ways to the Company, also gave power and responsibility to their clerks, who in many ways seem to have held positions analogous to that of the Company's secretary. In recognition of the power clerks held, the Vintners' Company, for example, required their clerk to take a special oath that included promising to keep matters secret. Clerks regularly wielded power through their control of company resources and their connections to clerks of other companies, and therefore the resources other clerks controlled.[31] Nor was this power limited to London companies. Secretaries and clerks of the Privy Council knew a great deal about the business they recorded, and they were treated as very knowledgeable—being asked for their advice at times by privy councilors. These men had to swear special oaths (almost identical to those sworn by the privy councilors they worked for) and there were policies in place to pass on necessary information to incoming clerks. Given that they collected all petitions to the Privy Council, their fingerprints were literally and figuratively on all aspects of the Council's business.[32] Whether in companies or the Privy Council, therefore, secretaries and clerks were power brokers.

Despite holding a powerful position, the Company's secretary was almost entirely invisible in the Company minutes—records that the secretaries themselves kept—in the early seventeenth century. The secretary was not named in the list of committees attending each meeting. When he did appear in the written record, it was generally in notes recording matters he was charged to deal with or notes of funds disbursed to him in acknowledgment of some completed task. The minutes referred to him no differently than any other person to whom Company funds were disbursed, or committees charged with particular tasks. Indeed, when they appeared, secretaries often identified themselves as "Mr." rather than "Secretary," eliding on paper their separation from the court of committees.[33]

Thus only the seemingly disparate court of committees and generality made up the recorded East India Company. They were parts of the same whole, yet record-keeping conventions separated them on paper, and the rules of when and how each took part in Company business separated them institutionally. Incumbency and reelection kept the ranks of Company leaders relatively closed as well, though some men did move into and out of the court of committees.

Perhaps it was because Company leaders and the generality were not as sharply separate as the records suggested (and as Company leaders may have wished) that Company leaders carefully cultivated the separateness of the generality through policies and practices. They referred to the generality as other, treating it as appropriate to shield members of the generality from the inner workings of the East Indies trade—despite what the members themselves might wish. When it came to the mysteries of the trade, the generality was part of the rude multitude, of the public, and Company leaders saw their role as guarding the secrets of the trade from this group.

The meaning of "public" as an adjective in the Company archives was ambiguous, and could indicate something positive or negative depending on the circumstance. The public benefit of the East Indies trade was something Company leaders were proud of, for instance, but when "public" appeared in conjunction with information, it was almost always dangerous and negative. Public knowledge in these latter instances represented what Company leaders could not control. Exactly who was alluded to when Company leaders mentioned "public" knowledge or the like is hard to say. "Public" was a useful and elastic adjective that Company leaders could use to refer to various groups, both inside and outside the Company. These multiple senses of "public" included the nation as a whole, other merchants and the City of London, and even the generality of the Company itself, which in essence redefined a part of the Company as "public."[34]

Defining part of the East India Company as "public" had consequences for the political life of the Company. It meant that Company leaders envisioned an ongoing distinction between themselves and the wider corporation, or between the court of committees and the generality. It meant that Company leaders took active steps to manage their relationship with their internal public (the generality), and it meant that Company leaders and their public could sometimes be at odds with each other. The best tool available to the leaders to manage the generality was the restriction and regulation of information. In courts of committees, Company leaders debated what information might be shared publicly—that is, in general courts—and what was to be kept secret. Secrecy was their best means of asserting their control and constituting their authority over the generality.

Secrecy and Access

Secrecy was an essential characteristic of any early modern political body. Government and authority in the early modern period relied on maintaining secrecy and controlling access to information. From the mysteries of state that Elizabeth I and James I warned people away from to parish accounts kept in locked chests, early modern authorities constituted authority through the restriction of access. Secrecy was a measure of early modern authority, delineating the boundaries between those who governed and those who were governed, between who was authority and who was part of the public. As one historian put it, "secrecy protected existing structures of authority," casting a veil over the inner proceedings of government and restricting access to those inner sanctums.[35] The concerns of Company members with secrecy, access, and the openness of government were at their heart political concerns and were shared by members of many other institutions, from other London corporate bodies to the Privy Council.[36]

The Company's court of committees was constantly exercised about questions of secrecy. Mentions of how various pieces of information were intended to remain secret and questions of how information that the court thought was secret had become public peppered the Company minutes. Newly elected committee members were reminded of the required secrecy as soon as they took their oaths and before business discussions were begun, and they were informed that "when a business of secrecy is recommended to their cares, and so recorded," they were to show "greater care and conscience" to keep it from being "discovered and spoken of abroad."[37] A marginal note on one record, for example, summed up the entire account as "secrets not to be divulged."[38] These repetitions of the need for secrecy highlighted not only the care the court of committees took to maintain it, but also the fact that secrecy required vigilance because it was both powerful and fragile.[39]

As a company with proprietary rights to the Eastern trade, information about and from the East Indies was a valuable and dangerous commodity. Company regulations gave extensive directions for how factors in the East Indies should keep records, and how and when to send their accounts to England. The two principal factors were supposed to keep letter books containing copies of all correspondence sent and received between factories. They were supposed to keep journals, to set down the "notable occurrences" of everything they did day to day. Additionally, the principal factors were expected to collect accounts from other factors of the doings in their factories and forward the accounts to the court of committees.[40] In the letters and accounts themselves, factors were instructed to "use care and exquisiteness in keeping and making up their accounts." Those accounts should be sent to England "perfectly finished" and legible. These various letters, letter books, accounts, journals, and bills of lading and invoices were supposed to be sent "verbatim" with the yearly fleet and any other "such ships as shall return."[41]

Once these various records made it back to England, Company leaders tried to keep them close. All news from the East Indies was supposed to be read first in closed committee sessions. The court of committees monitored access to the letters and journals that the captains and factors had been so carefully instructed to keep.[42] They also decreed that the "sundry journals and letters of intelligence," with their precious information on the "places and commodities fit for trade," were to be entered into the Company books, "and none of them lent abroad to any man before such time [as] an entry be first made."[43] The court of committees, therefore, took numerous steps to keep information from the East Indies both as complete as possible and in their control. When the court of committees' directives were followed, therefore, they would know at all times where their letters and ledgers were and who had seen them.

This concern with correct record keeping, access to records, and the control of information was not limited to the East India Company leaders. In London, other corporations, as well as guilds and vestries, made similar rules to sequester documents and restrict access to them. These rules and regulations were not even solely English concerns; similar practices and concerns shaped procedures in Swiss city governments as well, where civic authorities commissioned special cabinets and chests to properly house municipal archives.[44] Additionally, historians have long recognized that attention to the collection, control, and use of information was a hallmark of almost all European overseas activities—especially in, but not limited to, European colonialism.[45]

However, enforcing their regulations proved difficult for Company leaders on numerous occasions. When, for example, it appeared that some journals had been lost because they had been loaned out before they were entered in the log, the court of committees could only reiterate that the journals were to be entered in the log first, so that their access could be monitored and their location tracked. The rules notwithstanding, "the journals themselves have been lost, to the great prejudice of the Company, and some things known which are not fit to be published." The court of committees resolved that in future, "the journals shall be kept and not lent forth at all, until they shall be first entered in the books." Once entered, the "principal" members of the Company might take the books, but all others would be able to see them only in the Company's offices.[46] Similarly, decrees about the proper place for reading letters newly arrived from the East Indies were at odds with how the letters were sometimes treated in actuality. After the arrival of several ships from the East Indies in 1622, for example, the court of committees noted that the newly arrived letters should be opened in the appointed location and not in public places like the Royal Exchange: Company leaders "misliked . . . that any letters out of the Indies should be opened upon the Exchange, but always in the place proper, that is to say, either in this court or by order or direction of the same."[47]

Members of the generality certainly seemed to want and expect greater access to information from the East Indies than the decrees of Company leaders would allow. In 1621, for example, a committee reported that many members of the generality were coming to the counting house, expecting to see the letters, "and do take it ill to be refused them."[48] He observed that he had sworn to prevent anyone except other committees from reading the letters and requested the court to "settle it that they might either read them or not read them so he might be free from blame." The court of committees' discussion highlighted the distinction Company leaders made between themselves and the generality and why restricting access was so important to them. The leaders argued that they were bound to secrecy but the generality were not, and thus if the letters were readily accessible, "the principal secrets of the trade" would be open to members who might speak of them too freely. They decreed that the letters could not be read unless by order of the court, and even in such cases, any copies that were made must first be "purge[d]" of "such things as shall not be held fit for every common eye."[49] The decision reflected not only the concern of the court of committees with controlling access to information, but also its belief that the expectations of at least some members of the generality were coming into conflict with the desires of the court of committees. The "principal secrets of the trade," the court of committees thought, should be kept even from the general members of the Company.

Sometimes the court of committees restricted information to particular members of the generality. In 1631, when one member asked that a recent letter from Persia be read in a general court, he was refused. The "public reading" would reveal some materials that were "better to be concealed than divulged" to the entire general court.[50] Adventurers in the first Persia voyage, however, could repair to the counting house and see the letter there. Thus the Company leaders drew distinctions within the generality of who had access to what information at what times.

Company ledgers and account books were subject to similar problems and regulations. The court of committees periodically restated restrictions on access to the court minutes. In late 1632, for example, after receiving a complaint about access to Company letters and court minutes, the court of committees "observed how dangerous it is, that the counting house and secretary's office should be open to any of the Company to ravel [or delve] into the accounts." They decided to limit access, so that "no freeman of the Company but those that have the government thereof be permitted to see and peruse them." The person who had brought the complaint had not wanted the leaders to take that particular course of action and argued that every member of the Company took an oath "to conceal and not bewray [or reveal] the secrets of the Company," though the rest of the court of committees was unpersuaded.[51] Months later, the issue resurfaced. This time Company leaders noted that too many "secrets are divulged and an ill use made thereof." They decided that "from henceforth no person whatsoever (the committees only excepted) should be permitted or have the liberty to read or take copies of their letters, consultations or acts of court or to ravel or dive into their accounts without the consent of allowance of the court of committees." Someone then informed the leaders that some members of the generality came daily to access these documents, sometimes making copies of them. Company leaders ultimately ordered that adventurers could see the documents directly relating to their adventure, though that still required the consent of the court of committees.[52] The fact that Company leaders were dealing with this issue again in 1632 and 1633, despite earlier decisions limiting access to these records, demonstrated how hard it was to police the boundaries of access. The ideal for Company leaders may have been to keep access restricted, but over time the restrictions inevitably loosened, only to be tightened again.

A category of letters from the East Indies that Company leaders worked especially hard to control were private letters from factors in the East Indies to their friends and family members in England. The general of the returning fleet in 1614 brought all such letters "to private friends" to Company committees, who conferred on what to do with the letters. They read the superscriptions and decided to have most of the letters delivered, though they sent for the addressee of one, and the minutes noted that the letter would be "opened and read before him."[53] A few weeks later the issue of private letters came up again, and the committees decided that no private letters would be delivered without being read first. They had found, they claimed, that "the Company are much wronged by the bringing home of letters by private men to their great prejudice," and they decided to insert a clause in their commissions prohibiting "captain, master, nor other officers" from bringing and delivering letters "to any private persons" without first presenting them to be read by the governor.[54] Private letters were not forbidden, but they were monitored and probably somewhat discouraged. Certainly almost no private letters from the period have survived, and no estimate can be made of the numbers that were written and sent, or the number that were not allowed to be passed on.

The trouble with private letters was not only that they might spread valuable and sensitive information, but that they might be used to facilitate private trade. In the early seventeenth century, private trade meant illicitly imported goods that the returning mariners and factors brought with them, thus diluting the Company's monopoly on importation and provision of East Indies goods.[55] The letters the Company confiscated might just as easily have contained details on how and when to unload smuggled goods in England, as sensitive information from the East.[56] The court of committees desired neither sort of information disseminated. Thus, for example, when Captain John Saris returned in 1614, the Company confiscated two of his letters, one to his brother and one to a cousin who conveniently worked in the custom house. Saris had sent his brother instructions to come to Gravesend with a closed litter and two trusty watermen and mentioned sending letters with someone else who had left one of the ships before the Company's men arrived. The letters raised the suspicions of the court of committees, and they resolved to send two men to stay aboard the ships and make sure neither Saris's goods nor "those of others' letters" were landed before a full inventory of the returned goods was made. To help ensure compliance, they also requested the customs agents not to release any goods before the full ships' inventory was turned in. The entire situation was "to be kept secret."[57] This case was one of the most obvious examples in which the ability of Company leaders to control information reflected their ability to control the trade.

Controlling access to information, both about proceedings in London and further east, was one of the main concerns of the court of committees. Not infrequently, committee members were taxed with finding out how "some things [were] delivered abroad" that "were given in charge by Mr. Governor to have been kept secret."[58] In one case, considering the gratuities to two Company members who had served as commissioners to the Netherlands, the court of committees decided to keep the matter private "because no exceptions should be taken by the generality who have no means to consider of the causes."[59] The generality could not know the full matter and therefore might not understand that the gratuity was well deserved; overall, it was better to keep the whole matter secret.

Company matters still under discussion were not supposed to be disclosed outside the court of committees. Information that had been "delivered abroad" yet had been "given in charge by Mr. Governor to have been kept secret" led to a reiteration that only the elected and appointed committees were to be present for sensitive discussions: "none but committees to be permitted to be present in court when any business of import were handled."[60] Likewise, when the governor shared the news that he was working with Secretary of State Sir Ralph Winwood to have a clause inserted into the captain's commission granting him the power to take possession of any English ships in the East Indies on the Company's behalf, he prefaced the announcement with a desire to keep the news secret. Furthermore, he wanted to discuss whether the commission, with its new inclusion, should be made public—"whether it were fit to have it published or kept private"— if it were granted. Committees spoke on both sides; some claimed that making the commission known would discourage would-be interlopers from sailing, while others thought that it would only keep them from the common ports and thus make them harder to surprise and catch. Ultimately, all agreed to keep the measure quiet until it had to be made public, as "it were best to conceal it, that no suspicion may be had of them until some act shall give cause to have it known."[61]

The injunctions for secrecy and restriction of access to information were constantly repeated throughout the early years of the Company. Restricting access was both a practical and a theoretical issue. In the abstract, restricting access—without regard to the value of controlling any particular piece of information—showed the power and authority of those who ordered the restriction. The constant reiterations of the need for secrecy were part of how Company leaders constituted their authority over the generality. On a practical level, information from the East Indies was one of the most valuable commodities the Company possessed. Known too widely, the value of the Company's information might diminish. On occasion Company leaders worried that incomplete knowledge of their activities might lead members of the generality to misunderstand and wrongly suspect them of mishandling the Company's business. Thus, the restriction of access to information also served concrete ends, giving Company leaders greater control over the East Indies trade and protecting them from criticism.

Authority, Reputation, and the City

The court minutes testified to the clear sense that the actions of the Company were known and judged on a public stage, with consequences for the Company's reputation and its ability to fund the joint stock (that is, to get

adventurers to pay). This sense of public performance was part of the impetus behind the attempts by Company leaders to keep information about
the trade and their actions secret. It also led the leaders to monitor their
public reputations and defend themselves when they learned of public
criticism.

Company leaders acted on their perceptions of public judgment. For example, when the East India Company had a disagreement with the Levant
Company in 1614, the East India Company court of committees agreed to
negotiate—in part to end public disagreement between the two. The court
of committees "wished that a friendly end might rather be made than to
have two such companies to contest in public." They wanted the matter resolved "privately and peaceably betwixt them."[62] And when a "scandalous
imputation" was made about the Company for selling adulterated indigo
dust in 1622, the Company appointed a committee to oversee the indigo,
"for the satisfaction of the world."[63] In another case, a note in 1602 for the
Company to force adventurers to pay their promised contributions specified
that the Company did not want to be discredited by a "discovery being
made so public, as well as to our own country as to strangers in foreign
parts."[64] It was not just Londoners who they feared would be unfavorably
impressed with the Company, but also rivals much farther afield.

Talk "abroad," whether in London or Europe, was a concern to Company
leaders. Once information was abroad in London it was as good as abroad
in Europe for the court of committees; once information was public, they
could no longer control its spread. Indeed, the Company employed men in
the Netherlands to collect and report the same type of talk abroad—in this
case, news about the Dutch East India Company—that they sought to prevent circulating in London about themselves.[65]

Company leaders knew that people outside the Company were paying
attention to its doings and took some actions with the expectation that they
would be known widely. In 1614, Company leaders debated applying to the
Privy Council for aid in acquiring some seized Portuguese goods they felt
were due to them. They thought that knowledge of their actions would be a
deterrent to others in future, stating that even "if nothing be recovered yet
it will daunt others finding their power to prosecute matters at home as well
as abroad."[66] Company leaders thought action by the regime on their behalf
would gain them a great deal, though not necessarily in material terms. If
the matter were decided in their favor, "although it were but to have a key of
the door where the goods be," it would "gain a great reputation unto the

Company, and terrify others to do the like, when they shall see that they can neither find peace abroad nor at home."[67] In other words, access to the goods was the small return, while the symbolic message was the major one.

When Company leaders thought the reputation of the Company was at stake, they took aggressive action to protect it. The seized Portuguese goods had come to the court of committees' attention because "a knight abroad"—most likely meaning abroad in London or in England, rather than outside the country—had "cast many imputations upon this Company, for monopolizing as he pretended the sole trade into the East Indies."[68] Redress was necessary, therefore, to prove a point not only outside England, but also in London. A few months later, a writing was "set up abroad." Here, "abroad" signified London. The writing, which seems to have appeared anonymously, questioned the East India Company's right to some goods, and therefore, to Company leaders, its patent privileges. The Company's solicitor was "appointed to go and get a copy of the said writing" and to hire a proctor to lay claim to the goods "by virtue of his majesty's grant in their patent." Furthermore, the court of committees ordered two of its members to get an order from the Privy Council about the affair, "which will bring a reputation and honor to the Company, that shall make it appear to the world that they do not favor their cause, nor his courses."[69] The public rebuttal was necessary to protect the Company's reputation.

Of all public places, one was given special weight in the Company minutes: the Royal Exchange. The Exchange was the heart of commercial London. It was modeled on the Bourse in Antwerp and had been built in the late 1560s. As St. Paul's was the center of news exchange in London, and Paul's Cross was the pulpit of the nation, so the Exchange was not only a place where actual trade was conducted, but also a public forum for commercial and mercantile matters. Rules governed how and when trading took place in the public forum, and merchants of different nations had their own spaces in the Exchange, "so that those who have business with them can find them more easily." Information spread as merchants mingled. Letters could be delivered to merchants at the Exchange, and one contemporary account noted that "one regularly hears the news of other countries and regions, which is a great convenience for those who traffick in merchandise across the seas." It was here that "merchants stroll in fine weather and talk business."[70] Contemporary images depict the Exchange as a bustling place full of activity, with hundreds of conversations taking place among people from many nations, and by the early seventeenth century it was a popularly recognizable London place—referred to, for example, in a number of contemporary plays.[71]

The Company had an extensive presence at the Exchange. Some of the Company warehouses—particularly the pepper warehouses—were nearby.[72] The keys for the East India Company warehouses were brought daily to the Exchange, leading one committee to complain about the great distance between the Exchange and the deputy governor's house, where the key was kept when it was not at the Exchange. He requested that the key be kept at the house of a committee who lived closer to the Exchange.[73] As the daily bringing and returning of the key might suggest, the Exchange was the physical space where the private business of the Company intersected with the public presence of the city, not only practically but also symbolically. The Exchange was the physical locale of the City public that the East India Company dealt with.

Aspersions cast upon the Company in the Exchange had greater weight than those made in other places. Certainly the Exchange was one of few sites regularly mentioned by name in the court minutes. A committee in 1609 who "despitefully and viciously abused" another committee "publicly in the Exchange and at the full time thereof" was removed from his committee position as a result. Company leaders could not tolerate public dissent, especially among themselves. When Robert Bateman, then treasurer, reported that he had learned of a rumor alleging that he was false and had not correctly kept the Company's accounts that was circulating upon the Exchange, the rest of the court of committees assured him of their support. They also sent for the man who had told Bateman of the rumors to try to find out with whom they had originated, so the court could pursue further action as necessary.[74]

Challenges to the Company that appeared in the Exchange elicited special responses as well. When a group purported to set itself up as a "new East India Company" by means of a "bill set upon the Exchange," the governor informed Lord Zouch, a member of the Privy Council—who, according to the court minutes, promptly sent for the bill and took it to a meeting of the Council. To the court of committees' gratification, Zouch made a fuss about the matter, wondering that the lord mayor of London allowed it "to be set up so publicly about the city to the discountenance of this Company."[75] The Council agreed to take the issue to the king. The Company referred to in the bill was almost assuredly the short-lived Scottish East India Company, which is discussed in detail in Chapter 6.

When Sir Randall Cranfield—newly made master of the mint and the brother of Lionel Cranfield, the Earl of Middlesex—made "uncivil speeches" about the governor, deputy, and committees, notably in the Exchange, the court of committees debated how to respond. Part of the difficulty was that Sir Randall Cranfield criticized not just the governor, deputy, and committees as people, but also the government they represented: he "reached higher than to them as particular men, and trenched deep into the government."[76] Because he aimed so high in his criticism, it was "fit to be taken notice of," as the criticism surpassed what might be ignored. He gave "indignities not to be borne of private men, much less by the governor, deputy and committees." How best to pursue the matter was the question. Some Company leaders wanted to address the matter at a general court, while others wanted to take the matter outside of the Company, to the lord treasurer, because the criticism of the government of the Company was being "taken notice of by the gentry of the Company."[77] In other words, the complaints, due to their manner and content, questioned the authority of the members of the court of committees as men and as leaders of the Company, and the speech was made by a well-connected man to other well-connected men. Therefore, it could not be ignored. One committee promised that he could testify to the content of Cranfield's accusations, and although members of the court were still not sure how to pursue the matter, they decided that if they made a case of it, it should be "pursued effectually for precedent's sake to affright others from the like."[78] The location of Cranfield's criticism, as well as its substance, demanded action by Company leaders.

The Company's reputation in the Exchange could be endangered not only by critical speeches, but also by what Company leaders considered unseemly behavior or objects that they thought reflected on them. In 1615, the Exchange was the site of "great speeches" about "certain books" one captain brought back. The books, possibly pornographic by English standards of the time, "caused the Company and Mr. Governor's house to be censured." Company leaders confiscated and burned them, with the provision that "such as have heard derogatory speeches used upon the Exchange, and elsewhere, should now likewise be eyewitnesses of the consuming of them in the fire"—a course of action they hoped would "give satisfaction to any honestly affected, that such wicked spectacles are not fostered and maintained by any of this Company."[79] Those who had heard of the scandal were required to see the end of it.

The Exchange may have been the most symbolically important London location, but Company leaders also had no doubt that word on the street could have a significant effect on the Company's affairs. Word of the return of a fleet could spur investments, and quickly. John Chamberlain, writing to Sir Dudley Carleton, informed him of the enthusiastic investment after the return of a fleet: "the good return of our East Indian ships hath put such life into that trade, that our merchants mean to go roundly to work"—within two weeks, he reported, they had been promised £400,000.[80] Given that neither Chamberlain nor Carleton were members of the Company, the former's comments testified to the spread of the news (Chamberlain collected much of his news at St. Paul's); the accepted effect it had; and even, by Chamberlain's use of "our," the fact that the trade itself belonged not only to the merchants who carried it out, but also to men not directly part of the Company.

Negative public perception could work to the Company's detriment as easily as positive news could work to its benefit. In early 1622, when the Company petitioned the lord keeper about a case of private trading, he was sympathetic to the leaders' case but gave them some words of caution. The minutes reported, quite frankly, that the lord keeper, "told them that the East India Company is not generally well thought of." He advised them not to make too much fuss about private trade, lest by "carrying too strict a hand," they failed to attract worthy men to their service.[81] However, when a member of the generality reported that rumors were circulating that private trading had enriched men abroad who had gone out "scarce worth £20," the governor explained that the court of committees had taken action to investigate and invited members of the generality to take part in the investigation. He wanted them to know that their adventures were being properly cared for, and that the Company employees abroad had sufficient oversight, lest a perceived slackness discourage investments.[82] The court of committees reiterated the importance of dealing with the matter, as "this business is of much consequence, and . . . many eyes are upon the court of committees to observe their charge herein."[83]

Attacks on the Company could come from without or from within, and in the latter case, the response made by the court of committees had to be especially visible. Criticism from within belied the image of a unified company and provided public evidence that the Company was at odds with itself. In addition, depending on the topic, Company leaders viewed criticism that arose from Company members as more damaging than rumors on the Exchange or the like.

The particular danger of public criticism arising from a Company man was evident in an example from 1615, when word reached the court of committees about public criticism of the Company, and specifically of the court of committees, delivered by one of its own members. Two elements were especially noteworthy about the case: first, the criticism highlighted the real or perceived division between the court of committees and the generality, and second, the criticism had special weight because it came from within and was aired in a public forum.

In a meeting of the court of committees on 8 September 1615, Company leaders were "informed of a gross imputation and great scandal cast upon the committees by Mr. Burke." He had made his charges "at a public dinner, amongst many merchants and others of good account, and sundry women then present." Burke's accusation focused on an action of the committees regarding the seventh voyage, when they had, without consulting the generality, provided additional, necessary money—which Burke claimed was to the "great wrong and prejudice" of the generality. According to the minutes, he was then and there contradicted, but he refused to recant. The minutes noted that the charge could be easily answered by "certain orders of court made by the generality themselves," meaning that the court's actions were legal and allowed and should be known by all. But Burke's actions had "too much scandalized" their "credits and reputations," and the court of committees required the governor to bring up the matter in a general court, so that Burke "may be censured according to his deserts to the example of all others that shall offend in the like nature."[84] Interestingly, the very secrecy with which they had cloaked their actions had opened them up to Burke's criticism. According to the minutes, in other words, though the committees were sure of the acceptability of their actions, the public nature of the charges of scandal required an internally public refutation—that is, a refutation before the generality.

The governor, Sir Thomas Smith, handled the presentation of Burke's perfidy to the generality, emphasizing that Company leaders had acted correctly. He treated Burke's accusations as serious. According to the governor's presentation of the matter, "a brother of this Company, a grave man, hath offered a great disgrace unto their governor, deputy, and committees." Even presenting the matter before the whole Company, the governor emphasized that the scandal was against the court of committees and leaders, not specifically against the Company as a whole. He elaborated that the brother, who did not appear in the general court minutes by name, had made "uncivil speeches publicly at a table in town where were present many gentlemen, merchants and divers women." The charge itself was the same as that discussed in the court of committees earlier, but the governor went into more detail about the effects of Burke's speech on the Company as a whole. The minutes noted that Burke had been contradicted but continued in his calumny, adding: "seeing it is not unknown how many enemies this Company have, who are too ready to heap disgraces and scandalous aspersions upon them, they ought therefore amongst themselves to be the more circumspect to give such an advantage to their adversaries especially by any of the Company themselves."[85] The governor read the order, including the date it was made, that authorized the court of committees' actions, adding that the leaders had indeed canvassed the generality for additional funds, and that the majority of these new adventurers—in terms of number and amount—were from the generality.

The governor's careful presentation bore the desired fruit: according to the minutes, the generality cried out for the instigator to be publicly censured. Assured of the generality's support of the court of committees, the governor put the least culpatory spin on Burke's actions—which was also one that emphasized the Company's strength. He attributed the impetus behind the criticism to the devil's meddling in the face of the Company's good fortune.[86] Though Burke remained nameless throughout this account, the court minutes asserted his grief before the generality over the incident, with the incident allowing for the reiteration of the Company's profitable ventures and God-blessed endeavors and the assertion of the "great pains for the good of the Company" taken by the governor, deputy, and committees. The Company leaders viewed incidents like this one as dangerous. However, a well-orchestrated refutation could not only refute a charge but also bolster the structures under attack. In other words, the charge allowed for an assertion of good conduct that might have seemed out of place otherwise. The court of committees organized a proof of good and responsible government—the reading of the order by the generality—to counter the charge of bad government.

Company leaders protected the Company's reputation outside of England no less assiduously, even against the actions of Company members. When the court of committees discovered that a Company adventurer was buying pepper and then adulterating it before selling it abroad in Naples, they "held it to be a great deceit, wrong, and scandal to the Company, disgrace, discredit, and disparagement to this nation." Despite the merchant's claims that "he had done the like before, and it was well accepted and went current without any exceptions in those parts where it was sold," the court of committees, "to maintain the honor of the kingdom and Company," impounded his pepper and admonished him to be "so mindful of his own reputation as not to force those things to public notice."[87] In other words, lack of consideration of his private reputation would have public consequences for the Company. The leaders decided to prosecute that merchant, Edward Lutterford, because in addition to the scandal of selling adulterated East Indies goods, he had chosen to make very public criticism of the Company. Lutterford was not an insignificant member of the Company. He was one of the original adventurers and he had served as a committee in 1610–11, though he was not a committee at the time of his public criticism. Company leaders wanted to make him an example to prevent others from insulting and scorning them, "as they are informed he did at a dinner at Drapers' Hall by a large relation." The court of committees took their complaint about Lutterford to the lord treasurer, the Earl of Suffolk, who found that "his Majesty is much wronged to have impost repaid for the said dust put in by Mr. Lutterford which will touch him nearly."[88] From being an issue of Company concern and reputation, the leaders reframed the issue into one that touched the king. Essentially, the court of committees brought down official ire on Lutterford for cheating the king, to punish him for insulting the Company.

Company leaders knew the stakes were high when it came to information that circulated about the Company's trade and their management of it. They attempted to restrict access to sensitive information about the East Indies to themselves, and to guard their and the Company's public reputation, at times staging rebuttals to criticisms of their leadership. They wanted their actions to be secret, hidden from the view even of their own generality. Yet the repeated examples of information that did not remain secret demonstrated how difficult it was to keep information from an interested public, and how fragile the control of information could be. Secrecy and the control of information helped consolidate the authority of the court of committees over the generality, but the veil of secrecy was rarely impenetrable, and members of the generality could—and at times did—push back against the control of the court of committees.

3

Wooing Adventurers

Membership and Useful Men

T HOUGH THE EAST INDIA COMPANY was founded as a
company of London merchants, by 1618 its membership was much
broader. In August of that year, a Company member, Robert Bell, wrote to
the English ambassador at The Hague, Sir Dudley Carleton, that the
East India Company was "composed of the greatest part of the Privy Council,
of the nobility, of the judges of the land, the gentry of the kingdom, and [was]
furnished with an assured stock of sixteen hundred thousand pounds
[£1,600,000]." Bell was not boasting; instead, the overall tone of his letter was
a mix of concern and aggression. He noted the Company's impressive membership to argue that, with such a number of important members, Carleton
"may well imagine" that the Company would not "endure such affronts and
disgraces" as the Dutch seemed to be offering them at that time.[1] For Bell, a
London merchant, the Company's mixed composition was a strength, giving
it a force it would not have without the stake in the Company's success that
he assumed its privy councilor, gentry, and noble members felt.

Aristocratic membership in the Company also had its downside. What
role gentry and noble members should play in the Company's government
was not clear to members at the time. Just a few weeks before Bell wrote the
letter quoted above, some members responded to the extensive gentry membership in the Company by floating schemes to formalize gentry representation in the governing body of the Company. They wanted to ensure that
aristocratic members had at least a certain percentage of seats in the court of
committees, but they were unsuccessful.[2] A year later, members of the court
of committees complained that "such gentlemen as have been taken into the

Company by courtesy do aim to get all the government into their hands."[3] From the merchants' perspective, gentry involvement in the Company could also be a weakness.

Despite any possible complications resulting from elite involvement in the East India Company, a significant number of aristocrats and gentry became members (and hence investors) in it during the early decades of the seventeenth century. As Bell's letter testifies, Company membership became overlapped with court circles. Some historians have suggested that gentry presence in the Company might have explained the continuing, if at times begrudging, benevolence of Parliament toward the Company and the Company's favorable reception at the royal court at the time.[4] Others, however, have seen the Company as distinctly separate from court, despite any shared personnel, and often the target of attempted royal manipulation.[5] But historians have rarely considered what gentry involvement meant for the Company, or why an overseas company might want gentry members.

Gentry investment in the East India Company did not occur unprompted; the court of committees actively recruited influential members of the gentry and aristocracy to participate in the Company. Company leaders courted, and sometimes were courted by, gentry investors who offered a variety of services and skills that the Company could use. Gentry membership in the Company came in waves, with the first great phase of elite membership in the Company taking place against a background of phenomenal profits and slowing down in the 1620s when profits did.[6] By the time profits declined and the appeal of Company membership might have lost some of its glow, a significant number of courtiers and gentry were already members. This chapter examines how the Company acquired gentry and aristocratic members, how Company leaders hoped to use them, and how they cultivated nonmember courtiers. It reveals that the large numbers of gentry and aristocratic members were the product of the actions by Company leaders to benefit from the interest, abilities, and connections of influential men by offering them membership and the chance to invest in the Company.

Aristocratic and Gentry Membership in the Company

Aristocratic and gentry involvement in the overseas trading companies grew in the late sixteenth and early seventeenth centuries. Scholars have put forth a variety of answers to the question of what drew these elite groups—

whose income and high status traditionally derived from land and royal office rather than commerce—to companies like the East India Company and the Virginia Company. Ranging from the lure of rich profits without actually having to engage in trade to a commitment to a particular religious and / or imperial vision for England, the spurs for gentry involvement in the overseas trading companies were multiple and varied, and aristocratic members turned up in a number of companies.[7] The founding members of the Muscovy Company, for example, were an illustrious group, more so than the founders of the East India Company. Of the 201 people named in the 1555 Muscovy Company patent, seven were peers, eight were knights or esquires who held high positions at court, and there were also more than ten aldermen and a number of merchant knights.[8] Both the Spanish Company (founded in 1577) and the Barbary Company (1585) had two of Queen Elizabeth's most prominent advisors—Robert Dudley, the Earl of Leicester, and Sir Francis Walsingham—on their charters.[9] Additionally, the 1606 patent of the Virginia Company, which unusually named only eight people, included none who were primarily merchants (although had a list of the first subscribers survived, it would likely have named far more people, including many merchants).[10] These were not the only companies that had gentry and aristocratic investment; others included the Africa, Providence Island, and Bermuda Companies.[11]

Yet extensive gentry involvement in the East India Company in particular was not a given. Most gentry involvement in overseas companies was concentrated in the various Atlantic companies, where colonization was a priority. It was only in those joint-stock companies that gentry membership topped 25 percent of the whole. The Levant Company had few gentry members, and even in trading companies where there was initial gentry investment, nonmerchants seem to have played little role in the ongoing functioning of the institution. Several companies allowed nonmerchants as honorary members only, with no formal role in the trade.[12] In 1600 the East India Company's original patent named almost 220 adventurers. Only one of them, George Clifford, the Earl of Cumberland, was a titled peer—though at least one other man was ennobled later.[13] Another three were knights, all part of the City elite (all three were aldermen); four were esquires; and several others were knighted after 1600. The overwhelming majority of the original adventurers were merchants of London, with many from the civic elite of the City, and a few who had ties to the regime or positions at court.

When the Company was founded, there was no formal mechanism for enabling gentry investment. In the early seventeenth century, no one could invest in the East India Company trade without being admitted to the Company—becoming a "brother" of the Company or gaining the "freedom of the Company," in the parlance of the time. Buying and selling East India Company shares in the stock market was a development of the later seventeenth century.[14] In the early seventeenth century, only someone who was "free of the Company" could adventure in the joint stock—that is, invest money. Some adventured as little as the minimum required amount of £100. Others adventured thousands of pounds. In 1621, for example, Company governor Sir Thomas Smith noted that he had adventured almost £20,000.[15] All transfers of whole adventures or parts of adventures came before the court of committees for approval and were supposed to take place only between Company members, though they could also be transferred via inheritance. This was not merely a matter of form—Company leaders reserved the right to decline a transfer out of concern that, without oversight, fraudulent transfers of adventures might take place.[16]

The Company's patent had acknowledged that the original Company members might need or want to admit new people to the Company and specified only that new members approved by Company leaders had to make a corporate oath.[17] In the early years of the Company, several ways of becoming free of the Company became standard and were eventually codified in the 1621 *Laws or Standing Orders*. One method was through patrimony, meaning the right of founding and admitted members to pass the freedom of the Company to their sons when they reached the age of twenty-one. Another was through serving an apprenticeship of seven years. A third was by purchase, with set "fines" for people of different stations. A merchant could purchase admission to the Company for a fine of £50; the fine for anyone else was 100 marks (approximately £66). New members were supposed to be admitted on the same terms as the founders, "as if they were expressly mentioned in the said charter."[18] Like the founding memberships, freedom via fine, service, or patrimony therefore was heritable.

A final means of gaining freedom existed: becoming free gratis, by grace or kindness of Company leaders. This type of freedom usually cost the holder nothing more than a payment to the Company's poor box. It was not officially heritable, though that proscription does not seem to have always been upheld.[19] This was the means of gaining freedom of the Company used for almost all gentry and aristocrats (though a few merchants also received it, and a few gentry members did not). It did not exist in the early years of the Company's existence. However, it had become regularized by 1621, when it appeared formally in the *Laws or Standing Orders*—though court minutes mentioned gratis membership in conjunction with aristocratic members before that date.

Beyond the original members, the first (surviving) record of admission of gentry or aristocratic members did not take place until the Company was almost ten years old. A grant of incorporation secured on 11 May 1609—when James I renewed the East India Company's charter even though the fifteen years granted by Elizabeth I's original letter patent had not yet expired—led to the decision on 30 May to admit the Earl of Salisbury, then the lord treasurer; the Earl of Nottingham, then the lord admiral; the Earl of Worcester; the Earl of Southampton; and various other "lords, knights, and gentlemen" whom the records specified as being "favorers of the Company and no mere merchants." The note, timing, and fact that the admission was being granted to these men without their having sought it (the court minutes did not record any petitions by them to be made members, and the minutes did generally record such petitions) had the feel of thanks for services rendered. In addition, the court of committees gave the governor permission "from time to time to admit such and so many other lords, knights and gentlemen favorers of the Company and no mere merchants, as he in his discretion shall think meet."[20] When George Calvert (later Lord Baltimore and one of James's secretaries of state) was admitted several months later, the minutes referred to the "order formerly made the 30th of May last for the admission of lords, knights and gentlemen." The order continued to be cited in later years—for example, in 1610 when Thomas Marbury, a gentleman usher to the lord chancellor, was admitted "by virtue of the former order given to Mr. Governor for admission of lords, knights and gentleman."[21]

This 1609 admission of aristocratic "favorers of the Company" was the beginning of a period of growing aristocratic membership in the Company. Though missing volumes of court minutes make it impossible to compile anything close to a full list of all people granted freedom of the Company, the surviving evidence suggests that membership (aristocratic and otherwise) grew unevenly from 1600 to 1634, with periods of high activity during which Company leaders admitted many new members and other years in which they admitted only a few. The first years of each new joint stock, for example—in particular 1614, 1617–19, and 1628–29—seem generally to be correlated to the greatest increase in members. This makes sense given the nature of adventuring in the Company and when opportunities for large investment would be most readily available. Gratis memberships, which accounted for the vast majority of gentry and aristocratic admittances in the period, were significantly higher in the years 1609, 1614, and 1617–19, though they did not rise in the late 1620s. Any other given year before and after these years saw no more than two gratis freedoms, and sometimes none, while there were at least eight in 1609, six in 1614, twenty-four in 1617, thirty-two in 1618, and sixteen in 1619.[22] The lack of a big increase in gentry membership in the late 1620s may have reflected the cooling relationship between Charles and the Company, explored in detail in Chapters 8 and 9, and the slackening of profits in the 1620s.

Altogether, these numbers show that the 1610s were the period of greatest growth of gentry and aristocratic membership in the Company. Besides the opportunities that the first years of a new joint stock always presented, this decade was also one in which the Company did spectacularly well financially (the 1620s were less rosy for it for many reasons). In the ten years after that first 1609 admission of lords, knights, and gentlemen, dozens of aristocrats and gentry became free of the Company. As these men approached Company leaders for admission, Company leaders scrutinized their suits, trying to determine how these men might be particularly useful to the Company.

Company leaders did not accidentally or passively secure the majority of their aristocratic and gentry members. Their acquisition was part of a thought-out and acted-upon policy, as Company leaders purposely cultivated new members, carefully considering what strengths each of them would bring to the Company. People may have been drawn to the Company by the promised returns, but the Company was drawn to specific men for very different reasons, as leaders noted meticulously with each application. They did not offer gratis membership to all gentry applicants: some gentlemen paid the standard fine for their freedoms. The court minutes never mentioned any special qualities or connections of these men.[23] In other words, any gentleman might be welcome to adventure, but it was the useful ones who were worth cultivating by Company leaders. The culmination of their policy of aristocratic and gentry recruitment was that within a few years, the membership of the Company read like a who's who of early Stuart England. Even the chamber of London (essentially the city of London) invested in the East India Company.[24] It was in the context of this boom of aristocratic and gentry membership that Bell wrote the letter to Carleton discussed at the beginning of this chapter.

Both noble suitors to the Company and Company leaders were figuring out what roles nobles should play in the East Indies trade, and the understanding of their roles changed over the decade. When the Earl of Southampton was admitted in 1609, as a thank-you he sent the Company "a brace of bucks to make merry withal." A few months later, William Parker, Lord Monteagle, asked to join the Company on the same terms as Southampton, promising a brace of bucks every year at election time.[25] These were symbolic gifts, meant to be used by the Company for corporate feasts. These types of commensal events formed a key part of the institutional life of many livery companies in the early modern period.[26] By giving gifts for such an event, Monteagle and Southampton were showing support to the Company, but doing so in a way that emphasized the Company's ties to the livery companies. It highlighted the ways in which lords, knights, and gentlemen were outsiders to the normal life of the Company. As time passed, however, gentry members and suitors emphasized those differences less when approaching Company leaders, and Company leaders explicitly considered the political ways they might benefit from such august suitors.

The committees of the Company were active in recruiting useful men to become members of the Company. One Mr. Bayley, clerk in the court of Exchequer, was allowed his freedom because "such kind of men may be beneficial and helpful unto the Company in their suits and otherwise."[27] A few years later, one Dr. Poe wanted to turn his freedom over to a friend who had bought out his share of the adventure, but the Company—"knowing how near he is about the noblemen at court"—were unwilling to have him turn over his freedom, and to keep him as a member gave his friend freedom of the Company gratis.[28] Though the court of committees later tried to limit the practice, on occasion the leaders let friends of influential members in as a favor. For example, they admitted one Mr. Haines, appointed by the Earl of Southampton to manage his adventure, noting that "they would be pleased for [Southampton's] sake to admit [Haines] of the Company."[29] In 1614, in preparation for the upcoming Parliament, the Company admitted Sir James Stonehouse, "a courtier, one of the King's Privy Chamber," noting that he was "a civil gentleman who is daily attending about his majesty." Members of the court of committees were very open about their motivation: they "were willing to have some such [of] their friends about the king, that should be tied unto them by some kindness especially, against this time of

the parliament." They gave Stonehouse his admittance gratis.[30] At the end
of the month they let in two more useful men, William Fanshawe, a politician and frequent member of Parliament—"they conceiving that the Company shall have need of such persons' assistance against the parliament"—and
Sir Henry Neville, "a very worthy gentleman" who "may do many good
offices for the good of this Company."[31] Neville was a politician, member of
Parliament, and former ambassador to France. Sir Anthony Agar was admitted gratis "for the good offices which he hath done for the Company,
and expectation of the kindness in parliament house." Agar had served in
the 1614 Parliament and was an investor in several overseas trading ventures.[32] In 1614, Sir Anthony Palmer, a knight, was admitted gratis for being
"a gentleman that the Company expect to receive some kindness from."[33]
Sir John Digby was admitted before leaving for Spain, where he was to take
up the position of ambassador, on account of past services: while he was
posted in Lisbon, he had helped secure the release of English captives taken
at sea by the Portuguese who had been employed originally by the Company. Digby's letters promised that he would provide whatever future aid he
could, members of the court remembered his past help, and they thought it
might be useful to have someone well placed to give "advertisements from
the court of Spain or Lisbon."[34] They could expect him to continue his at-
tentions and keep them informed of news useful for matters of trade, such
as when the Portuguese and Spanish fleets returned.

Sometimes Company leaders admitted men in high places without
specific note made of their "good offices," just suggestive mentions of their
positions and connections. Thus, for example, "Sir Thomas Merry of
London, knight, clerk comptroller of his Majesty's house, as also Sir Thomas
Lake, knight, secretary to his Majesty" were admitted gratis.[35] The minutes
gave no specific explanation of what the court of committees might hope to
gain from them, but both men enjoyed close proximity to the king and held
positions that might aid the Company in securing royal access. Lake was a
privy councilor and one of James's secretaries of state, and thus a man of
considerable power and influence. Company leaders admitted Thomas
Trevor, "the prince's solicitor," in early 1618.[36] Richard Dorrington of Stowe,
the "register in the Chancery," was also admitted gratis.[37] When Company
leaders admitted the ambassador to France, Sir Thomas Edmondes, they did
not note specific reasons, but they doubtless had an expectation of future
usefulness; an incident earlier that year involving a French East Indies
voyage backed by English investors must have made the influence of the

English ambassador in France attractive indeed.[38] William Trumbull, ambassador to the archduke's court at Brussels, was admitted gratis.[39] Sir John Villiers—the brother of George Villiers, then Earl of Buckingham—was admitted in 1617 with no specific reason given, just the mention of his relationship to Buckingham.[40] When an unnamed privy councilor was late with a payment, the court of committees waived the fines, noting that the favor was requested by "a great person, a privy councilor."[41] Their flexibility was due to his position.

Soon the Company was being courted by increasingly powerful and well-connected men. Sir Edwin Sandys, the well-known advocate of English expansion and colonization and a member of Parliament, requested the court of committees to admit the doctor who had saved his life, promising in return "that he himself would study to deserve their loves." They acceded, "esteeming Sir Edwin a very good gentleman who hath deserved well of the commonwealth and worthy to be respected."[42] Sandys himself had been admitted some time before.[43] When Sir Julius Caesar—privy councilor, master of the rolls, and sometime member of Parliament—approached the Company and assured its leaders that he was "as willing and ready to do as great kindness for the Company as others are or can be," they happily let him in. They hesitated to allow him to adventure quite as much as he wished to but "were unwilling to deny his request being a person of that eminency and place."[44] And when Sir Francis Bacon approached the governor, "having heard of the justice of this Company and their upright carriage in managing their affairs," about joining, he supposed "it will not be offensive to have him admitted" and hoped it might be on the same terms, "with the like favor and privilege for adventure that they have granted unto some others his peers."[45] After he helped smooth over some legal difficulties the Company was having with the Scottish patent and helped the Company sway James in their favor, the court of committees admitted Bacon.[46]

These examples in the court minutes revealed that knowledge of what other courtiers were offered and allowed circulated at the royal court. The admission of useful men was not a private but an (at least partially) open pursuit. Men of high rank approached the Company not only wishing to be admitted, but to have the same terms and opportunities offered to them that had been offered to their fellows. William Lord Paget, for example, had heard that the Company had allowed in gratis a servant of Lord Cavendish, who could then inform Cavendish of what occurred when he was unable to attend, and Paget wanted the same privilege for himself. He "desired the like favor . . . pretending the like occasions, and promising to deserve their loves in what he may." Since he had "knowledge of such a precedent," Company leaders decided to accommodate his request.[47] Another noble requested the same privileges "afforded to some other noblemen"—in this case, the chance to have one of his men admitted to keep him informed of the proceedings of general courts. The court of committees agreed, "considering that it is no more than hath been granted to some other noblemen."[48] Men wanted the same terms they saw their peers granted. Quite quickly, therefore, Company membership had become a measure of status and favor among the aristocracy.

Company leaders gave freedom to a number of members of the royal households. They admitted, for example, Sir Thomas Howard, "knight master of the prince's horse"; Robert Rigdon, esquire, "gentleman sewer in ordinary to his Majesty"; and Sir Marmaduke Darrell, "cofferer to his Majesty."[49] The already mentioned Sir Thomas Merry, "clerk comptroller of his Majesty's house," was another person made free of the Company, as was David Bennet, "keeper of St. James, the prince's house."[50] When Theophilus Field, "doctor of divinity, and his Majesty's chaplain in ordinary," requested membership, even though the court of committees had decreed a hiatus on new membership, it allowed him anyway, no doubt because of his privileged position with regard to the king.[51] The king's bedchamber, the king's household, and the prince's household provided numerous members, but the queen's household had a much smaller, though not invisible, presence. One of the queen's gentlemen of the privy chamber, Edward Fitton, was admitted gratis.[52] Members of the royal household could be instrumental in securing physical access to the monarch.

Those "useful" men could use their expertise on the Company's behalf, both symbolically and in practice. Two other Company recruits, Sir Henry Hobart and Sir Henry Montague, were both lord chief justices. Hobart had approached the governor for membership, "hearing so well of the Company and their just and upright carriage of business." Sir Thomas Smith took this individual meeting as an opportunity to put some of the Company's legal concerns to Hobart in his capacity as a common-law expert. Hobart gave his opinion, even promising to consult with the new solicitor general, Sir Thomas Coventry, upon one matter, "to clear it according to law." The governor secured free legal advice for the Company, and Hobart got membership and the chance to adventure £2,000 (less than he had wanted, but still a considerable sum that he could expect would bring him considerable profit in 1617).[53] After Hobart was sworn in as a member before the court of committees, he was again consulted on legal matters—this time before the whole court of committees—and he promised "his best advice and furtherance" in settling the matter.[54] In other words, after a private consultation between Hobart and the governor, with legal advice given in return for a promise of membership, the governor and Hobart performed the giving of legal advice before the court of committees. The minutes recorded that "Mr. Governor then desired his Lordship's opinion (being now a member of the Company) in some particulars."[55] The court of committees even bumped up Hobart's adventure, to the originally requested £3,000.

This type of performative advice giving and the giving of informal free legal or other advice were not atypical. For example, Bacon, former attorney general and then lord chancellor, in thanks for the free membership given to one of his servants, reiterated his willingness to help the Company: "his Lordship [Bacon] would be ready to deserve and confirm by some real testimony unto all the Company in general, or to any of them in particular."[56] The advice could be private, but Bacon was willing to speak to the whole, to "deserve" their kindness.[57] Bacon was one of the regime's most prominent representatives as well as one of the great legal minds of the age, and his advice and influence could be expected to be worth something.

Montague did not return to be sworn in until a few weeks later, but when he came, he brought Sir Henry Yelverton, the attorney general, with him. They were both admitted, "being such persons as the Company would not deny both in regard of their place and council if occasion should be permitted." Montague even requested that a few servants of his be admitted too, including another attorney.[58] Around the same time, Hobart requested that freedom be granted to Henneage Finch, "a councilor at law," which the court of committees did.[59] Thus in a few weeks in 1617, the Company acquired the services of several of the great legal minds of the day.

The only person at court the Company was resolute about not admitting was the king. The Company leaders were willing to admit many well-connected courtiers, but what role the monarch should have in the Company was unclear. In some ways, the possibility of having the monarch as a member was a natural extension of the policy of allowing other gentry and aristocratic members. If earls could want and gain freedom of the Company, why not kings? Yet on several occasions the monarch offered to become a member of the East India Company, and on each occasion Company leaders demurred. Neither the patents nor the *Laws or Standing Orders* directly addressed the question of whether or not the monarch or other members of the royal family could adventure money in the Company. In 1618, Prince Charles approached the governor requesting freedom of the Company and the chance to adventure money with them. The court of committees granted his request. Some of the court's members, however, wondered if followers of the prince had spurred him to apply in hopes of increasing their own chances of membership in the Company.[60] When Charles desired to invest several thousand pounds with the Company the following year, his request " was very willingly yielded unto."[61] Yet the decision to allow the prince to adventure did not resolve the bigger question of whether the monarch could.

The question was a fraught one for Company leaders. Certainly contemporary opinion was not much in favor of the monarch's directly engaging in commerce. For example, in a 1608 essay Bacon commented on the long-standing sense that it was inappropriate for the king to engage in commerce, and that commerce was well below the majesty of the king: "For merchandizing it is true it was ever by the kings of this realm despised, as a thing ignoble and indign for a king."[62] Traditionally kings did not directly engage in commerce. However, when increasing numbers of courtiers were gaining admission to the Company, it was not inconceivable that a king, especially one as cash-strapped as James, might wish to do so, and on several occasions in the 1620s, both James I and Charles I broached the possibility of a royal membership.

The problem for Company leaders was that, as they understood the issue, admitting the monarch to the Company brought the viability of the entire East Indies venture into question. They were sensitive to the ways they might benefit from counting the monarch a member, but they were also aware of the possible complications of doing so. It also did not help allay their concerns that offers by the monarch to join tended to come at moments when they felt that the Company was particularly vulnerable. Both James and Charles offered to become adventurers as monarch, for example, at times of crisis for Company leaders as they tried to resolve problems caused by the events at Amboyna in 1623, and the monarchs presented joining as an action they could take to show support for the trade.[63] Additionally, James's original offer in 1624 came only a few months after the dissolution of the Virginia Company and its reformation under the crown, which many East India merchants had seen firsthand and which may have added to the feeling of vulnerability in the Company after Amboyna.

Company leaders decided they could not and did not want to admit the monarch. This was an opinion they reiterated every time the proposition was put to them. The main reason they gave was that in consultation with their lawyers, they had learned that a subject could not be in partnership with the king; if the king were admitted, the whole trade would belong to him.[64] One committee warned that if James—and more importantly, James's money—became involved, "that account will never be at an end." He suggested that accepting the monarch's offer would be a disincentive to people considering investing with the Company.[65] In response to James's offer, Company leaders suggested that they were refusing it to protect him, as "they cannot conceive how with his honor it may be done, the condition of partnership in trade being a thing too far under the dignity and majesty of a king."[66]

The reasons used to refuse Charles on the two occasions he offered to become an adventurer were much the same. His offer in late 1625 was slightly more pointed than James's had been. James claimed he had offered to become a member to show support to the Company. Charles posited that membership was a condition of his support; he offered because, "if they would have him interested in their cause this was the way."[67] The governor's answer was a carefully-worded rejection. He spoke of how the Company was made up of people of different qualities, including lawyers who had informed the governor that the king's proposal "could not be allowed," as it was "contrary to the laws for that no partnership can be held with the king, and being admitted an adventurer, the whole stock is presently in his Majesty's power to dispose of," which was why they had denied James' request.[68] When Charles offered again in 1628, Company leaders stuck to their legal excuse that "the whole right of the Company's stock would devolve to his Majesty for there can be no partnership held with the king." Though privy councilors assured Company leaders that the king's offer "was done not to deceive, but thereby the better to protect the Company," they held to their refusal.[69]

To discuss the monarch's offer—and then refuse it—required Company leaders to be sensitive to considerations of the monarch's honor. Neither James nor Charles directly commanded that they be admitted to the Company, but they could bring royal pressure to bear. For example, the Privy Council pressed the monarch's proposal on behalf of both James and Charles on Company leaders, sometimes explicitly.[70] Additionally, the monarch could try to set the terms for how the issue would be discussed in the Company. In 1624, for example, James wanted his offer shared with the generality as soon as possible—he did not want the court of committees quietly deciding against it. There was some debate about who would present James's offer to the generality, with the governor countering a suggestion of "some persons of honorable quality" with the statement that he himself would make the request known.[71] The court of committees was ultimately able to sidestep presenting James's proposal in a general court meeting, through careful references to the king's honor. A "great person near the king" had warned them that it would be a dishonor to him to have the matter refused in a general court, which is presumably what Company leaders wanted to happen. With that option closed, the leaders decided unanimously to answer James that though they understood the great honor his offer did to them, they would have to refuse on the basis of his honor, as trade was beneath what was rightfully due his honor.[72] James's honor became a means of circumventing his will.

The freedom of the Company was a precondition to adventuring in the East Indies trade. In the 1610s, a number of lords, knights, and gentleman gained freedom of the Company. Company leaders wanted these men for the skills and connections they brought, and these men wanted the freedom of the Company for the opportunities that it represented. The freedom of the Company was the deepest way the Company could tie influential men to it. Its leaders were still careful that ties to influential men not compromise the Company, which was the potential problem they saw in admitting the monarch to the body and why they so resolutely resisted it, despite repeated requests by the monarch.

Asking and Granting Favor

The ties of membership were not the only ones that Company leaders used to yoke influential men to Company interests. Both at court and in the City, Company leaders could curry favor through gifts and rewards ("gratifications," in Company parlance). When a new mayor, Sir John Jolles, was elected in 1615, the court of committees "gratified" him with some spices.[73] Likewise, when the clerks of the custom house requested a "remembrance" for their "kindness" toward the Company, the court of committees quickly voted to give them a reward.[74] Custom house clerks might not be obviously influential, but in terms of getting Company ships—and more important, Company goods—processed and released quickly, they were very important and worthy of monetary remembrance and occasional gifts of pepper and the like.[75] Sir Arthur Ingram, an influential financier at this time and still on the rise in 1617, received a £40 gratuity "for some kindnesses done."[76] The details were unspecified, and he could have performed almost any minor favor, given the relative smallness of the gift in Company terms. These monetary remembrances were codified in the Company's *Laws or Standing Orders*: their frequency and necessity were testified to by the presence of an entire section titled "Gratifications," which specified that the members of the court of committees could decide at their discretion to give gratuities of up to £100 without approval from the generality.[77]

Company leaders likewise could and did curry favor with influential members at court, even without the ties of membership. In 1613, for example, the East India Company, along with the City of London, the Merchant Adventurers, and the customs farmers (the wealthy London merchants who handled the collection of the kingdom's customs revenues and paid a yearly sum to the monarch in return for the lucrative job), sent plate as a wedding present upon the marriage of James's favorite, the Earl of Somerset.[78] A year later, in preparation for the upcoming parliament and to make themselves less vulnerable, the East India Company leaders ordered a gold cup worth £600 to be made for Somerset. The man in charge of the effort cordially wrote Somerset that he had heard the earl preferred fruit plates instead: if so, did the earl have a special request for the pattern?[79] In 1621, after the governorship left Sir Thomas Smith's hands after almost two decades, the Company thought of the "divers petty things to be given officers about the king's majesty and noblemen whose friendship this Company shall continually stand in need of" and requested Smith to "give note of the names of such."[80] The remaining leaders did not want to lose track of any of the useful men they had cultivated over time or risk alienating or losing the favor of any of those men about the king.

Privy councilors in particular merited special treatment by the Company leaders. In December 1621, when the court of committees decided to press late payers to produce their delinquent adventures, they decided not to press the lords of the Privy Council for payment. The minutes noted tersely that exceptions would be made for "the lords . . . of whose favors the Company may have present use of."[81] Similarly, though Company finances were tight that new year, the governor warned that the privy councilors to whom the Company usually gave New Year's gifts "might think themselves neglected" in the absence of such gifts. With a treaty with the Dutch under consideration,

Company leaders decided that to neglect the gifts would be "an unthrifty sparing" and that they must not "leave out any eminent person whose favor might be useful to the Company."[82] In 1630, the court of committees decided to give the gifts that at that point had become tradition, "howbeit they wished it might be sparingly done."[83] Recounting the giving of the Company's New Year's gifts in early 1624, the minutes recorded that they had been "well accepted" and had elicited a statement from James, who "expressed himself to be well satisfied of the benefit the kingdom received by the trade of the East Indies."[84] In this manner, the giving of gifts not only expressed the Company's thanks and obligation but also gave others an opportunity to reaffirm the value they found in the Company and its activities.

The granting of favors and gratifications could involve complex calculations of who owed exactly what to whom. The men who aided the Company sometimes wanted more than Company leaders wished to give. The men could be either members or nonmembers drawn into Company affairs. Their requests for gifts or gratuities could be quite open and highlighted the complicated nature of public and private office and aid.

The negotiations between Company leaders and Sir Dudley Carleton in 1619 over a gratuity demonstrated how this blending of public and private office and aid could lead to difficulties: both parties had to figure out how great a favor Carleton had done, and therefore how great a gift the Company owed him. Over the course of his tenure as James's ambassador to the Netherlands, for example, Carleton had aided the Company on a number of occasions. Both Carleton and his correspondent and close associate and friend, John Chamberlain, on occasion reminded the Company leaders of the debt they owed Carleton and how nice it would be if they would acknowledge it by means of a gift or gratuity.[85] For example, after Carleton's aid with the 1619 Anglo-Dutch treaty, he wrote Chamberlain to complain that the "prime instrument" of the negotiation (meaning himself) was being forgotten. He noted that the commissioners had received liberal gifts, but he had received nothing at that point.[86] On one occasion, in the midst of high-stakes negotiations between the Dutch and English, Chamberlain wrote to Carleton that "yesterday by good hap I lighted on Morris Abbot [then deputy governor of the East India Company] and in conference of East India matters I told him how little you were beholden to them considering your care and pains in their business." In other words, Chamberlain had issued a friendly but sharp reminder of the many efforts Carleton had made on the Company's behalf, and how little its leaders had given him in return. Chamberlain added that Abbot "confessed you were forgotten because you were not in their eye, but he would put some in mind of it that might see it amended," and he promised that "if you hear nothing of them before I return I will cause Sir Thomas Smith to understand it one way or another."[87] In short, Chamberlain had reminded the deputy governor, Abbot, about the Company's obligations to Carleton and assured Carleton that if the matter was not rectified, he would approach the governor on Carleton's behalf. What was at issue was not a simple gratuity, but what Chamberlain and Carleton both viewed as fair recompense for services rendered—essentially, an unofficial but legitimate payment.

A few months later, the Company still had not delivered a reward to Carleton, and Chamberlain addressed the matter again, this time noting to Carleton that "I have little acquaintance with any of them, so that I cannot promise much in their behalf, but when Sir Dudley Digges comes to town, I will set him on work, who is gracious among them, and understands their courses, and I know will be ready to do any good office in whatsoever may concern you."[88] Having approached the governor and deputy governor, Chamberlain would now contact Digges, who was a courtier and close Company associate, and whose facility with the Company along with his good will toward Carleton would, Chamberlain hoped, secure the desired reward.

A month later, Chamberlain sent an update to Carleton, informing him that he had spoken to Digges, who had told him that "there was no mention of you during all the treaty." Similarly, Chamberlain had heard from someone else who had "cast out speeches of their [the Company's] neglect towards you, but found all very cold." He had promised, however, to "deal further with Sir Thomas Smith who is *primum mobile* in all these businesses."[89] Chamberlain had not abandoned his quest for Carleton's reward, though it was slow going at the moment.

Chamberlain and Carleton recruited others to help Carleton secure a reward from the Company. The former ambassador to France, Sir Thomas Edmondes, wrote days later that he had reminded Smith of the Company's obligation to Carleton. Edmondes explained that he had "not been unmindful to cause Sir Thomas Smith to be mannerly remembered of the error, which they had committed, in having forgotten . . . the extraordinary care and pains which your Lordship had formerly taken" on the Company's behalf in the matter of the treaty negotiations with the Dutch. Edmondes wrote that Company representatives had explained that their "omission" arose from thinking that Carleton would shortly return to England, and "that then their meaning was to visit your Lordship, acknowledging their obligation to be great unto your Lordship," and arrive at a suitable recompense for Carleton's "special merit." Smith had been sick recently, however, and the matter had lagged. But after consulting with Abbot and Bell, Edmonds could assure Carleton that "it is really intended to give your Lordship very honorable contentment."[90]

At the end of the month, Carleton asked Chamberlain to remind Digges of how much Carleton had done on the Company's behalf in the late negotiations. Thus far, all he had received was a token from Lady Smith (the governor's wife)—which, incidentally, he had yet to see.[91] He wrote Chamberlain that he was writing Digges as well, and that he was offended by suggestions that he had done no more than was expected: "though the saying what I did was by the King's commandment should be no more applied to me than it might have been to the commissioners."[92] Digges wrote weeks later that the Company finally had decided to present a "small remembrance" to Carleton and that Digges hoped he would accept it.[93]

When Carleton wrote Chamberlain to acknowledge that he had accepted the East India Company's gift, he still expressed reservations. He did not know what the gift was, and though Digges had encouraged him to accept it, Carleton noted that "we say a man must not take a pig in a poke" and worried that "it may be such a lean pig that it were a shame to see it." Carleton asked Chamberlain to discover more, but Carleton did not want to draw too much attention to his attention, lest the gift turn out to be insufficient. Such a gift would only demonstrate how little he was valued: "I will not put the matter to other men's censure, nor myself to the hazard of going less in my credit with these men when they may have knowledge how slightly I may be valued at home."[94] When Chamberlain told Carleton that the gift's arrival, care of Digges, was imminent, he wrote that the Company "had at last remembered you and themselves."[95] The gift Carleton demanded, therefore, was not only as a return for services rendered, but a public affirmation of his worth and credit.

The next gratuity the Company gave Carleton required no extensive letter-writing campaign. In light of ongoing negotiations with the Dutch in 1623, Company leaders sent an additional £200 with Lady Carleton, who was about to leave to join her husband in the Netherlands. When the court of committees had considered the £200, the governor had mentioned how important Carleton was to the Company's cause, and that "they can now send over no man that shall be able to give a good account of his employment if he be not countenanced by [Carleton]." The motion for the cash gratuity was quickly passed.[96]

These gifts and the negotiations about them demonstrate both the complicated nature of public office and private aid and how knotty the issue of "the fruits of office" was.[97] No one, not Company leaders nor Carleton and his friends, doubted that he should receive something from the Company. The only question was when and how much. The gifts were unofficial wages, payment for services rendered—not only sweeteners to curry favor. In Carleton's view, the services he provided for the Company were predicated on his position as a royal ambassador but were outside of his normal work as a royal ambassador: he was not a private man acting for the Company, but a state office holder, and the gift he required was in recompense for the extra services he had provided.[98]

Company members themselves sometimes asked for specific favors from Company leaders. In 1615, when Charles Howard, Earl of Nottingham and lord admiral, requested oil, feathers, and some other goods, most of which the East India Company itself did not import, the leaders supplied the oil and made a note to check with the Muscovy Company about securing the rest for him.[99] When Robert Cecil, Earl of Salisbury and lord treasurer, requested the Company to "take a shop of his in his New Exchange to be furnished by them with East India commodities," they did not demur, presumably to keep Salisbury's good favor. Salisbury had gone directly to the governor, who now found himself £300 out of pocket for the venture.[100] These were some of the Company's useful men, and the willingness to do these sorts of favors for them was a recognition of just how valuable the men were.

Sometimes, however, these men asked for more than Company leaders were willing to give. Figuring out which favors to agree to and under what circumstances led the leaders to catalogue recent favors done for them, to determine out what was reasonable. Thus, when the lord chancellor petitioned to have a man of his bedchamber admitted to the Company, the members of the court of committees agreed: "considering that they have many matters at present depending before his lordship," including a writ of *Ne exeat regnum* that they hoped to secure, they decided "that his lordship cannot well be denied at present."[101] They agreed to give the membership and allow the adventure, but they also decided to ask the lord chancellor, if possible, "not to move the Company for any further request in the like kind."[102] Ultimately, the number of men who "could not be denied" was too great, and the court of committees decided to "discourage all of the Company hereafter to mediate for any friends." They decreed that in future, members who wanted to bring in their friends or followers would have to provide the adventures out of their own adventures (in other words, to turn over a portion of their adventure to the new suitor), as the joint stock was full.[103] Widely granting memberships to friends of members without a guarantee that those members would be useful to the Company was an unfair favor, granted without sufficient return.

Cultivating the king ran the greatest risk of all of being asked for more and more and more. Company leaders did cultivate the monarch, but there was a constant calculation of what the monarch wanted and needed and what the Company could give. The Company was none too keen to allow the monarch to personally adventure money in the joint stock or be a member of the Company. But while the members of the court of committees were eager to keep the king legally as separate from the Company as possible, they did not hesitate to court his favor in other ways. One of the enduring problems of the Stuart court was a lack of funds: its ordinary income simply could not keep pace with its expenditures. James frequently requested or demanded money from the Company, and on occasion, Company leaders even granted it unsolicited. In 1614, with Parliament having produced little revenue for the crown, Governor Smith suggested that the time might be right for a financial gratuity to the king. Events had conspired so that Smith had "frequent[ed] the court very often of late," and he had noted "that the king's occasions are very many to use money." This need made it "a fit time for this Company to show their affections unto his Majesty by presenting him with some remembrance thereof as a benevolence; to be delivered into his own hands which he [Smith] doth conceive would be taken very kindly by his Majesty being a time now especially seasonable for such an action, wishing all present to keep it private to themselves as a secret"—presumably because the suggestion that the Company was trying to buy the king would hardly reflect well on it. The stated reason for the benevolence was that "this Company shall daily have need of his Majesty's favor to countenance and protect them against their many adversaries that do oppose them." All present agreed, with the amount still to be determined.[104] Another time the Company, along with the Middleburgh merchants, agreed "to furnish the Exchequer with £50,000," an enormous sum at the time. James devoted £12,000 of that sum to Ireland, and spent £8,000 for artillery arrears, £17,000 for various lords, and £4,000 for a masque for Charles. That loan was not private, if it was ever meant to be, and news of it was sent to Carleton.[105] The accounting of where the money went demonstrated the ways loans to the regime helped enable the state to function.

Though Company leaders sought to give loans primarily by their choice, they were clearly concerned that money might be coerced from the Company. When news circulated in 1620 that the Company had loaned James £10,000, much to the disapproval of various members, the governor was quick to point out that though he and some others had loaned James £10,000, the money was their own, not the Company's. Though he would have preferred not to reveal the particulars of the loan, disclosure was preferable to the rumors of misuse of Company funds, and indeed the governor claimed that he and the other lenders had loaned the sum to keep James from demanding it from the Company: "the common report was spread abroad that this Company had lent £10,000 of the Company's money to the king whereat they were much discontent, thereupon Mr. Governor and Mr. Deputy made known (which otherwise they would have concealed) that it was true that Mr. Governor did lend the king £10,000 but it was none of the Company's money, nor procured by their seal, but lent by particular men out of their own purses, and upon their own credit to free the Company of the demand made unto them for the same."[106] Emphasizing in this case that the money was given privately underlined the ways in which the Company was vulnerable to unwelcome requests from monarch.

Loans by the Company or gifts in kind of supplies for use by the state also showed how fine the line could be between a gift given to cultivate favor and a coerced donation. Company leaders supplied the state with timber, labor, and other specialized goods and services. These were not gifts to any one individual, and both the request and the loan of the goods made the public purpose of the gift or loan explicit. For example, in February 1615, the lord admiral requested the loan of Company timber for the rebuilding of the naval ship *Vanguard*. Company leaders declared themselves "ready and willing to furnish his Majesty's service by their best means" and sent a committee to assess their stock. They provided more planks to the king at cost in November 1618, and in April 1625 they provided a mast for a ship at cost.[107] The Company sold five thousand feet of sheeting boards to the commissioners of the Navy at cost in May 1625, since "neither his Majesty's stores nor the wharves upon the river can furnish them so speedily as the service requires."[108] These goods underscored the usefulness of the Company to the state and the ways it bolstered the abilities of the regime and helped it achieve its objectives.

Yet the donation of goods and services was not always entirely by choice; sometimes it was in response to state demands, especially when the regime was at war. Company builders, carpenters, and sawyers were impressed to work on naval ships, for instance, sometimes to the detriment of the Company's business. Their service was recorded both as a loan of their labor and as a loss to the Company. The five thousand feet of sheeting boards mentioned above was actually only half of the amount requested, but since Company sawyers had already been impressed to do naval work, Company leaders could provide no more.[109] Indeed, demands by the regime on Company laborers in the weeks after Charles's accession, with so many immediate preparations for war, proved difficult to square with the Company's commercial calendar. In April 1625, for example, Company carpenters and shipwrights were impressed to work for the state, stalling preparations for a voyage to Persia. Company leaders questioned whether all of the men were really needed, but they conceded that "if the service of the State be so urgent and of importance that their servants must still be employed therein," then "they are ready and willing to bestow their utmost labors, endeavors, and estates." However, the cost might include the cancelling of that year's voyage to Persia.[110] In September 1626, twenty-two Company workmen, including fifteen master workmen, were impressed to work on naval ships, with promises from the regime that they would be returned in fourteen days, along with forty other workmen.[111] The fear that ships as well as men might be impressed led in January 1627 to the Company's dispatching ships (and the men on them) as quickly as possible upon receiving knowledge that a "press [would] shortly come forth for the king."[112]

The relationship between the Company and lords, knights, and gentlemen was complex. Men of power and influence at the English court and abroad could help the Company in myriad ways. Company leaders recognized this and were eager to tie those men to the interests of the East Indies trade. Sometimes that meant granting them the freedom of the Company and the chance to adventure, and sometimes it meant currying their favor through judicious gifts. When the monarch sought to gain admission to the Company, however, its leaders found themselves treading a fine line—needing to deny but not alienate the monarch. In general, Company leaders were happy to oblige gentry and aristocratic men who wished to adventure in the Company, and by 1620, a key group of privy councilors, courtiers, and influential knights and gentlemen had gained admission. The watchful eyes of the members of the court of committees kept track of the ways these men could benefit the East India Company, as well as the ways courting them might cost it.

4

Division within the Company

The Problem of Faction and Representation

ON 2 JULY 1619, a man named John Holloway brought a ballot box
to the yearly election meeting of the East India Company. It was a
hopeful gesture on his part: there was no guarantee that members of the
Company would agree to elect its governing body by secret ballot. In fact,
precedent was against Holloway, since the Company had never voted by
secret ballot in its nineteen years of existence. Holloway asserted that the
ballot box would allow for a freer choice than the current method of
election, which was by raising hands. Those against the change in voting
procedure argued that the box was a dangerous innovation, a "novelty" introduced only to "disturb the whole business."[1]

Holloway's ballot box was not a makeshift object put together in haste,
but something he had planned in advance and invested money in. Though it
had not been commissioned by Company leaders, it had been designed with
the Company's use in mind.[2] For example, it was decorated on one side of
the front with a crown and the initials of James I, and on the other side
with the arms of the East India Company. Under the lid was inscribed the
year 1619. Painted designs including dragons, birds, and flowers that imi-
tated Chinese and Japanese styles and pagoda-like structures on the lid—
presumably a nod to the Company's East Indies trade—decorated the box.
The object as a whole was substantial, almost eighteen inches high, seventeen inches across, and twelve and a half inches deep.[3]

The functional purpose of the box was to enable secret voting. Three
drawers, each four and a half inches across, five inches wide, and ten inches
deep, would hold ballot balls. The box was set up primarily for voting

between two choices: a conical projection at the front allowed the voter to insert his hand into the box and drop the ball either to the right or the left, so that the ball would be funneled to the right or left drawer. In the case of a vote between three choices, a removable panel allowed the voter to deposit the ball further back, so it would fall into a middle drawer. In any case, no observer would be able to see what the voter's choice had been.

The Company membership rejected the use of the ballot box for the 1619 election, but it was not the last time someone brought a ballot box to a Company election. Such boxes appeared with some regularity at the yearly election meetings, almost always put forward at times of division—what Company leaders sometimes called "faction"—within the membership. Time and again, leaders strongly resisted modifying the yearly election procedures to include the ballot box, though they used it with little hesitation or alarm to determine certain types of votes within courts of committees.[4] It was not the ballot box per se that they rejected. Rather, it was what the ballot box so frequently represented at the yearly election meetings that they sought to reject. Proposals to use the ballot box were a sign of what Company leaders saw as dangerous division within the membership and of competing claims to legitimate political representation. This was the real challenge that Company leaders tried to overcome by discouraging the use of the ballot box, both in 1619 and the other years when someone brought or suggested using such a box at the yearly election.

Open talk of faction had rarely occurred in the East India Company court minutes before 1619. There had been earlier mentions of scandalous imputation, aspersions, and charges that someone had jeopardized the Company's reputation, but rarely of "faction" or "division." The choice of words suggested that the problems of 1619 were more widespread than, for example, the public disparagements of the Company by Mr. Burke discussed in Chapter 2. In 1619 and after, Company leaders identified and discussed the presence of both "faction" and "sedition" in the Company, making frank assessments of the damage that faction could cause to the body—including to its reputation.

Tracing division within the Company is difficult, as the surviving records present only one version of the contestations between unhappy members of the generality and the court of committees. It is likely that not all dissatisfaction among the generality came to the attention of the court of committees. It is also possible that court minutes characterized unhappy members in ways they would not have agreed with. Based on examples recorded in the court minutes, division within the Company almost always pitted groups within the generality against the Company's leadership, rather than dividing the court of committees. Though there was no one coherent faction over time, "factious" or "divisive" members cited a common set of concerns over time. Division also frequently reflected social divisions within the Company, with elite members prominent among those desiring change.

The policies that Company leaders used to consolidate their authority over the generality were the same ones that received the most challenges. The policies of restricting access to Company accounts and letters, maintaining the secrecy of the deliberations of the court of committees, and sharing with the generality as little information as possible could cause resentment and unhappiness among some members of the generality. Episodes of division within the Company exposed differences of opinion among members about the Company's government and how representation within the body should work. The critics of the Company leadership disliked the tight control over information that the court of committees exerted, and they challenged the secrecy that kept Company affairs concealed from their eyes. They wanted greater transparency in the Company's affairs and the opening up of the Company's government to include new people among the elected leaders, sometimes suggesting precisely who those new people should be. Faction in the Company therefore was almost always linked to questions of transparency and authority, with the challengers demanding greater access or a reconstitution of the Company so that different groups might have access to its internal government.[5] In short, they were contesting the nature of the Company's representative government, debating what form of government would best secure the interests of the whole Company, and citing concepts like "freedom" and "liberty" to do so.

This chapter examines the problems of self-government within the Company, probing the types of challenges that members raised to the elected leadership and the types of solutions they proposed. The Company was a body with a diverse group of members, who ranged from small shopkeepers to privy councilors, and from people with adventures of £100 to those with adventures of thousands of pounds. Its leaders, therefore, had to deal with a variety of interests.[6] This proved difficult, and the yearly elections could become occasions for disputes about what proper and good government looked like. The elections could reveal the anger of some members of the generality and the desire for change in the Company's leadership. However, on multiple occasions election-day disputes proved not to be the most effective way for frustrated members of the generality to change the leadership. Rather, they illustrated the tools at the disposal of Company leaders for maintaining their control.

What proved harder for Company leaders to withstand were proposed procedural changes to the Company's government, especially when they were not limited to election day. Advocates for procedural reform could argue that they were not targeting specific leaders, but rather the rules that governed the Company without reference to individuals. Some of the rule changes they wanted would necessarily change the composition of the Company's leadership, particularly rules that limited incumbency and re-election. However, many of the proposed changes spoke to more general concerns, such as the limitations on access to Company records that the court of committees wanted but that were often resented by members of the generality. By no means were proposals for change always successful, but proposals for procedural reform sometimes succeeded, and debates about proposed changes revealed how and when members of the generality and the existing leadership could mobilize wider support to either insist upon change or bolster the status quo.

Contested Elections

The 1619 election was the most contentious one the Company had held to that point. In the run-up to and even during the election, members debated a variety of issues to do with Company governance, ranging from the constitution of the Company's leadership, to voting procedures, and to the transparency of the court of committees' actions. These issues and the debate surrounding them revealed much about tensions within the Company, and how Company leaders sought to control division and faction within the corporation. Some of these issues were specific to the Company, arising out of the particular circumstances of its constitution—for example, its mixed membership of merchants and aristocrats. However, others spoke to larger abstract political questions not limited to the Company, such as the transparency of government and how representation should be apportioned.[7]

A few weeks before the 1619 election, unease among some members of the generality came to the attention of Company leaders. In mid-June, the treasurer informed the court of committees that his accounts were being "questioned and suspected" by some of the generality. He wanted new auditors appointed to allay any suspicions, but the court of committees resisted, responding that they already had auditors who inspected the books "from time to time," and these were "gentlemen of such sufficiency and without exceptions of partiality"—which should satisfy the misgivings of any members of the generality.[8]

What the increased interest in the Company accounts prompted in Company leaders was a reassertion of the importance of secrecy and of not giving members of the generality access to the accounts. The court of committees concluded that it was unfit for those members to read the account books because it would lead to "some things not to be seen commonly to be divulged abroad." Thus, even though the accounts held nothing "to be ashamed of," the court of committees did not want to allow access to them.[9] The incident pointed to tension already present between the court of committees and some members of the generality. It also showed that Company leaders were essentially resolute about not changing their actions in response to any dissatisfaction of the members.

A few days later, the court of committees became worried that the particulars of the election itself might be contested. Some members of the court of committees had heard that members of the generality were upset with the traditional timing, location, and manner of the election. They had composed a petition "to have ten days' respite before the election to solicit their friends to be present." They also wished to meet in "some larger hall than [Governor] Sir Thomas Smith's and that it will be present to have a balloting box." Elections were usually done by show of hands, with the choice of each member clear to others. The minutes never provided individual votes, just the consensus. The logic was to reduce the potential of division by keeping voting public.[10] The use of a ballot box was not prohibited by the bylaws or charter of the Company, but it would have been a new introduction to the common procedures of the Company at that point.[11]

These challenges to the standard voting procedure elicited some debate, though no committees were very sympathetic to the requests. Some responded to the suggestion of using a ballot box by labeling it an "innovation and alteration in the government of the Company to the endangering of the subversion thereof" and supposed that the suggestion had been made by some "busy spirits" who had come up with the notion at a "privy meeting."[12] They equated use of the ballot box with private interests and labeled it an innovation—a term of condemnation in the early modern period. Others responded that their duty was to "oppose whatsoever may tend to the disturbance or ruin" of the Company or trade, and "although the election [is] in the power of the generality yet the manner thereof or for them to alter at their pleasure is not." They decided to hold the election on 2 July in a manner consistent with the previous elections. Their only concession to the petition to delay the election was to delay it by one day and find a larger place in which to hold it, but only if "the assembly shall be found so great, more than Mr. Governor's hall can hold."[13] In the face of a procedural challenge, the court of committees was willing to admit no power of members of the generality to change the means or method traditionally involved in the election.

The reasons for the defensive stance of Company leaders became evident at a later meeting. They were concerned because the "disturbances and innovations intended at the court of election" were coming at a sensitive time in the negotiations between English and Dutch commissioners to settle terms between the respective East India companies. Beyond that, however, committees identified what they saw as the real cause of the proposed changes: a group within the generality wanted to change the Company's government, putting different people in control of the trade. There was no reason for individual committees to "take these things to heart," as no particular committees were being targeted for replacement. Instead, the sitting Company leaders noted a far more chilling prospect: the existence of faction within the Company, which they identified as arising from "such gentlemen as have been taken into the Company by courtesy [and who] do aim to get all the government into their hands, which [was] a business properly for merchants, and gentlemen [were] inexperienced to manage business of that nature."[14] This was the first time the nature of the conflict in the Company was explained in the minutes.

Though this type of tension—between merchant leader and gentleman investor—had arisen before, rarely had it been presented in such starkly oppositional terms. In earlier cases, when the court of committees had refused to allow some Company positions (for example, positions of authority in Company fleets) to become part of court patronage networks, the court of committees had presented its motive as one of preserving the appearance of a merchant-run enterprise—meaning that it was competently led by people with practical expertise.[15] The tenor of this exchange in 1619 was starkly different, with resentment rather than prudence the dominant motif. Thus, here were "gentlemen as have been taken into the Company by courtesy" who sought "to get all the government into their hands." The gentlemen remained unnamed, though the court of committees clearly seemed to have specific men in mind.[16] Indeed, just months earlier, an election in the Virginia Company had ousted Sir Thomas Smith from the leadership of that body and replaced him with Sir Edwin Sandys, in essence transferring leadership from a merchant to a courtier. It is possible that the committees assumed a similar attempt was under way in the East India Company. This tension between elite members of the Company and the court of committees was one of the unforeseen consequences of the growing numbers of courtiers with freedom of the Company. Elite membership here was directly tied to division within the Company.

However, the more important division was not between gentlemen and merchants, but between the court of committees and the generality. Rumors suggested that some members of the generality wanted to overhaul the entire government of the Company. The unhappy members of the generality were ready to contest the claim that only the court of committees could, according to the patent, handle the business of the Company. These members were upset "by reason of some speeches formerly let fall by Mr. Governor, that by the Company's patent, all business are [*sic*] to be managed by the committees, and not by the generality (the truth whereof they doubt)." If the patent indeed was found to support the governor's claims, these members reportedly wanted to change the patent. The investigations by members of the generality into the accounts were part of the same larger challenge to the Company leadership. The court of committees was willing to appoint a few new auditors from the generality, which they hoped would "dash and quell all other plots." The court of committees had nothing to hide in their accounts "because nothing is done by the Company but will justify itself."[17]

Company leaders decided that their best hope of defeating the proposed changes was to emphasize the importance of continuity to the generality. They planned to underscore the need to present a unified front to the Dutch and keep any divisive issues, like recent gratifications to the court of committees, off the agenda. While acknowledging that they could not control the election—could not, in their words, "prevent" the gentlemen from trying to get the government in their hands—yet they "ought to endeavor to withstand" the efforts of those men. They needed, they thought, "some person of countenance to qualify matters with jeweled terms" to present their side and emphasize the importance of the continuing leadership of merchants in the Company. They needed to convince the generality that "the business hath now as great need (if not more) of the help of such men as have been of best experience and observation."[18] They hoped to make the incumbent leadership (that is, themselves) seem like the sensible and safe choice.

These debates in the court of committees showed that Company leaders had at least some awareness of the growing unhappiness of some members of the generality. The leaders knew what those people were suggesting and the complaints they had. They tried to gauge how serious the unhappiness was and whether they really needed to take action to answer the charges. They discussed the complaints and possible responses to them on multiple occasions. As leaders, they were not divorced from the generality—each time they considered rumors current in the generality was proof that they were monitoring the feelings of that body—though the specific complaints of the discontented suggested that they were too separate. Company leaders worked hard, and sometimes unsuccessfully, to avoid precisely the division that was so evident at the election meeting later that afternoon.

The election meeting was long and contentious, with the division within the generality openly acknowledged and discussed. The meeting opened with a reminder from Governor Smith that its purpose was limited to the election. He added that he "wished them to be very considerate, and well advised in the elections to make choice of such as shall be fit to manage so great a business," directly reminding them of the business of the Company and urging them to choose their leaders according to the needs of the business. Addressing the unhappiness directly, he acknowledged that the court of committees was aware that "many of the generality are discontented and desirous to have the business for the election to be carried in another form than formerly hath been." He added that he knew the discontent involved himself and other members of the court of committees. Since the matter should be addressed properly, he requested that "some of the generality might be appointed to deliver those grievances, hear the answer made, and make report of them at [the] next general court." In other words, in acknowledging the problem and discontent as important, he was able to label it important enough to warrant a formal list of grievances that could be answered at a separate court meeting. This suggestion neatly divided grievances from the business of the current meeting and reduced the danger at the election meeting of the spread of resentment or, for that matter, of a serious challenge to the sitting leadership. Thus, by acknowledging the grievance in one area, he attempted to limit it in another.[19]

What happened next in the election meeting was a dramatic demonstration of the fact that royal court connections were not solely in the hands of the courtiers in the Company's generality—the regime was also invested in the established government and leaders. The court of committees had spoken about the need for a "person of countenance to qualify matters with jeweled terms." After charging the generality with electing a fit governor and stating that thus far, the Company had always acted "with the approbation of his Majesty's state," the governor was interrupted by just such a person. Whether by fortuitous coincidence or by plan, a representative from James came forward to deliver a message of support for the current governor, deputy, and court of committees from the monarch.

James's representative, Lord John Digby, was a member of the Company though not a member of the Company leadership, and he had only recently returned to England from a diplomatic mission to Spain. The message he delivered from James was one of strong support for the current leaders of the Company and of opposition to sudden changes in the leadership. James's message directly backed the existing model of government, emphasizing the ways in which the king's favor was key to the success of the Company but was not something that members should expect to remain with them if they heedlessly changed the government. The message touched on the ways that exposing the internal workings of the Company's government to prying eyes outside the Company could have wide-ranging effects, including on the Anglo-Dutch treaty negotiations and other state affairs of relevance to the Company.

The message from James flattered, warned, and underscored the ties between the regime and the Company. According to Digby, James was concerned about the effect that a change of leadership might have on the Anglo-Dutch commissioners. As he presented the matter, James was aware that the Dutch treated the East Indies trade as "a matter of state," and he was concerned that the election difficulties would "expose" the English East India Company's involvement as that of "but private merchants, and too unequal a match (in that respect) to contend against them."[20] In other words, the power that the generality held over the leadership, via the election, would announce to the world that Company activities were merchant rather than state affairs—even though that was not the case. That false perception would compromise the reality.

James's message openly supported the government of the Company and pledged the support of the regime. The Company was "a great ornament and strength unto his kingdoms, whom he hath and will maintain." With his aid, he "doubted not to procure them in some convenient time their every own desires in the Indies, which if the Dutch should deny, that quarrel should be no longer the Company's but of the state." In short, with James on the Company's side, its endeavors, even against the Dutch, had the weight of state matters and would be accorded James's direct efforts and oversight—which in this case was presented as a positive thing. If the Dutch did not cooperate, James would instruct the Privy Council to take up the matter. He would instruct the Council "to cause an act of Council to be entered to make it appear to be his act, approving the government of this Company (which he hath taken knowledge of) to have been hitherto very good, and performed with much quietness, not doubting but business have [*sic*] been carried well, with great content unto the general Company." The key part of that comment was the note that he would instruct the Council to act and "make it appear to be his act," thus signifying the monarch's protection of the Company.[21] How better to prove that this business was not one of merchants' affairs but one of matters of state than the open approbation of the king?

Most importantly in terms of upholding the existing leadership, James's message freely admitted the personal connections that he had to the governing members, and the importance of those connections in securing his aid for the business. His message explained that "many of them having had often and free access unto him, he knows the facts of some of them well, Sir Thomas Smith and some others, and will not have any alteration of them." Having delivered James's message, Digby added that he agreed that no one deserved a place in the court of committees by "inheritance," yet "this is no convenient time now for alterations, but rather to have things continued this year as they were, because distraction may much hurt the business, and the Dutch may take advantage of innovations, having given out that they have as good friends at court as the English."[22] The time was ripe for continuity, he asserted, not change.

It is impossible to know how much of Digby's interruption with James's message was a planned grand gesture. The governor's comment about the man of consequence who could speak in jeweled terms suggested forewarning and planning, though there is no further evidence to confirm it. The episode had the feel of a carefully stage-managed performance, from the governor's tentative opening speech to Digby's timely interruption with word from a concerned and caring monarch. Even the notes that James's message hit hardest—the dangers of "alteration" of personnel given the situation with the Dutch and the importance of the Company to the state—were the same aspects that the governor had highlighted in his speech to the generality. The evidence certainly suggested that the very convenient message of support was planned in advance; the correlation seemed too perfect to be a matter of chance.

At this point, after the nominations for governor were made, Holloway came forward with his ballot box. It is worth noting that the only member of the generality named in all of the minutes dealing with the trouble with the 1619 election was Holloway, as the presenter of the ballot box. This innovation was the one that had caused the worry about faction in the Company. Holloway claimed that he had been promised the year before that a ballot box would be used, and thus he had brought one for the election.

Once again, the challenge to normal practice was met not with an objection from the committees but from various "lords and others present," who made the committees' points for them. Those gentlemen labeled it a "novelty not formerly used nor known in these elections, but a means to disturb the whole business standing as they did distracted abroad." Worse still, they

> did judge the author thereof [Holloway] worthy of blame, that did present it to interrupt the course intended by so gracious a message from his Majesty and therefore caused it to be taken away, and concluded by erection of hands, to have it put by for this year, and election to proceed according to the old manner without any alteration, or innovation, which notwithstanding did not tie the Company's hands, but left the Company to as free a choice as they could have by any other means.[23]

The gentlemen's concern, therefore, was that the innovation of the ballot box would "disturb" the business with the Dutch and possibly circumvent the intention of James's message of support. Also evident, however, was a direct challenge to the idea of the supposed benefit of the ballot box. Even without the innovation, the Company would have "as free a choice as they could have by any other means." If supporters of the ballot box were arguing that its use would allow a freer choice by making the voting anonymous, the defenders of the old way were asserting that voting by erection of hands did not constrain freedom of choice.[24]

Rejecting the claims to freer choice, the majority of the generality spurned the ballot box and reaffirmed the existing leadership. Smith's re-election as governor, recorded in the minutes a few lines later, was described as "by general and free consent, with erection of hands." Both the deputy governor (Sir Morris Abbot) and the treasurer (William Harrison) were reelected as well.

The members of the generality had rejected a wholesale change in the Company's leadership, but they proved more sympathetic to concerns about the composition of the court of committees. Some of the members had begun to perceive incumbency, though that term was not used, as a problem. At this election, in this year of so many innovations, some men presented a "grievance from the generality, that there is a perpetuity as it were amongst the committees." They complained of the lack of turnover, that the same men were holding the same positions year after year, and wanted a mandatory number of committees to change each year. They suggested that half should be changed, "or at least six or eight," so that the generality "may not be kept in ignorance, but some new to grow up with the rest in experience."[25] The committees for the upcoming year had yet to be elected, so change was still possible at that point.

Even more obviously than in the debate on the form and format of elections, the concern motivating this proposal was that the court of committees was acting without due consideration of, or due openness toward, the generality. Additionally, these unnamed men wanted not just different merchants chosen, but specifically "some gentlemen and shopkeepers." In response, the petitioners were told that shopkeepers were already part of the court. Furthermore, some gentlemen (again unnamed though identified as gentlemen) reminded the generality that "if gentlemen be chosen whose occasions hold them much in the country, the service is not like to be performed with that care as by merchants, whose knowledge is most proper in merchandizing affairs, and can best judge of those things which may concern the good of the trade."[26] Here gentlemen were advocating for the merchant leaders, pointing out that both by experience and lifestyle, merchants based in London were better suited to the governing of the Company and the trade.

In the end, the general court adopted a compromise. A special group of gentlemen would be given greater access to meetings and records, but few day-to-day responsibilities. They would be "gentlemen at liberty to be committees at large, to come to courts when they please, to satisfy themselves of the carriage of business and see what is done."[27] Sir Edwin Sandys, Sir Dudley Digges, Sir John Wolstenholme, Sir William Russell, Sir William Smith, Sir John Suckling, Sir John Merrick, and Levinius Munk were chosen.[28] Digges and Wolstenholme were long-standing supporters of the Company and closely allied to the governing merchants.[29] However, the inclusion of Sandys suggests that this group of committees at large was not entirely predisposed toward the governing merchants, as Sandys and Sir Thomas Smith were already at odds in the Virginia Company and Sandys had unseated Smith from the leadership of that corporation in April. Indeed, one account of Sandys's election to Parliament from Sandwich a little over a year later noted that the East India Company was a "pernicious matter" to them as a port city outside of London, and that Sandys was "against that (as he said)."[30] Sandys was not known to be a friend of the Company's leadership, despite his investments in and involvement with the Company.[31] His presence in the group of committees at large, more than any other, testified to divided interests in the generality and suggests that the creation of these positions might have been an attempt to manage division.

Divisions within the generality with regard to the composition and turn-over of the committees and the balance of merchants and nonmerchants may have been particularly apparent in the 1619 election, but they were not unique to that year. Similar proposed reforms had been suggested in the 1618 election. In that year, members of the generality had floated various proposals for standardizing what proportion of the court of committees should be new each year, ranging from the simple call for all twenty-four committees to be new to a more complicated plan of requiring one-fourth of the committees to be new, while allowing up to three-fourths to be old. Other members had argued that since the Company's membership was made up of three types of people—nobles, knights, and gentlemen; merchants; and shopkeepers—all three ought to be represented, so as "not to rest so much upon the merchants."[32]

The specific reasons given for these schemes varied. A common thread running through all of them was the idea that change and greater circulation of people through the elected leadership was necessary to effect transparency in the Company's government, as well as to properly balance the roles of merchants and nobles in the Company. Some members claimed that as matters now stood, the Company's leadership "remaineth as a perpetuity in most of the old, whereby the rest of the generality continue ignorant." Others argued that with more knights and gentlemen as committees, "the nobility and gentry may the better be satisfied of the upright carriage of the business," while still others contended that "it is a business most proper for merchants, who are best skillful to manage merchandizing affairs." Considering that "upon the shoulders of the committees all the burthen of the business depends," some suggested that the nobility and gentry were not capable enough, "yet held it unfit to make any order to refuse them."[33]

In accommodating some of the concerns expressed in 1618 by compromising with the creation of committees at large in 1619, Company leaders had taken steps to limit and neutralize the effects of internal Company division. Nevertheless, news of the 1619 election difficulties did not stay within the Company. Within two weeks, John Chamberlain was reporting to Sir Dudley Carleton that the Company had "with some difficulty" chosen Smith as governor again, reporting also that James had sent a timely message that it "was not fit to remove him."[34] Likewise, the news of the business with the Dutch, which had been such a key component of the defense of the current leadership, was appearing in newsletters.[35] The Company's difficulties were known, if not in detail, to people who followed London news.

In 1620, the Company suffered from election-time problems again, and it found a solution that was comparable to the one used in the 1619 election. Unfortunately, the court minutes do not survive for the year from July 1620 to June 1621, so the events of the election are unknown. However, a letter from Chamberlain to Carleton suggests that a similar situation developed— or at least, that Company leaders had prepared for a similar situation. Chamberlain reported that Smith had been elected governor again, "by reason of a letter from the king wishing them not to alter their officers and committees." Chamberlain also wrote that Smith had been reelected "without any contradiction," so it is possible that either the tensions at the last election were repeated, or Company leaders were simply prepared with a letter to head off difficulties.[36] While the exact nature of the difficulties at the 1620 election cannot be known, the device of a letter from the king was the same as the year before.

The East India Company was not the only trading company dealing with faction in the late 1610s. The Virginia Company was riven by faction in the same period, its membership divided over the direction and form the colony should take. Surviving evidence from this time reveals the Virginia Company to be a body even more fractured than the East India Company, and to be in the grip of what the regime considered the dangerous exercise of popular politics and popular government.[37] In a 1625 proclamation on Virginia, for example, Charles explained that the company's patent was taken away in large part because James had realized that ordering affairs by the "greater number of votes and voices" and governing via "popular government" were antithetical to the good and quiet government he prized.[38] The turbulent affairs of the Virginia Company led the monarch to call in the company's patent and make Virginia a royal colony in 1624. Given the overlap of membership between the East India and Virginia Companies (at least half of the East India Company's twenty-four committees elected in 1618 were members of both companies, and at least fifteen of the committees in 1619 were, as were Governor Smith and Deputy Governor Abbot), the East India Company's leaders knew firsthand of the bitter factional conflict racking the Virginia Company. Indeed, one of the main conflicts in the Virginia Company was between Smith and Sandys, who was also active in the East India Company.[39] Upheaval in the Virginia Company was a subtext of the difficulties in the East India Company.

The fundamental difference between the factional conflict in the two companies was that the East India Company survived it, while the Virginia Company did not. Many of the elements were similar—tensions about what direction the company would take, between the governing merchants and the noble or gentry investors, and over the use of the ballot box—yet in the East India Company, the tensions led to a reaffirmation of the ties between James and the merchant leaders, the balloting box was not used, and the Company survived. Conversely, the Virginia Company had a major change in leadership in 1619 and was dissolved in 1624 after aspersions of dangerous popular government and the frequent use of the balloting box exacerbated division in that body.[40] The difference between the two was the nature of the monarch's involvement, with James taking an active role in propping up the existing leadership of the East India Company.

Perhaps the East India Company survived also because these troubled elections were not the rule. After three years of controversy, the election in 1621 was untroubled, even though the leadership changed from Smith to Alderman William Halliday.[41] In reporting the change in leadership, Chamberlain did comment that Smith was "at last removed from his warm seat of being so long governor".[42] This sense that the election saw an incumbent toppled from power was not noted in the court minutes. Likewise, the reelection of Halliday in 1623 was uneventful, as were the majority of election courts in the early seventeenth century.[43]

Proposals for Procedural Reform

Elections were not the most successful time or place for members to express their discontent. Election-day contestations—including calls for the use of the ballot box, a change of leadership, and greater access to Company records—provided obvious signs of division within the Company. These contestations drew attention to the unhappiness of some members of the generality. News of contested elections could and did spread outside the Company and were proof of trouble in its body politic. Yet election days were also a stage for enacting support of the existing leadership. The provident royal messages of encouragement and the crying down of dissent by supporters of the leadership could sway members of the generality as effectively as the actions of the challengers did. Additionally, while some of the most vocal proponents of change at the election days were nominated for elected positions, few of them were elected. For example, Holloway was nominated as a committee in 1619 but was not elected.[44] In short, agitating on election day brought attention to grievances but did not effect much change in the leadership of the Company.

Often more successful in prompting deeper debate about the need and reasons for change, and sometimes (though not always) in effecting change, were proposals for procedural changes that took place during the year and were not tied to criticism of particular leaders. This was the tack that unhappy members took in the late 1620s and at other times. These motions for change often arose from a particular person or group of people. They took aim not at the current leadership per se, but at the rules and regulations that governed representation and access in the Company. Invariably, the proposals these members put forward would change the Company's leadership if passed, but because they did not target the existing leaders as pointedly as the election-day contests did, the proposals were harder to reject reflexively. Additionally, because the debates about the proposals took place over several meetings, the kind of set-piece defense of the existing leadership that was rolled out in July 1619 was out of place in this context. Like contested elections, proposals for procedural change were not common and tended to be put forward at times of stress in the Company, when the continuing viability of the trade seemed in question due to either political or economic considerations. Company leaders still called these proposals evidence of faction, but it was faction that usually manifested itself more subtly than the division that was so evident at some elections.

The first sustained attempt to modify the procedures that governed representation in the Company came six months after the 1619 election. In early 1620, Digges wrote Carleton that "factions and dissensions in the Company [have] . . . have almost torn that body in pieces."[45] The court minutes before that date made no mention of trouble, but Digges was one of the committees at large chosen at the 1619 election, and consequently he had an insider's understanding of the problems facing the Company.

A general court held just days after Digges wrote to Carleton provided proof of his assertion that division still roiled the Company. The court was discussing the fact that a number of investors were behind in their payments. In discussing these delinquent adventures, members of the generality again raised concerns about the proper prosecution of the business and the lack of transparency alongside questions about how representation within the Company should work that had been aired at the election meeting months before. Some members commented that the small amounts were paid "to cast an aspersion (of seeming neglect) upon the Company, than that it can any way be approved and justified." Instead of consulting with the committees first to resolve the issue, members had gone directly to the general court, so that their complaints might be "divulged to the disgrace of the Company, without cause."[46]

At this point in the debate, Digges claimed that as a committee chosen to oversee the "carriage" of the business, he saw no problem with it. He stated firmly that "all is carried fairly, and upon very good terms, and that his Majesty is very gracious unto the Company and satisfied with the upright and plain dealing of the Company." As for the disturbance and lack of faith evident in the meeting, he could "ascribe [it] to nothing but the jealousy conceived here at home, and sundry faults imputed and bruited, without just ground." In other words, Digges saw the forces of evil and divisive faction at work. He added that he "thought (and wished) that, if there were any error conceived, they ought to be righted (with discretion) by the committees, without malice, partiality, or faction, that as it is fitting fraud should be avoided in the government, so faction in others, to prosecute matters."[47] Digges affirmed that as far as he saw and understood the mercantile aspects of the business, it was being conducted correctly, and he recommended that the proper way to resolve grievances was not in the more public general court, but in the more select court of committees.

Not everyone agreed with him. Other members (particularly one Mr. Mellyn) brought up older Company history to say that the dispute was rooted in real matters, not an attempt to destabilize the current government—except insofar as pointing out mismanagement was destabilizing. Wolstenholme, another of the committees at large picked in the 1619 election, characterized Mellyn's comments as entirely factious: Mellyn had spoken "seditiously, and scandalously, both here and in other places, to deprave [or vilify] so worthy and grave a government." Mellyn's actions were so bad that the Company should consider disenfranchising him, according to Wolstenholme, who suggested that Mellyn might be "an instrument to ruin the Company."[48]

Calling for disenfranchisement was unusual: very few adventurers had been disenfranchised in the first decades of the Company's operation. Yet not only Wolstenholme but also Governor Smith and other members of the generality came forward to condemn Mellyn's actions. Smith suggested that appointing auditors to prove Mellyn wrong to the generality was necessary, so that "the main action may not suffer by cruel division which must needs bring ruin to the whole Company." Nevertheless, he agreed that Mellyn's membership might be in question. The danger of faction and division was being taken particularly seriously. Another member of the generality, a Mr. Cotton, explained that he had heard aspersions like Mellyn's elsewhere and thought they damaged the Company as a whole, since they made people doubt and distrust it. He cited himself as an example. He had heard "the government of the Company much condemned" so intensely that it had made him start to question the integrity of the elected leaders. Hearing the matters discussed in the general court, however, he realized that the aspersions came only from "some factious persons," and that their charges were baseless. Even baseless, though, the charges had damaged the reputation of the Company.[49]

More telling than the particulars of this debate was its language: unusually, the court minutes recording the meeting gave the names of numerous speakers. Anonymity was abandoned not to leave a record of division, but to record support for the Company's leadership. In almost all instances where a speaker was named, the person was speaking in support of the Company's leaders. Numerous supporters of the Company's leadership were cited, and though the concerns of members of the generality were recorded, the minutes obscured the number of dissenters. The only critic named was Mellyn. Singling him out in this way and raising the possibility of his disenfranchisement acknowledged the danger of his actions but also localized their threat. He alone was the poison in the body politic, even if other unnamed members had joined him temporarily.

Ultimately, the court of committees did not follow through on the threats to push for Mellyn's disenfranchisement. However, his factious behavior continued, and at a later general court meeting, the generality voted to bar him from Company meetings until he proved himself less divisive. Mellyn's case prompted the Company to debate the proper mode of response when confronted by people like him, people "of such a turbulent spirit, so indiscreet in [their] carriage, violent and factious in [their] behavior."[50] Given the mentions of disenfranchisement and the comments in the general court about why exactly Mellyn's behavior was so bad, Company leaders seem not to have known the right response to make. If they were too harsh, other members of the generality might condemn them, but if they were too lenient, they might invite further conflict.

The essential issue that Company leaders were debating here was the nature of the representative government of the Company. Aside from the turbulent spirit, indiscreet speech, and violent and factious behavior already mentioned, Mellyn was also charged with instigating others "to disturb the peace of the business, and endeavor the ruin and subversion of the Trade, contemning the authority of a court of committees, and disturbing the general proceedings of the Company by his bold and uncivil behavior." Adding to this list of charges, the leaders noted that he was "but a very small and mean adventurer," more uncivil than other much greater investors, who had "ten times as many thousands in adventure as he hath hundreds." For these great investors, it was important to "uphold their business, and not suffer it to be disturbed, by every idle humor, knowing that peace and love raiseth small action to become great, and discontents, malice and hatred are means to overthrow the greatest." In other words, the Company owed it to the great investors to keep the business in order, as the actions of a discontented small investor could eventually lead to the overthrow of the trade. Neither Smith nor Abbot much liked Mellyn by this point—the deputy governor adding that Mellyn disturbed whatever meeting he attended and that he was "unfit to be admitted into any of their civil Company."[51] Whether Abbot meant that the Company should remove Mellyn from the Company entirely or simply ban him from general courts was unclear, but other members' discomfort with the action implied by Abbot's statement was immediately evident. After all, Mellyn was not the only "factional" member of the generality, and what was done to him could be done to others.

At issue was also how the Company esteemed, and should esteem, small versus large investors. Members of the generality uneasy with the idea that a small investor deserved less consideration than a large investor sought to decouple Mellyn's behavior from his status as an investor. Some members argued that the size of a man's adventure should have no bearing on his right to express his opinion: "although a man hath but a small stock, yet they supposed it should be no bar to withhold him from delivering his opinion upon occasion." However, Governor Smith disagreed, saying that the amount of investment was absolutely relevant, and the opinion of a large investor ought to be considered more than the opinion of a small investor because a large investor would be more affected: "there ought to be a great difference put, that a small adventurer should not oversway a great adventurer, seeing it concerneth the one so much more than the other." Nonetheless, he added that no one would be barred from speaking his mind, so long as it was done "peaceably and quietly."[52] Mellyn had been neither peaceable nor quiet.

It would be too facile to say that Company members were having a debate on the nature of the early Stuart political nation. They were not self-consciously discussing the topic by proxy. Yet the ideas on display here were some of the central concerns in the political nation at large. Who had the most stake in the well-being of the commonwealth? Were some men by training or circumstance better able to ensure the prosperity of the body? Could someone's beliefs or actions disqualify him from political participation, and if so, under what conditions? Were the leaders of the commonwealth right to guard secrets of state? Was public critique of their leadership appropriate or a sign of dysfunction? Here too there were no easy answers.

As Mellyn's case demonstrated, procedural and constitutional issues could arise from the "factious" behavior of an individual. What to do with one vocal person, in this case, inspired discussion about the nature of the Company's representative government and how the different interests of different types of investors could best be managed. Mellyn had not proposed specific changes, stating only his desire to have more insight into and say in Company affairs. However, the debate about him raised questions about whether or not certain investors should automatically be understood to have a greater stake in the Company's government, just as they had a greater stake in the Company's stock. Though the governor intended to "call him in question in another place," he did not move to have Mellyn disenfranchised, "as some wished." Instead, Smith advised the members that they would be wise to bar Mellyn from their courts: the governor "was of opinion they should do themselves right, to forbid him their courts hereafter."[53] Ultimately the generality voted to bar Mellyn from the general court until he submitted himself to the court of committees.

For a number of years after the Mellyn affair, the level of division and faction in the Company seems not to have reached the heights it did in 1619 and 1620. Perhaps the minutes simply did not record low-level discontent that never was openly stated. Perhaps the corporate body was indeed more at peace. Perhaps one of the two missing volumes of court minutes for the 1620s would have revealed more division. In any case, the next substantial evidence of further division in the Company does not appear until the late 1620s.

In spring 1628, William Bonham and Henry Polstead presented a petition to the court of committees, requesting that a general court be held. Both men presumably were engaged and active members of the generality, though neither was currently a committee. The petition had been signed by more than a hundred members of the generality, and, though Bonham and Polstead were evasive about the precise purpose of the meeting they sought, they promised Company leaders it was for the good of the trade. They wanted to deliver some information and opinions about the Company's affairs.[54]

Company leaders were not pleased with this demand for a meeting by members of the generality. They commented that "this example is without precedent" and were unwilling to grant the request without knowing if the reason for it was "for or against the Company"—by which they meant for or against themselves. For the court of committees, at stake in their decision to grant the petition or not was the wider question of whether members of the generality should be able to demand a meeting to discuss the trade. It was, essentially, a referendum on how transparent to the generality the court of committees' activities were required to be, and how much input the generality would have on the decisions of the court of committees.[55]

This requested general court meeting did take place within the month, with the stated purpose of answering the petition. Governor Abbot first wanted to read the petition and ask each of the undersigned to avow it or not. Casting doubt on the legitimacy of the petition, he explained that he had heard rumors that some of the signers were not adventurers, were dead, or were not members of the Company. Those who had signed the petition affirmed having done so when it was read and claimed that many others supported it but had not signed. One man claimed, however, that he had signed only to request a general court—not because he agreed with the propositions that now appeared to be appended to the petition, with which he said he was unfamiliar.[56]

The propositions turned out to be a wholesale criticism of the leaders of the Company and the decisions they had made in running the trade. The debate that ensued was acrimonious, and the criticisms personal. Only a few of the petition's signers seemed to be in full agreement with these propositions—the minutes listed just two men as openly supporting them. Other signers seemed uncomfortable with the extent of the personal attacks. Some tried to quiet the leading critic, Thomas Smethwick, but another man said that "if men might not have free liberty to speak," then the meeting might as well end. Smethwick was therefore able to give his complaints full rein. The governor suggested that if people were so unhappy with his leadership, they were welcome to choose another leader at the yearly election, which would take place in a few weeks.[57]

Although at the end of the meeting the participants cleared the committees of "all manner of improvidence," the meeting revealed deep unhappiness among the generality with the Company's leadership. The debate at the meeting had become so rancorous that Sandys, who had himself come into conflict with Company leaders in the past, spoke in favor of them now, saying that "he was sorry to see these personal disputes," since everyone agreed on the end they sought to achieve: the success of the trade.[58]

The petition that Bonham and Polstead delivered to Company leaders in 1628 raised overarching questions about the Company's representative government. In this case, the question was how accountable, on an ongoing basis, the Company's elected leaders should be to the wider generality. In calling the general court that the petitioners had demanded, Company leaders effectively accepted the view that members of the generality had a right to call court meetings and speak about the decisions the court of committees had made. The leaders implicitly acknowledged that they were immediately accountable to the generality, not only at the yearly election.

Members of the generality sought to expand this concession a year later, calling for mandatory regularly scheduled general courts to give them an ongoing say in the Company's actions. In March 1629, the governor reported to the court of committees that at a meeting of some adventurers, one group had made three demands for procedural change: They wanted four quarterly general court meetings a year, in addition to any such meetings that the court of committees might find necessary. They wanted a ballot box to be used at the election day. Lastly, they wanted auditors to give an appraisal of the state of the Company's affairs at each quarterly general court.[59]

The adventurers cited by the governor had met about a different matter altogether than procedural reform. They had been debating whether and how to combine the second and third joint stocks. One group, including a number of "lords and gentlemen," looked likely to lose the argument. Faced with this prospect, at least one of them, Lord Saye and Sele, raised the question of whether the generality had the authority to decide the question. As it became increasingly evident that the group of old adventurers would not carry the day, they became "discontent . . . alleging that they come not to this court for justice." Governor Abbot reminded the unhappy adventurers that the Company had a patent to govern it, and that all decisions and procedures had to comply with the requirements of the patent. In this case, that meant that the court of committees would abide by what the generality voted. The result was not what the old adventurers had wanted (to combine the two joint stocks), though it was what Company leaders had desired.[60] The vote was the spur for further meetings of the unhappy adventurers, which in turn led to the demands for procedural change that they brought to the governor.

The fact that Saye and Sele asked the question about authority is interesting and not entirely surprising, as he was one of the most vocal defenders of the Petition of Right just months before, when he had claimed that the petition did no more than recognize the rights of subjects. In 1626 he had supported the rights of the peerage against the monarch when Charles I wanted to exclude the earls of Bristol and Arundel from Parliament (to keep them from voting on the duke of Buckingham's impeachment). In other words, Saye and Sele had long-standing convictions about the proper location of authority and a willingness to press the issue. And as this case and his actions in other cases in the Company throughout the 1630s demonstrated, he was committed to applying his convictions to the structure of the Company as much as to national politics.

The court of committees debated the adventurers' proposals for procedural change. They referred to the patent once again, deciding that it was not for them as the Company's leaders to make such a decision. Nor, however, was it "the opinion of private men"—presumably men like Saye and Sele—that should determine Company procedures. Instead, they decided to put the motions to the general court and be guided by its members' vote on the proposals.[61] This identification of their challengers as "private men" and as such ill-suited to decide how the Company should be governed pointed once again to the ongoing tension between public and private within the Company. By identifying their critics as private men, Company leaders implicitly named themselves public men with the best interests of their commonwealth at heart, though in other contexts they themselves were suspected of private motivations.

Members of the generality ultimately decided to implement several of the proposals. They voted to hold a general court meeting on the Friday of the last week of each quarter and agreed to the use of the ballot box, but they decided that expecting auditors to report on the Company's accounts four times a year was too much. Instead, they agreed on having such a report once a year. They also decided that the new quarterly general courts would not have any greater weight than a general court called by the court of committees. Decisions made at a quarterly court could be modified at any general court, and changes need not wait until the next quarterly meeting.[62] From this point on, there were four quarterly general court meetings a year.

The quarterly meetings remained contentious, particularly when Company leaders tried to undermine them. Conflict between some members of the generality and the court of committees came into the open again in 1632. A missing volume of court minutes makes it impossible to understand the full contours of the problem, but some exchanges recorded in general courts in the months before suggested that division was growing once again among the generality over the distribution of power within the Company and how much access to power members of the generality had. Debate about the usefulness of the quarterly general courts helped focus discontent. In February 1631, at the beginning of one such meeting, Governor Abbot mentioned that the meeting was being held "rather to observe order," as it was the day assigned for the general court, than because there was any particular business to share with the generality.[63] Abbot seemed to think that the meetings were of limited use, and the minutes of the June quarterly meeting that year noted that no one spoke up when asked if they had business to discuss. This silence suggested to Abbot that members of the generality felt as he did about the utility of the regular general courts. However, after the silence, one member came forward to express support for the quarterly general meetings. He stated that he knew that some people disliked them, but he argued that that they were important: "for by this means they have the opportunity given them to meet the more often to debate of their affairs, and to make known every particular grievances [*sic*] as there shall be."

Indeed, he chided members who did not come forward with their complaints, when he knew that they were "free enough of their speech" when "privately together." After he spoke, some people did come forward with concerns.[64]

Though exchanges such as this one demonstrated uneasiness among the generality, they did not represent a call for change. However, a conflict that evolved in 1632 involved fundamental challenges to the Company's government and how the Company's leaders were chosen. Though the full minutes for the year have not survived, a few surviving documents give the outline of a highly contentious debate. One is a copy (possibly a draft) of the minutes for the May 1632 quarterly general court, and another is a draft of a letter from the court of committees to Secretary of State John Coke that gives details about the challenges and the response of the generality.[65] The fact that Company leaders were writing to Coke suggests that the regime was either keeping tabs on affairs within the Company or had been asked to mediate in some way.

The conflict challenged the way power and representation worked in the Company by disputing the 1621 *Laws or Standing Orders*. This was yet another conflict that pitted particular members of the generality (in this case, the easily identifiable members were Saye and Sele, Lord Brook, and Thomas Smethwick) against the sitting court of committees and particularly the governor (in this case, Abbot). Both Saye and Sele and Brook were extensively involved in overseas ventures: by 1632 they had worked together on several colonial ventures, on Providence Island in the Caribbean and in New England (where the town of Saybrook—now Old Saybrook, Connecticut—was named for them). Smethwick's tie to these two men was less clear, as was the identity of any other agitators. What set this challenge apart from others were its terms and how the challengers and the committees presented the nature of power and representation within the Company.

The 1621 *Laws or Standing Orders* had governed the Company's procedures for over a decade when, in February 1632, a member of the generality came forward to argue that the orders were essentially illegal. In the debate that followed, some members argued that the court of committees had no authority to implement the orders listed in the printed document. The perspective of the court of committees was that the rules had successfully governed the Company for over a decade, had been implemented in a time of what the court's members described as "disorder," and had been "so well compiled for the government of the Company's affairs" that "there was no reason to question the said orders." Over a year of consideration had gone into the making of the book of orders, and the court of committees was convinced that it had put together the orders with consideration of the monarch's patent and the powers granted therein.[66] It is possible, in fact, that the disorder mentioned was the division and factional conflict that characterized the Company in 1619 and 1620. Nevertheless, a select committee of twenty-four members of the generality was appointed to review the orders. The letter to Coke did not record all of their names, though it did note that Saye and Sele, Sir Edward Wardour, Holloway (of the ballot box), and Abraham Chamberlain were among the group.[67]

Over the course of several meetings, some members of the select committee determined that the book of orders was invalid as it had never been voted on by the generality and proposed a series of new orders. If implemented, these orders would fundamentally change the government of the Company. For example, one of the proposed new orders placed a limit of one year on the term of the governor and deputy governor and prohibited their reelection for three years. Another required that the eight longest-serving committees be changed each year, and that no more than four of the committees could be members of the Levant Company. A third required that any member of the generality could have free access to the letters and books of the Company and could come into a court of committees and give his opinion, though he could not vote. Others challenged different aspects of the Company's internal practices. Collectively, these proposed orders would force the Company's leadership to turn over far more quickly than it currently did. They would necessarily create greater transparency and limit the ability of the court of committees to mandate and enforce secrecy, as the number of people who governed the Company would increase dramatically.

The select committee eventually boiled down the twenty-one possible new orders, deciding to bring four to the full Company. They wanted the governor to serve no longer than one year; to require that any governor have already served as a committee; to have six committees (down from the eight originally mentioned) change each year, including four of the longest serving; and to require the deputy governor to be one of the twenty-four committees (in effect reducing the number of elected officials by one). Saye and Sele presented these four proposed orders to the full generality at a meeting on 11 May 1632.[68]

The proposed orders and their implied invalidation of the *Laws or Standing Orders* elicited immediate and heated debate. The challenge came at the opening of the meeting. When the minutes of the last general court were read, a member of the select committee (a Mr. Chamberlain) objected, stating that the book of orders mentioned in the minutes had never been voted on by the generality.[69] Unusually for minutes of a contentious debate in the Company, the copy that survives noted names in the margins for who espoused what position. For example, we know that Thomas Mun, a committee and a defender of the Company in print, observed that the court of committees had expended much care on the making of the printed orders, adding that they were well suited to governing the Company's activities both in England and the East Indies, and that therefore the hostility some members were showing to the *Laws or Standing Orders* was unfair.

Those who objected to the printed orders did so on a variety of grounds. Sir John Bankes argued that the orders misused the patent and power delegated by the monarch. He maintained that they were "against the laws of the kingdom and good of the Company"—though when he was pressed, the only example he could give was the oaths the Company required its employees to take. He had consulted a lawyer, who had suggested that the Company's patent gave the Company power to administer oaths only to the governor, deputy governor, and committees. Other members responded that the Company had administered oaths since its beginning, "even to the very porter of the gate who is no brother of this Company," while the governor added that the person currently inveighing against the Company's oaths had recently attended a court of committees and insisted that all Company employees take an oath as a means of combating private trade.[70]

Saye and Sele made a very different argument about the provenance of the printed orders that echoed some of the contemporary critiques of absolutism. He maintained that the "orders for government of the Company ought to have their confirmation from the general court." The printed orders did not, which explained the necessity for the select group and the four orders it had proposed. He acknowledged that members of the generality might confirm or change the proposed orders in any way they wished. In short, he argued that orders governing the Company (that is, its laws) drew their authority from the consent of the people they governed, and that without that consent they were invalid.[71]

Members who responded to Saye and Sele's challenge argued that history and tradition conferred their own authority. For example, Digges pointed out that people had known about the printed orders and referred specifically to them for years. In all that time, nobody had challenged the authority of the orders. Instead, they had been "never yet contradicted by the generality," even though all members had known that "the method for government of all the Company's affairs" was included in the printed orders.[72] Another committee, Alderman Anthony Abdy, noted that though some members were saying that the printed orders were not actually binding, yet "the Company hath been ruled and governed by them these 10 or 11 years." Their force in practice proved their legitimacy.[73]

Yet another committee, Alderman Henry Garway, conceded that it might be proper for the generality to have some say about the orders that governed the governor, deputy governor, and committees, but given that most of the printed orders covered other aspects of the Company's government, it was appropriate only for the court of committees to make them. Abdy added to Garway's point by noting that the four proposals were the work of a day only (according to Saye and Sele), and governed only one day each year—the election day. In contrast, the printed *Laws or Standing Orders* was the work of a year and governed all of the Company's year. Whatever the legitimacy of the rules they had, Saye and Sele's proposed orders might leave the Company without the means of governing itself.[74]

Of the proposed orders, the one stating that the governor must change every year monopolized the debate. The argument by the members of the select committee was that the patent required a yearly change. Saye and Sele stated that there were two questions for the generality to decide: whether the patent supported the group's reading, and whether the yearly change would help the Company's business. The second was hardly a neutral question to Saye and Sele, and the way he framed the question showed that he feared that the generality would put profit (that is, continuity in leadership though the reelection of the governor) above right and freedom. As he asked it, the question was "whether they will always put the government of the Company into the hands of one particular man and he to be perpetual dictator?" Saye and Sele argued that changing the governor was "an exercise of that liberty granted by the patent" and would benefit both the Company and the person chosen to be governor. The Company would benefit by the greater transparency that the frequent changes would enable, as no one person would be able to secure a widespread power base. The people chosen would benefit by being able to share the honor and reputation that accrued to the man holding that position.[75]

Opponents of the proposal argued that the members of the select committee were misreading the patent and requiring Company members to restrict their liberty of free choice in a way never required by the patent or monarch. Thus, while the proponents of the proposal saw an annual change in leadership as a sign of the free choice of the generality, the opponents of the proposal saw the requirement that a change should happen as a sign of the lack of free choice of the generality. Anyone who wanted to reelect the governor should be able to. The deputy governor noted that most London companies reelected the same person to lead year after year. It was not unusual for a group to do so, and this had long been the Company's practice. Other members concurred. Lord Lovelace, trying to accommodate both sides, reminded everyone that as long as the reelected governor took the oath anew each year, he was no different from a newly elected governor.[76]

The issue of the reelection of the governor was so contentious that none of the other three proposals got to be debated. Governor Abbot remained quiet through the debate. He spoke only at the end to assert that he actually had little personal control over the decisions the court of committees made, and he had never abused his power in the way that some proponents of the proposal had suggested. When he framed the question for the generality to vote on, however, he also tied the idea of freedom and free choice to reelection and not to change. The minutes recorded him as saying: "As many of you as think fit to leave the Company as free as formerly they have been, and not to restrain their privileges in the election of their governor etc. but to maintain them according to the tenor of the Company's charter, hold up your hands." The motion passed. Once again breaking with usual practice, the minutes included a small editorial comment, noting that the generality had voted to "continue their ancient privileges and not to admit of any innovation or other manner of election."[77] In the account of the meeting that the members of the court of committees sent to Coke, they characterized the proposals as "an innovation and of so dangerous consequence for the government of the Company as being put to the question, they were by a general consent rejected."[78]

The members of the select committee did not give up but met again to consider the full printed book of orders. The proposals they came up with this time were more numerous but less politically charged. The proposals touched on what time of day meetings should start, what constituted a quorum, and how often the treasurer should report on the Company's debt. Despite the less controversial nature of these proposals, they never received a hearing in a general court. The original authorization for the select committee required that ten of the appointed twenty-four members meet to make a quorum, but only eight could be brought to meet.[79] As of October 1632, the challenge to the existing leadership was over, and sometime before March 1633, the court of committees received a message from the king, delivered by a privy councilor, that he did not wish the Company to "suffer any innovations in their government, whereby to weaken their power, or alter their ancient customs."[80] As a sign of just how firmly the proposed changes had been voted down, the election in July 1633 was held without incident, "in a very fair and peaceable manner without the least contradiction," though the commentary on the peaceable manner suggested the tumult was still fresh, and the designation of fair was a judgment made by Company leaders, who were hardly impartial.[81]

The challenge to the *Laws or Standing Orders* in 1632 was the most sustained and coherent attempt to remake the Company's government. It was the one most likely to succeed, given that it was an organized attempt. The reforms' proponents had spent time and effort to lay the groundwork and cultivate other members of the generality for support. Though a few people had been the prime movers of the effort, their suggestions reflected concerns that many members of the generality shared.

Both sides had used the language of freedom to argue their position. For the challengers, freedom meant freedom from the continuous government of one individual or group of individuals. As Saye and Sele put it, freedom meant not allowing one person to rule as "dictator" over the Company. For the governor and court of committees, however, freedom meant the freedom for members of the generality to choose exactly as they wished, and thus the freedom to elect the same person over and over again. The governor's formulation of the question directly cast a vote for the continuation of the status quo (the ability of the generality to choose) as a vote for freedom, and a vote for the proposals as a restriction of freedom.

Competing definitions of freedom were not the only ways to understand this conflict. The letter that Company leaders sent Coke presented the matter in a very different light. In this context, the challenge to the Company's government became a direct referendum on the monarch. The leaders were not subtle in presenting this interpretation. According to them, "some of our Company backed with a few of the nobility took the boldness to frame propositions to change the government of our Company, not only to the disordering of our affairs, but to the prejudice of his Majesty's power and authority."[82] This was the most direct reference to the way the Company's government reflected the monarch's authority; indeed, it could hardly have been more direct. This formulation transformed the dispute within the Company into an attempt by the agitators to strike at the regime. It also suggested, therefore, that the current Company government reflected and upheld the monarch's power and authority—a suggestion Company leaders may have been keen to make, in light of Charles's dissatisfaction with the Company in the 1630s.[83]

It is probable that the proponents of change meant to return to the rest of their proposed orders and a greater reformation of the Company's government once they had amended the procedures governing the yearly election. Their other proposals would have drastically reduced the power of the court of committees, allowing far greater involvement of members of the generality in the ongoing business of the Company. The proposals would have abolished the court of committee's ability to keep Company documents secret and might have opened the door to more oversight by the generality, as well as what Company leaders would likely have considered more meddling and second-guessing of their decisions. Yet the proponents of change had misjudged either the amount of support they had or how compelling their case was, and by losing the fight over the first four proposals, they lost their chance for greater change.

Some unhappiness with the restrictions of access to Company accounts and letters remained, and on numerous occasions over the next few months, members expressed frustration with those restrictions. Though the generality had reaffirmed the structure of the Company's government, some members still wanted greater access. But Company leaders reacted to the recent challenge and the fact that the challengers had used information gleaned from Company accounts to help craft their challenge and stoke unrest (as the leaders claimed) to further restrict access to accounts and letters. They had agreed to let some interested people make copies of various documents, and this had created problems. Henceforth, only committees would have "liberty to read or take copies of their letters, consultations, or acts of court, or to ravel or dive into their accounts." The men who had taken to coming daily to the counting house and inspecting the books would no longer be able to do so without first getting the approval of the court of committees. They could see the accounts directly related to their own adventure, but nothing else.[84]

Though this restriction was no different than what the court of committees had decreed on earlier occasions, it elicited a considerable amount of anger and frustration on the part of some members of the generality. At a general court meeting in November 1633, a member complained about the restriction and the fact that it kept him from correctly assessing the state of his own affairs. Company leaders explained that no one was being kept from the documents related to his own adventure, but this assurance did little to reduce frustrations.[85] A year later, Company leaders once again announced that they would restrict access to prevent members from "prying" into Company accounts, and members of the generality again raised the same complaints, this time in part due to the fact that the combining of the various joint stocks and adventures into a single joint stock that had recently been voted had complicated people's accounts.[86] The unrest and outcries were great enough that Company leaders debated whether they could and should abolish the quarterly general courts, which in their opinion did "beget nothing but quarrels and debates."[87] The idea of discontinuing the meetings was more a wish than a possibility, however, and although Company leaders continued to toy with the idea over the next year, they never took action to get rid of them. Indeed, in November 1635, when they discussed the idea again, they acknowledged that as the quarterly meetings had been approved by the generality, only the generality could abolish them.[88]

At the heart of the various instances of faction and division in the Company between 1619 and 1635 and of proposals to change the Company's government were attempts by members of the generality to shape the body they were part of but had such limited control over. Their challenges and concerns were reactions to the policies of secrecy and restricted access that Company leaders considered essential and reflected different ideas about how power and representation should work in the Company—a situation that Company leaders not infrequently diagnosed as a consequence of the socially mixed membership of the body.

The challengers to the Company's leadership had limited success. Attempts to change the leadership that centered on election days were the least likely to succeed, in part because the court of committees could often marshal the support of the regime in its defense. The challenges that focused on policy, in which members of the generality proceeded step by step, were more effective in spurring debate and avoiding the presence of a royal thumb on the scale in favor of the existing leadership. These challenges were not always successful, but at least they allowed members of the generality to bring attention to their concerns. The Company's leaders generally kept their control of the Company's government, but on occasion they did so by meeting the demands of members of the generality. The outcome of factional conflict was as much about the court of committees' managing the generality as the generality's changing (or even influencing) the court of committees.

5

Merchants, Trading Companies, and Public Appeal

R O B E R T   K AY L L was no friend of the East India Company, and he made his position clear in a 1615 pamphlet titled *The Trade's Increase*. He thought that the East Indies trade was a misuse of the nation's resources. Despite claims by Company members that the trade helped enrich England, Kayll suggested that the Company was impoverishing the state with its trade in luxury goods that required so much bullion. "Let the common people say that [the East Indies] commodities are unnecessary," he wrote, and "let the whole land murmur at the transport of treasure."[1] However, Kayll targeted not just the uselessness of the trade, but also the form and government of the Company. "How tedious and costly they, and all other companies, make [the trades]," he complained. He argued that other nations did not restrict trade to companies and benefited from allowing all subjects to trade in all places. The crux of his quarrel with the Company was that it placed unfair restrictions on trade and made unneeded distinctions between people, allowing some and prohibiting others to engage in the trade. "How much more we, murmuring at this iniquity," he asked, "may affirm that we are all Britons, all subjects to one royal king, all combined together in one natural league, and therefore not to be barred from trading equally to all places?" Though he assured the reader that his purpose was not to abolish all trading companies, he certainly did not support them.[2]

When Lord Saye and Sele asked in the Company's general court in 1632 "whether they will always put the government of the Company into the hands of one particular man and he to be perpetual dictator?" he was asking a question no less (and maybe more) provocative and damaging than Kayll's challenges.[3] Saye and Sele was tapping into concerns among some members of the generality about the Company's government and the extensive power that was in the sole hands of the governor. He was not the only Company member in the early seventeenth century who criticized its internal government. There was a crucial difference between his dissent and Kayll's pamphlet, however. Company leaders handled the concerns of Company members in meetings of the general court; as much as possible, they tried to resolve problems within the Company's membership among themselves. Saye and Sele's comments had taken place in the context of an intra-Company debate. He did not castigate the Company's government outside the halls of the general court, and Company leaders also responded to his charges in the general court.

When Kayll wrote so critically about the Company, he did so in a pamphlet available to anyone to purchase. Unlike Saye and Sele, Kayll wanted to draw widespread attention to the problems he saw with the Company. He hoped his pamphlet would effect change not just in the Company, but in the nation's overseas trades as a whole. Kayll's primary concern, in fact, was the herring trade, though he made his case in part by contrasting it with companies, particularly the East India Company.

Printed attacks on the Company prompted Company leaders to respond in kind—in print. The decision to do so was not automatic. Company-backed writers produced printed pamphlets rebutting critics and defending the East Indies trade. However, they did so only after considerable debate within the Company about the utility and appropriateness of responding in that fashion. In deciding that they could not handle an external complaint internally, but that they also could not leave it unanswered, Company leaders began to experiment with the tools of public appeal to refute public critiques. Thus while Saye and Sele's complaint about the Company's government was addressed in debate in the general court, Kayll's printed critique prompted a printed public response.

In the early seventeenth century, a flurry of pamphlets appeared concerning the merits and flaws of the East India Company and England's overseas trades more generally. The writers who supported the Company—Sir Dudley Digges, Thomas Mun, and Edward Misselden—all had direct and strong ties to the Company. The writers who condemned the Company—most notably Kayll, along with a few others—were more varied in background, but alike in their distrust of the Company.

For writers on both sides of the issue, the essential question was how to reconcile public benefit and private interest. They also discussed a related question: how best to govern a trade. For those who disliked the Company, it represented a restricted trade that encouraged private interest at the expense of public benefit. For those who defended the Company, charges of unfair restrictions prompted them to develop new arguments about the relationships between private interest and public utility and between the economy and the state. Private interest for defenders of the Company became not a vice to guard against, but a means of harnessing initiative and resources for the commonwealth. The features of the Company's internal government that limited access to the trade—which some critics labeled monopolistic—could, in this formulation, actually prevent the untrammeled exercise of private interest, funneling private initiative into an institution that benefited the commonwealth. Although they were not the same as the positions advocated by factions within the Company, these arguments in essence addressed the same debates that were taking place in the Company— about the management (or mismanagement) of trade and the concentration of power and resources in the hands of the few. As had happened within the Company, Company writers in public drew on absolutist conceptions of the English state, demonstrating how wider political concerns framed and influenced ostensibly nonpolitical debates in a nascent public sphere.

Merchant Pamphlets and Public Appeals: A Case Study

Before it was the title of a pamphlet, the *Trade's Increase* was the name of a very large ship. Consistently referred to in the Company minutes as the "great ship," it was truly impressive for its time—at 1,100 tons, it was the largest merchant ship ever built in England to date.[4] Company leaders planned an elaborate event for its launch.

In 1609, the Company was running short of the money required for the upcoming East Indies voyage: only £43,000 of the needed £60,000 had been subscribed. But Company leaders hoped that the fame of the new ship would help boost subscriptions. Happily, James I had an "inclination to be at the launching of the great ship and to give her her name." The court of committees was heartened by this sign of interest and the "great encouragements" to the flagging adventures it would provide.[5] No expense was spared. One committee, for example, was taxed with providing "a silk ancient" for the ship, "with the Company's arms in silk or metal."[6] The

Company leaders also hired the purser of one of the king's ships to put the masts up and do the rigging of the ship, noting that they would have to entreat the lord admiral to spare the man from his service to the king for the job.

As the launch drew closer, the event grew more elaborate. In December, when the time had come to set an actual date for the launch, the court of committees debated whether it would be good policy also to throw a banquet for the king, ultimately deciding that it was "fitting" to do so. In the end, however, everything ended up quite rushed. The king confirmed that he would attend only at the last minute. The launch was set for 30 December. On 29 December the governor explained to the court of committees that just the day before the Earl of Salisbury, then the lord treasurer, and the Earl of Nottingham, then the lord admiral, had told him "that his Majesty was pleased to be at the launching of the great ship at Deptford tomorrow [30 December] about one of the clock in the afternoon." With one day's notice, the court of committees set about securing the necessary china dishes and assembling "such tapestry and chairs as shall be needful" and wine "of such sorts and quantity as shall be fitting," all to be sent to Deptford on borrowed barges in the early morning. For an appropriate start to the event, they arranged for salutes to be fired to announce the king's arrival.[7]

The Company leaders were in luck—not just the king but also the queen and Prince Henry came. One newsletter account described how "the king, queen and prince went this morning to the launching of the great East Indian ship newly built, where they were to have a great banquet, and Sir Thomas Smith to be graced with a great chain of gold and a medal to be put about his neck by the king's own hands."[8] For the Company's part, the attendance of members of the royal family at the launching of the biggest merchant ship ever highlighted the royal favor given to the East India Company's venture and the royal family's interest in it. The placing of a chain around Smith's neck by the king himself was a mark of high favor and emphasized the direct personal ties between the governor of the Company and the monarch. On James's side, giving Smith a great chain of gold emphasized not only that Smith was a vassal of the king, but also that he held his office at the hands of the king and through the power of the prerogative. The launching and naming of the ship at the king's hands also underlined the fact that the ship, though commissioned by the East India

Company, belonged to the king and the state. As public ceremonies went, the event was therefore relatively successful.

In many ways, there was nothing extraordinary about how Company leaders orchestrated the launching of the *Trade's Increase*. The visibility of the event was unusual, but the types of public ceremony on display were in keeping with other public events that punctuated life in the city of London. The launch of the *Trade's Increase* made sense in the world of lord mayor's shows and other civic spectacles. The East India Company and the East Indies were even featured in some of these early seventeenth-century processions, and merchants played a prominent role in funding parts of the royal entry when James became king in 1604.[9]

Despite the opulent ceremony in 1609 and the feast, salute, and royal attention, the voyage of the *Trade's Increase* had several dire problems. It turned out that the sailors could not manage to properly launch the ship, as its huge proportions made it almost too big for the docking berth.[10] The rest of the ship's maiden voyage proceeded in line with this beginning: the *Trade's Increase* never made it back to England, being wrecked in the East Indies in 1613. However, news of the loss of the ship made it back to England in 1614, with one newsletter noting it as a "great pity, being the goodliest ship of England and never made voyage before."[11]

The pamphlet *The Trade's Increase* was published by Kayll only months after news of the wreck reached England.[12] It openly referred to the fate of that ship, the single failed venture, and the large quantity of English lumber thereby wasted on a fruitless voyage. The ship might have spurred the publication of the pamphlet, but the thrust of the argument went far beyond one lost ship. Kayll provided a point-by-point attack on the East Indies trade, blaming on it the drain of resources and bullion, the high mortality of the venture, and even the loss of the Muscovy trade as merchant interest was redirected to the East Indies. He addressed the trade and Company as "you," framing his criticisms as direct accusations—that is, you have done this and that—and included information about and assessments of all past East Indies fleets. He juxtaposed this with an account of the benefits that would accrue to the nation—from more and better ships, more money, and more poor people employed—if the English could only be persuaded to commit to the fishing trade. The pamphlet ended by promoting the English fishing industry (primarily the fishing of herring), following the Dutch model.

Company leaders were not sure how they should respond—and even whether they should respond—to Kayll's pamphlet. It represented a marked departure from the public ceremonies that Company leaders knew and ushered them into unknown territory. The records of their debates about the appropriate response to a printed pamphlet that attacked them are some of the most revealing ones in existence about how people in the period were beginning to conceptualize the role of print and public appeal. There was no immediate consensus on the proper response. There was not even an immediate consensus on exactly how serious a threat a printed pamphlet was.

For the court of committees, there were several issues at stake when considering Kayll's pamphlet: not only what they should do about the pamphlet and how they should respond, but why the pamphlet had been allowed to be published in the first place. Beyond debating the pamphlet themselves, they sought outside expertise, approaching George Abbot—the archbishop of Canterbury, the deputy governor's brother, and no stranger to printed polemics—for his advice on the matter. Smith sent the archbishop a copy of the pamphlet and asked him whether the Company ought to take action to have the pamphlet suppressed. Abbot sent his chaplain, who had authorized the pamphlet's publication in the first place, with his answer. He advised the Company leaders that the pamphlet "should rather be suffered to die, than a stop to be made which will cause many men to seek after it the more earnestly." But if the court of committees was set on having it suppressed, he would secure a warrant. Letting the book have its fifteen minutes of public attention and then quietly die did not sit well with many members of the court of committees. Some members wanted harsher and more visible punishment: they "were of opinion to have the author rather punished which will quickly be bruited abroad and thereby discover the dislike the state hath to such pamphlets that shall tax what the state hath approved." The court of committees appointed two committees to read the pamphlet and meet with the attorney general, Sir Francis Bacon (at that point not a Company member) to get his opinion and find out whether or not the case might be raised before the court of Star Chamber.[13]

The legal authorities the Company leaders consulted seemed to support taking aggressive action against the pamphlet in the courts. Bacon and another lawyer—unnamed but "much esteemed for his judgment"—agreed with the leaders and in the pamphlet "found some points very near unto treason, and all the rest very dangerous." The court of committees decided to check also with Sir Henry Yelverton, the solicitor general, and then prosecute the author of the pamphlet depending on his advice. Meanwhile, Sir Dudley Digges, a member of the Company and an up-and-coming man at court, wanted "to have a book set forth in defense of the East India trade, and to make known the benefit that it brings to the commonwealth."[14]

What is fascinating about the situation is the variety of responses that Company leaders considered. The type of printed attack and public appeal that Kayll's pamphlet represented was a fairly new phenomenon in the early seventeenth century.[15] The question of how to respond was therefore also new. The court of committees considered ignoring the attack, responding in kind, or pursuing retribution through legal mechanisms, outlining what each course of action might achieve. Archbishop Abbot's advice took the pamphlet not as a simple act but as an act still in progress, and therefore best ignored—since the Company's reacting to it would compound its effect. Meanwhile, Digges was suggesting that the Company print a book of its own that would specifically defend the trade and show its benefit to the commonwealth. He took the pamphlet as a critique that had to be answered, but only with a defense of the trade. The committees who consulted with the royal common lawyers focused on the treasonous aspects of the pamphlet. This approach emphasized not the defense of the trade, but the defense of the state and focused on Kayll rather than the specific contents of the pamphlet.

Company leaders gave the topic much consideration over the next few weeks. In a court of committees, the governor considered "what wrongs and scandal the Company is subject unto, by the envious eyes that do depend upon them." The great profits the Company made came at great risk, though "the malice of some is ready to take advantage upon the least occasion to disgrace either the principal members of this body or the whole Company itself." Kayll's pamphlet was one of the incidents Smith mentioned of an author who had "so maliciously and unjustly written in public disgrace of this Company."[16] Smith wondered whether the Company might be best served by following the Dutch example in responding to printed attacks. According to him, the Dutch so zealously guarded their East Indies trade that they had special laws to keep people from making "invections" against the Dutch East India Company.[17]

There were no equivalent laws in England, but the court of committees did get a sympathetic Privy Council to take up the matter. The Council summoned Kayll and asked him to answer for his pamphlet. When he did not give them sufficient satisfaction, they remanded him to the Fleet Prison until he did so—which he did almost two weeks later, on 17 April, by petitioning the Council with "his humble suit and submission, wherein he very justly condemneth himself." His submission acknowledged his wrongdoing and that he was now "admonished both of his duty to the commonwealth and to your lordships."[18]

The response that Company leaders eventually settled on was the one recommended by Digges. Within a few months he had published, under his own initials, a rebuttal titled *The Defense of Trade*.[19] This pamphlet included a ten-page extract from Kayll's pamphlet (which, since Digges' entire work was only fifty pages, meant 20 percent of the whole publication was given over to Kayll's words) before responding point by point to Kayll's accusations. In his pamphlet, Digges identified himself as a member of the Company—though he said he was writing as a concerned private citizen to correct the misinformation that Kayll had so maliciously spread. Digges's *Defense of Trade* ran to two editions, suggesting that more than a few people bought it. The Company's ultimate response was therefore two-pronged: Kayll was taken to task by the Privy Council, and the Company responded publicly in kind to his pamphlet. However, given that Digges included a long extract from the portion of *The Trade's Increase* that was most critical of the Company, he arguably provided considerable oxygen to Kayll's fire.

The actual effect of Kayll's pamphlet on contemporary opinion about the Company cannot be known. As with any printed work, it is almost impossible to ascertain with any certainty who read it. The pamphlet may have run to two editions. We know that it made its way into a number of aristocratic collections: for example, both Sir Nathanial Bacon and Sir Edward Coke possessed copies of it in their libraries.[20] Beyond this anecdotal evidence (which, as anecdotal evidence goes, is not bad), little can be known about the popularity of Kayll's pamphlet.

Whatever its actual impact, Company leaders always thought that their actions were viewed and judged on a public stage, one that extended beyond the generality. In the case of Kayll and his pamphlet, they seemed to have definitive proof that they were being viewed and judged in that way. The discussion among the leaders about how they should respond to Kayll and what they hoped to accomplish by responding revealed their uncertainty about directly engaging the public. In the end, they decided to deliberately enter the public forum to rebut Kayll's aspersions. *The Trade's Increase* and the question of how best to respond to it marked the beginning of the Company's experiments with the tools of public appeal.[21] It demonstrated

Company leaders' realization that public appeals could be employed by or deployed against the Company, and their decision to participate in a newly developing type of politics that depended on appeals to the public.

The Problem of Private Interest and the Defense of Government

The Trade's Increase was not the only printed challenge to the Company to appear, nor the only item to which Company writers responded in print. Over the next decade, Company writers ventured into print several times to defend their trade. Though the particular criticisms of the Company varied, they were united by a common distrust of the Company and its government. The authors of the critical pamphlets were not members of the Company, but their challenges were analogous to those made by Company members at annual elections and the attempts to change the Company's government by procedural means. Internal Company divisions differed in aim and tone from the pamphlet critiques but shared with them an unease about lodging so much power and money in the hands of a small group of men. Internal Company critics sought to redistribute that power within the body of the Company. Critics who published pamphlets wanted to redistribute it in the body of the commonwealth.

Very little is known about the writers of the critical pamphlets. Kayll left few clues about his life. Nor can much be learned about Tobias Gentleman, author of the 1614 pamphlet *England's Way to Win Wealth*, or a third author identified only as E.S., who published *Britain's Busse* in 1615 (a busse is a herring fishing boat).[22] Their pamphlets all appeared in either 1614 or 1615. All three authors wrote primarily in support of the herring trade and hoped to encourage English participation in that venture. Their works might be seen as a late addition to a collection of pamphlets on the same topic that had appeared periodically during Elizabeth's reign.[23] Distinguishing them from the earlier works, however, was the fact that the authors of these three pamphlets also devoted considerable effort to critiquing England's developing East Indies trade, seeing it as responsible for a lack of interest in their pet project.

There were logical reasons for why authors advocating herring fishing would focus on the East India Company. In 1609 Hugo Grotius published *Mare Liberum*, which argued that no European nation could claim to control the seas, and consequently no European nation could forbid others from trade and commerce in the East Indies (a line of argument that defenders of the Company had made for years). It provided a theoretical defense of Dutch (and, by extension, English) activity in the East Indies. One of the earliest responses to Grotius was published in 1613 by the Scottish jurist William Welwod, who saw Grotius's work as a "subtle treatise" that really endeavored to justify fishing by Dutch fleets in British waters—that is, the herring fishing trade.[24] There is no evidence that Kayll, Gentleman, or E. S. had seen either Grotius's work or Welwod's, but like Welwod, they linked the herring trade and the East Indies trade. For these three authors, herring fishing and the East Indies trade represented a fundamental choice between different economic priorities and different national ambitions.

Both explicitly and implicitly, these pamphlets debated the relationship of private interest and public benefit. For example, the three authors claimed that developing a herring fishing trade would represent the triumph of public benefit over private interest. The basic theory behind the pamphlets was that England could make untold thousands of pounds—one author cited the figure of £600 profit per trip per ship—by following the Dutch example and engaging in off-shore herring fishing. The herring trade, these writers claimed, brought such wealth to the Dutch state that the English should try to emulate it.

According to these authors, this new enterprise would marry public and private benefit. The English commonwealth would profit, as would the individual men who participated in the enterprise. E. S. stated that the herring trade would enrich the king and commonwealth, adding that it would be to the "private and peculiar benefit and advancement of every private undertaker therein."[25] Gentleman highlighted how much the scheme would benefit England's poor, but he also noted that merchants would gain. As proof of the possible riches, he included the example of one busse owner who cleared £1,000 after a single summer's work.[26] E. S. gave a full list of the expenditures and profits that someone could expect in the first few years of setting up a busse. After the initial expenses, E. S. suggested that the profit in the first year would be £62, jumping in the second year to almost £900. He acknowledged that the "private gain to every undertaker" might seem too good to be true but insisted that it was so.[27]

For these authors, the herring fishing trade represented the virtues of trade, while the East India Company represented its vices. For example, the fishing trade was English from start to finish, including the waters in which it took place and the mariners employed in it. Its benefits would accrue to the whole realm, since ships could set out from a number of ports. In contrast, the East India trade depended on foreign commodities from far away, did not particularly help the ports, and supposedly killed more mariners than it employed. One writer emphasized the high human costs of the East India trade—the mariners who were sacrificed to obtain unnecessary commodities—and used the high mortality of the trade to argue that it weakened rather than strengthened English maritime abilities. Likewise, he argued that the resources used in the East Indies trade—including the timber used to construct the ships, the provisions needed for voyages, and the silver coin sent to buy goods—were wasted. England might get pepper slightly cheaper, but the country would be hard pressed to assemble a fleet to oppose an armada like that of 1588.[28] In this view, the East India Company represented the misuse of English resources for the private profit of merchants.

The authors had a range of opinions on the value of companies in managing trades, and using them to govern trade. Gentleman did not mention companies directly, though his suggestions that everyone could and should take part in the herring trade might have been a subtle knock at restrictions on trade. He treated the ability of subjects to engage in business and trade activities as a right, encouraging all Englishmen to take part in the herring fishing trade. He stated that he "shall not need to prove that it is lawful for us that be his Majesty's own subjects to take with all diligence the blessings that Almighty God do yearly send unto us . . . in our own seas."[29] Wrapped in this praise of the blessings enjoyed by England was a statement that all people should be able to access them—which amounted to an implicit criticism of the restrictions on individual action that patents and monopolies represented.

In contrast, E. S. acknowledged the benefit of incorporation in managing the proposed herring trade. He suggested that the king might be willing, if "some of our noblemen, and some of our gentry, and some citizens, and others of ability" petitioned him, to "incorporate them with privileges, immunities, and authority." The new company would be able to choose its own officers, make laws for itself, and manage the nation's herring fishing trade. Yet, lest readers of the pamphlet think that E. S. was advocating that the herring fishing company model itself too closely on the East India Company, he specified key differences between the two. There would be no jointly funded busses: each man would be able to send out his own ships and sell his own fish, so long as he did so in accordance with the company's regulations.[30]

E. S. drew even more direct comparisons with the East India Company. Unlike in the East India Company, for example, he stated that the herring fishing company would tie up members' money for only a year at a time. There would be no investment for years in the "common treasury," with company officials able to require men to pay in more, and every adventurer would be able to take his money out after a year. The government of the herring fishing company would also differ from that of the East India Company. The full company would gather each year for the elections, and all officers would change every year. Additionally, all payments to officers would have to be approved by the full company. In arguing that this model would better govern the company, E. S. was necessarily suggesting that the Company's model of government was not the best way of running a company and did not protect the interests of the generality. He may have been aware of the critical note his suggestions struck, and he added a statement about how easily the Company could support his venture due to its economic benefit. "I think the East India Company will liberally further this work," he wrote optimistically, "for that thereby some of their greatest wants are like to be supplied."[31]

Gentleman avoided mentioning the Company, and E. S. critiqued it only in a relatively conciliatory fashion, but Kayll took direct and unabashed aim at the Company and its government. He faulted the East Indies merchants for the failure of the Muscovy trade, suggesting that they had left a profitable trade for England out of self-interest. He likened the East Indies trade to an illusion of prosperity and appeal, which proved decayed and rotten upon inspection. The ships built to carry the trade, Kayll argued, were wasted and of no benefit to England except as a means of abusing its natural resources (he called it a "parricide of woods").[32] Merchants benefited at the commonwealth's expense by using timber and wasting the lives of mariners. Kayll suggested that the profits to the merchants must be very great to justify such wastefulness of the commonwealth's resources, making it clear that he disapproved. He spent page after page detailing how the East Indies trade misused not just timber, but men and every other resource as well. The East Indies trade, he explained, was like a bird that cloaked itself in stolen feathers, benefiting from beauty that did not belong to it. After discussing several Company voyages and identifying how they had faltered or not profited, he suggested that in fact the survival of Company ships was the exception, rather than the rule. Indeed, except for an early statement that there were enough herring in the sea to make every Englishman rich, he did not return to the herring trade until he had discussed in detail the Company's manifold faults (as well as what he considered the weaknesses of England's other trades).[33]

According to Kayll, incorporation was at the heart of England's trade woes. He argued that the way to remedy England's faltering overseas trades was by allowing "freedom of traffic for all his Majesty's subjects to all places." Such an act would increase customs, shipping, and employment and would benefit the commonwealth overall. Anyone would be able to be a merchant and benefit from trade: "the universal body of the subjects of the land [would be] content, in that they may become merchants, being very ready in this adventurous world to make new discoveries."[34]

This would be a stark contrast to the current system, which Kayll suggested limited innovation by limiting access to trade. As it stood, with trade "settled in companies," merchants were limited by "private orders," and as a consequence, he asserted, "their trades fail them." Interested men could take part only by submitting to the rules of the existing companies, which Kayll viewed as essentially a restriction that tied future generations to the tyrannical control of the past. It was simply wrong, he argued, for "subjects and equal citizens in this great monarch, to be so serviceably tied and subject one unto the other." Privileges were supposed to be temporary rewards, not for "the eternal benefit of a few, and the wrong of all the residue." Yet companies used those privileges to exert excessive control over access to commodities or places. For example, the Virginia Company claimed control of so much territory that "many honest and able minds disposed to adventure are hindered, and stopped."[35]

The East India Company drew special criticism, and Kayll described all the ways that it unfairly restricted trade. He suggested that the Company was not that good at managing the trade, and that was why it relied on restricting access to keep the trade going.[36] The rules that governed the trade in effect prevented men from acting freely. They manipulated the trade to keep prices up, reexporting goods so that people in England did not benefit from cheaper prices.

The essential problem with the East India Company, according to Kayll, had to do not with any particular commodities it traded or resources it used, but with the form of regulated trade that it represented. The problem with the trade was one of government. The Company and other similar corporations made trade too "private"—which did an especial disservice to people outside the companies, who had no choice in the matter. The greatest loser was the commonwealth, for "the commonwealth being made private suffereth by all." Kayll compared England to other countries, which he claimed placed no similar restrictions on the movement and activities of their people, stating that "the like fashion of companies and societies is not used in all Christendom else." Other nations let people trade and travel as they liked. This led to his view that all subjects of James should be able to trade the world over: "we are all Britons, all subjects to one royal king, all combined together in one natural league, and therefore not to be barred from trading equally to all places." Indeed, Kayll stated, the king and Parliament had already made this the case for trade with Spain, Portugal, and France. In an early modern version of the claim that information wants to be free, Kayll argued that privately held trade was the opponent of progress, for "if the world in his infancy had been resolved to have held private what they had in possession, and to have concealed what they knew, there had not only been no civility, but no society."[37]

Kayll clarified that it was not government of trade as such that he was opposed to, but the perpetual limiting of trade. Allowing those who discovered or established a trade alone to enjoy its benefits as a reward for the discovery or establishment was acceptable, "and no man would grudge it." The problem was when someone tried "to keep others out for ever, unless they pay, and submit themselves according to their order, and to their government." A company trying to extend its privileges to more places would also deserve to be criticized.

With these qualifications, Kayll suggested that his proposals were not so radical. He believed that there was a role for government in trade: "my proposition is not any way so tumultuous, as that thereby I would exclude all order and form of government in trades." Misguided people who wanted "promiscuous" action in trade and who did not understand that there should be "an economical and discreet partition and proportion among members" misunderstood his position.[38] In explaining that it was not government in trade that he challenged (in spite of his numerous statements to the contrary), he emphasized that it was the East India Company in particular that he took issue with. It was the prime example of the misuse of trade restrictions and of the detriment to the commonwealth that arose from companies. When Kayll wrote, the Company's patent had been in force for only fifteen years; yet for Kayll, it was the prime example of an untrammeled private interest that too zealously guarded a trade—well beyond the reasonable guaranteed returns that he said discoverers of a trade should receive.

Neither of the two Company defenders of the trade, Digges and Mun, denied the claim that private interest played a role in the East Indies trade. Instead, both authors responded to the larger notion that subjects' pursuit of private interest necessarily meant loss for the commonwealth. For Mun and Digges, private interest played a role in promoting trade. They defended the Company by arguing for the positive influence of private interest.

The response penned by Digges—the response Company leaders had debated extensively before it was written—presented a radically different image of the East Indies trade than those provided by Kayll, Gentleman, or E. S. Digges was a courtier and active member of the Company in the 1610s, though when he wrote in 1615, much of his Company involvement was still ahead of him.[39] Digges's response was formatted as a letter to Smith, the Company governor, by "one of that Society," giving the letter the appearance of a private communication about the nature of the East Indies trade as opposed to a public defense of the Company.[40] Digges reproved the "busy" author of *The Trade's Increase*, who had spread malicious untruths about the Company. Digges concluded that anyone who would seek to besmirch a corporation such as the East India Company, which engaged in "blessed endeavor, with good service to the state," not only detracted from the state himself but must be doing so for private ends. In contrast, Digges claimed he had carefully measured his words, omitting much "secret of merchandise" that "comes too near matter of state."[41]

Much of Digges's pamphlet was a point-by-point rebuttal of Kayll's charges. Digges emphasized that the charges were merely slander. Correcting Kayll's assertions might well make too much information about the nature of the trade public, but as the Company could not allow the charges to appear unanswered lest they be thought true, Digges therefore alluded to the troublesome nature of public debate in print. In engaging in it, the participants risked revealing state secrets or other information better kept private: "I dislike as much as any man to see one . . . steal occasion to censure all our trades, and give intelligence what ships of ours, how manned and at what seasons yearly pass from place to place, with such particulars of our sea states decay, as must be either true, and so the secrets, or false, and so the slanders, of our country." Digges even questioned the wisdom of revealing information on the as-yet-unimplemented herring fishing trade, even though he was quick to comment that the information provided by Kayll on this subject too was likely to consist of the "fond reports of idle fellows," as "false in these particulars, as we know they are in our East India matters."[42]

In addition to rebutting Kayll's points, Digges developed a positive justification for the Company. The East India trade, he asserted, was like the actions of industrious bees and the hive.[43] Merchants were the bees, and "from furthest parts abroad, they fetch and bring the honey to the hive, laborious bees, they cloth and feed the poor, and give the willing man employment to gain with them, and with the commonwealth, the honor and the riches." He viewed merchants as helpful bees, in contrast with those who would present merchants as spiders that set traps and lay in wait for victims to come to them. The East Indies trade, he argued, had first brought wealth to the Venetians by means of the overland trade, and then to the Portuguese when they developed the sea route. Now was the time for the English to benefit, too, and it was this very goal that motivated the "famous fellowship" to start the East India Company. With little effort, the East India merchants would be able to turn London into an entrepôt in northern Europe, "a staple of commerce for all the world," that would in turn lead to "much life and quickening to the navigation and affairs of this whole land." Digges cited the successful return of the East India Company's ships the year before, and noted how their arrival had spurred economic activity in the capital. In his view, the Company was undertaking "voluntary hazards" in the form of such long, costly, and dangerous voyages for the sake of the "reputation and revenue of the commonwealth." He argued that the self-sacrifice of the members of the Company for the sake of the public good was such that they must be commended even by "their enemies' concession."[44]

Digges therefore refused to accept the characterization of the East Indies trade as wasteful and selfish. It was envy and ignorance at best, and evil and maliciousness at worst, that made others criticize the Company. Envy and ignorance might explain the charges that the Company was "killing mariners and carrying out the treasure of the land," since Digges was sure that an examination of the information would reveal the true situation and resolve the question in favor of the Company. He addressed the objections made to the East India trade one by one. He countered the charges that the East India trade had diverted merchants' interest from the Muscovy Company by arguing that Smith, governor of the East India Company, was still heavily involved in the Muscovy Company, and that the latter company still made enough to defray the cost of the current embassy to Russia. To charges that the development of the East India trade caused a diminution of the trade through the Strait of Gibraltar (the "Straits" as it was referred to then) and into the Mediterranean, he answered that as long as the kingdom gained, it did not matter if it gained via the Cape of Good Hope or the Straits, and moreover, now that the Dutch were also involved in the sea route to the East Indies, if the English decided not to use it that would not revitalize the more expensive straits trade. Who could think, he wrote, "that while the Dutchmen hold their trade, there will be any more spice brought from Turkey? Certainly that course is now forever overthrown."[45]

Digges took special care to address Kayll's charges regarding the East India Company ships. Digges responded in detail to the claims that the ships' construction wasted English timber and that they would be too far away to be summoned quickly if they were needed for the defense of the nation. He explained that the Company had bought the oldest and most decrepit ships and fixed them up at its own expense (using not English but Irish timber). He listed the Company's ships one by one, giving the condition in which they were bought, how they were refurbished, and the voyages they had undertaken. With regard to the charge that the ships were inaccessible if they should be needed, he argued that once home they could be made ready quickly, and that ships arrived each summer and were available in winter while they were being made ready for a voyage. Most importantly, the king had no problem with the amount of service the Company rendered, as it operated according to letters patent granted by him—and therefore no one else should have a problem with it either.[46]

As for the high mortality of the trade, Digges maintained that death was an inevitable part not just of trade, but also of life, and it was only to be expected that men would die in pursuit of the trade. He claimed that a death in pursuit of the commonwealth's benefit was to be preferred than for a man to die idle at Wapping while waiting for employment.[47] Nevertheless, experience had taught and would teach the Company to manage their residences abroad better so that mortality would go down.

Digges explored the relationship of public and private from the position that the state could and should encourage private action for public benefit. He asserted, for example, that the commonwealth had a right to the bodies of its people, and that those bodies were the kingdom's greatest treasure. Refusal to venture Englishmen in pursuit of trade was misguided:

If we look upon it, for itself or for ourselves, to stay away from sea for fear of death, and starve at home, or pine away in poverty, were foolish superstitious cowardice. But as we are the bodies of our king, and of our country (though in truth their greatest treasure, witness Powhatan, or Virginia, without them yet). This [is a] necessary relative of sovereignty. Living bodies, unemployed, are nothing. And if unhealthiness or danger or mortality should keep us from a course wherein we may enrich us, or our masters, or serve the king, or good the commonwealth [*sic*]; who then shall live in Rumnie-Marsh, or Holland, or our Cinque Ports, or cities visited with sickness or go unto the war?[48]

A marginal note explained that Powhatan was a "poor naked king" and that Virginia would be the "goodliest country in the world, were it well inhabited," further underlining the link between the bodies of subjects and the strength of the state.[49] A land or king without men, or a king whose men who were unwilling to venture forth, was a land or king whose full potential had not been realized.

In Digges's formulation, the question for the monarch or commonwealth was how to get private men involved in public matters that would have a long-term benefit, given the disincentives of death or sickness. For Digges, the answer was honors and privileges: "perfect wisdom in all commonwealths hath honors, pay and privileges to invite the private man into such dangers, for the public good."[50] In the situation as Digges described it, the monarch was responsible for promoting trade. The best way for him to do so was to promote the kind of actions by trading companies that Digges had been defending. Appeals to private interest were an essential tool for a monarch trying to ensure the public benefit.

Mun picked up these questions of private interest and private benefit in his two pamphlets defending the East India Company, the 1621 *Discourse of Trade* and the 1628 *The Petition and Remonstrance* (which he authored on behalf of the Company, and which appeared under the corporation's auspices). Neither pamphlet was a direct response to the herring fishing pamphlets that had spurred Digges's work, but both of Mun's pamphlets developed themes similar to those used by Digges to justify and explain the East Indies trade. Mun did so by reframing the nature of England's overseas trade. He was in a good position to speak authoritatively about the Company's trade as he was an active member of the Company's court of committees almost without interruption from 1615 to 1635, and he even served as deputy governor briefly in 1624.[51] He defended the trade by redefining what the costs and benefits of overseas trade were. In Mun's formulation, there was no easy trade-off between fish and pepper, or between a busse and a merchant ship. Instead, the question was whether the reader could be persuaded that overseas trades, and the long-distance overseas trades in particular, were, as Mun claimed, the most profitable to the kingdom, and the true and only means of enriching the commonwealth.[52]

This was an argument that applied to proponents of herring fishing and dissatisfied members of the Company alike. For example, introducing a new topic in *The Petition and Remonstrance*, Mun posed a question that, he said, even "many of our Adventurers do not well understand": how could the commonwealth profit even when merchants involved in the East Indies trade made a loss? This, Mun assured his readers, was possible and far more likely than the opposite case, where merchants made a profit at the expense of the commonwealth.[53] Mun argued that one had to think about more than just the English commonwealth in assessing the impact of the East Indies trade. He distinguished between the types of commonwealth that could benefit or suffer. Before judging the trade beneficial or injurious, he wanted his readers to factor in the effect that a given action or policy would have not only on the English commonwealth, but also on England in relation to the rest of Europe and Christendom. Thus, though detractors might claim that Christian money was being spent on infidel cloth when Company leaders imported cloth from the East Indies, this underestimated the beneficial effect of moderating the excessive prices charged by the Dutch for cambrics and linens. Likewise, accusations that the sea trade depressed the earlier robust overland trade did not consider how important it was to strike a blow at the Turk, since the sea route to the East Indies circumvented the caravan trade through the Ottoman empire and the Mediterranean.[54] Mun went one step further, pointing out how the development of the sea route also depressed trade between the East Indies and the Red Sea and the Persian Gulf to the benefit of Christian traders; therefore, the East Indies trade providentially allowed for a shift in Eurasian politics, since the Cape route seemed to smack of God's favor to Christian commerce—hurting Indian and Ottoman trade to the benefit of Christian trade. Mun thus situated the benefits of the Company's activities in an international, not just a domestic, context.

Mun also made a determined stand against the oft-cited charge that the East Indies trade impoverished the nation for the sake of luxury goods like spices and dyes. He challenged the charge on two counts: first, such goods were not actually luxury goods at all, but needful and necessary commodities; and second, they allowed for increased or better production of English commodities. The supposed luxury goods, Mun argued, actually consisted of medically valuable rare herbs and medicines. "Who is so ignorant in any famous commonwealth," he asked, "which will not consent to the moderate use of wholesome drugs and comfortable spices?" He painted the detractors as fanatics and presented himself as the voice of moderation. Thus the East Indies trade became not a luxury trade, but a means of acquiring useful and good commodities. East India goods were "as things most necessary to preserve their health, and to cure their disease," and Mun cited several herbals and medicinal tracts to lend his claim credence.[55] Anticipating charges that many nations lived without those same healthful herbs and medicines, Mun stated that either those people did not know what they were missing and so suffered, or they were simply unable to procure the herbs and medicines. The English, of course, both knew and were able to secure supplies.

For Mun, the East India commodities belonged in the same category as other goods acquired abroad. He argued that if one wanted to forgo East Indies drugs and spices, one might as well forbid all the other goods that England had enjoyed for so long. Many of these were goods the English had long made part of their daily lives. While others were luxury goods more easily labeled as unnecessary, even those were harmless enough. "Objectors" to the East India Company "might as well deny us the use of sugars, wines, oils, raisins, figs, prunes, and currants, and with far more reason exclaim against tobacco, cloth of gold, and silver lawns, cambrics, gold and silver lace, velvets, satins, taffetas," yet "moderate use" of all of these goods "hath ever suited well, with the riches and majesty of this kingdom."[56] Thus, Mun made East Indies goods analogous to any other imported good, regardless of origin or degree of luxury. Pepper, wine, and gold lace, which came from three different places and by the transport of at least two companies, were linked together and collectively found a useful, or at least unobjectionable, place in English consumption patterns.

Mun argued that East Indian commodities could actually benefit English commodities by changing English production patterns. Indigo and raw silk could make English woolens more esteemed and desired, in turn spurring the production of English woolens that used the products and employing large numbers of the poor. Mun referred to various silk projects being explored at the time, asserting that if they survived and flourished, they would likewise make the nation flourish. This had been demonstrated, he claimed, in many Italian states, France, and the United Provinces.[57] Thus, Mun tied the imported East Indies goods to domestic industry, and even to stimulating a little healthy intra-European competition. In short, he challenged charges of self-interest by querying the terms of the debate. Self-interest in a complicated economic system could not be easily isolated.

In the 1628 *The Petition and Remonstrance*, Mun more fully explored the relationship between private and public benefit. He asserted that the greater the distance involved in the trade, the more profit it brought. Not every foreign trade was equal, and some benefited the commonwealth more than others; but, as a general rule, he wrote, "the remotest traffic is always most beneficial to the public stock." Mun argued that the English made more profit off the East Indian trades than the East Indians did: "whereby it is plain, that we make a far greater stock by gain upon these Indian commodities, than those nations do where they grow."[58] The East India Company was well positioned for public profitability. Once again he emphasized that England's economic relationships were complicated. Mun was a devoted and eloquent fan of the reexport trade. English profit was contingent, he argued, on the English buying the commodities not just to consume but to resell—that is, on being prepared to act as middlemen in the East Indies trade in Europe.

For Mun, there was no less honor or money in the reexport trade than in a simple import trade. Reexporting was a fair means of increasing profit. The wealth gained by reexporting commodities produced in other nations was no less to be valued. The wealth generated by the East Indies trade was also, Mun explained, to be valued in terms of national honor. Expanding the East Indies trade brought as much honor to England as the greater production of English commodities: "neither is there less honor and judgment by getting riches in this manner, upon the stock of other nations, than by an industrious increase of our own means, especially when this latter is advanced by the benefit of the former, as we have found in the East Indies."[59] This assertion was important in light of the claims that many of the writers (regardless of their viewpoint, and including Mun) made in their pamphlets of God's having blessed the English with such a wealth of resources and production that England could be self-sufficient without need of foreign trade.[60] This was not the same as wealth, though. Mun did not seek to challenge this assertion of English self-sufficiency but instead presented an alternative way to make an honorable profit.

According to Mun, foreign trade was the way to enrich the commonwealth with the fewest negative consequences, and trade was the only way of creating new wealth in the kingdom. He pointed out that lacking mines, England could not increase the nation's treasure from its own resources. Long-distance trade goods, provided that a good proportion of them were reexported, would bring treasure into the kingdom. The East India trade had the greatest potential and therefore did "excel all others." Reexportation meant that the balance of trade was not bipolar, and bullion sent from the country to fund the trade did not necessarily result in a net loss of bullion from the country.[61] If trade was the source of the nation's wealth, then merchants' self-interest in promoting trade might indeed lead to the nation's benefit.

Mun went beyond the divide between the public and the private to explore the relationships among Company, crown, and public benefit. Many of the critics of the East India trade had posited a simple bipolar relationship between private and public benefit, so that when merchants benefited, they must be doing so at the expense of the public. Mun was not the first apologist for the East India Company to argue that this explanation was not correct, but he also explained that the relationship between trade, merchants, and profit was complex. The bipolar public / private divide became the tripolar Company, crown, and commonweal. For Mun, the East Indies trade had three types of potential gains. First, the commonwealth gained, which would happen even if the merchant lost. Second, merchants gained, which could occur even if the commonwealth lost. Third, the crown gained, and this would always occur because an increase of trade always meant more money to the crown from customs and duties.[62]

Therefore, what separated Mun and Digges from the authors who favored the herring fishing trade was not just their attitudes about the East India Company, but how they understood private interest. For the proponents of herring fishing, private interest was what drew people to and kept them investing in the East Indies trade. It was what lured people away from a new fishing trade that, in the authors' opinion, would so clearly benefit the English commonwealth. Focusing on the herring trade did not necessarily mean abandoning organized companies, though that depended on which pamphlet one was reading. E. S. suggested that those interested in the fishing trade should try to secure company privileges to enhance the private benefits that a work so beneficial to the commonwealth would accrue. In contrast, Kayll saw organized companies as part of the problem, since they protected private interest at the commonwealth's expense. Although these two authors drew opposite conclusions, both of them believed that the link between organized companies and private interest was clear.

Neither Digges nor Mun contested the claim that private interest helped fuel the East Indies trade. Nor did they address Kayll's challenge to governing trade in companies or his claims that trading companies unfairly restricted trade and protected private interest. Instead, both Digges and Mun responded to the larger assumption that private interest meant the commonwealth's loss. Rather than simply denying that the East Indies trade benefited private interests, Mun and Digges crafted arguments to explain why private interest was a tool in the arsenal of the monarch.[63] Digges argued that the monarch had to harness private interest for the public benefit, and that the drive for profit or status and office were some of the mechanisms by which individuals could be enticed to become involved in the overseas trades. For Mun, trade was more complicated and profit was more nuanced than a simple zero-sum relationship between public and private profit. In short, private interest was not necessarily the commonwealth ill that the advocates of herring fishing suggested. Mun and Digges defended their company by defending the supposed vice it promoted.

An Absolutist Defense of Companies

There was another way of responding that was very different to that of Digges and Mun: focusing on the political rather than the economic implications of Kayll's critiques. In 1622 in *Free Trade: Or, the Means to Make Trade Flourish*, Edward Misselden answered Kayll by defending trading companies as reflections of monarchical power.[64]

Misselden was connected to the East India Company, though less directly than Mun or Digges. Little is known of Misselden's early life, but by 1615 he was a member of the Merchant Adventurers, which exported cloth to the Netherlands. As early as 1621 he promised the Company's court of committees to do them whatever service he could. *Free Trade* helped inaugurate Misselden's association with the Company, though the work was not directly authorized by the Company. The fact that writing a pamphlet could gain someone the Company's patronage suggests that despite misgivings among Company leaders about whether taking part in public print debates was good, they recognized how such publications could help them. Thus, participation in a print debate could be a means of currying favor with

Company leaders.[65] By late 1623, Misselden had been formally employed by the Company to serve as its agent in Delft, where he also served the New Merchant Adventurers. For years he wrote to Company leaders, keeping them apprised of news and events in the Low Countries, and on occasion he acted on their behalf.[66]

Nearly half of Misselden's *Free Trade* examined the various roles of government in trade, including in the chartered companies. Misselden expanded the meaning of government in trade beyond the question of how a trade was regulated (the definition used by all the other contributors to the print debate). "Government" for him was not just the regulation of trade, but also the representation of the majesty and authority of the king in trade. Since government was a reflection of the majesty of the king, any governed body, Misselden declared, was invested with some portion of the king's honor. With their direct ties to the monarch on account of their patents, the chartered companies were especially favored, and those trades that operated under a charter did "much advance and advantage the commerce of this commonwealth," doing much better than any ungoverned trade.[67] Misselden was standing up for the chartered trades, though with some caveats—since he admitted that the misuse of government in trade could turn an orderly governed trade into a monopoly, which he agreed was always bad.

In *Free Trade*, Misselden was nothing if not methodical. He outlined how both government and the lack of government affected the trades— concepts which were necessarily related to monopolies—and the distinction between public and private restraint of public liberty. Misselden created an argument for government's playing a role in trade on the basis of likeness, or similarity. Just as the state and subject benefited from the presence of government, so did trade. Government in any form became a means of expanding the king's honor: its presence endowed the king's honor into something that would not have it otherwise. It was a commonplace, he said, that the best argument about the want of government was the benefit of government itself, and he contrasted the English with the Dutch. The Dutch, he argued, better understood the need of public involvement in trade (by which he meant government restraint of trade), and valued it over a misplaced emphasis on particular (by which he meant private) gain, "for they wisely consider, that their interest is involved in the public, where, in our nation, men commonly prefer their particular, to the common good." The forms of trade existed on a spectrum—from chaotic at one end, where anyone could take part in the trade, even to its detriment; to monopoly at the other end, where the trade was restricted to the point of excessive exclusion, and the monopolist rather than the commonwealth benefited from the application of order and government to the trade. The ideal situation was in the middle, where judicious application of order and government kept the trade from both chaos and undue restrictions. Lack of restriction allowed people who did not understand the trade to ruin it: "for want of government in trade, openeth a gap and letteth [in] all sorts of unskillful and disorderly persons, and these not only sink themselves and others with them, but also mar the merchandize of the land . . . there can be nothing in trade more prejudicial to the public utility."[68]

The restraint of public liberty, therefore, could be beneficial to the state under the right circumstances. Misselden argued for the restraint of liberty by the state to limit access to a particular opportunity to those best able to take advantage of it. This was in many ways an absolutist argument, relying on common understandings of how prerogative power functioned.[69] The state could order this type of beneficial restriction of the public liberty, for example, when it issued patents to encourage and reward innovation. Public liberty could be restrained by public authority, as when the state restricted it; or by private authority, as when—in Misselden's description—a few people kept a trade entirely in their own hands, unofficially and without public endorsement.[70] Public authority for the restriction of trade could be either through the prerogative of the king or an act of Parliament, though Misselden made the distinction that the king's prerogative granted privileges while an act of Parliament prohibited the actions of others. The king gave, and Parliament restricted. Indeed, Misselden argued that the king could grant something that Parliament had earlier prohibited, provided it was not *malum in se* (evil in itself), since the particular scenario might not have been considered by Parliament when it passed the prohibition.[71] Thus in Misselden's formulation, the exercise of prerogative power of the monarch could be a corrective to parliamentary acts that might have been well intentioned but incorrect.

Wrong notions about equality in trade were the cause of popular resentment of companies that relied on patents and the prerogative, according to Misselden. People perceived that a patent was robbing them of the freedom to engage in a trade that they thought they should enjoy. Whether the restriction arose with a parliamentary prohibition or the monarch's patent, this sense that a previously held right was being taken away led "so many [to] plead the freedom of subjects and press, or rather oppress, that plea of equity." Though Misselden did not mention Kayll, this was almost exactly the way Kayll had framed his objections to trading companies, down to the appeal to the rights of all subjects under the monarch. Yet what these angry people did not understand, Misselden claimed, was that their ideas of equality were flawed. Equality did not mean that "all should be merchants at their pleasure." That was a false equality: "for that's not equal, that may seem profitable to one, and be hurtful to many." Instead, equality in this case was served by having membership in the trades equally open to everyone with the proper means, not by having no restrictions.[72]

For Misselden, the form and structure of trading companies were a clear good. Limiting trade was necessary and beneficial to the commonwealth. England had long organized trades into companies for good reason, as "there cannot be any greater bane to a well-governed commonwealth, than ill-governed and disorderly trade." Misselden came out in strong support of crown grants of privileges as the basis of the trading societies, writing that if people only thought about it, they would realize the good sense of having corporations founded on crown proclamations, and that the "gracious grants and privileges of His Majesty, conferred upon societies, would not seem so much a restraint of the common liberty as a prudent ordering and accommodating thereof unto the public utility." Misselden's conclusion overall was that the ends justified the means: as long as public utility was better served by having restrictions on trade, then restraining public liberty, either by the crown or by Parliament, was permissible and indeed desired.[73]

The crown was key to the trading companies in part because it was the king and not Parliament who guaranteed and secured rights outside the kingdom. Parliament was involved in adjudicating liberty within the kingdom, but national law could not bring into being or govern a trade that relied on foreigners. Laws gave rights within the kingdom, but "it is the king that must enable men to trade without the land." Arguments about free and closed seas might help open or restrict the waterways, but trade itself was conducted based on the amity of kings and treaties of peace made by the king "by his own authority," and without, Misselden noted, "the assistance of his Parliament." The international trades likewise specifically affected the king, touching his honor and revenue. Trade could affect the king's honor generally: for example, a slow-working legal system or unnecessary lawsuits reflected badly on the king. Trade could also affect the king's honor specifically, as when a particular trade failed or suffered setbacks—such as had recently happened with Dutch depredations against the Company in the East Indies. Government of the trade likewise reflected on the king. A trade that was too strictly restricted (in other words, a monopoly) abused the king's prerogative, while a chaotic and ungoverned trade projected the wrong image of the king and English government abroad, for strangers unfamiliar to England and English government would necessarily judge the English by the actions of the king's subjects abroad.[74]

Misselden did not limit his defense of government in companies to the theoretical. He provided numerous examples drawn from actual English companies to show how beneficial companies with government had been. The Merchant Adventurers, the Eastland Company, the Levant Company, and the French Company were all mentioned, with Misselden noting how each had served England. For example, the Levant Company, "by their trade under government," had helped build England's naval defenses. The East India Company received special mention, and Misselden referred to earlier pamphlets by Digges and Mun. He praised their works vindicating the Company and added his own defense: "this I say, that this great and noble society by the benefit of government, hath set on foot a very mighty trade, far beyond any other company of this kingdom."[75] Envy alone led people to doubt the accomplishments of the East India Company.

To contrast these stories of success, Misselden also gave examples of how trades failed through lack of government. In this section of his pamphlet, Misselden again seemed to be responding to criticisms like the ones Kayll made, though without mentioning him by name. For example, Misselden referred to the "ordinary objection" that other countries in Europe did not organize trade into companies and societies and still did fine. He countered that objection by noting that most countries had some form of government of trade even when that form was not called a company. For example, Italian trade was mostly organized by families, Misselden said, which played a role analogous to that of a company by similarly organizing and restricting a trade. He also argued that when a trade did not have government it generally failed, citing as an example the poor performance of the Spanish trade in England, "that hath no company nor restraint." Indeed, he wrote, "those that trade without order and government, are like unto men, that make holes in the bottom of that ship, wherein themselves are passengers."[76] Government of a trade was that trade's best defense and would secure its benefit for the commonwealth.

A series of pamphlets about the herring fishing trade drew the East India Company into the printed arena in the early seventeenth century. Company leaders knew they were entering a public debate, and they chose to do so even though they had reservations about responding in such a forum. The pamphlets did not simply advocate the development of a new trade (herring fishing). They also took aim at the East Indies trade, challenging the type of restricted trade it represented and its utility to the commonwealth. In defending the form and function of their trade, writers supporting the Company developed arguments justifying the role of private interest in trade and how the overseas trades brought wealth to England. What others saw as unfair restrictions on trade, these writers lauded as the government of trade. Companies were set up by the monarch to order trades (not restrict them), and consequently delegating a particular group of people to conduct a trade was a proper exercise of power. Thus, writers with ties to the Company were able, in conceptual terms, to justify the government of the East India Company and the motives of its members.

Whether answering the generality or writing for print audiences, Company leaders grappled with how to answer the protests of the "public." How Company leaders answered challenges from the generality differed from how Company writers answered challenges from printed pamphlets, in part because the challenges differed in type and content. Nonetheless, the challenges were not so dissimilar. Unhappy members of the generality thought that Company leaders neglected the public of the Company. Critics who wrote pamphlets thought that the Company failed to guarantee the interests of the public of the commonwealth. In both cases, Company leaders and Company writers had to defend the authority and function of the Company against assertions that in some essential way the Company did not represent the interests of those whom it should have served. Vital to the Company's defense was the argument that its government was sound and appropriate.

What the proper government of trade looked like was a question that Company leaders grappled with repeatedly and in many contexts. It was behind the challenges that members of the generality made to the leadership of the court of committees, and it was mobilized to support the existing structures of power. It was crucial to the contentions of critics like Kayll, even as it prompted new explanations of what government meant in relation to the Company and how the Company fit into the commonwealth. In short, the proper government of the Company was a dominant motif of its early history and was at the heart of the Company's corporate identity in the early seventeenth century, whose origins were firmly rooted in the Company's patent.

The history of the East India Company in the early seventeenth century reflected the political culture of the period. Concerns with access and transparency, and with order and authority, were common motifs of the time. The steps Company leaders took to manage these issues were generally in line with the steps taken in other institutions. One area in which the Company's uniqueness was especially evident was in its relationship to the English state. The ways that relationship could shape actions and events within the Company have already been explored. How that relationship shaped and was shaped by the Company on the national stage is the central question of the next section of this book.

Part Two

THE COMPANY
AND THE STATE

This part of the book sets the activities of the East India Company against the background of wider political events of the early seventeenth century to uncover both the interplay of actions overseas and domestic policy and the constant negotiations between the Company and the regime required by the business of state. The cases examined here are organized chronologically and reveal the issues and political maneuvers that drew Company leaders and members of the regime together.

Part 2 thus charts the Company's changing relationship with the monarch and Privy Council, from periods when Company leaders and privy councilors worked together to periods when the relationship was tested. The cases discussed here demonstrate the extensive interactions between the two as Company needs were balanced against the objectives of the regime. A few themes recur in these cases, like the exclusivity of the patent and the relationship of military activity overseas to policy at home, yet their treatment was always determined by the political needs of a given moment. There was no guarantee that the monarch and Privy Council would accommodate the demands of the Company, but there was an expectation that they would work together.

Chapter 6 returns to the patent (previously examined in Chapter 1), treating the acquisition of privileges beyond the original patent and the meaning of the patent years after its initial granting. The example of the short-lived Scottish East India Company demonstrates how the Company and crown could have different understandings of what one had granted to the other and of what the patent required of each party.

Chapter 7 looks at the Company's martial engagements abroad, particularly the Company's role in the fall of Hormuz. These activities abroad raised questions about how Company affairs fit into English affairs. There were practical considerations (Did the Company owe money to the lord admiral?) as well as conceptual ones (To what extent were Company men acting as representatives of the English state when they were abroad? Were Company military engagements necessarily English military engagements?).

Chapters 8 and 9 focus on the consequences of the often-strained relationship between the East India Company and the Dutch East India Company, particularly after the death of several Englishmen at the hands of the Dutch at Amboyna in 1623 (the so-called Amboyna massacre). The events at Amboyna led Company leaders to press the regime to secure restitution from the Dutch, at times when neither James I nor Charles I were amenable to doing so. Company leaders employed a number of tools of public appeal to try to shape public opinion about Amboyna and compel action by the regime. These appeals did not succeed, and the continued failure of the regime to secure restitution led members of the Company to explore ending the trade—though ultimately Company members reaffirmed their dependence on the crown for their success.

Chapter 10 reveals the breakdown in the Company-crown relationship in the 1630s. Frustrated by the continued push by Company leaders for restitution for Amboyna as well as the failure to shape the Company to better suit his aims, Charles developed and supported schemes to create alternatives to the East India Company that were more obviously imperial in aim. Even though the Company was not as strong or influential as it had been, it proved more difficult than Charles might have thought to disentangle the state from the business of the Company.

6

The Changing Patent

Negotiating Privileges between Company and Regime

I N M A R C H 1618, a Dutchman named Isaac Le Maire approached James I and the Privy Council about securing a patent. He hoped to establish a company in England to take advantage of his new discovery: a previously unknown route to the East Indies. Rather than the more common Cape Route—to the East Indies via the Cape of Good Hope—or even the less common passage to the Pacific through the Straits of Magellan, Le Maire's new route went around the southernmost tip of South America, past what he had named Cape Horn.[1] The patent he sought would guarantee that no Englishman unauthorized by his company could sail to the Indies via the southwest passage, as the Cape Horn route was known, or could import into England goods acquired by use of the southwest passage. It would mean that Le Maire and his fellow investors could develop an East Indies trade to rival that of the eighteen-year-old East India Company.

The leaders of the Company were not pleased with Le Maire's request. They petitioned James I to turn Le Maire down, arguing that if the monarch wanted someone to carry out a trade via the southwest passage, they would do so—not under a new patent, but through the privileges already granted them in their current patent. They even suggested that Le Maire's route already fell under their geographical control and that "they conceive this passage, and all others which soever beyond the Cape of Bona Esperanza [are] discovered, or that may be discovered, to be sufficiently and in express words granted unto them, by your Majesty's gracious letters patent."[2]

Thus, they argued that James had already granted the Company the south-west route before it had been discovered.

James challenged this expansive reading of his earlier grant to the Company. "But to that point of power which the Company claim by their patent," the minutes of a court of committees recorded, "he was a little amazed thereat, demanding whether he were like Pope Alexander, who divided and distributed the whole world." Instead, he informed Company leaders, he thought it more "reasonable that the right of discoveries should be to such as made them."[3] The Treaty of Tordesillas notwithstanding, the globe was not something he could or would partition for the Company's benefit, forever protecting its supposed privileges. Rather, new discoveries might very well change the scope of the Company's powers, and not necessarily in its favor. In the case of Le Maire's petition, the Company was ultimately successful: neither Le Maire nor other rivals of the Company received a royal patent for the southwest passage, and Le Maire dropped out of the Company's records. Le Maire was not the only challenger to the Company's patent in the early seventeenth century, however.

Despite the appearance of permanence and transparent meaning that a written patent gave, the patent—and exactly what its grant encompassed—was always fluid, with both Company and crown understandings of it changing in response to political realities. Patent negotiations between the crown and the Company years after the initial grant of the patent revealed how both parties could use the patent as a political tool to compel the other to act in particular ways, as well as the mechanisms by which they negotiated with each other. The negotiations show how Company leaders effectively mobilized the language of the state to secure Company interests. Following the process through which the leaders obtained privileges and then attempted to protect them uncovers the wider working relationships between Company leaders and the regime, and how the leaders worked with the king and Privy Council. These processes and relationships could be tense, but they were the cornerstone of the Company-crown relationship in the early seventeenth century.

The example of the short-lived Scottish East India Company of 1617–1618 puts these processes of negotiation between crown and Company on display. It reveals how the grant of a rival patent could become the grounds for a complex give-and-take between Company and crown with stakes far beyond the original patent. Company leaders brought pressure to bear on the regime to secure their ends, while the king and Privy Council did the same to the Company, and the matter of the Scottish patent ultimately brought into play loans to the monarch, an embassy to Russia, and a decision about whether the East India Company represented just England or both England and Scotland. The meaning of a patent ranged far beyond the privileges it granted.

Patents, Privileges, and New Authority

Patent privileges were mutable. Their physical nature—the documents were often formally embossed, stamped with a seal, and kept as valuable physical objects—suggested permanence and transparency, but in fact they existed in a constant state of negotiation. A patent and its privileges were flexible and subject to interpretation. Even the privileges ostensibly written out and included in the patent were subject to competing constructions. Additionally, either grantor or grantee could move to change the patent, expanding, clarifying, and even revoking existing privileges.[4] Thus, not only the meaning of particular privileges, but even what privileges the Company had, changed over time. Lastly, patents were given for only a limited period of time. All patents were limited term grants.

Patents were not static or singular things, though the terminology historians have used—"the patent" or "the charter"—tends to obscure that fact. Even the use of those two terms changed over time. The terms had similar meanings in the early seventeenth century, though for the first thirty years of the Company's history, its minutes used "patent" in preference to "charter." Both detailed the powers or privileges granted to the Company by the monarch. Company minutes could use "patent" to mean the sum of the privileges granted to the Company, including to refer to the document that set out how the Company was organized and governed. The minutes also referred to specific patents, meaning specific privileges that they had been granted—such as the power to export set amounts of silver each year, or the power to use martial law abroad. In contrast, "charter" always referred to the sum of all privileges. There was no plural equivalent for the charter of the Company, in comparison to the "patent" or "patents" that appeared in the minutes. In the early decades of the Company, the minutes were more likely to refer to the Company's "patent" or "privileges" than to its "charter." Only in the 1630s did "charter" become the term more commonly used to refer to the sum of the Company's privileges and the document setting out its organization and governance.[5]

The patent granted to the Company in 1600 by Elizabeth I was only the first patent the Company received. Company leaders negotiated a second patent in 1609, which replaced the 1600 patent. The main difference between the two was that the 1609 patent removed the fifteen-year term of the first patent, though the monarch could still revoke the Company's patent with three years' notice. Even after the renewal, Company leaders did not see the patent as a completed thing. In 1614, for example, Governor Smith suggested that when the leaders next renewed the patent, they might wish to try to get a privilege to tender oaths, such as the Muscovy Company had. Other committees contended that the Company might already enjoy this right. This exchange testified to the sense that the patent was a living document, as well as to the fact that its interpretation was not always clear.[6] Beyond the main patent of incorporation, the Company had other patents as well, which granted it other privileges. For example, in 1615 James granted the Company the privilege to transport foreign bullion, and this grant was added to its patents.[7] In July 1616, it received a grant to sell ungarbled spices.[8] This grant was likewise added to its patents.

All new privileges represented exercises of royal authority. However, some of them were also transfers of authority to the Company. Expanding a company's privileges sometimes meant that it was permanently or semi-permanently being granted powers or authority that otherwise would have belonged solely to the crown. In the early decades of the seventeenth century, Company leaders slowly acquired a number of privileges that augmented the power of the Company. For example, the monarch granted it certain governing privileges for each Company voyage—particularly the authority to impose martial law and even conduct executions if necessary. These were powers the Company required to govern its fleet, but they were not ones granted by the patent, and therefore a new application to the monarch was required on behalf of each voyage. Elizabeth granted James Lancaster, the commander of the Company's first fleet, the right to use martial law to govern it while away from England.[9] Company leaders had to apply for similar grants for each subsequent voyage.

In 1614, however, Company leaders sought to remedy "some defects in their patent" and get a more permanent grant of the authority to govern themselves abroad and apply martial law. They wanted to "strengthen them[selves] with power to authorize their servants that shall be sent abroad immediately from them, under some great seal to be procured without troubling his Majesty for every fleet."[10] Thus, the authority for governing the fleet abroad would come directly from the Company and indirectly from the monarch, rather than directly from the monarch. The leaders' ability to grant this authority to their servants directly would require a new privilege from James. They were clear that they needed "to procure privilege from his Majesty by obtaining power for a seal of their own whereby they may give leave to their servants to govern their men with sufficient and absolute authority."[11] They sought with this privilege to increase their existing power over their men in the East Indies.

This transfer of authority arose from an expressed desire to simplify the preparations for readying a fleet, and certainly the minutes highlighted this aspect of the situation, but actually obtaining this authority from the king represented a significant augmentation of the Company's power. The English in the East Indies were now to be governed by the king via the Company, not directly by the king. What Company leaders sought was the power to grant of their own accord "sufficient and absolute authority" to their servants to govern their men. The securing of this privilege would de facto bolster their power as a corporation; it gave them quasi-state powers abroad and made them essentially a law-making and law-enforcing group.[12]

A few years later the Company sought and received another privilege that enhanced its powers of enforcement: the power to arrest English ships in the East Indies. The Company's governor, Sir Thomas Smith, claimed that this power already belonged to the Company through the patent. In 1614 in conjunction with the secretary of state, Sir Ralph Winwood, he arranged to add a clause to a captain's commission that gave Company ships the explicit power to "take any English ships abroad that shall attempt to go into the East Indies."[13] Exercise of this power would make the East India Company the de facto policing power of all English activities in the East Indies and would give it the power to enforce its monopoly where the monarch's oversight was distant. This power to police the sea lanes was another one (like the power to apply martial law) that lay at the heart of Company's authority by the late seventeenth century but was not in the original patent.

The nonstatic nature of the royal grants of authority that the Company relied upon was further demonstrated by the fact that informal privileges supplemented the powers and privileges formally held by the Company. The patents the Company received represented grants of royal authority for it to exercise for its benefit, but not all exercises of royal authority and state power that the Company used were officially granted as privileges. The exercise of royal authority on behalf of the Company with regard to diplomacy and ambassadorial representation was one such case. Unlike martial law privileges, in which the crown signed over ongoing power to the Company, diplomacy remained an area where the Company and the crown shared power. It was a state power that the Company needed, but one that the regime would not formally sign over.

Diplomatic representation was not a power that the Company ever formally had. There was no ambiguity about whether or not diplomacy fell under the purview of the crown, nor about what constituted official representation—only the crown could appoint a diplomat. Diplomacy was incontestably a state function, but it was one that seemed to Company leaders to be enmeshed with mercantile aims, "seeing all princes that have commerce each with [the] other have their ambassador."[14] The need for an official ambassador to the Mughal court engendered considerable internal debate in the Company about how it and the state could share a diplomat and the dangers of turning over control of Company affairs to a courtier. Though the Levant Company had sent and funded ambassadors to Constantinople since the 1580s (the Ottoman court required a standing embassy from its trading partners), the East India Company's first foray into official diplomacy did not come until the 1610s. Up to that point, the Company had secured letters from James appointing official agents or representatives, but not an official ambassador.[15] The Company's trade in the Mughal empire was still on shaky foundations, and merchants had represented the Company at the imperial court. In 1614, however, Company leaders decided to send a courtier, Sir Thomas Roe, to represent them at the imperial court, rather than another merchant agent.

A royal ambassador for the East Indies presented Company leaders with two major concerns: the problem of the ambassador's influence over the Company's commerce in the East Indies, and the problem of the crown's influence in Company affairs in London. The leaders worried about the power the diplomat would have over their activities, goods, and men—in short, "the power which [ambassadors] will assume unto themselves in those heathen countries, to command the Company's goods without control and subject the lives of their men at their pleasure."[16] Limiting the ambassador's influence in the East Indies was the easier of the two problems to solve. To protect their business interests in the East from the interference of their ambassador, Company leaders decided that the ambassador's official commission should direct him to follow Company instructions. The official state instructions should order him to comply with Company decisions:

"for the ambassador there must be a commission procured from the state, which must direct him to the articles and instructions that shall be drawn by the Company," and they warned Roe "not to intermeddle with their business and merchandize"—a direction that Roe found difficult to follow.[17]

The leaders faced a far greater concern: an ambassador chosen and funded by the Company and appointed by the king might one day become an ambassador funded by the Company and chosen and appointed by the king. This concern appeared even in the earliest debates about the possibility of using an ambassador. Some committees worried that in choosing an ambassador rather than a merchant, the king might someday foist an unwanted ambassador on them: "but another doubt arising whether it will be fit to have such a person for their ambassador, or a merchant rather, lest time may work to have such an one put upon them by his Majesty who may bring to pass those things which are not so much doubted." As they expressed it, the concern was not that they might lose their ability to choose an ambassador, but that the monarch would choose someone unsuitable to the trade in general. However, other committees responded that history was on their side; in the past (that is, in his interactions with the Levant Company), James had never sent ambassadors who had not been chosen by the concerned parties.[18] Smith got James to agree that the Company leaders would choose their own ambassador "because the charge is to be their own." The leaders were comforted by the knowledge that as long as they were paying for the embassy, the choice of ambassador was theirs.[19]

This strange division of responsibility between crown and Company drew contemporary attention; people outside the Company recognized the unusual nature of the East Indies embassy. Other people at James's court readily acknowledged Roe's strange status, as an ambassador appointed by the crown but chosen and funded by the Company. John Chamberlain wrote Dudley Carleton (also an ambassador) that he had heard that Roe was to be sent as ambassador "as from the king by the East Indian [*sic*] Company to the Great Mogor [*sic*]," mentioning that if Roe's salary was as high as reported, it was more than any of James's own ambassadors, going "far beyond the best ambassador the king hath abroad."[20] The Company's use of martial law elicited no such commentary about the sharing of power between crown and Company, though it represented no less of a collapsed distinction between Company and state.

Diplomatic representation and martial law were both powers that belonged to the monarch, yet their acquisitions presented different challenges to the Company. Seeking a patent that granted the Company an enlarging of its powers to govern its men abroad was one of many such requests by Company leaders to acquire more privileges in the name of better running the East Indies trade. According to Company minutes, these requests generally were presented and granted with little delay. Diplomatic representation was a different matter, and one that required extensive discussion within the Company about the balancing of Company and crown requirements—especially in the absence of the guidelines that a formal privilege provided. Ambassadorial representation was not a privilege signed over to the Company to employ at its leaders' will, but one that showed in real terms the monarchical power that enabled the East Indies trade.

The Company existed because of the patent and privileges granted to it by the monarch. Yet those privileges were not granted irrevocably. They were subject to negotiation and interpretation by both Company leaders and the crown. From the founding of the Company to its careful acquisition of additional privileges, its leaders grappled with the meaning of privileges and the responsibilities that accompanied their use. They learned to cast the possession and use of privileges in terms of benefit to the commonwealth, an ideal that underlay the whole patent system.

Policing the Patent and Rival Ventures

Acquiring privileges was only part of the story, since a privilege was only as valuable as the monarch's commitment to upholding it was reliable. The most essential and valuable privilege the Company possessed was its exclusive access to the East Indies trade, including the sole right to import East Indian goods into England. It was a privilege the Company had to defend throughout its lifetime, as contemporary critics challenged patents in general—and its patent in particular—as examples of illicit monopolies.[21] Defending this privilege under James also meant sometimes challenging the monarch and persuading or coercing him to uphold the privileges he had granted them against the claims of groups the Company viewed as interlopers, whose licenses often also came from the monarch.

Company leaders intervened in political negotiations, made use of political leverage, and even on occasion challenged royal authority to protect the Company's privileges, especially those making its men the only legitimate English East Indies traders. They did not target foreign East India Companies—they did not try to prevent the Dutch East India Company

(VOC) from trading in England, for instance. Their focus was entirely on preserving their Company's place as the only outlet for English investment in the East Indies trade. Company leaders expected theirs to be the only company trading in the East under James's aegis. Yet cases arose that greatly tested how far the Company could force the king to uphold the privileges he had granted them.

James's attitude toward the Company's patent was not straightforward. Certainly he did not view the patent as inviolate. In 1604, James licensed Sir Edward Michelborne to trade with Cathay, China, Japan, Korea, and Cambodia—a patent that directly contravened that of the Company. James gave Michelborne the right to trade in the named areas regardless of any previous grants prohibiting access to those areas—that is, despite the Company's patent that gave it rights to those same areas—so long as no trade had yet been developed in those regions.[22] Michelborne had been one of the original subscribers to the Company but was disenfranchised in 1601 when he did not pay in his promised adventure.[23] Newly armed with James's patent, Michelborne left England in 1604 and returned a few years later with goods from and knowledge about the East Indies. Company leaders began a suit against him in the Admiralty Courts in 1607, presumably to protect the Company's patent and dissuade others from trying to follow in Michelborne's footsteps. They dropped the suit later that year, supposedly concerned about expense, but they noted that they could always sue Michelborne later if necessary. Surviving records do not allow much further examination of his venture, including what negotiations Company leaders had with the regime or why James granted the patent to Michelborne in the first place. Michelborne did not sail for the East Indies again, and he died in 1609. It is possible that he would have, but it is also possible that he was already in the process of negotiating a settlement with the Company— possibly to turn his patent over to it in some way. Certainly in early 1608 he met with Company leaders to give them an account of the best places for trade in the East Indies, and a few weeks later, Company leaders discussed employing two East Indians then in Michelborne's service. Both actions suggest a rapprochement between the two parties.[24]

The patent to Michelborne was the only one James granted that directly contravened the privileges granted to the Company. It is unclear why the monarch chose to challenge the Company at this point and not again. Michelborne's patent was granted in the early years of the Company, after the return of only a single fleet. Perhaps the Michelborne patent was a test of how protective of their privileges Company leaders would be and thus an experiment on James's part for how much latitude he had with the East Indies venture. Perhaps the king intended the Company to buy out occasional rivals, and James's grant was thus a way of rewarding someone through Company coffers (as he seems to have done years later with the Scottish patent discussed below). With so few surviving records, it is impossible to know how either James or the Company leaders understood this challenge.

Whatever the cause, James did not grant other patents to people that infringed so clearly on the Company's grant. Thus, for example, a 1609 petition to James by John Midnall for privileges to trade in the Mughal empire failed, despite Midnall's care in his petition to note that the trade he wanted was one that the Company "did not regard."[25] The Company already traded in the Mughal empire, though in 1609 its trade had only recently been established. Few petitions for directly competing privileges exist from the 1600s and 1610s, possibly because few people actually challenged the Company through those official pathways at that time (and not because petitions have not survived). Equally possible is that as courtiers became adventurers in the Company in the 1610s, their influence at court prevented James from testing the Company's patent too far.

Although James stopped openly licensing rivals after Michelborne, he continued to test the Company's expansive reading of its privileges. He happily considered requests for privileges for activities or places on the edges of the Company's trade. Isaac Le Maire's petition for a license for the southwest passage fitted this mold. Though Company leaders believed that Le Maire sought a competing privilege, it was not a straightforward challenge to the Company's patent. James treated Le Maire's route as a new discovery and thus eminently patentable. Another similar case had occurred in 1607, when James granted a patent to Richard Penkevell to find a northwest passage to China, Cathay, and the Moluccas.[26] Company leaders certainly saw the northwest passage as falling within their jurisdiction, given how they had tried to defend themselves against a possible claim by the Muscovy Company to the northwest passage if it was discovered under that corporation's aegis. Like Le Maire's southwest passage, however, it was arguably beyond the scope of the Company's patent. Penkevell's grant was for seven years, though no voyages seem to have been launched as a result of the grant. Had Penkevell made it to the East Indies, his patent would have given him the right to claim possession of new lands, which would have given him a distinct edge over the Company. The right to claim possession was a power the Company did not have.[27] In contrast to the case of Le Maire, it is unclear whether Company leaders knew of the grant to Penkevell, and given that Penkevell never made or authorized a voyage, it never intruded on their attention.

When James granted a commission in 1612 for a Persia voyage to Sir Henry Thynne, Company leaders took steps (albeit not until 1614) to quash Thynne's expedition.[28] They asked the Earl of Nottingham, then lord admiral, to stop Thynne's ship from leaving England, which he did—even intervening on their behalf with James on the matter.[29] Friends and relatives of Thynne took up his cause with the Company, arguing that Persia was not included in the Company's patent. Unsurprisingly, their argument did not convince Company leaders.

The Company's aggressive defense of its privileges led to some criticism. For instance, Roe, its newly chosen ambassador, suggested in 1614 that Company leaders at least buy Thynne's ship after stopping his voyage, to counter "the scandal that is cast upon them abroad (although unjustly) that gentlemen cannot pretend a voyage to any place but must render an account unto the East India Company thereof."[30] Sir Carew Raleigh, Thynne's stepfather, argued that the Company "crossed all gentlemen so as they could not intend a voyage but they must yield an account unto [the Company], whither they go, and what they carry."[31] James's responses to the Company's claims regarding Le Maire, Roe's warning about popular opinion, and Raleigh's angry challenge all suggested, directly or indirectly, that the Company constantly risked overreaching the grants of its patent. However, the responses also testified to the Company's apparent ability to enforce its expansive understanding of its patent.

The most attractive option for English merchants who sought to trade in the East Indies outside the Company's control was to trade under the authority of a foreign monarch. Le Maire's attempt to petition an English monarch for privileges when he could not secure them in his homeland had its counterpart in attempts by English merchants to secure privileges from various continental powers. Several groups of merchants pursued these trades in the 1610s, when the Company's profits were at a height. In 1614 in particular the Company found out about several proposed voyages: one group of investors planning a voyage under the authority of the French monarch came to light in March; another group planning a voyage out of Ireland was discovered in July; and a second proposed voyage for France was uncovered in November. In each of these cases, Company leaders followed the same plan of action. They gathered information, particularly the names of investors; consulted privy councilors; and explained to the king and Council why the proposed voyage was illicit.

Although James neither had nor claimed any jurisdiction over other monarchs' East Indies ambitions, Company petitions to James about these rival ventures emphasized that he did have sovereignty over any of his own subjects who might become involved in such projects. Rumors in March 1614 of an East India voyage that would leave from France but was underwritten heavily by English investors led the Company to consult members of the Privy Council. The Earl of Somerset, then lord chamberlain, and the Earl of Northampton, then lord privy seal, asked for a list of the names of the investors who had "become so unnatural to their own country, and unrespective to their king." The two lords promised to let the potential investors "know how much they have wronged his Majesty and the state."[32] When the second French voyage came to the attention of Company leaders in November, Winwood, the secretary of state, assured them that James would give his support, would "afford all lawful favors," and "will prohibit all his subjects from carrying a trade from this land, under the protection of a foreign prince."[33]

Challenging an Irish venture, the Company's governor argued that the "English nation" had a good reputation in the East Indies, "known to proceed in peaceable manner like merchants," in contrast to the proposed Irish venture—which planned to depart "with only powder and shot," and thus could be "no other than pirates, to rob and spoil those country people." He argued that the venture out of Ireland would bring scandal and dishonor to "this nation." The privy councilors agreed and promised their aid.[34] Deterring the rivals, therefore, not only reaffirmed the Company's privileged position, but it did so via appeals to what was due James and England. Circumventing the Company's monopoly by going abroad challenged the monarch and state, not just the Company.

When questioned, the investors in the rival ventures admitted their desire to challenge the Company's control. The court of committees tracked down some of the presumptive investors and confronted them. They confessed that they had pursued the project "to join together and use their means to break the neck of the business [that is, the English East India Company]." Upon "finding the state to distaste the course that is intended," some agreed to give up the project in the hope they would be made free of the Company gratis, though others persisted in their opposition.[35] One of the hopeful investors in both the first and second proposed French ventures offered to reveal "more of those plots [to challenge the Company] than the Company shall be able to learn by any other means."[36] Company leaders lamented the plots that seemed to spring up with such frequency and the "wrongs and scandal the Company is subject unto, by the envious eyes that do depend upon them."[37] Yet despite their complaints, Company leaders proved remarkably able to fend off challengers by enlisting the aid of the state—particularly the Privy Council.

In framing opposition to the Company as a matter of disloyalty, Company leaders turned their opponents into detractors of the state. Company matters became matters of state. For instance, during attempts by Company leaders to stop the first French voyage, they had appealed to the Privy Council. The Council ordered the rival investors to appear before it for questioning. One of the conspirators fled to Flushing, in the Netherlands; another appeared before the Council but refused to sign a reconciliation with the Company before its members. In his refusal, the latter investor "questioned the clerk of the Council's authority, would show no reverency nor respect unto him, and refused to enter into bond to appear before their lordships at the Council table." Not only was he refusing the Company's terms, therefore, but he was impugning the authority of the Council via his treatment of its clerk. For his behavior the Privy Council deemed him "worthy of imprisonment, and committed him close prisoner by warrant to the Gatehouse." Other investors who appeared before the Council were told the "heinousness of their offences" by both the Council members and Sir Francis Bacon, then the attorney general, and freed only after submitting "on their knees craving pardon of the state" and promising to stop pursuing the trade. With such an extreme example to hand of the dangers of trying to circumvent the Company's patent by going abroad, the court of committees decided to have an order drawn up concerning the whole affair, to "remain as a precedent hereafter upon any occasion that might hereafter be presented of the like nature."[38]

By resorting to the Privy Council, Company leaders had made it nearly impossible for opposition to the Company not to be seen as opposition to the regime. The way the investors were pardoned was telling: they were pardoned by physically submitting to the authority of the Council and begging pardon of the state, not the Company, for their actions. Similarly, the jailing of the one recalcitrant investor revealed the overlap of Company and state. He was imprisoned not for refusing to submit to the Company's terms, but for challenging the authority of the Council by showing disrespect to its clerk and denying the Council's authority to command his physical presence. The success of Company leaders in guarding their privileges thus arose in part from their abilities to convincingly identify the Company with affairs of state.

The Scottish East India Company

The example of the Scottish East India Company (1617–1618) demonstrated that Company leaders could, to a great degree, coerce James into enforcing his grant to them, even according to their expansive understanding of what he had promised. They did so, however, only by paying a (sometimes literal) price and cooperating with the crown on other matters—in this case, a loan on James's behalf to the tsar of Russia. Cases such as this hinged on the leaders' ability successfully to employ the language of the state and commonwealth to justify their continued protection by the regime; in other words, on whether they were able to frame their opponents as dangerous and damaging to the state. The cases also revealed that sometimes the cost of the crown's aid was concessions on the part of Company leaders in return.

The Scottish East India Company tested not the limitations on English subjects acting abroad, but the limitations on James's other subjects, the Scots, and what the English East India Company meant for Scotland. James was king of two kingdoms, and though the Union of the Crowns in 1603 yoked England and Scotland together under one monarch, it was a composite monarchy, with each realm governed by its own laws and institutions (and in the case of Scotland, a mostly absentee monarch). Despite James's wish to create a unified Great Britain, the kingdoms remained distinct. Politicians and advisors pointed out that a legal union would void all English and Scottish treaties and laws, which raised the specter of legal chaos if a true union was pursued, and popular antipathy to a greater union was strong.[39] Even keeping the kingdoms mostly distinct, however, raised questions of how to balance English and Scottish interests and influences. The East India Company had been founded as an English venture, but what that meant in the context of the regal union was not clear.

When it comes to short-lived Scottish East India Companies, the Darian Company of the late seventeenth century may be the better known of the two, but it was not the first.[40] In late 1617, Company leaders learned that Sir James Cunningham, a Scottish courtier, had secured a patent with "sundry new privileges for the East Indies, wherein the southeast passage is included."[41] The Company leaders' first response upon hearing of the proposed Scottish Company was to gather information. They appointed a committee to get a copy of the patent, they "being desirous have a sight of [it]."[42] Having accurate knowledge of what privileges the king had granted a rival was key. The court of committees soon secured a copy of a letter from James to Cunningham, with details of the privileges he was granting. If the patent encompassed everything mentioned in the letter, Cunningham's company could traffic throughout the world and bring its wares to any of James's kingdoms; indeed, the letter named the East India Company as the model Cunningham should strive to follow.[43]

Detailed news of the Scottish patent became widespread in early 1618, though the Company had first heard of the Scottish East India Company in November 1617. By late January, the news had filtered through court and city circles widely enough to reach Chamberlain, who wrote of it in a letter to Carleton, then ambassador at The Hague. Chamberlain sent a detailed account of the terms of Cunningham's grant beginning with the basic facts: "the king hath given a patent to one Sir James Cunningham a Scottish knight to raise an East Indian Company there." According to Chamberlain, the grant was to Cunningham and his family. His company differed, therefore, from the English East India Company, which was an incorporated group of merchants—though Chamberlain did not explicitly point out this difference.[44]

The grant promised Cunningham's company a wide geographical reach, encompassing the East and West Indies, Turkey, Muscovy, and Greenland. More importantly, Chamberlain had heard that the Scottish East India Company would be able to sell its wares not only in Scotland but also in England; not only could they outfit their ships in England, but also they "may vent their commodities here." Membership was not limited to Scots, and Chamberlain found the whole situation troublesome: "it seemed to me most strange that not only Scots, but English or any other stranger may be admitted into this society, and yet it must be called and accounted the Scottish Company, with a number of other large privileges which do directly infringe former grants, and cross the whole course of our traffic." The best news he had heard was that investors were reluctant to commit to the new company, and he suspected that the whole venture would end with

Cunningham and his partners selling their rights to the English East India Company: "they do only yet make a noise and show, and seek all over for partners and adventurers which come slowly in, and as I hear would fain compound and sell their rights and interests to the East Indian Company."[45]

What was especially notable about Chamberlain's letter was not only how detailed was the information about the venture that was circulating— which indicated either that Chamberlain or his sources were particularly well informed, or that the knowledge of the Scottish grant was widely known—but his conviction that James's grant to Cunningham violated previously granted privileges. Company leaders certainly made claims of infringement, but their aggressive defense of their privileges in other contexts had drawn criticism. This letter, neither written by nor addressed to someone with demonstrable formal ties to the Company made similar claims about infringement of the Company's patent, albeit in less detail than the Company soon would.

Members of the court of committees might have known nothing of what Chamberlain was writing to Carleton. Several days later, though, they learned that a notice about the new East India Company had circulated publicly in the Exchange. They spoke to Lord Zouch, a privy councilor, about it. He took the information to the other members of the Privy Council, who, according to the Company's minutes, were gratifyingly abashed by the matter and "wondered that it was suffered by my Lord Mayor to be set up so publicly about the city to the discountenance of this company." This move was especially surprising, Lord Zouch claimed, as the Company was one "which his Majesty and their Lords have been so tender over to preserve and cherish as a trade which hath gained honor and profit to his Majesty and dominions." The members of the Privy Council promised to tell James of their feelings on the matter: to "send to his Majesty to let him know how ill they all do conceive thereof and to crave reformation."[46] This account was the Company's version of its leaders' meeting with the Privy Council. As with all of the court minutes, it is impossible to know what was actually said, rather than what the governor reported and what the secretary recorded. The Company's account portrayed the news as prompting the Privy Council to emphasize the importance of the Company's trade, condemn the public nature of the grant and its effect on the Company, and comment on the past care that the king had expended to "preserve and cherish" the East India trade, which served here as synecdoche of the English East India Company. The account never accused the monarch of neglecting the Company, yet it showed the Privy Council seeking to preserve the Company even in the face of the king's mistake or absentmindedness, contrasting James's earlier "tender" care with the Company's current "ill" usage.[47]

In an early March meeting of the Privy Council, James agreed to recall Cunningham's patent. The meeting took place in the presence of a number of merchants as well as privy councilors and culminated with James's promise not to grant such a patent again without the Company's prior approval.[48] The Company account of the meeting and the entry in the Privy Council register differ in a few key particulars: the Council's account emphasized the role of the Muscovy Company in the negotiations, as Cunningham's first proposed voyage was for Newfoundland, while the Company's account made no mention of it at all (though Company minutes later acknowledged that the Muscovy Company had done the heavy lifting on the matter).[49] Smith was governor of both companies at the time and thus attended as a representative of both.

Smith was perhaps presenting a particular account to his East India audience. In his account to the court of committees, James's agreement to withdraw Cunningham's patent was somewhat reluctant. The Company account noted that Cunningham had promised to pay 5 percent customs duty on imported goods, and this was an attractive reason for the king to continue his patent; nevertheless "his Majesty purposed to show his tender respect and regard unto this company, and not to be swayed by words nor fair promises against them." Smith also reported that James had promised in future not to grant anything in Scotland that would injure the English East India venture: "Mr. Governor found his Majesty's favorable respect, in that sundry passages that were offered, assuring the Company that if any beneficial grant should be made for Scotland that might be approved prejudicial for this land, his Majesty would cancel it."[50] Bacon, then lord chancellor, was sworn in as a member of the Company within a week, suggesting that he had been influential in having the matter settled. The Company minutes noted that "the troublesome business for the Scottish patent is ended."[51]

Contrary to Smith's account of special consideration shown to the Company, the account in the Privy Council register emphasized that the king and Council had found the Scottish patent legally questionable and counter to James's objectives. This account highlighted the role of the Council (the "mediation of this honorable board") in effecting the revocation of Cunningham's patent. James revoked it "out of his incessant care of the welfare of his subjects of this kingdom" and because the petitioners "offered to his princely consideration" many reasons to convince him that the patent was "neither in the form, nor in the execution warrantable by law, as [Cunningham] pretended, nor agreeable with his Majesty's intention."[52] In the Privy Council record, the Muscovy Company played a central role in the resolution of the Cunningham matter. James claimed that he had meant Cunningham's grant to be a mark of favor but had never intended to discommode the Muscovy Company. The Muscovy Company offered to allow Cunningham "or any other Scottish gentleman or person of worth of that nation into their society to trade with them in their joint stock if they pleased, paying nothing for their admittance, a courtesy which they did not usually afford to others."[53] Cunningham declined this offer. In the end, the only recompense he received for losing his patent was being allowed to sell his partially outfitted ships to the Muscovy Company. The record made no mention of Cunningham's reaction to the summary cancellation of his patent.

The details of the negotiations differed, but in both the Company's and the Council's accounts, James made the same promise to preferentially treat the patents and privileges of his English subjects against his Scottish subjects. The Company account noted that the king had said that he would revoke a Scottish grant if it proved "prejudicial for this land."[54] The Council account was more explicit, describing an elaborate handing over of the patent to Smith with a public promise not to do such a thing again:

> His Majesty delivered the same [Cunningham's revoked patent] to Sir Thomas Smith, knight, governor of the Company aforesaid, and promised upon his princely word that the like should not be granted again, before they were first made acquainted with it and without their consent: which his Majesty's gracious promise was afterwards related unto divers of the merchants of the Muscovy and East India Companies by the Lords of the Council Chamber, who seeming well satisfied therewith for their own parts, did undertake to communicate the same to the rest of their Company.[55]

Smith and the other merchants were to circulate the news of James's pronouncement, which would help cement the Company's rights and dissuade others from attempting to circumvent its patent by following in Cunningham's footsteps.

Details of what would happen to Cunningham's fleet still had to be settled. James had appointed a group of courtiers to carry out this task. In the negotiations that followed, the interested parties were able to spin James's decision to revoke the Scottish patent in different ways. A few days after James's order, in a commission to the men assigned to appraise Cunningham's ship and goods, the Privy Council labeled James's order for Cunningham to cancel his voyage as arising from a "reason of state." A few months later, however, addressing the Muscovy merchants who proved slow or reluctant to pay the agreed-upon sum of money to Cunningham to reimburse him for the charges of the voyage, the Privy Council's tone was modulated. Their letter did not mention the "state" as an entity at all; instead, it described Cunningham's patent as one "pretended to be very prejudicial to the state of that [the Greenland] trade."[56] This letter, with its downgrading of "state" to "state of that trade," had been signed by members of the Privy Council, but it "was brought ready written and signed by Sir James Cunningham," which may explain the councilors' apparent reluctance to couch the revocation of Cunningham's patent as a matter of state: Cunningham would have no incentive to mobilize the state against himself.[57] This fluidity of expression—a dangerous fluidity, in the eyes of Company leaders—undermined the certainty that they thought they had secured.

Chamberlain's next update to Carleton on the matter testified to the confusion that implementation of the king's decision had sown about exactly what threat the Scottish East India Company represented. Chamberlain noted that the king and Council were "much troubled" by the Scottish patent and had consequently had "many meetings, debatings and consultations" on the matter. As he reported to Carleton, the king had dissolved the project because it was "found so prejudicial to the East Indian, Muscovy, and Turkey companies," and if it had been allowed to reach fruition, it "would apparently ruin them all, and bring confusion into all trade and intercourse, breeding moreover distraction and separation instead of union twixt us and them [the Scots]."[58] English liking for the union would suffer from Scottish competition. Different interpretations of what had happened in the Privy Council thus only became more garbled as the news spread across London. Chamberlain's account, like that of the East India Company, emphasized the Company's preeminence as the prime mover and affected body, aided but not led by either the Muscovy or the Turkey Company. This discrepancy between the Privy Council act (which named the Muscovy Company) and the other accounts (which named the East India Company) was probably due to the clout of the East India Company: in 1618, it was on a far sounder financial footing than the Muscovy Company and thus might figure larger in the popular imagination.

The calling in of the Scottish patent brought the East India and Muscovy Companies together in unexpected fashions. Members of the court of committees found themselves grappling with the question of how extensive a role, especially financially, the East India Company was supposed to play in the resolution of the Cunningham patent and in the Muscovy Company's trade. Smith reminded the court of committees of the "burthen having laid hitherto upon the Muscovy Company for maintaining the charge of resisting this new patent," and since the Levant and East India Companies also benefited from the repeal of the patent, "they ought in equity to contribute unto the said charge." However, some members of the court feared that they were being shaken down. Rumor had it that someone or some group was leaning heavily on James not to repeal Cunningham's patent after all, and "several flying reports [rumors] have possessed many in their opinions to believe that a great sum of money is given to his Majesty to check and subvert their proceedings." Other members were convinced that the entire operation was an elaborate plan by James to funnel money and support from the East India Company to the Muscovy Company: "yet it is not unknown that the especial drift of his Majesty in giving way to disannul the same is for the hope he hath of having the Muscovy Company to be upheld and maintained either by private adventures or some public companies."[59] What all these possibilities had in common was an acknowledgment that the Company's involvement with the Muscovy Company was not over.

Indeed, James's support of the Company in the matter of the Scottish patent was predicated on a sketched-out quid pro quo, according to which the Company would supply money to the struggling Muscovy Company now, and in return James would withhold his future support from schemes like the Scottish patent. Smith urged the court of committees to "break the neck of all other patents (which his majesty by his Royal word will be very chary of hereafter)" by the simple (if pricey) expedient of helping fund the Muscovy Company's joint stock. The court of committees agreed to do so, with the note "to have it remembered unto his Majesty that this Company had condescended conditionally that his Majesty would be pleased to call in the former patent, and not to grant any other hereafter to their prejudice."[60] A week later Smith reiterated that "his Majesty granted the recalling in of the new patent in expectation, that the East India Company should join with the Muscovy Company," and that the Company's decision to do so would be "a most acceptable piece of service unto him."[61] At a meeting of the court of committees dedicated to the business of joining with the Muscovy Company, the governor reiterated that it was James's wish for the Company's involvement and the matter of the Scottish patent that necessitated the joining: "the inducements . . . were in respect of his Majesty's desire, and surrendering up the new Scottish patent wherein they have been given to understand his Majesty's gracious intents and promises."[62] Company leaders were making a deal with James, with the patent and its future cousins as bargaining chips.

The financial entanglements between the two companies ultimately had two elements: a new joint stock of £60,000 funded equally by the East India Company and Muscovy Company to support joint ventures for the next eight years; and a major loan on James's behalf to Tsar Michael I that was also funded equally by the two companies. The new joint stock required £30,000 each year from each company, and it would also be responsible for any financial obligations to Cunningham.[63] Aside from the fact that the joint venture was mandated by James, its management did not involve the crown in an ongoing fashion. In contrast, the loan highlighted the overlap of Company and regime and the ability of each to require the other to comply with particular demands.

Even as Company leaders were meeting with the Privy Council about the matter of the Scottish patent and agreeing to the new joint ventures, the Muscovy Company's merchants were pressing James to agree to make a large loan to the Russian tsar, whose ambassadors had sought to receive 100,000 marks (approximately £67,000) from the English monarch. The Muscovy merchants presented a list of reasons why James should agree to the loan, which enumerated the ways the Russian ruler could benefit English merchants.[64] James agreed to send the money, "although it be rare and unusual to furnish other princes and allies upon any occasion with supplies in that kind," but he now expected the Company to "apply themselves with all readiness to make good and perform the payment" of half the amount.[65]

The funding of the loan quickly became wrapped up in the patent revocation and merger of the companies that had been discussed only days before. Details of the deal between James and the East India Company became widely known. Chamberlain's account to Carleton, for example, made the link between loan, merger, and patent revocation clear, explaining that "here is a great business agreed upon yesterday betwixt the East Indian and Muscovy Company, for the furnishing of the Emperor of Russia with a hundred thousand marks by way of loan. . . . The Muscovy Company was not able to undergo the burthen without the assistance of the East Indian merchants, who for their assurance are to have an equal stock and adventure for eight years . . . and for their better encouragement the king hath recalled and delivered into their hands the Scottish patent I wrote of."[66] Chamberlain's account framed the event in decidedly benign terms; the king revoked the patent as a douceur, and the Company secured an equal stock in the Muscovy trade for eight years. Sir William Lovelace, writing to Carleton a few days later, gave a much less benign account of the loan than Chamberlain's, instead reporting that the loan was "imposed by his Majesty upon the East India Company."[67] An account from a few years later connected to the separation of the two companies noted that the East India Company had been "commanded by his Majesty's royal letters" to join with the Muscovy Company and "assist" it in funding the loan.[68]

On the one hand, James's ability to compel the Company to fund a loan to another monarch, presumably in James's name and with the revocation of the Scottish patent as leverage, would seem to suggest both James's power over the Company and his creative means of exerting it. On the other hand, the loan would not only to help fund the tsar's war against Poland but would also secure the trading privileges of English traders in Muscovy.[69] Additionally, Company leaders were able to ensure that the money ended up where it was supposed to. When the news began to circulate about the proposed loan, it was accompanied by news that Sir Dudley Digges, a known Company man often appointed to press Company matters at the royal court, would travel as ambassador along with the money.[70] For example, Lovelace explained that Digges was to travel to Muscovy as ambassador, with the Company funding the embassy.[71]

The note that the Company would be defraying the cost of the embassy suggested that the Company would have some influence over the embassy and the ambassador. Certainly it had exerted a similar power in like situations, such as Roe's embassy to the Mughal court. Indeed, a few days later, members of the court of committees decided to confer with the returned ambassador to Muscovy, Sir John Merrick, and solicit his opinion on what appropriate gift they could make to Digges "in his Majesty's name."[72] This discussion took place a month and a half before Digges formally received his warrant from the king. In other words, Company leaders were confident at this early stage of their control of the situation. When James had compelled the Company to do as he willed, he had also granted them definite concessions in turn and endowed them with aspects of his prerogative power. It is unclear whether James picked Digges as ambassador knowing that Company leaders would accept him, or whether Company leaders had suggested Digges. What is clear is that Digges was a Company man: when he met with the Privy Council to receive his instructions, he was accompanied by Company merchants, and his instructions made it clear that he was in part representing merchant interests.[73]

The loan continued to give Company leaders leverage as negotiations stretched on about the extent of their financial obligation to Cunningham. The revocation of his patent had come with a demand by the king that Cunningham be compensated for his monetary outlay in outfitting ships that now would never sail, and that he should be repaid directly. The Privy Council's letter to the Company had included a note on how much Cunningham had spent—which, according to various sources, was some £600.[74] The Company contested the amount, which Cunningham within days was claiming was closer to £800. Company leaders wanted to repay only the £124 that Cunningham was able to itemize.[75] To speed the resolution of the affair and influence the decision in their favor, members of the court of committees decided to petition the royal favorite the marquess (later duke) of Buckingham to aid them, claiming that they had already paid more than the provisions were worth.[76] Buckingham turned out not to be as reliable an ally as they had anticipated, instead advising them that he expected them to speedily pay Cunningham a sum now grown to "900 and odd pounds." The court of committees demurred, suggesting that Buckingham either stop pressing repayment—on account of the "good service the Compan[y] have thereby performed for the honor and good of the king and state," an oblique reference to the loan for the tsar—or refer the matter back to the Privy Council that it might be heard again.[77]

Company leaders got their wish for the matter to go back to the Privy Council, and in August 1618 they submitted a petition from themselves and the Muscovy Company. They argued that while Cunningham claimed that the Company owed him £800, his claim had always been just that: a claim, not acceded to or acknowledged by the East India Company. It was a "relation of what he demanded," but his demands had little bearing on what they and the Muscovy Company legally owed him. In their version of the case, James's and the Privy Council's order had been to pay only for the provisions

Cunningham had already bought—which they had done to the tune of £5,000, and from which they had never benefited, as the provisions were "wholly lost." Because of their "faithful zeal and humble obedience to his Majesty," they had done a number of other singular services for James in recent months, including funding the loan to the tsar; funding Digges as ambassador; and paying for the other costs of the embassy, including presents. All of this, they claimed, was done in James's name, at no light cost to themselves: "which although they proved heavy burthens unto them, yet they did in dutiful manner undergo, believing that those services were well accepted by his Majesty and their lordships." Cunningham's claim for an additional £800, though the amount was small in the scheme of the Company's finances, was one claim too many. It was dissuading members from bringing in their adventures.[78] The Company leaders requested the Privy Council to heed their claim and convince James not to press them for this additional £800.

In December, Cunningham approached the Company, still attempting to secure his money.[79] Returning to James's court, Smith and several committees learned that James still expected them to pay Cunningham directly, "if for no other respect, yet for [James's] sake." They finally agreed, provided that Cunningham would absolutely release his rights to the Scottish patent, as he was claiming, upon legal advice, that "he can take forth a duplicate thereof, and will not thus end that business." James also once again promised that neither the Scottish patent nor any other patent would "hereafter hurt the Company." With assurances from James and the Privy Council that Cunningham would indeed fully release his patent upon payment, the Company leaders agreed to settle. In consideration of the number of people urging them to do so, they "held it fit to make satisfaction for his majesty's sake, and put an end to that troublesome business." The only requirement they insisted on was that they would draw up, with legal advice, a release for Cunningham to sign.[80] This release would fully settle any obligations between Cunningham and the Company, and they required that he sign it before they paid him the £800. Thus ended the Scottish East India venture.

When historians have considered this brief experiment with a Scottish East India Company, they have focused on it either as one of a number of Scottish ventures, to analyze James's attitudes toward the needs of his northern kingdom, or as an example of James's inconstancy to city merchants.[81] Andrew Nicholls looked at it as one of many failed attempts to institute companies in Scotland that paralleled those in England. Citing Robert Ashton, Nicholls argued that James more or less granted Cunningham the charter to secure leverage to extract money—in this case, a loan of £20,000—from the East India Company. Ashton presented a picture of the Company at the mercy of the crown, with James essentially forcing it to give the loan, and said that the events of 1618 showed that the Company needed strong backing at court to protect it against the infringements of the crown. Ashton also used the 1617 document examined at the beginning of this book as evidence of the "crown's willingness ruthlessly to exploit its position vis-à-vis the Company."[82] In contrast to Ashton's reading, I do not think that the events in 1617 and 1618 point to the intensely adversarial relationship that he claims existed. In simplifying the story, Ashton left out the leverage the Company had. Both Ashton and Nicholls confused James's various requests for money to the Company. James requested two large loans from the Company in 1618, but the Company granted only one request: the loan described above made in James's name to the tsar. The requested loan cited by Ashton and Nichols was for £20,000. That loan was unconnected to the Scottish patent, and the Company did not grant the request.

When the Privy Council approached the Company in December, praising it as the "greatest, rightest and most flourishing in the land, and the very column of the kingdom, and therefore of best ability to do his majesty a pleasure," it requested the Company "to supply his [James's] present occasions for Ireland by lending £20,000 for a year." The Privy Council also applied a little pressure, suggesting that Company leaders surely "will not deny his majesty this kindness having found him so gracious unto them in all their requests, and therefore hold them bound in duty, to show some retribution, for his care and good will towards them." It cited the Russian loan as a precedent for the Company's giving loans to monarchs: "having lent greater sums to a foreign prince, without absolute hope of recovery, their Lordships do believe they will do it to so gracious and loving a prince."[83] Some members of the court of committees wondered whether they ought to loan the money. The Privy Council seemed to be suggesting that having already lent money to a foreign monarch, they could hardly refuse their own monarch a loan.

The court of committees' ultimate response, however, was to play a delicate game of threat and counterthreat. In their response to the Privy Council, Company leaders claimed that they could not vote on their own to give such a loan—the request would have to be made of the generality of the Company. More important, they did not have such a sum on hand. They repeated that any request for additional funds would have to be made through the generality. Such a request at a general court meeting, however, was "like to be published abroad throughout the land, as well amongst strangers and English," and if the general court decided not to give the loan, "if amongst [James's] subjects [it] should be denied, how dishonorable and disgraceful it would be, and therefore [they] durst not attempt it without their Lordships' consent." In other words, the court of committees countered the Privy Council's threat that the Company might be criticized for loaning to a foreign monarch but refusing James money with its own threat that the loan would have to be requested in a general court meeting, and that as news of the request would undoubtedly become public, so would rejection of the request. On previous occasions, Company leaders had voted to give loans to James that they kept secret, not sharing information about them even with the generality. Presumably the Privy Council was hoping that they would follow this course of action again. Instead, faced with the threat of the request—and its rejection—becoming public, the Privy Council backed down. Acknowledging the Company's "reasonable and sufficient answer," the Council next tried to get half the requested amount. Company leaders did not budge, and the governor made the same answer as before, offering to open the matter before the general court, "and concluded with an absolute negative, that the Company cannot do it." As the governor reported to the court of committees, he was convinced "that the thing itself, in Mr. Governor's opinion, will never be further moved nor urged again."[84]

This interaction between Company and Privy Council highlighted how effectively Company leaders could use the tools of public appeal against the Privy Council. Both Company leaders and privy councilors knew what was at stake, with the allusions to the consequences of requests made to and then rejected by the generality. This book began with an examination of how the patent bound private and state interests together. Publicity and public appeal were tactics that could be used to resist the obligations of private individuals to accede to the demands of the regime. Company leaders had learned from their engagement with Robert Kayll and other writers a few years before (see Chapter 5), and they now showed their comfort and competence with using the threat of publicity.

Thus, both regime and Company could apply pressure to try to compel the other to act, but no one side dominated the relationship. The large loan the Company had given James for the tsar was used partly to benefit itself: in return for money it lent, the Company secured its choice of ambassador to accompany the money. Meanwhile, the Company was able to mobilize new forms of persuasion in refusing the later loan of £20,000. The balance of power between regime and Company was constantly evolving.

It turned out that some of the Company's money would soon be returned to England. Digges returned unexpectedly in October 1618, only a few months after his departure. Chamberlain reported that Digges's return was due to political unrest in Muscovy, as armed hostilities were threatening to break out between Poland and Russia. He reported that Digges returned with £11,000 of the £27,000 he had carried in coin, having left the rest of the money, as well as other commodities worth a total of £60,000, in "some trusty hands there" (presumably in the hands of someone who could deliver the loan to the tsar). Chamberlain suggested that Digges had gone to Muscovy somewhat against his will and was now seeking office in England, which perhaps explained his precipitous return: "as he went in a manner against his will, so he had the *animus revertendi* and so without question lingers after some better employment here at home."[85]

The Company leaders did not hesitate to press Digges for information about his mission, in fact earning themselves a request from Digges to cease condemning him before he had even reported to either James or them. He complained "that some have dealt hardly with him in censuring his return openly upon the Exchange" and asked that judgment be withheld until he could give his reasons to the Company, which he could do only after he had first met with James.[86] Despite the appearances of a failed embassy, implied by Digges's overly hasty return, it emerged that he had secured some very important privileges in Muscovy. John Pory, one of the best known London newsletter writers, wrote to Carleton that a messenger from the East had vindicated Digges and reported that he had secured the overland silk trade from Persia through Muscovy via the Volga, for the East India Company. He had traded the loan, which was given in James's name and which the tsar would use to pay for his war with the Poles, for privileges for the Company. This was the true outcome of Digges's apparent "defeat in Russia and his return home."[87]

Digges wrote to the Company a week later, letting its leaders know that he was ready to answer any questions they had with regard to his actions in Russia. He would also answer "any particular objection or exception," a concession that acknowledged their interest in and shared authority over his embassy. He was sending his accounts and instructions on the matter and requested that they evaluate the information and decide how much to award (that is, pay) him for his work—a request that openly acknowledged the ties between his embassy and the Company. The court of committees concluded that "he hath performed good service" and "therefore wished him to believe that if the state be satisfied for his return, they are."[88] This formulation epitomized the awkwardness of Company and state "sharing" Digges's embassy. Digges conceded the Company's interest in his work and its right to evaluate it, especially as he hoped for payment. The Company did evaluate him, and on its own grounds. However, Company leaders also had to acknowledge that if the state was satisfied with his service, they must be as well. Ultimately, the Company decided to award him 1,000 marks despite any concerns they had had about the service he had actually performed.[89] The settlement must have been sufficient for Digges, as he resumed his roles of courtier and Company sympathizer. He made clear his continued willingness to act in the Company's interest.

The concerns Company leaders expressed about the potential hazards of diplomatic representation, specifically about the choice of diplomats and the funding, were very real concerns. Once again, the personal nature of the relationship between crown and Company was at the heart of the problem. James reserved the formal right to choose diplomats—or if not to choose them, then to veto a choice—but he did not force a candidate on the Company. Thus, while he had required the Company to fund a loan to the tsar, the Company was granted some power over the ambassador's agenda. In appointing Digges, James chose a courtier who was a known Company man and could be expected to have a care for Company interests. In Digges, James appointed an ambassador with appropriate rank, known political experience, and Company sympathy.

James had given the full status of a royally appointed ambassador to someone with strong Company ties. This was not the only occasion on which he did so. The Roe embassy to Mughal India would never have occurred without Company initiative. Thus the Roe embassy to the Mughal court and the Digges embassy to Muscovy demonstrated a willingness on James's part to allow the Company a participatory, financial, and sometimes guiding role in this matter of state. In other words, while one could view the Roe embassy as an instance in which James had no real interest in or commitment to a royal embassy, and thus presumably had minimal scruples in allowing the Company choice in the matter (given that he did not sign away part of his prerogative powers), the Muscovy embassy was a different matter. Even when James, not the Company, was the prime mover behind the endeavor, he was still reconciled to a diplomat chosen by the Company, or at least openly sympathetic to it.

Over the first two decades of the Company's existence, Company leaders and the regime established patterns for how Company and crown worked together. The basic Company objective of safeguarding its exclusive privileges led to numerous cases in which the Company resorted to the authority of the crown and Privy Council to enforce its desires. Sometimes this aid was given willingly, especially when the Company's case could be framed as one that touched on James's ability to control the actions and loyalties of his subjects. At other times, the king's aid had to be secured via negotiation, especially when the case pitted one group of James's subjects against another, as with the Scottish patent. Even with the Scottish patent, where the price of the continued exclusivity of the Company's patent was to fund an international loan in James's name, the Company was able to keep a measure of control over how its money would be used and its interests represented. In sum, the Company, crown, and Privy Council worked in concert: an apparent lack of autonomy on one hand (the loan to the tsar) might be coupled with heightened authority elsewhere (choosing Digges as ambassador with the power to determine the amount of the loan in situ).

Ongoing negotiation was necessary because the meaning and use of patents and privileges were not stable. Other objectives were often more pressing for king and Council than enforcing the Company's patent. Yet by the 1610s, Company leaders had managed on multiple occasions to protect their privileges and even add to them. The king might have tested how far he had to respect their patent, and on occasion he told them exactly what he expected them to do, but he consistently backed the Company and its patent. Despite hiccups along the way, including the Company's outright refusal to lend the king £20,000 in December 1618, the norm was for Company and crown to work together, with each relying on the resources of the other.

7

"What His Men Have Done Abroad"

Martial Engagements and the Company

O N   T H E   F I R S T   D A Y   of March 1624, both houses of Parliament
turned to the subject of the fleet of East India Company ships waiting
to leave England. The topic was both unusual and unexpected: the coming
and going of merchant vessels was not normally part of parliamentary business. However, Parliament was considering a war with Spain. The members
present determined that the mariners, gunpowder, and money assembled
in the East India Company's fleet might be needed for that war and so ordered the ships not to leave.[1]

Company leaders suspected that the stay of ships had less to do with a possible war with Spain and more to do with Hormuz, in particular an ongoing
legal case between James; the lord admiral, the Duke of Buckingham; and the
Company. The case concerned how much and to whom the Company owed
money for their part in the conquest of Hormuz, which it had undertaken
in alliance with the Persians against the Portuguese in 1622. If Company men
had acted under letters of marque from the lord admiral, then the Company
owed the state 10 percent of its profits. If not, then the Company had acted
apart from the state and owed it nothing. The dispute therefore turned on the
legal relationship between Company and state actions, and it ended only when
the Company agreed to pay £10,000 each to James and Buckingham. Shortly
after this agreement was reached, in late April, Buckingham lifted the stay
and allowed the Company's ships to sail for the East Indies.[2]

In 1626, the fall of Hormuz resurfaced, playing a prominent role in Buckingham's impeachment trial. One of the charges that Parliament leveled

against Buckingham was that he had abused his power as lord admiral to extort money from the East India Company in 1624. The charges specifically mentioned both the stay of the ships, supposedly arranged by Buckingham, and the £10,000 payment as examples of the duke's corruption.[3]

No one in the East India Company could have anticipated the curious afterlife of the Company's role in the conquest of Hormuz, but events like Hormuz forced the Company and the regime to grapple with the question of how actions taken in the East Indies fit into wider English foreign (and even domestic) policy. Clear precedent did not exist for dealing with English activities in such faraway places, though increasingly the actions of English people abroad could have consequences at home—as Sir Walter Raleigh, for example, learned to his detriment. The structure of the East Indies trade, which was dependent on authority granted by the royal prerogative in the form of a patent, raised ongoing jurisdictional questions about how much oversight the state should provide, and what else the regime could license people to do in the East Indies besides trade. In the case of Hormuz, no one knew whether a Company military action abroad should be considered a state military action abroad, and neither the regime nor the Company knew to what extent the state was responsible for the Company's military actions in the East Indies. Related questions also arose: for example, if the Company was primarily a trading company, could the state license another body to take advantage of the nontrade opportunities the East Indies offered, like piracy? When the regime licensed a group of men headed by Sir Robert Rich (later the Earl of Warwick) to do just that, the Company scrambled to prove its answer (a resounding no) to just that question. The answers to these questions would determine the parameters of Company and state authority when multiple groups could claim to be acting by authority of the English state. In the cases of the fall of Hormuz and the licensing of non-Company vessels as privateers in the East Indies, events in the East Indies became the starting point for protracted domestic debates about the limits of Company and state authority.

As evident from the afterlife of Hormuz and cases like it, the Company's relationship to the state was only one consideration for the merchants and statesmen involved. More than any theoretical legal issues, it was the political and financial requirements of the late 1610s and 1620s—that is, the influence of favor and financial need—that informed contemporary interpretations of these events. Parties such as the king, prominent aristocrats like the Duke of Buckingham and the Earl of Warwick, and Parliament had widely divergent understandings of how events in the East Indies could and should fit into the actions of the English state. They questioned the limits and exercise of the authority of Company representatives. The meaning and consequences of events in the East Indies were entangled with the political debates of the early 1600s, even as they set precedents for the Company's future actions. At stake were the bounds of the regime's authority, England's diplomatic relations with other European states, and the sustainability of the Company and its ability to trade in the East.

Privateering Ventures in the East Indies: The Company and the Earl of Warwick

Trade and commerce were not the only objectives that an English ship abroad might have. A privateer, for example, did not aim to engage in either trade or commerce. The difference between a privateer and a pirate was that the former had a letter of marque from the lord admiral—in other words, a state license—which turned the taking of a ship and cargo at sea into a legitimate and legal activity.[4] Privateering was a routine feature of European sea voyages in the seventeenth century, and English privateers had long been active in European waters. In the early 1600s, however, multiple parties approached the English crown to try to secure letters of marque as privateers in the East Indies.

The Company's patent, from the perspective of the court of committees, seemed definitive in its prohibition of English access to the East Indies outside of Company control. Both the patents granted by Elizabeth I and James I specified that not only did the Company enjoy sole rights to trade and traffic in the East Indies, but that the monarch, while the patent was in effect, would refrain from granting those rights to others. For example, Elizabeth's patent prohibited any of her subjects outside of the Company from trading in or traveling to the East Indies:

> by virtue of our prerogative royal, which we will not in that behalf have argued, or brought in question, we straightly charge, command and prohibit, for us, our heirs and successors, all the subjects of us, our heirs and successors, of what degree or quality soever they be, that none of them, directly or indirectly, do visit, haunt, frequent or trade, traffic or adventure, by way of merchandize, into or from any of the said East Indies . . . other than the said Governor and Company of Merchants of London, trading into the East Indies.[5]

James's patent granted the same rights and prohibitions, and extended the grant in perpetuity.[6]

Despite the Company's patent and various royal proclamations upholding its sole right to "trade, traffic or adventure" in the East Indies, an enterprising challenger to the Company's exclusive privileges could find loopholes. For example, the patent did not specifically prohibit unaffiliated Englishmen from other activities in the East Indies, so long as they did not trade there and import commodities to England. The charter granted that the monarch would not allow any other of James's subjects to "visit, haunt, [or] frequent" the East Indies, but in specifying "nor the Islands, havens, ports, cities, towns or places thereof [in the East Indies]," it could—if interpreted with a certain amount of flexibility—be taken to mean that travel to the lands of the East Indies was prohibited, but not travel to the seas of the East Indies.[7] This flexible reading of the grant allowed for the possibility of privateering ventures to the East, provided the ships avoided the prohibited land.

Another loophole for an English subject was to sail under the authority of a foreign crown. English merchants looking to circumvent the Company's patent had approached the French monarch for a charter in 1614, promising to set up a French East Indies trade run by English merchants. The English East India Company successfully quashed that venture, but the investors behind that proposal were not the only people to see the possibilities of securing foreign authority.[8] It was this loophole that a group of aristocrats, including Sir Robert Rich, sought to take advantage of when they sent ships armed with letters of marque to the East Indies in the late 1610s. Their letters of marque came not from James, but from the Duke of Savoy.[9]

This venture came to the attention of the Company—at least, to its factors in the East Indies—in the autumn of 1617 when the privateers seized their first ships. Captain Martin Pring, commander of the Company fleet, wrote to the court of committees from Surat, in the Mughal empire, that Company ships had prevented two ships belonging to Rich and a merchant, Philip Barnardi, from taking an Indian junk belonging to the Queen Mother, meaning Emperor Jahangir's mother. Pring explained that had the ship been taken, the Company would have been held responsible and expected to make restitution for the actions of the non-Company Englishmen. The Company's preventive measures seemed to have gained it favor at the Mughal court; Pring was happy to report that Sir Thomas Roe, the English ambassador, had written to him that "never was anything more kindly taken at the court than the rescuing of this junk."[10]

The incident came to the Company's attention as part of a general concern that Rich and his fellow investors were attempting to find a way around the Company's monopoly privileges by appealing to the Duke of Savoy for diplomatic protection. The source of the news was unclear, but "some flying reports" had reached the court of committees.[11] The reports did not mention the averted diplomatic imbroglio that Pring's letter had described, instead focusing on Rich's European connections. Rich's ships had captured a carrick, the rumors reported, and were headed for the Red Sea carrying petitions from the Duke of Savoy. The court of committees wanted to present the cases to the king and Privy Council as a problem of James's control over his subjects: Rich and his fellows "have sought foreign protection, to [the] dishonor of his majesty, prejudice of their country and great damage of both these companies."[12] They did not mention a diplomatic problem with the Mughal empire; instead, the problem was that English subjects were seeking protection abroad from hands other than James's.[13]

Rich saw strategic, targeted piracy—not trade—as the ultimate goal of England's overseas activities. In Virginia and the Caribbean, for example, Rich and his father, the Earl of Warwick, wanted to use the colonies as bases for pirating expeditions, rather than as the seed of territorial plantations.[14] Staunchly anti-Spanish, Rich was chiefly concerned with targeting Spanish ships in the New World, not with developing trade or agriculture. His actions suggest that he was pursuing the same goal in the East Indies though clearly in a less particular manner, as it was not Spanish or Portuguese ships that his men had seized. The emphasis the Company's factors placed on the damage Rich's activities could do to diplomatic relations and trade in the East spoke to the greater question of what English activity in the East Indies would look like: trade with local powers or piracy against them. In the Company's view, it could not look like both.

For the next several months Company leaders and Rich attempted to build cases against each other. Members of the court of committees claimed that Rich had begun collecting evidence against them, having mariners examined, "searching into the Company's actions abroad," and generally seeking to "disgrace and damnify them."[15] Any goodwill Company leaders might once have felt toward Rich was gone; when he requested their aid several months later in getting his seized ships and men to London, they responded huffily that they would "not meddle with a business of that nature and quality, which may concern the state, being yet unknown what his men have done abroad."[16] Company leaders then mobilized their court connections to act on their behalf. For a grant of membership, for example, Sir Lionel Cranfield, then one of the masters of requests, agreed to present the Company's case to the king. The account the court of committees put together for Cranfield emphasized the damage Rich's actions did to both the Company and England: while it was "to the hazard" of the Company, it was the "utter disgrace of our nation." With their account, they added, "his Majesty may be fully possessed with the truth."[17]

Initial public accounts of the event, carefully put forward by Company leaders, emphasized the Company's role in preventing the depredations of the privateers. John Pory, a newsletter writer, reported that the commander of the East India fleet had forced Rich's ships to return a "prize worth 100 thousand pounds." Through this action, Roe and the Company merchants posted at the Mughal court had "purchased themselves much favor," and Pory concluded that "this is the fair tale which the East India Company do tell for themselves."[18] Company leaders' framing of the story to reflect well on themselves and poorly on Rich and his associates—framing that Pory acknowledged with his comment about the "fair tale"—was successful enough that Buckingham caused a delay in the granting of another patent with which Rich was involved, to trade in Guinea and Binney in west Africa. Buckingham wanted Company leaders to first confirm that this patent would not be to their detriment. The court of committees "held themselves much bound to his Lordship for his honorable favor" and warned him that Rich and his fellows might use the patent to harass Company ships in the Red Sea.[19]

The arrival of news from the East confirming the Company's actions and elaborating on the loss of Rich's ships prompted Rich to question, and the Company to defend, its actions.[20] Rich directly challenged the legitimacy of the Company's actions in seizing his ships. His representatives reported that "his Lordship supposeth he hath received a great deal of wrong" and wanted to know "whether it were done by the Company's authority and that they would justify the act." Rich had intended no harm to the Company, he claimed, and in fact his men in the East had no instructions to seize ships as they did. Members of the court of committees responded that with or without his instructions, the outcome was the same, and they stood behind their men's actions. They claimed that the Company had acted within its rights: "but for a present answer the Company made known, that they must and will justify the action, having done no thing but what they had power from his Majesty, by his letters patents."[21] Far from targeting Rich specifically, "whosoever had come in their way, they would have done the same unto them, and will do the like hereafter, upon the like occasion."[22] Indeed, months earlier, Roe had written to Pring with similar sentiments, explaining that he knew that the Company's patent prohibited others from piratical activities in the East Indies, and "if it [the patent] prohibit it, it consequently giveth power to execute such prohibition, else were it in vain." Roe added that he took this position even though he was a supporter of Rich, stating flatly that "Sir Robert Rich is my friend; but I am now a public minister, and cannot see anything with those eyes." Roe was not targeting Rich but representing the "king's honor" to the best of his ability, which in this case came at Rich's expense.[23]

In early 1619, opinion seemed to favor the Company. Rich made his displeasure at the Company's seizure of his ships widely known, but most observers had little sympathy for him. One letter writer observed dryly that "my Lord Rich takes it ill of the Company of the East Indies that took his prize from him."[24] Another letter by the same writer a few weeks later elaborated how James wanted Rich to settle the matter with the Company, probably in arbitration, while Rich stubbornly wanted to take the Company to court. According to the letter writer, "my Lord Rich was very earnest with his Majesty that he might have the benefit of a subject to wage law against them, but the king would not yield to it."[25] When Archbishop George Abbot wrote shortly thereafter to Roe at the Mughal court, he thought that the matter was settled and that "you shall hear no more of him there." Far from discouraging legal action, however, the archbishop argued that the Company could have pursued the matter even further. In his view, they should have dealt with Rich directly and put his men on trial, in addition to going to king and state: "it was the fault of our merchants that they began not with [Rich], not only by complaining to the king and state, but by putting his men to trial whither the law against pirates would not take hold upon them." Buckingham, the archbishop assured Roe, had promised the king that no more such commissions would be issued.[26]

As of February 1619, therefore, the Company was the clear victor in its case against Rich. The king had promised to cancel the Company's financial liability in the case, and Company leaders scheduled a general court to announce the news and to "let them [members of the generality] know how gracious his Majesty hath been unto the Company in my Lord Rich his business."[27] In the meeting a few days later, the governor announced that his Majesty had "been so gracious, to hear the cause himself. He approved

of their doings, and willed their Company not be discouraged in their proceedings." Thus, the Company highlighted the direct and personal oversight of James in this matter, to the favor of the Company. As a further
show of support, James increased the amount of coin the Company had license to export, to advance the growing trade.[28] This monarchical support
testified to the successful selling of the Company's version of what had happened in the East, with its actions not only accepted but lauded.

Yet the Company's position of strength was not unassailable; favor at
court could and did change quickly. The ultimate resolution of the matter
between the Company and Rich (who became earl of Warwick in 1619) took
almost a full decade. In 1619, when Warwick's venture received official disapproval and the Company leaders may well have assumed that they needed
to take no further action, they were in a position of strength, but their fortunes were soon reversed. Warwick was able to use his ties at court and in
Parliament to keep his challenge to the Company alive, eventually receiving
£4,000 compensation from the Company in 1628. The protracted negotiations
between Warwick, the Company, the monarch, and Parliament demonstrated the political and financial considerations that shaped the resolution
of the conflict.

James's approval of the Company's actions grew less enthusiastic after
Warwick signed over half-ownership of his ships to the monarch in 1619. A
legal gamble, this change of ownership had James viewing the Company's
seizures less sympathetically. In mid-May, the Company received a letter
from the king requesting half of the goods taken from Warwick's ships in
the East Indies, "which doth belong unto his Majesty."[29] By the end of the
year, attitudes at the royal court toward the episode had changed enough that
when Roe reported to the king and Privy Council at the end of his embassy,
he attempted to take full responsibility for the seizure to shield the Company.
Far from the earlier narrative of the Company safeguarding the trade, Roe's
explanation emphasized his own accountability "to ruin that business of my
Lord of Warwick, [and] he took it wholly upon himself and told the Lords,
that it was his own act, and he is ready to make answer for it, and justified
the same."[30] He cloaked the Company's actions with his own authority as
ambassador.

Official opinion on the Company's actions had shifted fundamentally.
James's new solution attempted to propitiate both Warwick and the Company. He informed the Company that he required it to pay for Warwick's
losses—James had signed his moiety back to Warwick—but simultaneously

absolved it of any wrongdoing in the matter. He acknowledged that the Company "had done no more than what in justice was lawful." Nevertheless, he wanted it to pay Warwick because he asked it to do so this one time: "he set this account apart by itself." In James's construction, legal rights were beside the point, and indeed he promised future aid in prosecuting similar cases.[31] Company courtiers including Roe and Sir Dudley Digges warned members of the court of committees that opinion at court was not in their favor. Reminding the king and Council that months ago "his Majesty and the Lords of the Council seemed to be well satisfied" with the Company's innocence would do no good. Instead, the courtiers urged the Company to rely on its patent as justification, "as Sir Thomas Roe hath satisfied *many* of the Lords," and to try to negotiate an acceptable compromise.[32]

It quickly became evident, however, that an acceptable compromise with Warwick was impossible. Warwick's monetary claims against the Company had been a nasty shock; he estimated the worth of the ships, goods, and wages at £19,466, which the minutes noted was "too too exceeding great."[33] Company estimates of the value of the ships and goods were in the hundreds rather than the thousands of pounds.[34] Given the discrepancy in the estimates, members of the court of committees found themselves less optimistic about arbitration, and the Company members appointed to meet with Warwick had instructions to keep the matter out of arbitration if possible. Roe, who was one of these members, assured the court that he would attempt to persuade Warwick "to make reasonable demands according to the intent of his Majesty's letter."[35] Meeting with Warwick revealed little common ground, however, as he insisted on half of the claimed sum and pushed for arbitration in the absence of agreement.[36] The Company leaders were willing to negotiate the exchange rate for the value of the seized *reals* but not to pay half of Warwick's claim for over £19,000.

Since compromise looked unlikely, some committees brought up the question of whether the Company should begin soliciting legal advice to determine what James's rights were to a prize taken in the Indies. They "wished to have some civil lawyers' opinion" about "how far his Majesty's part may extend by law, upon a prize taken in the Indies." However, others thought it was too early to begin to make such inquiries, "until it shall be found how my Lord will press the business."[37] This unresolved question about the state's authority over Company activities in the East Indies would return to haunt the Company, especially with regard to its role in the conquest of Hormuz and the disposition of the prizes taken there. With regard to Warwick in 1619 and early 1620, however, the Company decided not to pursue this legal avenue.[38]

Negotiations between Warwick and the Company dragged on, with no resolution. Both sides managed to secure James's assurance that he did not mean them to be losers in the situation. Warwick's argument for the £19,466 was that since the Company had at one time had his ships in its possession, it was liable for the full value of the ships. The Company's argument was that since the ships were broken and unserviceable, and in fact had not made it back to England, they had not profited from the ships and thus were not liable for their value. The minutes laconically noted that "there grew a long dispute."[39] The Company agreed to pay for what it took and managed to keep, but not the rest. Warwick appealed to James, who sent a letter to the Company demanding a resolution to the business. The letter stated that the matter should be turned over to two arbitrators, "indifferently chosen." If the two sides could not agree on arbitrators, James would chose an "umpire." The court minutes noted that the letter also promised that Warwick "should be no loser by the voyage," which suggested that James did not favor the Company's case.[40]

When Company leaders appealed to James only weeks later, however, they received as encouraging words as Warwick had. They promised that they would not "be gainers by [James's] loss," echoing the language of Warwick's letter. Company representatives delivered a petition to the king, and court minutes described how James drew out the letter, "read and commended [it] twice," and praised it as a "judicial and well-penned letter." He explained that "his intents are not the Company should suffer for his Lord of Warwick's attempt or become losers for his action." It was time, however, for all of this to be concluded, "that his Majesty might be no further troubled with that business."[41] Taking his favor as evidence of royal support, Company leaders agreed to meet again with Warwick—but this meeting too was unsuccessful.[42]

Even when a conclusion to the matter finally appeared near, the different objectives of Warwick and the Company stood in stark relief. Warwick came to the Company ready "to make a peaceable end with them" in March 1620.[43] The court of committees decided to offer him £1,019, which they now listed as the sum they had gained in the matter. The concern of Company leaders in dealing with Warwick was to satisfy James with their behavior. Thus, the minutes noted their consideration of how and when they should "let his Majesty know" what they were offering, with the ultimate hope that James would not command them to give more, "lest they should be drawn and overruled, to a greater [settlement] by his Majesty."[44] The new twist to the story, however, was that some committees now reported that Warwick was privately offering to acquit the Company of responsibility in the entire matter if it would only allow him to send a pinnace into the East Indies, "to get what he can." The court of committees was sure that he would be unsuccessful in the business, even without its contrivance, "yet knowing their intents unlawful (who put on such a business) they would by no means hearken to such a motion."[45] The irony of the suggestion was evident: Warwick was essentially suing the Company for preventing his piracy and was promising to give up the suit if they would allow him to engage in piracy again.

There the matter rested for years, with no real resolution. The Company and Warwick had made preparations for arbitration in 1620, despite the Company's reluctance, but either the arbitration did not take place or it did not succeed.[46] Five years later, in early 1625, the Company received another letter from James, telling the Company and Warwick to enter arbitration.[47] Warwick was threatening to go take the case to Parliament—he was "resolved to fly to a parliament"—and the Company was prepared to let him.[48] Rather than negotiate a settlement with arbitrators, Company leaders wrote to James expressing "the Company's desire to be judged by a parliament."[49] Part of their willingness to take Warwick's case to Parliament may have been that public opinion at that time was strongly with the Company in the aftermath of the Amboyna massacre (see Chapter 8). They might have hoped or assumed that Parliament would be more sympathetic to them in 1625 than it had been the year before.[50] Meeting with James on the matter, they explained their reasoning and requested that he would refer the matter to a parliament.[51] However, James died less than two months later without having taken any further action.

The Company's faith in Parliament had flagged by the time the House of Lords took up the still-unresolved disagreement between the Company and Warwick in 1628.[52] In contrast to their request in 1625 for James to turn the case over to Parliament, in 1628 they requested that Parliament not adjudicate the question; they suspected that Warwick had more allies than they did in the House of Lords.[53] For example, some of the lords suggested that the Company had already had ten years to settle the matter and told it to "make some fair overture to his Lordship" or accept a parliamentary vote.

Their proposal and tone did not promise much sympathy for the Company.[54] Though Company leaders tried to argue that James had favored their side secretly, as he had foreseen "the inconvenience that would happen to the whole trade if his Lordship should be admitted to question his regal power granted to the Company by his letters patent," this was not an argument that convinced members of Parliament, and the matter went into arbitration.[55]

The parliament-mediated negotiations dealt in sums of money the Company leaders had never expected to pay. The lord president, the Earl of Manchester, offered himself as mediator, citing his affection for the Company and close kinship with Warwick. He suggested that the Company come up with an "indifferent sum"—perhaps £10,000—and settle the matter. Compared to the £28,000 Warwick now demanded, £10,000 may have seemed indifferent to Manchester, but the sum was far from the £2,000 the Company was willing and able to offer. Several lords concurred that £10,000 was a fair amount, but Company leaders could not agree. The lords suggested £8,000 if £10,000 was too high. Company leaders responded that they could offer an additional £500. After more debate, the lords suggested £5,000, and the leaders departed to consider the matter. After considering in private, they sent for the lord president and said that they could offer £3,000.[56]

The negotiation between the Company and the lords in Parliament showed how Company leaders were not at as much of a disadvantage as they might have feared. Warwick was better connected in the upper house of Parliament. Meanwhile, the Company's past history, and even its defenses for its actions, highlighted its ties to the monarch and monarchical power rather than Parliament or the common law. The power of the prerogative was hardly the most compelling argument to make in Parliament in 1628, when representatives were struggling to compel the regime to redress a set of grievances that touched on questions of monarchical power and prerogative rights, like ship money and the forced loan.[57] However, the willingness of the lords who were negotiating to adjust the settlement amount and their avowed "affection" to the Company highlighted the fact that at least some of the lords in Parliament were favorably disposed toward the Company, particularly if they were members or had been the objects of cultivation by the Company in the past.[58] The reduction of the "indifferent sum" from £10,000 to £5,000 showed a willingness to actually negotiate, despite the warnings that the lords as a whole might not favor the Company in a suit against Warwick.

Nevertheless, internal Company debate on the proposed settlement emphasized the difficult position Company leaders felt they were in. After the business had "slept many years," Warwick had petitioned the House of Lords, asking for £28,000. The Lords had multiple hearings on the matter and had shown Warwick "extraordinary favor." Company leaders stood behind their actions, using their patent as defense. The governor, Morris Abbot, reported that James had only expected the Company to enter into bond for £5,000 when mediation had seemed a possibility, which suggested that he had agreed that the Company were liable for only that amount. Although by the Company's calculations, Warwick's £28,000 was actually only £3,000, this "final" offer was not judged sufficient. Company leaders felt that they had to end the affair, even if not on terms they liked. Members of Parliament were not neutral arbitrators, and if the matter went to a vote in the House of Lords, Company leaders felt the Company was sure to suffer. The parliamentary committee ultimately suggested £4,000, which both parties accepted, and the matter was finally settled after a decade.[59]

The case that had dragged on for years revealed how the consequences of aggressive actions taken by Englishmen far from England—"what his men have done abroad," in other words—were mediated by the political situation at home. The twists and turns of the Warwick affair demonstrated how quickly favor could seem to settle a matter and reopen what had seemed to be a closed matter, and how favor and connections could change who had the upper hand in negotiations. Custom and precedent for the prosecution of the Company's trade and liability were scarce, and events thus could easily be caught up in the ebbs and flows of court favor.

Buckingham and the Conquest of Hormuz

The wrangling over events at Hormuz showed just how dramatic the changes in court favor could be when the most influential aristocrat and the king were closely involved in the matter. Hormuz and its aftermath revealed the difficulty of reconciling Company actions abroad with state affairs in Europe. Warwick's piracy had pitted competing visions of English activity in the East Indies against each other in both the East Indies and England, and how people in England understood it and treated it was in part mediated by court politics. Hormuz added the additional dimension of the wider European diplomatic situation. It set state affairs against Company affairs, raising conceptual and practical questions about the consequences of what Company men did abroad.

In 1622, the island of Hormuz was an object of intense desire. For over a hundred years, the Portuguese had held the castle and fortress of Hormuz, situated at the mouth of the Persian Gulf, and used it to control military and commercial traffic.[60] Both the Persians and the English coveted the island and the strategic access it represented. The Persian emperor, Shah Abbas, had explored a variety of ways to oust the Portuguese or change the relationship between them and the Persians, all with limited success. A military conquest of the island was out of the question, for as one observer noted, though "the king of Persia quarrels with the Portugals for what they possess in the Gulf of Persia," he "hath no shipping" and "will doubtless be able to do little hurt unto Hormuz."[61] From the East India Company's perspective, almost as soon as Company factors had begun trading in the Mughal empire, they had written to London about the possibilities of opening a trade in Persia.[62] This trade would provide markets for English goods and held out the promise of easier access to overland silk routes, which normally passed to Europe through Ottoman territory. As long as Hormuz remained in Portuguese hands, however, English trade opportunities were limited.

To overcome their respective weaknesses, Shah Abbas broached the possibility of using a joint English-Persian force to remove the Portuguese from Hormuz in early 1622. The Persians would supply much of the manpower, while the English would provide several ships for battle as well as a small number of fighting men. On behalf of the Company leaders in London, the factors in the East jumped at the chance. The parties first spelled out each of their responsibilities in the venture, including who was allowed to attempt to convert whom and how power and authority in the town would be divided should the effort succeed. Several months later, a combined English-Persian force ousted the Portuguese from Hormuz, captured goods worth an enormous amount, and divided the plunder.[63] However, this tidy division of the spoils was not the end of the story of the conquest of Hormuz.

The conduct of international affairs fell within the bounds of the sovereign's prerogative, as did the granting of charters and letters patent. At times, the monarch's pursuit of the former could conflict with the exercise of privileges granted in the latter. English foreign policy had rarely concerned areas outside of Europe, but the long-distance trades managed by chartered companies in the early seventeenth century introduced new complications. As long as the East India Company was able to enforce its patent rights, it was not only the sole English trading presence in the East Indies, but the sole English presence in the region. The Company's men became de facto official representatives of England in the East Indies—the Company was the English state abroad. In the fall of Hormuz, the Company's action resembled state action, complicating the diplomatic relations of the state back in Europe. In the aftermath of this event, both Company and state had to evaluate how the Company's activities fit into English foreign policy, and to what extent its employees acted as representatives of the state. Ultimately, though, as with Warwick, political considerations and favor framed the conclusion.

The distance of the East Indies from England severely circumscribed both the king's and the Company's power to direct the actions of Company men abroad. Information traveled slowly. News of the capture of Hormuz reached England piecemeal and was at first unconfirmed. Sir Henry Wotton, the English ambassador at Venice, wrote to Secretary of State George Calvert in August 1622 that a rumor had reached Venice that seven English ships had helped take Hormuz, but he added a note later in the letter that the castle still held out, though under siege.[64] By December, news of the capture of Hormuz had reached England from multiple sources. A letter from Madrid in that month confirmed the capture: an overland express messenger had arrived with news that Shah Abbas, with English aid, had taken Hormuz, which news "hath made a great noise here, and doth trouble [the Spanish court] much."[65] Also from Madrid, the Earl of Bristol wrote that there was "much murmuring in this court about the taking of Hormuz" and that the success of the action was due to English assistance. He added that he had heard news of this event from England but had not believed it until the arrival of the express messenger. Given the importance that the Portuguese placed on Hormuz, the news had created "much storm," and the earl promised his aid in calming that storm.[66] In Spain, he defended English actions in the East, acknowledging the friendship between the monarchs in Europe but arguing that the open hostility between the English and Portuguese in the East justified any actions the Company had taken.[67]

The diplomatic fallout from the capture of Hormuz was immediate: as was already evident, the Spanish were not pleased. Wotton's first letter in August recording the early rumors about Hormuz's capture had noted that, even in Venice, people were wondering what effect the capture would have on England's ongoing treaty negotiations with Spain.[68] James was trying to secure a Spanish bride for his heir and thereby acquire a Habsburg alliance as well as a rich dowry, though many people at court had no desire for this match on religious grounds. A major diplomatic incident between the two nations would put the match in jeopardy.

The high stakes meant that careful handling on the part of the regime was necessary. The Spanish ambassador in England soon approached James and the Privy Council demanding justice, which he claimed the Spanish had not gotten in the Admiralty courts.[69] When Bristol wrote with an update from Madrid, he let Calvert know that several courtiers had been appointed to deal with the Hormuz business, including the Marquis of Montes Claros and the Count of Gondomar, who had until recently been ambassador to England.[70] Bristol also wrote that with the Spanish court so troubled by the taking of Hormuz, he daily expected "a relation of the whole business," which he would promptly send to James.[71] The matter dragged on unresolved, however, and James made no official move on it until half a year later, when he passed the matter on to Calvert for his "judicious handling." The king's instructions emphasized that Calvert was to make the Company understand the "serious and grievous complaints" of the Spanish ambassadors. His instructions noted that "these complaints are new" and "can do new hurt."[72] Within two days, Calvert had passed on the information to the Company and planned a meeting with its governor to discuss the situation.[73]

This message from Calvert to the Company seems to have been the first formal notice the Company had that there would be official difficulty over the business at Hormuz. Indeed, it was also virtually the first mention of Hormuz in the Company minutes.[74] Calvert's message immediately put the members of the court of committees on their guard. A number of them had met with Calvert in the Star Chamber, and he had informed them that the Privy Council had received several letters from the Spanish pressing the king to take action about Hormuz. It is unclear from the court minutes exactly what Calvert expected the Company to offer. The committees reported that he wanted them to "send unto Mr. Secretary Conway in writing such satisfaction as they can at present give, taking knowledge of what he had said unto them." The Company leaders decided to err on the side of caution and not submit anything in writing. Instead, they sent representatives to meet with Conway.[75] They learned that someone had made complaints to

James, but Conway "did not perceive that it is much pressed at the instant" and promised to let them know if anything changed.[76] The situation would require action, but it was not yet a crisis.

Trouble came from an unexpected source: when James summoned several committees to meet with him a week later, it was the complaints of Buckingham, then lord admiral, and not the Spanish ambassadors, that concerned the king. In a private meeting, James informed the Company's officers that "he had understood from the Duke of Buckingham that the Company had before his going promised to gratify him." James urged them to pay the gratification now, while Buckingham was in Spain with Prince Charles, "because thereby it would appear they had been mindful of him." The gratification they had promised should take into account the conquest of Hormuz, and now that the ships involved in that action had arrived in England, richly laden, the Company would be well able to pay.[77]

These kinds of gratifications were common. Basically cash bribes, they were occasionally given by the Company in expectation of or thanks for some singular service. The amount could range from a few hundred to a few thousand pounds, and though the Company might deliver the money noting that it was for such and such a purpose, these were not contractual payments. In considering James's words to them, for example, members of the court of committees cited Buckingham's past favors, "the continual use they shall have of his favor" to the Company, and his assistance in matters of negotiation with the Dutch. They also noted that "this business of Hormuz (how well soever to be answered of the Company's part) may find a strong opposition" and that it was "fit to gratify him and it appears to be expected at their hands." Thus, "to sweeten him for their future occasions, and particularly for that of Hormuz," they decided to give him £2,000 and let the king know they were doing so.[78] A set of notes made by a Privy Council secretary gave a slightly different version of the meeting; according to the notes, the Company was ordered to pay Buckingham the £2,000.[79]

If it seems that Company leaders were caught flat-footed as far as what response to make to the events in Hormuz, it is because in part they were. There was a reason the Company minutes were so silent on the matter of Hormuz: the action had not been directly sanctioned. The court of committees had not planned for it or laid the groundwork in London to prepare the king and Council for it. It is possible that Company leaders were as surprised as anyone else when news of the conquest began to trickle back to Europe.[80] Thus, in the summer of 1623 when the fleet returned, the court of committees questioned the returning factors and captain closely, especially concerning by what authority they had made the decision to ally with the Persians and offer military aid, and how valuable the spoils were. One factor explained that it was James's own commission "to defend and offend" that had empowered them, and that the factors and captain had consulted on the matter in Surat. They saw it as a perfect opportunity to repay the Portuguese for their treatment of the English in the East, not to mention the fact that the Persians were preventing English trade in Persia until they gave their aid.[81] As for the spoils, the factor explained that the Portuguese had expected some sort of siege and removed goods beforehand; thus, the acquired valuables were not as great as they might have been.

If the immediate downside of the affair for the Company was dealing with a situation for which its leaders had not planned, the upside was a huge influx of goods—even if such a windfall brought its own problems. Letters began carrying news out of London of the arrival of the rich fleet, as well as the Spanish ambassador's displeasure at the arrival. The Venetian ambassador priced the spoils at £2 million in gold, and John Chamberlain noted that "our East India Company was at a low ebb, but is now somewhat afloat again by the arrival of three ships richly laden"—a common enough response to the arrival of ships from the East Indies. More unusual, though, was Chamberlain's next comment, that he heard "a whispering that the Spanish ambassador hath a meaning to arrest them upon pretense of the business of Hormuz."[82] The good news, therefore, was qualified. Additionally, James still insisted that the Company pay the ordered (or agreed upon) £2000 to the still-absent Buckingham.[83] Thanking James for showing them a way gain Buckingham's friendship—for being "so gracious unto them as to direct them a way to gain so noble a friend as the duke"—Company leaders agreed to pay the £2000, though the king responded with a simple, "it was well, and asked when it should be paid." However, the acquisitive tone was coupled with a promise to "prepare" Buckingham to "requite" the gift. The leaders also promised James an accounting of the Hormuz business, and the king seemed content with their plan for the spoils, a large part of which consisted of piece goods.[84]

The court of committees began to seek legal advice about what to do with the spoils and to whom they belonged. Members of the court consulted some of the top legal figures of the day, including Sir Henry Marten of the Court of Admiralty and Richard Zouch, the common lawyer. The immediate issue was whether the mariners should be paid a wage or receive only a share of the spoils, and to resolve that point the question of how to categorize the events at Hormuz had first to be answered. The preliminary report from the lawyers noted that the spoils from Hormuz were not the same as prizes taken at sea, though they resolved to consult further on the matter.[85] The issue of payment neatly distilled the ambiguities of Hormuz. If the mariners' role in the conquest of Hormuz was part of their normal Company duties, then the mariners should receive only their expected wages. But if the conquest was part of a state military action, then the mariners were due a share of the spoils.

As the newly returned sailors bragged of their victory and flaunted their spoils, the Spanish ambassadors renewed their petitions. The "braving speeches" of the captains did little to soothe the ambassadors.[86] Their complaints described the "excess of the East Indies Company's ships." The newly acquired riches were stolen goods worth £500,000, they wrote. They noted that even the lowest Company men might now eat off dishes of silver and possess priceless jewels, and that the men had rejoiced in rumors that the Spanish match had been called off, firing cannons in celebration and throwing their hats into the sea. Their actions cast doubt on the amity between James and Philip IV, and the ambassadors requested that James seize the ships and make restitution to Spain.[87] These complaints apparently moved James, who ordered that the men in the harbor be examined and court officials sequester the ships for the time being: if the ambassadors' information was right, then the Company's actions would have been in error, and presumably the Company would be ordered to offer restitution.[88] Since the courts were in recess at the time, however, James claimed that he could not proceed further, but he would begin an investigation. Justice would be done, he assured the ambassadors, and nothing would be allowed to weaken the amicable relationship between himself and Philip.[89]

Several factors may have influenced James's actions in late 1623, including his relations with Spain and a new sense of the enormous wealth of the spoils of Hormuz. He abandoned his earlier contentment with the Company leaders' accounting for Hormuz and its spoils and pursued further investigation. This examination gave James and his advisors time to consider possible actions. With Prince Charles and Buckingham in Spain exploring the possibilities of a match with the infanta, this was not the time for a major diplomatic controversy between the two countries. Although the prince's trip to Spain ended with the match conclusively out of the picture, it is not certain when James accepted this outcome. Thus, James's concern with the situation might have echoed that of the Spanish.[90] Another possibility, however, was that as higher estimations of the value of the spoils came to his attention, as well as information about the possible yearly revenues from Hormuz, James wanted more time to consider the fate of Hormuz. This was not the moment to act impulsively about the future of the fort. A document (undated, but likely from this time and among the state papers relating to the East Indies) calculated the possible profits Hormuz could bring the king, citing £400,000 as the yearly revenue it had brought the Spanish monarch and could conceivably bring James.[91] Given how cash-strapped the Stuart monarch was—a large dowry was one of the main lures of the Spanish match—the revenues from Hormuz must have looked very tempting. With the Company's penchant for secrecy and the delay in receiving information from the East, it is entirely plausible that the true value of the capture of Hormuz, in immediate and future terms, was not evident to James until he received the extravagant and possibly inflated complaints from the Spanish ambassadors.

By December 1623, the regime began proceedings in the Admiralty courts to determine the value of the prizes taken, so the amount that the Company owed the regime could be calculated. Admiralty courts usually ruled on matters of prizes taken at sea and were supposed to render judgments on whether seized goods had been lawfully taken before they could be sold. The idea of the court hearing a case that involved the seizure of goods belonging to a rival sovereign was not extraordinary. However, it was also not extraordinary for the regime to attempt to circumvent admiralty procedure and authority and employ the court as an arm of the executive rather than as an independent court. The Company seemed to have suspected that this was the case in this situation.[92] Over the course of a month, Marten examined five newly returned officers from the East Indies fleet. The examinations investigated the chain of events and the reasoning behind the men's actions. However, most of the questions focused on the type and quantity of goods seized from Portuguese ships at Hormuz.[93]

Whether the prime mover behind this investigation was James or Buckingham was unclear. Both would benefit from an Admiralty court decision that the Company had acted piratically (without a letter of marque). What we do know is that the account of goods in the Admiralty court encouraged Buckingham to examine his options more closely, as his men began to explore the financial possibilities that Hormuz offered the lord admiral.[94] A report prepared for Buckingham by Sir John Coke described a variety of

possible courses with regard to Hormuz. It assessed the monetary value of
the spoils as at least £100,000 and noted that there were two ways to interpret the Company's action in the East: the spoils had been taken either by
piracy or else as "reprisals" from enemies. In support of the piracy interpretation, the report argued that England and Portugal were not at war, nor
were the English at war with any of the "infidel" nations of the East Indies.
Though the Company had a warrant to defend its trade, Coke noted, the
warrant was not to assail other powers. This claim was in opposition to
what the one factor told the Company, that he and other factors in the East
understood their commission to permit both defense and offense. If the regime deemed that the Company had acquired the goods piratically, then
the spoils and captured ships belonged to James—the entire prize would go
to the monarch. However, the report continued, if England's friendship
with Spain did not extend so far, this would clear the Company of piracy
charges, and if infidel nations restricted English access to trade, they could
be deemed to be enemies. In this construction, the Company had acquired
the goods as reprisals from enemies. The Company's estates would not be
forfeit to the crown in this case, but by ancient custom, one-tenth of the
total would be due to Buckingham as a customary tithe to the lord
admiral.[95]

The easiest and best solution, the report concluded, would be to agree to
settle claims with the Company for a tenth of the whole. Accusing the
Company of piracy might gain his majesty the goods, but it also might
cripple the Company permanently and possibly lead to its dissolution. Since
the Company was rich, prosperous, and influential, this course might not
be the most desirable outcome. In contrast, settling with the Company
would have none of those detrimental outcomes, and a settlement would be
easier to secure, especially since Company leaders had already offered some
money to Buckingham.[96] Though the report did not state this explicitly, it
implied that by offering the gratuity months before, the Company had acknowledged Buckingham's authority over the action.

By early 1624, the uncertain status of the Hormuz action was compromising the Company's negotiating power with the regime. When James
requested that Company leaders defray the costs of a visiting ambassador's
stay in London, his letter "gave a touch that the Company were yet under
the account of Hormuz." In a similar vein, the committees wrote to Buckingham wanting to discover "whether they be malefactors or not" on account of Hormuz before they spent time and money developing the trade

there.[97] As February 1624 progressed, the Company still had not received an answer about an official decision, and indeed all evidence from Buckingham suggested that he was considering asserting the lord admiral's rights to a tenth of the goods. A representative of the duke, who asked to remain unnamed in the Company minutes, came to meet with Company leaders, and the minutes of the meeting described it as "a proposition made darkly to the Company concerning the lord admiral's right for goods taken in the Indies."[98]

This meeting galvanized the leaders, and they began to explore their legal options in case Buckingham pressed his right to a tenth. There was some precedent regarding the lord admiral's tenths of prizes taken by the Company in the East Indies. In 1603, for example, the *Ascension* had arrived in England having captured a prize in the East. The committees had discussed the lord admiral's share as a matter of course, referring to "the tenths belonging to my Lord Admiral for the prize which the Company's ships have taken in the East Indies."[99] If and how they paid the tenth was not recorded, yet it is important to note that the lord admiral's right to a tenth was assumed without contest. However, the prize the *Ascension* took was taken from the Portuguese at sea, not on land.[100] It followed a much more standard pattern: sea engagement, prizes taken, tenth paid. To the court of committees, the case of Hormuz did not.

Company representatives canvassed various civil and common lawyers on the matter. Instead of giving particulars, the Company first presented a general scenario to the lawyers. In it, merchants with a commission directly from the king set out to discover and open new trades. Hostile actions interrupted their voyages, so the merchants abroad took reprisals. In this case, the Company's leaders asked, did the admiral of their home country have a right to a part of their reprisals? The first expert they consulted told them that customarily a tenth belonged to the lord admiral if he gave the merchants any commission. If he had given no letter of marque, however, he could not claim the tenth. Upon being informed that the Company wanted to know this information in relation to the current lord admiral, the lawyer refused them to give them any more information; he would not give advice against Buckingham. Even though the Company men explained that they had no desire "to wage law" with the lord admiral—they wanted only to know where they stood when they met with him on the matter—the lawyer refused to advise them further: they "used other motives to induce the delivery of the doctor's [lawyer's] opinion, but all would not avail." He would add only that there was no written law for cases where the lord admiral had not given a commission, though he explained that the admiral's jurisdiction extended through all seas and oceans.[101]

The Company's leaders next showed their patent to Zouch, who examined it and told them the admiral had no legal basis for his demands, while acknowledging that customarily, they would owe him a tenth if they had letters of marque. Unlike the first authority they consulted, Zouch agreed to give them his legal advice in writing. The leaders and Zouch discussed some of the possible cases that might be brought to bear, again asserting that they did not seek to wage law with the duke but confirming that theirs "was a single case without precedent." Zouch requested a copy of the patent and promised to "inform himself" about the matter and write up his opinion for them. A third jurist advised them to delay the proceedings entirely and get that year's fleet off first, before dealing with the mess.[102] The court of committees decided to send representatives with the reasons set down by Zouch and to insist that the £2,000 they had already given Buckingham was sufficient payment for Hormuz.[103] Unsurprisingly, Buckingham was not satisfied with the £2,000.

As Company leaders drafted a new petition to Buckingham, they debated how best to approach him. Sir John Coke had declined to represent the Company to Buckingham and left the leaders to their own devices. They decided to emphasize their need for official support in the aftermath of the fall of Hormuz, resolving to remind Buckingham that the situation in the East Indies was dire, as "the Portugal arms in earnest and is filled with anger and revenge by the late defeats they received in the Indies." Consequently, "if the English shall be subject to question for what they do in their just defense it will dishearten all seafaring men from doing service to the Company." In other words, the Company's actions in Hormuz had issued a challenge, and the leaders needed to show even more strength in the East as a result. Further questioning of the Company's actions would show a lack of support by the state. Additionally, the Company needed new, explicit letters of marque for the ships about to sail, if indeed the regime concluded that the Company's ships in the past had acted implicitly under letters of marque.[104]

The actions the Company requested would have the benefit of settling the issue of who owed whom for what definitively for both the Company and its mariners. Some committees wanted to accept a decision by the regime about jurisdiction provided it was clear, stating that "if it please the duke as he is admiral of England to grant letters of marque, the Company will willingly allow him his right." The "double good to the Company" that this course would have was that "they shall know what is theirs and be free from question." Internal debates showed Company leaders had agreed to treat the duke civilly, but to point out that the Portuguese were ready and willing to move against the English. However, other committees wanted to assure Buckingham that if he would waive his claims of right to the Hormuz spoils, they would be generous in return. It is not possible to know how much they would have offered Buckingham if he had waived his rights. Certainly the waiver would have been worth a great deal to the Company, as it would allow the leaders to leave the legal issue undecided and open to future interpretation. Even though their civil lawyers had just reported that they were "of opinion that for goods taken beyond the line the lord admiral has no jurisdiction and therefore can require no tenth," the Company decided not to push the issue of who had the right, but rather to settle the case with mediation.[105] This idea about the geographic reach of the English state's authority versus that of the Company's authority—or more properly, no one's authority—would have been a provocative legal argument to follow, had Company leaders pursued that line instead of mediation.

While still trying to come to a consensus about the best course of action, Company leaders found themselves the subjects of public criticism. Buckingham soon seized the initiative, and on 1 March 1624, days after the leaders had been debating how to approach Buckingham, a parliamentary conference committee of both houses passed a motion to stay four Company ships waiting to depart for the East Indies.[106] Parliament in 1624 was particularly unsympathetic to trading companies; the motion—which Buckingham seemed to have a hand in—came after the House of Commons had already spent days debating and criticizing trading companies and what members of Parliament labeled "monopoly" trades.[107] Not all of the supporters of the motion to stay the ships were Buckingham's men— instead, antimonopoly sentiment found broad support among members of Parliament. Additionally, many members were agitating for a war with Spain and argued that allowing Company ships to depart for the East would prevent those ships and their men, gunpowder, and cannons from taking part in an English war effort.[108]

The Company's acting governor, Morris Abbot, and deputy governor, Thomas Mun, worked both openly and behind the scenes to sway Parliament, but with little success. Abbot was a member of Parliament, and in the

House of Commons he had addressed the damage to the kingdom resulting from the stay of the Company's ships. Mun explained that "he had not slept in the business, but had done what lay in him to further their proceedings," also without success. What the Company needed, he said, was "a gentleman who [was] not in the Company's behalf (having no interest in the adventure)," but who would "for virtue's sake" take up the Company's cause. The unidentified gentleman they found to fill this role went with a few Company men to meet with Buckingham. The duke received them, but when they asked him to release their ships, he denied any responsibility for the stay, claiming instead that the motion in the House of Lords had so moved him, "he could do no less than give the order they had done."[109] With this somewhat disingenuous disclaimer of responsibility, Buckingham agreed to allow the ships to go as far as Tilbury, but no farther.

Parliament's hostility to the Company continued as members debated the stay of the Company's ships. Representatives repeated long-standing criticisms of the Company, especially regarding its export of bullion. Abbot's account of the events in Parliament revealed how vulnerable the Company leaders felt to parliamentary inquiry, and how the matter of staying the ships morphed so easily into a general inquiry into the entire trade. He reported how the house had questioned Robert Bateman, both a member of Parliament and the Company's treasurer, about the Company's finances. Bateman had been forced to admit that his presence in Parliament meant he did not know the particulars of Company business that had taken place during the body's present session. Parliamentary agitation reached such a pitch that some members "cried out, search the [Company's] books." Abbot was forced to offer his expertise to answer questions in an attempt to dissuade them.[110] He had provided the house with a short explanation of the economics of the trade, citing how much bullion the Company exported—£40,000 a year—and imported, and so forth. The pressure to answer this parliamentary inquiry may, in fact, have been the impetus behind Mun's composition of *England's Treasure by Foreign Trade*.[111] The question of the Hormuz spoils, according to the court minutes, did not arise at all. Despite this, Company leaders continued to see Buckingham as the author of their troubles. The minutes hinted darkly at Buckingham's role, noting that "in this court was a great dispute concerning the lord admiral omitted but remains to be seen in the original," though that original draft has not survived.[112]

Even as the leaders wrestled with Parliament, further examinations of the Company's actions in Hormuz took place in the Admiralty court at the insistence of James. These examinations coincided neatly with Parliament's debates, lasting from 4 to 10 March.[113] Marten once more questioned Company men, this time focusing on the escape of the Portuguese commander, Ruy Freyre, from Company arrest in Surat. His questions suggested Company negligence. In contrast, the Company's cross-examinations (which either had not occurred or had not been recorded previously) emphasized the common knowledge among the Company's men that the Portuguese had orders to disrupt or harm the English trade, making Hormuz an act of reprisal rather than piracy. For example, one witness noted that everyone knew the Portuguese had intended to "destroy and beat away the English nation from trade in the East Indies," and that he had heard stories about Portuguese oaths on the sacrament to target English trade.[114] The cross-examinations justified the actions of Company men while avoiding any talk of negligence. Shortly after the conclusion of the examination, however, the Company received an order from the court, in James's name, to pay the monarch £15,000 for the goods taken at Hormuz—which the court ruled had been taken piratically.[115]

A later set of notes produced for the Privy Council in June 1624 reveals in even more depth how dire the Company's situation was in March. With the Admiralty court case and the parliamentary stay of ships, the Company faced official opposition on multiple fronts. Informal channels of negotiation had failed, and its ships were stuck at Tilbury. Company leaders, the monarch, and the lord admiral met on 18 March. Buckingham claimed that he could not act until Parliament had resolved its position on the matter. While Buckingham's demands had custom and tradition behind them, James had little such justification; instead, the June document reveals that his claim was based on a questionable promise made by the previous governor, Sir William Halliday, to give him £10,000. To Abbot's response that the late governor might have spoken "something in general words on the expectation and rumor" of the news from Hormuz, but "nothing to bind the Company," James replied that he was no tyrant to fear the law, and the Company could take him to court if they found his demands unlawful. Just as Company leaders had hesitated to take Buckingham to court, they had no desire to take James to court.[116] In any case, what became clear during the 18 March meeting was that James and Buckingham each wanted

£10,000 from the Company. The Admiralty court order to pay £15,000 came days after the Company refused to settle with James for £10,000.

The account of the interchange between James, Buckingham, and Company leaders in these notes also reveals some of the underlying and not always concordant understandings of what the state and the Company owed each other in their partnership. Buckingham based the majority of his claims on a customary right, but he also mentioned that he felt neglected by the Company. Its leaders had not shown him enough gratitude for the many instances in which he had exercised his favor and influence on their behalf, and he was "very round with the governor at Whitehall expostulating his being neglected by the Company when the Governor let fall words that might give expectation from the business at Hormuz." James, with no customary right to the goods, justified his demands as fair recompense for his actions on the leaders' behalf, such as interceding for them with the Spanish about Hormuz, and he harangued them: "Did I deliver you from the complaint of the Spaniard and do you return me nothing?" Possibly out of pique or frustration, or to show that it was within his power to do so, James threatened to have all the spoils declared the lord admiral's.[117] A few days later, on 22 March, James delivered this opinion: the Company had acquired the goods either justly or unjustly. If unjustly, all the goods were forfeit, and if justly, they owed and had to pay a "right."[118] He never explained why this right was due to him, aside from the supposed promise by the dead governor, but he continued to demand £10,000. The Company leaders believed that they had promised nothing, and that the East Indies was so far away it was not clear that custom should apply. They were willing to offer gratuities, but only to a point—and not when they were compelled to do so in such a heavy-handed fashion. Each participant argued from a different understanding of what the shared enterprise of the East India Company entailed.

As time passed and the fleet still had not sailed, however, Company leaders grew increasingly open to negotiation. They began to worry that they would miss the year's entire voyage—if the fleet did not sail by the end of April, it would miss the winds for the East Indies until the next year. As their desperation grew, so did their willingness to pay the sums demanded. The continuing lack of resolution had long-term consequences, and the court of committees resolved to seek a permanent ruling once they had settled the case. They would "procure from his Majesty a declaration for the direction of their people in the Indies, that there be no place left for any further question concerning any occurrents there between his Majesty's subjects and any others whatsoever." Avoiding similar cases in future was paramount, and Company leaders began to treat Hormuz itself as a lost cause. They agreed to pay the £20,000, in return for a legally drawn up "discharge" or statement from the king. This discharge would set out what the standard policy on cases of the sort would be in the future.[119] By the end of April, the Admiralty court had concluded the case; discharged the Company; and released its ships, which sailed shortly thereafter, and the Company had made arrangements to pay both James and Buckingham.[120]

The aftermath of the Hormuz action was not over. The action remained at the center of interactions between Company and regime for weeks, as James and Buckingham pressed for prompt payment of the monies owed them. Not until news of the proceedings at Amboyna (see Chapter 8) reached London later in 1624 was the case of Hormuz eclipsed. Then the gristly events at Amboyna quickly superseded the riches of Hormuz both in the national imagination and in the attention of the Company and Council.

Hormuz made one last, unexpected appearance on the national scene. In 1626, the negotiations about Hormuz became a key piece of information in the impeachment trial of the Duke of Buckingham. As a man with considerable wealth, influence, and the ear of the king, Buckingham had acquired a number of enemies over the years, and in 1626 Parliament drew up articles of impeachment as a way to force him from power. Buckingham's receipt of £10,000 for Hormuz and the £2,000 gratuity before that constituted one of the charges against him in his impeachment trial. Although in 1624 Parliament had criticized the Company, in 1626 Parliament allied with it. The criticism of the Company that was so prominent in 1624 never emerged in 1626.[121] Some mariners did exhibit a petition that they had showed Parliament in 1624, and the Company was required to answer it in the House of Lords, but otherwise, the Company escaped negative parliamentary attention in 1626.[122] Instead, the parliamentary subcommittee investigating Buckingham sought the Company's aid in preparing for his impeachment case.

Open enthusiasm for the impeachment of the king's favorite on the part of the Company would have risked alienating the king, but the court of committees' circumspect aid to the parliamentary subcommittee suggested some enthusiasm for Buckingham's prosecution. Members of the court of committees spoke at length with members of the subcommittee and allowed them access to registered Company documents and records, including payment receipts for the £22,000 (£10,000 to James, £10,000 to Buckingham, and the original £2,000 gratuity to Buckingham). Subcommittee members ordered the Company's secretary to separate out the relevant records and "bundle them up apart, and to keep them safely in a box by themselves," in case anyone needed to consult them again. Yet the minutes presented the Company's aid in terms of required, involuntary action, disavowing Company agency or choice. Company leaders complied because Parliament was "of such a commanding power, as is not fit to be resisted or dallied with." The minutes carefully mentioned that the court of committees collected the Hormuz records separately for convenience and to preserve the secrecy of the rest of its affairs from the subcommittee, "and for no other cause."[123] The minutes omitted any mention of whether or not the subcommittee conferred at any other time with Company leaders.

Parliamentary debate on Hormuz in 1626 sided firmly with the Company. From the introductory question—"What ships have been unnecessarily stayed of merchants?"—the account of Hormuz presented in Parliament was highly sympathetic to the Company. The member who introduced the topic in the impeachment committee, Sir Edward Spencer, referred to the 1624 legal opinions that Buckingham as lord admiral had no right to a tenth of the goods. He presented the shortage of mariners and bullion—the ostensible reasoning Parliament used in 1624—as a blind to cover Buckingham's rapacious claims. At the end of Spencer's speech, the committee resolved that Buckingham's actions represented an "undue exacting and extorting."[124] When the full House of Commons took up the matter two days later, it reiterated Buckingham's "pretense" in staying the ships. It argued that the duke's right to a tenth, if it existed, would not have been negated if he had allowed the ships to go. By holding them to force the Company's compliance, Buckingham had actively extorted money from the Company.[125] This talk of "pretense" and "extortion" was not only a far cry from the hostility of two years before, but it also suggested that the parliamentary committee had indeed relied heavily on Company accounts of the event.

The treatment of the case in the House of Lords was even more pointedly in the Company's favor. Members discussed Buckingham's "unlawfully pretended" right to the goods. The Earl of Bridgewater argued that Buckingham thought Hormuz a "fit subject for him to exact and extort some great sum of money." His position as lord admiral had functioned as a springboard for malfeasance: Buckingham had used the "color of the said office of lord admiral of England, and out of his power and greatness, his office being used for a ground work of his design."[126] Bridgewater had done his research: His speech mentioned particular ships and the goods carried on them. He referred to the monsoons and wind patterns that would have prohibited the year's Company fleet from reaching the East Indies had Buckingham managed to continue his stay of the ships, and he recounted the day-by-day negotiations that led to the Company's agreeing to pay James and Buckingham in return for allowing the ships to sail. Lastly, he mentioned the names of Company members present at various meetings.[127] In short, his speech drew heavily on the Company records that the court of committees had made available.

The resurrection of Hormuz in Buckingham's impeachment trial marked the end of its afterlife. The Company never got its money back and Parliament never got its impeachment, as Charles dissolved it before the trial's conclusion. Nor did Parliament remain an ally of the Company, despite this moment of accord. English involvement in Hormuz had proceeded without a long-term plan or much thought to consequences. Political considerations at court determined its meaning in London, which altered as those considerations changed. By 1626 other events—notably, those at Amboyna—had surpassed Hormuz as an immediate concern for the Company. Yet at a fundamental level the English involvement in Hormuz forced the Company and state to grapple with their relationship. The positions each formulated were not clearly defined, nor were they always legally or logically consistent, but they illustrated how events at the fringes of English influence could play an unexpectedly large role in domestic affairs. The drawn-out struggle to determine what Hormuz meant attested to both the difficulties and the promises of integrating Company activities abroad into the political world of London and Whitehall.

The fall of Hormuz and Warwick's privateering venture tested both legal categories and customs. Like many other episodes in the early history of the Company, they ended with little conclusive resolution of the exact form and requirements of the relationship between Company and state. Indeed, cases such as these revealed just how complicated that relationship could be, as policy and jurisdictional issues collided with favor and influence at court. They showed the fine line in the relationship between Company and crown between being mutually beneficial and being coercive, with either side capable (at times) of coercing the other. Both the English involvement in Hormuz and Warwick's voyage helped determine how the regime and

Company approached each other in the years after the Company's establishment. Company leaders saw both as setting precedent for future actions. Yet it was the political requirements of the 1610s and 1620s, more than theoretical legal concepts, that shaped contemporary understandings of the episodes. Answers to conceptual questions, such as how the Company's activities abroad fit into England's foreign policy and to what degree the Company coincided with the state abroad, evolved to address specific circumstances in the period. The same interplay between domestic politics and East India affairs became increasingly evident in the aftermath of the events at Amboyna.

8

The Dutch East India Company and Amboyna

Crisis and Response in the Company

ON 9 MARCH 1623, ten English East India Company men were beheaded at Amboyna in the Moluccas at the order of Herman van Speult, the Dutch East India Company governor of the island. The Englishmen had been accused of plotting with Japanese mercenaries to overthrow the Dutch. They were shortly tried and executed, along with nine of their supposed Japanese co-conspirators.[1] When news of the legal proceedings and deaths of the English factors reached London in May 1624, it prompted an existential crisis for the Company about the meaning and purpose of the East Indies trade. This began a years-long attempt by Company leaders to secure restitution for the deaths of the ten Company men.

The problem of Amboyna tested the Company and the regime in different ways. For Company leaders and members, the event became a measure of the future viability of the East Indies trade, as they discovered how willing or unwilling the monarch was to protect the Company when that protection imperiled other aims of the regime. For the monarch, the Company's repeated insistence on martial reprisals against the Dutch endangered other political aims relating to England's role in the Thirty Years' War.

The events at Amboyna involved more than just the regime and the Company, however. More than any other event involving the Company in the early seventeenth century, Amboyna drew the attention of people outside the Company. Newsletter writers, diplomats, ministers, and others followed the event. They wrote their own meanings onto Amboyna, employing it to prove a variety of points about religion, trade, and war. Happy to use public appeal as a tool, as they had been since their initial forays into pamphleteering in the response to Robert Kayll in 1614, Company leaders also tried to promote their version of Amboyna, and thus their version of how the regime should respond.

Amboyna became the crucible in which the weaknesses in the mutually beneficial relationship between the Company and the regime that generally had characterized the first decades of the Company's existence were tested. This chapter examines the first attempts by the Company to secure restitution, when its leaders explored a variety of techniques and seemed to have public opinion on their side. When they first learned what had happened at Amboyna, the leaders announced that the state would respond swiftly and in favor of the Company. As months passed, however, first James I and then Charles I balked at pressing the Dutch for restitution. Company leaders tried to tip the scales in their favor, using tools of public appeal to keep the issue alive in the public imagination and compel action by the state. All their efforts, however well-executed and well-conceived, foundered as the king prioritized other diplomatic aims of the regime. The Company ultimately failed to secure the restitution its leaders wanted, leading many in the Company to question the viability of the East Indies trade and their trust in the monarch to protect their interests.

The English and Dutch East India Companies before Amboyna: Cooperation and Competition in the East

The events at Amboyna were not the opening gambit in Anglo-Dutch relations in the East Indies. Indeed, what happened at Amboyna was actually the culmination of years of intermittent skirmishes and failed attempts at diplomacy between the English and Dutch East India Companies, and between England and the United Provinces. It marked the inability of a treaty reached only a few years earlier, in 1619—which had taken almost a decade to negotiate and was intended to govern Anglo-Dutch relations in the East Indies—to prevent bloodshed between the two companies.

In the early 1600s, the Dutch, the English, and the Portuguese were the predominant European nations active in the East Indies, and thus they often viewed each other as commercial rivals. The English viewed the

Catholic Portuguese as their natural enemies but had more complicated attitudes toward the Dutch, viewing their coreligionists sometimes as allies and sometimes as competitors, depending on affairs both in the East Indies and in Europe.[2] The example of the Dutch had long proved a spur to English efforts in the East Indies.[3] The petition to start an East Indies company drawn up by interested English merchants in 1599 had mentioned the success of several Dutch voyages to the East Indies. It also noted that English merchants loved their country and commonwealth no less than the Dutch loved theirs, evoking the sense of rivalry that English merchants often felt toward their Dutch counterparts.[4] That rivalry did not abate with the establishment of English trading ventures in the East.

By 1609, tensions between the Dutch and English East India Companies in the East Indies had become matters for English and Dutch diplomats to discuss. In that year, commissioners between James and the States General (the governing body of the United Provinces) addressed matters including an agreement for how to share or divide the trade in the East Indies.[5] This agreement proved largely ineffective in the years that followed. In November 1611, Company leaders petitioned the Earl of Salisbury for aid in securing redress for injuries received at Dutch hands while seeking to "enjoy the benefit and freedom of trade" in the East Indies.[6] Sir Ralph Winwood, the English ambassador at The Hague, brought the complaints of the Company to the States General—though he doubted that the Dutch East India Company would follow its government's lead, observing that the corporation's leaders "will not acknowledge the authority of the States General more than shall be for their private profit."[7] This was one example of what became a familiar occurrence: the English ambassador to the Netherlands regularly received instructions, when he set out for his post or by letter, to address some complaint of the Company against the Dutch.[8] Furthermore, the Dutch were as likely to complain of English abuses against them in the East Indies as the English were to complain of the Dutch.

The friction between the English and Dutch East India Companies was due in part to the different styles of their commercial ventures. From capitalization to preferred mode of trade in the East Indies, the companies approached the trade differently. The initial capital that the Dutch East India Company raised was £550,000, in contrast to the £63,373 raised by the Company for its first voyage.[9] Participants in the trade on both sides noted the differences between the Dutch style of trade in the East Indies, which followed the Portuguese model and depended on fortifications, and the "simple trade" in which the English engaged, which proceeded without fortifications or open use of force.[10] Additionally, the differences in the governments of the two nations and the two companies led to the sense, at least on the English side, that the Dutch East India Company enjoyed greater support from the state than the English East India Company did. When comparing the two, Company minutes noted that it existed at the pleasure of the king, while the Dutch maintained its company with the state. An English writer outside of the Company observed that "the States [that is, the Dutch] look upon this trade into the East Indies as a high point of state."[11]

A greater source of tension between the two companies was the news that arrived with almost every fleet of skirmishes between the Dutch and the English in the East Indies. Conflicts between Europeans in the East Indies were not uncommon—each nation built its success partly on the failures of its European competitors. For example, the Dutch East India Company took Amboyna from the Portuguese in 1605 to consolidate its control over the spice trade, while an English victory over Portuguese ships helped persuade the Mughal emperor Jahangir to allow English traders into his realm. Initially the English and Dutch East India Companies cooperated in the East Indies. After the signing of the 1609 treaty between the Dutch and the Spanish, however, the Dutch had less need of their English allies in Europe, and there was open rivalry between the English and Dutch companies in the East Indies.[12] By 1619, the Dutch and English in the Indonesian archipelago were essentially at war.[13] One possible way to manage conflict was to negotiate some kind of diplomatic arrangement between the companies.

The form of diplomatic arrangement was open to discussion. One intriguing possibility was to join the companies in some manner. The plan was advocated sometimes by the Dutch and sometimes by the English, but never by both at the same time. The benefit of the plan, as one observer put it, was that the companies would then "live together in good amity, and . . . be master over the Portugal in those islands."[14] Whatever form unification might take, it would ease relations between the two rivals and allow them together to achieve an aim of both—to triumph over the Portuguese in trade and might. This union would not be a full integration of the two companies, but an agreement to share profits and expenses for defense in the East Indies and potentially to send their fleets together. It would also mean negotiating who had proprietary rights in different parts of the East Indies and therefore where each company would be allowed to trade.

Merchants in the companies and government officials in both countries put forward a variety of possible ways to unite the companies in the 1610s. Commissioners traveling between England and the Netherlands in 1613 and 1615 discussed the proposals formally, though with little resolution. Writing from The Hague in 1613, for example, Winwood informed the Company's governor, Sir Thomas Smith, that the Dutch commissioners were not authorized to promise much.[15] In 1614, between commissions, the leaders of the Company advocated joining the Dutch in a defensive league in the East Indies against the Portuguese, but otherwise more or less leaving each other alone. The Dutch ambassador in London, Sir Noel Caron, was interested in some form of union and remained so even though Company leaders warned him that James would not support an offensive league against Spain in Europe, only a league in the East Indies against the Portuguese.[16] The four English commissioners sent in 1615 included two men picked by the Company. An observer noted that James's nominees were sent "with two merchants" to handle "certain difficulties betwixt us and them touching the trade of the East Indies."[17] The Company leaders' aim at that point was to avoid a united joint stock, and though both James and the Dutch encouraged the idea, the second commission ended as the first one had—with no real resolution.

The Company's leaders continued to frame their opposition to a united joint stock in terms of their reluctance to become inveigled into participating in a war against Spain. Even after the failure of the 1615 commission, their information indicated that Caron was still promoting the idea of an Anglo-Dutch joint stock to the king, with James prepared to hear proposals on the matter.[18] The Company prepared a response emphasizing the different characters of English and Dutch overseas trade, with the Dutch pursuing a more martial approach: the Company argued that it wanted a "peaceable and quiet trade," while war with Spain was "the main scope and drift" of the Dutch Company.[19] Years later Caron still advocated the proposal, arguing that together, the English and the Dutch would be "able to give the law to others in the Indies," though the united joint stock was never fully realized.[20]

What aided Company leaders in their resistance were surges of popular anti-Dutch feeling that occurred with the intermittent arrival of news of Dutch depredations against the English in the East Indies. In 1618, for example, accounts of Dutch cruelties to the English in the Banda Islands prompted one newsletter writer to observe that "here is loud speech of ill measure offered by the Hollanders," and that "if matters be so foul as they are made [out to be], it will be hard to reconcile them, and in the meantime it breeds ill blood."[21] This type of news could change diplomatic alliances: in its wake, Spanish and Portuguese representatives made overtures to the Company's governor.[22] Meanwhile, Secretary of State Sir Robert Naunton wrote to Sir Dudley Carleton, the English ambassador at The Hague, that all of London was angry at the Dutch for their actions in the East Indies. His letters testified to the Company's success in transforming actions of the Dutch East India Company against the English East India Company into Dutch actions against the English, making the Company worthy of the monarch's protection. Naunton wrote of the "resentment which the Dutch have given to all that have any sense at all of the honor of his Majesty and of our whole nation."[23]

Anti-Dutch feeling was widespread among various groups and was encouraged by the Company. George Abbot, the archbishop of Canterbury and brother of Sir Morris Abbot, wrote to Carleton about the "insufferable" acts of the Dutch against the king and English nation, and Naunton wrote to Carleton that if the commissioners could not give satisfaction for the activities in the East Indies, he doubted "our people's patience will hardly be forced by the authority of the state to endure such foul insolencies and indignities unrequited."[24] Both of these writers presented the matter as one that touched the English state and as a crime against the king and nation—one that might provoke the king's subjects to actions that the authority of the state could not control. Presumably to further the anti-Dutch feeling of James and others, the Company made arrangements with a long-time employee to write "a relation of the Dutch towards the English in the Indies," though they did not elaborate on how they planned to use the manuscript.[25]

In the face of possible conflict, an Anglo-Dutch commission once again tackled the possibility of a diplomatic resolution to the difficulties between the two companies in 1619. James wanted this commission to end in a proper treaty, and he appointed several privy councilors to oversee the East Indies negotiations.[26] A number of Company men (including many of the leaders) attended the negotiations as English representatives, and though the main meetings took place at Merchant Taylors Hall, the English representatives as a whole (not only those who were also Company men) sometimes met at

Smith's house. Their presence and actions, and even the location of the meetings, highlighted the overt involvement of the Company in these affairs of state.[27]

Despite lengthy disagreements between the English and Dutch commissioners, in 1619 the two sides came to an agreement that became known as the Accord of 1619. Antonio Donato and Pier Antonio Marioni, Venetian ambassadors in England, both noted that only the king's direct intervention in the negotiations had allowed the two sides to reach a compromise.[28] James had pushed the Company to accept the treaty: "the King hath dissolved the difficulties of the East India business and by his own wisdom and authority brought them to accord, which being indeed said to be his own act, they are to acknowledge his gracious and pacifical disposition."[29] English observers were of two minds about the treaty. One wrote that "the other" (meaning the Dutch) had come out better in the negotiations, and that everyone suspected that the Dutch "have found great friends, and made much use of their wicked mammon." He added that "our men shall never have like means and advantage," and that the opportunity for a better settlement was "lost, and the heat cooled."[30] Another observer thought that the treaty was wonderful and hoped that within a few years "the interests of both nations in those parts will be so united and incorporated together as all further cause of difficulties or jealousies in that behalf will be taken away." He wrote that "all honest men here do rejoice" at the signing of the treaty, and he hoped that the treaty would be the first step to "renew the ancient amity and good correspondence" between the English and the Dutch.[31]

The accord was meant to govern relations between the English and the Dutch in the East Indies for the next twenty years. It did not unify the two companies but was supposed to end their competition in the East. The accord specified what share of the trade each nation's company would have in specific places. Thus, for example, by the terms of the accord the Company was supposed to have one-third of the import and export trade in the Moluccas, Banda, and Amboyna, while the pepper trade from Java was to be divided equally between the two companies. Each one was supposed to provide ten warships, and a joint council of defense with members from both companies would specify the numbers of smaller ships required of the two companies and coordinate their movements. Dutch forts would remain solely Dutch, but any new forts acquired through a joint effort would be held jointly. The English monarch and the Dutch States General would resolve disputes between the two companies when and if they arose.[32]

By 1619, Company leaders had already developed procedures for managing the seemingly inevitable conflicts between the English and Dutch East India Companies in the East Indies. The leaders resorted to the monarch for aid and had relationships with relevant diplomats. They were thus connected to wider state networks. Aside from official channels, they also sought to harness the anti-Dutch feeling stirred up by news from the East Indies. Indeed, they had even begun to explore ways they might create anti-Dutch feeling by preparing written narratives of their version of contested events in the East Indies.

Meant to last for two decades, the peace enacted by the 1619 accord lasted only years, though officially the treaty remained in force. The news of the execution of English men by the Dutch East India Company in Amboyna flew in the face of the amity supposedly secured by the treaty. It immediately raised the question of what exactly the Company's relationship to the state was, and exactly what the state owed the Company in terms of protection. When James sent a message to the Company shortly after the 1619 treaty was concluded, he had told them that it would, with time, achieve all their desires in the East Indies, and that if the Dutch should attempt to subvert those desires, "that quarrel should be no longer the Company's but of the state."[33] After Amboyna, however, as the Company sought aid first from James and then from Charles to secure restitution and did not get it, Company leaders came to think that they had very good reason to distrust what they saw as the regime's promise to back Company interests with the power of the state.

Amboyna: The Initial Response

Amboyna effectively changed the Company's political reality, as from that point on Company leaders saw securing either restitution or reprisals from the Dutch East India Company as one of their prime objectives, in the face of what they perceived as wavering support from the English state. The regime's continuing inability and disinclination to secure the restitutions the Company desired led many of the leaders to reexamine the relationship between their trade and the state and to question the ongoing feasibility of the trade when it relied upon such shaky support. Amboyna revealed some of the fundamental differences between the aims of the Company and those of the regime—even though, in the course of the negotiations, each ostensibly affirmed its commitment to the other.

The problem of Amboyna for the Company and the problem of Amboyna for the regime were not the same. For the court of committees, the events at Amboyna demonstrated the vulnerability of the Company's trade in the East Indies. The initial and subsequently repeated inability of Company leaders to secure restitution in the years after the event then revealed the fragility of the Company's position in England. This perceived weakness was an issue that Company leaders had to address to prove the ongoing viability of the trade to the Company's own generality and thus secure continued financial support by adventurers. The actions of Company leaders, therefore, had to persuade two different audiences—the regime and the Company's membership—of two different messages: to take action on the Company's behalf, and that the trade was secure for the future, respectively.[34]

For the regime, the calls for restitution for Amboyna constituted unexpected and unwelcome complications that might wreck the monarch's attempts to stay out of (in the case of James) or enter (in the case of Charles) a European war. James had spent most of his reign trying to avoid costly military entanglements. He balanced his pro-Spanish and pro-Dutch courtiers and officials and did not commit England to war, though after the outbreak of the Thirty Years' War, this became increasingly difficult. In contrast, Charles dearly wanted to ally with the Dutch and the Palatinate and enter the war. In 1624, it looked as though Charles and Buckingham would succeed in nudging James into the conflict. They had assembled a "patriot" coalition, a group of courtiers and members of Parliament united primarily by their desire to push James to enter the continental war. Most of these men were anti-Spanish, pro-Dutch, and pro-Palatinate. In 1624 under their influence, Parliament repudiated treaties with Spain and granted James large sums of money to go to war, and the proposed Spanish match for Charles that had been tentatively explored for a decade was definitively abandoned. Dutch commissioners spent the spring and summer in England, waiting to negotiate a treaty with James to secure his aid and involvement in the war. There was considerable and widespread support for war, though James still balked. In short, news of Amboyna and the wrench it might throw into proposed alliances and finely balanced commitments for those who either wanted or wanted to avoid war, came at a particularly inopportune time.[35]

The first word that all was not well in the East Indies arrived in England in late May 1624. The settlement with James and Buckingham for the spoils of Hormuz had occupied the Company's attention in early 1624, and the final payments to James did not take place until July 1624—but once news of Amboyna arrived, that eclipsed all other topics. On 28 May, Carleton wrote a letter to Secretary of State Edward Conway from his post in the Netherlands that included a relation of the events at Amboyna. On 31 May, Company minutes show that the court of committees had received letters describing those events.[36] And by that date, Company leaders had already informed the king of the business. As Governor Morris Abbot reported, he had

> made known unto his Majesty that which (as things now stand) he was sorry had so happened, and that was, that by letters out of the Indies the Company have been advertised that in the Moluccas the Dutch have without all humanity and contrary to the Treaty without a lawful trial before the Council of Defense of both Nations, upon evidences and confessions extorted to the violence of torments and no other witnesses than the heathens allied and linked with the Dutch put to death ten of the factors and servants of the English in the Moluccas upon pretense of a practice intended by the English against the Dutch in those parts, where the forces of the Dutch are so far above those of the English as there is no proportion between them.[37]

Abbot's account, as he conveyed it to the court of committees, related both abhorrence of the news and shock at what the Company saw as the illegality of the Dutch actions. He reported that James had expressed disbelief at such foul deeds, but Abbot had explained that the Company's information came from complaints made by the Company's president and council in the Indies—in other words, from factors they trusted in the East Indies and who, therefore, could be believed. James asked the Company to give copies of the complaints to Conway and assured Abbot that he would be pleased to act on the Company's behalf if the accusations were true: if "it be proved there will be ways now for his Majesty to force them to reparation."[38]

If the reports from Amboyna could be confirmed, and James did indeed push the Dutch for reparations, it would have presented a major setback for Dutch sympathizers at court who were trying to persuade James to go to war. The Company leaders were aware of and concerned about this possible source of opposition. The minutes noted that "it was said that the Company is much blamed by some, for that now in a time when his Majesty had resolved to aid the Dutch, the Company had published the putting of ten

English men to death in the Moluccas, which had made a stand in that resolution."[39] In other words, Company leaders knew they would be and were being blamed for hindering the efforts to convince James to provide material support to the Dutch in their rebellion from Habsburg Spain—or rather, that their decision to spread the news of the massacre just when it would do the most damage to the pro-Dutch group was being criticized. Only two weeks before, after difficult negotiations, Charles and the patriot coalition had been able to conclude a treaty with the Dutch that would pave the way for England's entry into the war.[40] The news from Amboyna delayed James's signing of the Treaty of London for at least several days.[41] The first notice of Amboyna in the letters from the Venetian ambassador in England acknowledged the political consequences, noting that those "in whom the old hostility and rivalry with the Dutch still flourish" were eager to condemn the events at Amboyna, and that the "Hispanophiles" sought to "increase the exasperation" and increase tensions between the English and the Dutch.[42]

Members of the court of committees rehearsed answers to the charge of stirring up anti-Dutch feeling. They explained to themselves that by the terms of the 1619 treaty, they were supposed to keep James apprised of the state of the trade, and that James himself had told them, when they attended him in his bedchamber, that "if he heard nothing of them, he should believe that all is well." To remain silent in this case would therefore be to deceive the monarch. As secretary of state, Conway in particular wished to know more of the business, and Company leaders resolved that "for the better manifestation of the truth," they would copy the protests about the "slaughter" and send them to him.[43] However, Conway was a firm believer in the Protestant cause and a member of the pro-Dutch lobby (he had named one of his daughters Brilliana in tribute to her place of birth, the English-garrisoned town of Brill), and he may have also been informing himself about the complaints he might have to rebut to keep James committed to a pro-Dutch foreign policy.[44]

The news from Amboyna left Company members feeling particularly vulnerable and prompted soul-searching about the objectives of their trade. The court of committees considered the trade itself, noting that "the Company suffers both by their false friends the Dutch abroad and common obloquy at home, where everyone cries out against the trade, and the Company suffers and is subject to common reproach." The one thing Company leaders were sure about was that they could count on James: they waited on "the pleasure of the state," certain that the regime'would act "to call for an account of the lives of the king's subjects."[45] At this point in mid-June, they did not seem doubtful that James would succor them in this matter, nor was there any reason for them to doubt. Thus, while they worried that various opponents targeted the Company, they trusted that the regime would protect, if not necessarily the trade per se, at least the English subjects who carried out the trade.[46]

The Company got new ammunition when two English ships arrived from the East Indies in June. John Chamberlain wrote to Carleton that the ships brought a "fresh cry against the tyranny and injustice of the Hollanders towards our men lately murthered or executed there."[47] The ships brought not just news, but also witnesses: several Company men sent home as prisoners and others who had been exonerated who could speak about the events. The Company resolved to send them to speak with Sir Henry Marten, who had handled much of the Company's legal business and was a judge of the Admiralty court. They also resolved to send the men to speak with one Mr. Skinner, whom they had appointed to write an account of the events. Skinner was to produce "some relation of the truth," as rumors were already circulating to justify the Dutch, claiming that what the Company regarded as a cruel murder was instead a just execution.[48]

As Company leaders waited on James, Amboyna was debated and discussed ever more widely in letters and at court. Chamberlain described the "barbarous" deed to Carleton and commented that regardless of the truth of the accusations against the men, they should not have been treated in such a way. The Company and its supporters, Chamberlain wrote, were disheartened by the news and "cannot speak nor hear of this their [the Dutch] insolence without much indignation."[49] Another observer reported that the Company was even considering ending the trade over this event because it was "so discouraged with the last outrage committed upon their factors." This observer also noted that the repercussions for the Dutch were dire, as the event made "the Hollanders to be very ill spoken of even by their friends."[50] Another writer shared similar impressions, repeating that Company leaders were "in consultation to relinquish their trade" and adding that the news had "distasted all sorts of people here and breeds ill blood."[51] The Venetian ambassadors to the Netherlands noted that news of the incident at Amboyna had severely damaged negotiations for English military aid to the Dutch. "This severity towards the subjects of a king who has acted as their benefactor, has excited much feeling in London," they wrote, "and will have delayed the king's signature to the treaty, despite the representations of the prince and Buckingham."[52] Thus, even without any effort by Company leaders to stir up feeling, the Company's disheartening troubles had become known, and the events at Amboyna were having a negative impact on Anglo-Dutch ties in Europe.

The court of committees officially informed the generality of the news at the court of election in early July, though given the circulation of news about Amboyna through London, many Company members had surely already learned of the event. The message to the generality as recorded in the minutes presented the matter as an "insufferable torment" and as "unspeakable tyrannies," and that although the Dutch might try to justify their actions, God was the "avenger of all such bloody acts." Company leaders assured the generality that they had taken what action they could. They still hoped "that the state will take care of the Company," but they had also "set [the story] down in writing to be published."[53] This was the first indication that Company leaders planned to publish their own account of Amboyna— presumably the one they had set Skinner to compose—to make a public issue of the executions, using skills they had developed in public appeals over the previous decade. A week later, when the writing was completed, the leaders called another meeting of the generality (which rarely met so frequently) to read the entire account out loud. It was so long that they could read only a shortened version of it, but presumably they read enough to get their interpretation of what happened at Amboyna across. They held copies of the account ready for distribution, but at this point no copies were to be released without permission from the governor, in an effort to control how and when their story would circulate.[54] Though these were manuscript copies, the idea of printing them was already being mentioned.[55]

The reading prompted a discussion in the general court of what Amboyna meant for the trade. Members declared that to continue, the Company needed both restitution and a guarantee of protection in the future as "it was held impossible for them to proceed in the trade, except a real restitution be first made . . . as also that security be given for the prevention of the like hereafter, all which if they may not be obtained there is no help, but the trade must be let fall." This blunt formulation made it clear that the members did not want to be bought off with just promises, and in the absence of "real" restitution, the trade itself would have to cease.[56] Company leaders resolved to petition the king to seek recompense, drawing the analogy that, as it was the Company's duty to seek reparation for the lives of its servants, so it was the monarch's honor to seek reparation for the lives of his subjects. Both parties had a responsibility to act.[57]

Days later a deputation of Company leaders delivered the petition and a copy of the Amboyna narrative to the king. They told him how disheartened they were by the fact that no action had yet been taken, and how tempted they were to leave the trade. James promised action and told them to proceed in good heart; he would, he promised, get them reparations "by the strength of his own arm" if the Dutch did not offer it themselves.[58] He then turned the petition over to the Privy Council, with instructions to resolve the matter within a month or he would take it into his own hands.[59] On later occasions James would repeat that he did not want the Company to leave the trade. He even offered to become an adventurer in the Company should that course appeal to the membership (this was the first of the offers of royal membership that the Company found so important and yet difficult to decline). Despite any concerns that Conway may have harbored about the effects of Amboyna on an Anglo-Dutch treaty, he also sent a message of support, informing Company leaders that the Privy Council wished "that the East India Trade be continued in so much as it is become a business of state."[60] In sum, the message that the leaders received from the Privy Council and king was that the regime would act decisively and quickly on their behalf, and that they had the full support of the state for their Company and trade.

At the same time that James, Conway, and other lords of the Privy Council were expressing solidarity with the Company, however, Conway was also cautioning Company leaders to be circumspect about fueling public feelings about Amboyna, and with whom they were sharing news. He sent them a copy of James's letter to Carleton at The Hague but warned them not to circulate it widely: "I doubt not," he wrote, "but according to your wisdom and good discretion you will use this copy with that moderation as is fitting a matter of state of so great consequence, not suffering it to be causelessly divulged." Only share the letter, he wrote, when there was real benefit to be gained by doing so.[61] In other words, Carleton was cautioning the Company against the type of public exposure they would stir up by publishing their Amboyna narrative.

The narrative, however, seemed to be working, at least with the very limited audience of the generality, king, and Privy Council. When Company leaders were called to the Council table a few days later, they read the entire lengthy narrative to the councilors. The governor reported that the narrative "moved passion in their lordships, and stirred them up to a good affection to procure that the Company be righted." If indeed that was the response engendered by the reading of the narrative, then it was as effective as could be hoped for, in that it predisposed the councilors toward the Company and moved them to resolve the matter in the Company's favor.[62] The councilors asked the Company representatives to report in a few days what they wanted the Council and monarch to do.[63] The same sort of effusive estimation of how affected the councilors were by the narrative entered into public knowledge, and one newsletter writer reported that when the matter was opened and the pamphlet read, "some of [the councilors] shed tears." He did not doubt, he said, that the Company would receive some satisfaction.[64]

A mixed court with committees and various members of the generality met to discuss the Privy Council's demand for specific requests with regard to Amboyna. Those in attendance agreed to reiterate their need for the monarch to give them "real protection": "that except the Company may have real protection from his Majesty as the French and Dane [*sic*] do to their subjects, there will be no possibility to proceed in the trade." In terms of retribution, they wanted several things. First, they demanded that the principal perpetrators be sent to England as hostages until reparations were received. Second, they asked for permission to seize Dutch ships in the Channel, by letters of marque if necessary, to make up for the English stock lost to the Dutch at Amboyna. Company leaders noted that if they could use force in the Channel, "it will give life to the business" and prove to investors that the Company was still viable.[65] Third, they requested the liberty to build forts and use them in the East Indies. The group of Company members added one last request: that the crown and Privy Council abandon the idea of joining the English and Dutch East India Companies, as the Dutch had proven untrustworthy.

While the Company postponed publicly printing its account of Amboyna, the Dutch were quicker off the mark. By August, the Company had received a Dutch printed book on Amboyna, along with an open letter to the Company from the Dutch East India Company. The book, dated July 1624, was in Dutch and, like the letter, portrayed the trial and executions at Amboyna as a logical course of action in the face of a possible plot.[66] Company leaders decided to use what they saw as a vicious mangling of the truth of the events to give urgency to their complaints. They took a translation of the Dutch book and the letter from the Dutch East India Company to the king and tried to use them to force him to give the Company permission to take Dutch ships at sea.[67] Company leaders also decided to print their account of the events of Amboyna, despite Conway's earlier suggestion that they not fuel public discussion of the matter. It would not be an anonymous libel, as the Dutch account was, they decided, but would be published with the full "avow" of the Company.[68] Their commentary on the events at Amboyna would have the force of the Company behind it, at least in the sense that the Company's name would be publicly associated with the printed account.

The original date that James had set for settling restitution for Amboyna was 12 August, yet that date came and went without any settlement. To try and "quicken" the matter, Company leaders took the translated copy of the Dutch book to court to show the king and lords of the Privy Council.[69] By September, however, some of the sympathy the Company had initially enjoyed after the news of Amboyna reached England had dissipated. Chamberlain, who had been so sympathetic to the Company earlier, noted that no solution seemed to content its leaders: "what answer soever they have, they seem not satisfied." Not only was sympathy evaporating, but the Company was starting to seem like the difficult party, refusing acceptable solutions. Conway, Chamberlain wrote to Carleton, seemed to be turning back to the Dutch side in the matter.[70] Another writer noted that the situation remained largely unresolved, and that he was disturbed by the indiscretion of the merchants, who seemed so set on revenge.[71]

What had started as an existential crisis for the Company—with members questioning whether or not to continue the trade—began to appear to some as more like a bargaining chip in negotiations with the regime. In discussions with James, for example, Company leaders still maintained that they would leave the trade, to which James's response was that he "utterly dislikes the Company's intimation." This did not stop them. They answered that they required proper recognition of their need for royal protection and support, and "that if this business of the Dutch might be righted, and the Company countenanced at home, they would pursue the trade royally." If James did not satisfy them, they would leave it. James once more promised to attend to the business, agreeing to appoint a number of lords to a commission to investigate the matter.[72] About the book they wanted to publish, he added that he would "like it well if it contained no bitterness against the States [that is, the Netherlands]." This demonstrated a distinct change in the tenor of how he viewed Amboyna and the Company, with his frustration at the Company's demands increasingly evident.[73] His commission, likewise, treated the court of committees with "rough entertainment and hard admittance" and had some of the proceedings from earlier courts of committees cast up to them for explanation.[74] As the court of committees learned more of this commission, Company leaders increasingly came to see it as a gesture rather than an actual solution. The commission was not under the broad seal, or great seal, but presumably under the lesser privy seal, and the chief justices and admiralty judge on the commission turned out to be there merely in an advisory capacity. Most important, the commission had authority only to "hear and report," not to "hear and determine." In other words, it had no teeth.[75] When Company leaders once more made noises about leaving the trade, they were told it was not their place to make this decision and that "it is not for a private company to contend with a state."[76]

After a confusing meeting with the commission in September, Company leaders did get one significant concession. The commission would not free them of the treaty with the Dutch, telling them the treaty merely needed to be fixed so that the "dangerous interpretation of the Dutch" could not be repeated. Yet despite not releasing them from the treaty, the commissioners assured Company leaders that James did want to fix the problem. That said, their protestations, as recorded in the minutes, had an air of defensiveness: "his Majesty is graciously resolved to right the Company really." The concession that James gave via the commission—and it was a substantial one—was that he had ordered the lord admiral to arrest any Dutch ships arriving or leaving through the Channel until "full reparation" was made.[77] This was seen as a concession by others, though the Company did not label it as such. As one newsletter writer observed, "the merchants of the East India Company have so far prevailed that the king signified his pleasure unto them" by ordering the lord admiral to seize Dutch ships.[78]

The concession meant a great deal to the Company. A Company representative asked Conway to have the order entered in the books of the Privy Council and for the Company to have a copy of it.[79] For Conway's aid in the matter, the Company presented him with a £100 gratuity.[80] Having made sure that the order was documented as thoroughly as possible, the court of committees then debated how to present this promise of action to the generality. Some members noted that the lords who had been instrumental in securing the warrant would expect that the Company be somewhat public about the warrant: "it is expected by some whose favor the Company hath used in this business." Others thought that the actual seizure of Dutch ships would be the best way to make the warrant public. The "work will publish itself," the court of committees noted, as its members did not doubt "but that his Majesty's purpose and promise of justice would be really performed."[81] Once again, this language hinted at an underlying anxiety about James's intentions, though overall, they still seemed to believe that he truly meant to support them.

Company leaders' anxiety about the regime's support against the Dutch was at odds with international perceptions of the regime's actions in the case. The letters of Venetian ambassadors across Europe reported a very different story from that of the Company. In early August, the Venetian ambassador to the Netherlands, Alvise Contarini, noted the determined attempts on the Company's behalf by Carleton, the English ambassador, as Carleton insisted "more than ever upon the punishment of the governor of Amboyna."[82] As Company leaders watched the original deadline of 12 August pass, Contarini noted that James continued to push for the Company, that he demanded punishment, compensation, and "reparation to his subjects whose honor he consider[ed] seriously impugned." Contarini emphasized once more Carleton's work for the Company, including that he had managed to get a Dutch East India Company book about Amboyna banned and publicly disapproved by the Dutch government.[83] Every mention of Amboyna by Venetian ambassadors at various locations expressed the view that James and his ambassadors were pushing hard for some resolution to the matter, particularly in terms of reparations to the Company. One letter from Contarini noted that Carleton pressed so hard, presenting a "very mordant paper" about Amboyna, that the Dutch had sent to France to learn if Carleton truthfully represented matters, with some suggesting that Carleton was hardly disinterested as he had many relatives in the Company.[84] Letters through the end of the year continued to mention that the English pressed the matter of Amboyna, though by mid-October they also suggested that James was being "mollified" by the Dutch government's promises to ensure satisfaction. From that point on, most accounts portrayed Carleton as acting more on the behalf of the Company than of the king in his ongoing efforts to secure restitution, as he continued to push in his role as English ambassador to the Dutch.[85]

In October, still waiting for any Dutch ships to be seized in the Channel, Company leaders debated printing a book that detailed the "cruelties of the Dutch." They could print five hundred copies for less than £13. Ultimately they decided to print two thousand copies and then make sure that the press was broken (so no unauthorized copies could be made) and that all copies were distributed directly by the Company. They would first send them to "principal persons of the nobility." A positive response to the work would allow the Company to distribute the remaining copies, and they anticipated that the ensuing benefit "will pay for the printing."[86] A few days later, they decided to print an additional thousand copies translated into Dutch and to send them to the Netherlands for sale. Lest anyone think the work was a libel, they decided to print the Company's coat of arms on the front of each book, "in token that they avow them to be true."[87] The leaders moved on this project quickly and soon secured a license to print the books. By mid-October, they were missing only the epistle to the reader, and they requested Skinner to draft one and show it to the court of committees.[88] By late October, the books were printed. The court of committees sent ten copies of the book to Carleton, their indefatigable champion in the Netherlands. They also ordered, "for the better distribution of those books," that each committee get five or six copies "for themselves and their friends." In addition, they planned to present the lords of the Privy Council and other prominent nobles "in and about London" with finely bound copies of the volume.[89] They were making plans, therefore, for a wide distribution of the books, producing hundreds if not thousands of copies, with a targeted rollout to make sure that the book ended up in the hands of the most influential people in the land.

The 1624 book was a substantial publication. Titled in full *A True Relation of the Unjust, Cruel, and Barbarous Proceedings against the English at Amboyna in the East-Indies, by the Netherlandish Governor and Council there. Also the Copy of a Pamphlet, set forth First in Dutch and then in English, by Some Netherlander, Falsely Entitled, A True Declaration of the News that came out of the East-Indies, with the Pinnace called the* Hare, *which arrived at Texel in June, 1624, Together with an Answer to the Same Pamphlet. By the English East India Company. Published by Authority*, it included an epistle to the reader, Skinner's account of the events, a translation of the July 1624 Dutch pamphlet, and a response to the Dutch pamphlet—altogether, almost a hundred pages. As the minutes had noted, the Company's coat of arms appeared prominently in the pamphlet. A woodcut depicting the tortures at Amboyna illustrated the pamphlet, and the title page declared it to be "by the English East-India Company," and "published by Authority." By the end of 1624, at least two editions had appeared, meaning that the work was circulating widely. Additionally, some copies of work were published with some of the words of the title published in red ink for increased visibility— for example, "Amboyna," "unjust," "cruel," and "barbarous."[90]

The distinctive woodcut at the beginning of *A True Relation* portrayed the Amboyna victims as martyrs, subject to an unreasonable Dutch authority and suffering cruel punishments as a result. The image showed three English victims, one spread-eagled and tied to a door while being tortured by flames by one Dutchman and forced to drink water as a torture by another; a second Englishman near naked and in agony; and a third, with arms raised in prayer or supplication, on his knees before a Dutchman swinging a sword. Anthony Milton has pointed out the similarities, surely intentional, between this woodcut and the illustrations in John Foxe's *Book of Martyrs*. One of the figures in particular, he noted, seems to have been copied from the 1570 edition of the *Book of Martyrs*.[91]

With the coat of arms and the prominently placed "published by Authority," the pamphlet made much of its official origins and explained in detail why it had been published and when. The epistle to the reader, which Skinner had also written, set forth the Company's reason for going public. The epistle directly addressed the months-long delay in printing the pamphlet and the concerns that news of Amboyna would turn English public sentiment against the Dutch. It acknowledged that its publication came months after the initial arrival of the news in England, claiming to come even months after its presentation to the king and Privy Council and attributing the delay to the Company's care of the "ancient amity and good correspondence" between the English and the Dutch. It also claimed that the Company did not want to divulge its "private injuries" and be responsible for the "distaste and disaffection, which might haply grow between these two nations," on the basis of a quarrel between two companies. Company leaders had therefore followed the correct procedure and written to the king and Privy Council about their grievances, "without publishing anything to the world in print, thereby to stir up or breed ill blood between these nations." The epistle contrasted the Company's actions with those of the Dutch, who had quickly published a pamphlet justifying the massacre and then published an English-language version to distribute in England, "to brave and disgrace us at our own doors, and in our own language."[92]

The Company presented its resorting to print, therefore, as a matter of national pride and a refusal to bear the Dutch accusations. The Company had been forced into the public arena ("to have recourse also to the press") to uphold not merely its own reputation, but also that of England. The pamphlet directly addressed the concern that others had expressed months earlier—that the news of Amboyna would jeopardize the anti-Spanish, pro-Dutch coalition. In fact the epistle, unique among Company documents, mentioned "patriots" by name and identified the problem that the Company and Amboyna constituted for the "patriot" coalition: the pamphlet informed readers, that "without doubt, reading this discourse, and being a true patriot of thine own country, and a well-willer of the Netherlands (as we presume and wish thee to be), thou wilt wonder how it cometh to pass" that the English received such ill treatment at the hands of the Dutch. The pamphlet attributed the Dutch behavior to the Dutch East India Company's aims in the East Indies, which, it claimed, were more martial and aggressive than the Company's insistence on peaceful commerce. Thus the Company appealed to a popular audience even as the pamphlet acknowledged the widespread pro-Dutch sentiments of 1624 that might lead readers to look unfavorably on the Company's claims.[93]

Appealing to an even broader audience, someone also printed a two-page ballad, the *News out of East India of the Cruel and Bloody Usage of Our English Merchants and Others at Amboyna, by the Netherlandish Governor and Council There*, illustrated by a woodcut.[94] The woodcut was the same one (or at least a crude copy of it) that illustrated *A True Relation*. The *News out of East India* abridged the *True Relation*, opening with an account of the tensions between the English and the Dutch in the East Indies and devoting a verse each to the tortures of the executed English merchants (some invented and not appearing in *A True Relation*), with a refrain of "Oh heaven look down, upon poor innocent souls." It included an account, in verse, of the storm and darkness that God sent on the execution day and encouraged readers and listeners in England to think with sorrow upon the sad deeds in Amboyna. For those readers or listeners who might be intrigued by the terrible tale, a note at the end of the ballad directed readers to *A True Relation*, pointedly informing readers that "you may read more of this bloody Tragedy in a book printed by authory [*sic*], 1624."[95] The ballad was printed anonymously, and it is not entirely clear who commissioned it.[96] The use of the shared woodcut and reference to *A True Relation* suggested an official tie to the Company, but the minutes did not record a decision to commission or print a ballad, and the reference to *A True Relation* was oblique rather than direct. It could be that the author or printer was trying to cash in on popular interest and used textual elements to allude to the official document (the reference to "authory" instead of "authority" echoed the Company's title page but suggested a certain inattention to detail). If this last possibility, then it would suggest that *A True Relation* was quite popular.

After this publishing blitz, with copies of the books making their way into influential hands and circulating more generally at this point, the court of committees received news of a well-laden Dutch fleet soon to sail through the Channel, and they waited eagerly for it to be taken by the king's ships. After all, Company leaders had received the king's promise to seize Dutch ships. Further news revealed, however, that James had not put a sufficiently large fleet in position to carry out his promise. His ships were outnumbered: there were three English ships to seven or eight Dutch ones, and after one of the three English ships was lost, only two were left to take the Dutch ships.[97] Company leaders were well aware that two ships were unlikely to take eight and complained to Conway. Conway's response was to chastise them for their unwanted commentary and to remind them that James had other options available: "his Majesty is not tied to any one way to right himself and his subjects," and "if they be not met upon the Narrow Seas," James could stop Dutch fishing in the North Sea or take their ships elsewhere or later. Buckingham, the lord admiral, also put the Company leaders off and said that if the English did not take the Dutch ships on the outbound voyage, they could take them inbound later on. When the leaders repeated their threat of leaving the trade, Conway told them frankly, "no, there should be no cause to quench the trade," and that "it must not be required that the state shall act things impossible."[98] Conway's and Buckingham's responses thus show that despite the Company's distribution of copies of *A True Relation* and attempts to curry support through that publication (and perhaps because of its distribution, given Conway's warning to Company leaders not to spread their grievances too widely), the leaders faced determined official opposition by this point.

As 1624 drew to a close, the tide of official support seemed to have turned against the Company. Though the conferences Company leaders had with Conway and Buckingham did result in James's ordering more ships to the Channel, the leaders were increasingly uncertain about whether they had the regime's support.[99] Their threats of leaving the trade had been more or less brushed aside by the secretary of state, so they explored what other pressure they could bring to bear. In an internal discussion, one committee suggested appealing to Parliament: "If the course now held do no good, the Company must acquaint a parliament with it." The king had promised to make reparation but had not yet done so, and, the committee said, "the world may see it is far from his thought."[100]

Other signs pointed to fear in the print shops of official displeasure at efforts to add to Amboyna's publicity. In January 1625 Samuel Purchas, compiler of *Purchas His Pilgrims*, approached Company leaders with a gift of his work. He explained that he wanted to include an epistle condemning Dutch actions and the Amboyna massacre. Purchas read the epistle to the court of committees and received suggestions on the content from its members.[101] However, even after securing a license to publish the epistle, Purchas could not get his printer to print it, or the bookbinder to insert it into the larger work. The bookbinder explained that he had asked around and had been "told it may be dangerous," and thus he was refusing.[102] These refusals showed that attitudes toward the Company and about the Dutch were sufficiently sensitive that printing even a licensed work might be dangerous. The sensitivity and possible repercussions of an anti-Dutch stance, even if it was a pro-Company stance, made waving the bloody shirt a difficult proposition for the Company when, given Purchas' experience, Company leaders might not be able to get even a licensed document published and circulated.

Even as Company leaders learned of difficulties in getting licensed materials about Amboyna printed, they learned that people unaffiliated with the Company had been using Amboyna to further their own agendas, without the Company's knowledge or permission. Almost immediately after the Company published *A True Relation* in 1624, it was reprinted at the English College in St. Omer, with a new publisher's note to the reader emphasizing Dutch abuse of the English nation. Printed in English, this work was distributed across the Channel, in England. Given the facts that the English College was Catholic and St. Omer was in the Spanish Netherlands, one can assume that this use of Amboyna was an attempt to drive a polemical wedge between the English and the Dutch.[103] Around the time Purchas was having such difficulty getting the licensed epistle bound into his book, Company leaders discovered that someone else in England had begun circulating a "printed piece of the several tortures in effigy of our men at Amboyna." An emissary from Archbishop Abbot spoke to the court of committees to discover if the members wanted to license that piece and print it on their own account.[104] It transpired that the aim of the printed piece was also not related to the Company at all. The archbishop shortly informed the court of committees that the picture had been printed abroad and brought over and circulated by Archduchess Isabella's ambassador—in other words, the

anti-Dutch possibilities of Amboyna were being exploited without any particular concern for the East Indies trade.[105] Like the St. Omer version of *A
True Relation*, this publication was almost certainly produced to cast aspersions on the Protestant Dutch rather than to support the Company.

Others in England also sought to capitalize on the anti-Dutch feeling
that the story of the Amboyna massacre presented. Thomas Myriell, a minister courting the Company's favor, came to its leaders with an epistle he
had written to attach to a reprint of a sermon. In fact, he approached them
with twenty-four nicely bound copies of the sermon and epistle: the work
was already a done deal.[106] The sermon, *The Stripping of Joseph, or The Cruelty
of Brethren to a Brother*, had been delivered before James years before by
Robert Wilkinson, now deceased. Myriell wanted the Company to approve
the epistle he had written, describing it as "a consolatory epistle, to the English East India Company, for their unsufferable wrongs sustained in Amboyna, by the Dutch there." The printer's note prefaced to the piece drew a
clear analogy between "Joseph's unnatural persecutions in Egypt by his
brethren, and the inhumane tortures of our countrymen in Amboyna, by
the either Atheistical or Arminian Dutch there." The epistle, which was
dedicated to the governor and the whole East India Company, focused on
the same issue of Christian brotherhood and the terrible things the Dutch
had done to the English.[107] Based on the reference to Arminians, the printer
and Myriell were apparently attempting to channel any anti-Dutch feelings
they could stir up on the basis of Amboyna toward a very different end than
the Company's—against Arminianism in particular, rather than against the
Dutch in general. However, the association could work the other way as well,
and the anti-Arminian message might channel sympathy toward the Company's more general anti-Dutch cause. The court of committees accepted
Myriell's offer, and surviving copies of the pamphlet include the Company's
coat of arms.

The Company also explored a variety of nonprint means to foster public
anti-Dutch sentiment. These included commissioning a painting by Richard
Greenbury, which was to be a large-scale indictment of the Dutch in terms
of both size and scope. The court of committees was carefully timing its
completion, probably to coincide with the sitting of Parliament, and even
instructed the painter "not too much to hasten the finishing of that picture,"
lest it be ready too soon. It included a depiction of a petition from the Dutch
to Elizabeth I asking for aid against the Spanish. The unsubtle message of
the painting—and Myriell's publication of Wilkinson's sermon—was to

contrast England's aid to the Dutch with its inhumane repayment. Green-bury might have included the petition without the Company's order, though even if he did, some members of the Company liked the conceit so much that they wanted James to see the picture.[108] At least some people outside the Company learned about the painting, and one newsletter writer noted that it included "the whole manner" of the tortures of Amboyna.[109]

The same writer also believed that the Company's efforts were working. He noted that a play describing the events at Amboyna was soon to be put on, and that the anti-Dutch feeling the Company was stirring up was causing a sufficient amount of concern among enough courtiers that the Privy Council had ordered the Company to put a halt to its activities.[110] Company minutes describing the same events recorded that some commit-tees had been summoned to the Privy Council, where councilors informed them that they knew about the printed picture, described as having "the quality of a libel"; the play; the Myriell epistle, and the Greenbury picture. All of these things, the Council informed the committees, were in bad taste and bad timing and were stirring up people's emotions. Company leaders claimed that they had not spread the printed picture—rather that it had been done by the Archduchess Isabella or her ambassador. They claimed (also truthfully) that Myriell had written the epistle and printed the book on his own. Meanwhile, the big painting was for their private enjoyment and was done "with much art," and thus was not in poor taste. The coun-cilors told the committees not to "publish" the picture or let anyone see it, at least not until after Shrovetide (Shrovetide-related riots and violence was common), and the committees agreed to order that the door be locked to the room where the picture hung.[111] In 1625, Shrovetide ended on 1 March, so they were promising to restrict access to the painting for at least a week.

The account of the same events that Chamberlain sent to Carleton in the Netherlands demonstrated that the Company's activities as well as the efforts of others indeed had succeeded in reanimating anger and indigna-tion against the Dutch, at least for some people. In previous letters Cham-berlain had shown less sympathy to the Company—his previous comment on Amboyna had been that the Company was being too difficult to satisfy on the matter—yet this letter expressed sadness at the affronts offered to the English in a much more emotional way:

I knew not how we that have been esteemed in that kind more than other nations do begin to grow by degrees less than the least, when the basest of people in matter of courage dare brave and trample upon us. I have known the time when [the Dutch] durst not have offered the least of those indignities we have lately swallowed and endured: but they presume upon our patience and somewhat else, otherwise they would have showed some resentment, or given some sign of their dislike of such barbarous cruelty by some notorious example upon the authors and actors, and not suffer the chief instrument the fiscal to walk up and down Amsterdam untouched without any thing said to him, as we hear he doth, and turn us over for satisfaction till the return of I know not whom out of the Indies God knows when, but they are every way too cunning for us and know that *chi ha tempo ha vita*, and understand every way to the wood.[112]

This comment showed Chamberlain's personal response: sadness both at the Amboyna massacre and at the continued lack of restitution for the English. Later in the same letter, Chamberlain acknowledged that letters of marque had been issued against Dutch ships but doubted that anything would come of them. Nevertheless, the Dutch had lost most of their friends in England, and the Dutch, he wrote, were concerned enough that they had informed the Privy Council of "divers ill presages," including the Wilkinson sermon, "which I know not what relation it can have to this late accident (for I have not read it) but the epistle or preface made by a minister is bitter enough"; the play, which was "ready to be acted"; and the Company's big painting. The Privy Council had suppressed the picture, forbidden the performance of the play, called the book in, and set a watch of 800 men to keep the peace over Shrovetide, when it expected anti-Dutch disturbances or riots.[113]

The picture was a sticking point. In late February, days after the Privy Council meeting, the Company received a summons from Buckingham to turn the picture over to him immediately: the picture, "done to the life and at large," was to be sent to Buckingham that same day.[114] When Greenbury came to demand payment for his work weeks later, Company leaders blamed him for allowing so many people to see the painting, for "not only that picture was taken away, but divers other conceits upon the same subject was [*sic*] quashed." In other words, in losing the picture they also lost all future use of it as an idea and recognizable image. They may also have been blaming Greenbury's artistic license, as the petition he had included in the painting might have been what offended the authorities—implying, as it did, that the Dutch as a nation, and not just the Dutch Company, were at fault for the events at Amboyna.[115] Though Company leaders may have pled ignorance about Greenbury's publicizing the picture and were now bitter because it was being suppressed, they had known about his addition earlier and been pleased enough to plan for it to be widely viewed after it was done.

The ultimate efficacy of the Company's various public maneuverings is difficult to gauge. Despite seemingly changing public opinion about the Dutch, James and Buckingham still allowed the Dutch ships to pass through the Channel unhindered.[116] The captain of one of the English ships in the Channel told Buckingham that there was no way he could have taken the Dutch ships, which were too many and too fast for the few English ships.[117] Thus, despite angering and saddening people about Amboyna, the Company did not succeed in its objective of making the regime take action on its behalf. Worse, by publicizing the Dutch violence against its men, the Company had also publicized its vulnerabilities without securing a demonstration by the state to prove that the vulnerabilities were not real—or rather, were surmountable.

At this juncture, James died. With the change in monarch, everything was in flux, including what position the new monarch would take toward the Dutch. James had acted to keep England out of a continental war; in other words, his lack of response to open demands for restitution had kept England's generally friendly relations with the Dutch from degenerating into open antagonism. In contrast, Charles desperately wanted to bring England into the continental conflict. For England's entry into the war, however, Charles needed the Dutch as an ally, not an enemy. His policy toward Amboyna, therefore, turned out to follow James's pattern of avoidance, though with a different objective.

With the passing of the monarch, the Company could safely emphasize the statements James had made that he would protect the Company and downplay his failure to actually do so. Thus, only days after James's death, Company leaders commented that James, "his Majesty that then was," had promised to "take the Dutch from off our neck." Charles, "his majesty that now is," had so far shown himself in agreement that the Dutch had acted badly. Although the Company was still in need of succor, its leaders rested easy, they said, confident that Charles would deliver on James's promises.[118]

Soon the Company received intelligence that a returning Dutch fleet would pass through the Channel, which would give Charles an opportunity to right the Company in regard to the Dutch. In anticipation Company leaders planned to "revive the business of Amboyna" and send the new king a petition about the matter. They also intended to meet with Buckingham and acquaint him with their news of the arrival of the Dutch fleet.[119] The Company even put together a set of directions for how the king's ships could best surprise the Dutch ships in the Channel.[120] Company leaders thought that they would finally secure restitution. Instead, however, they got news that the king's ships near Dover had been within a league of the Dutch ships and let them go.[121] Inquiry revealed that the ships' captains claimed that Buckingham had told them the matter was settled, and therefore they were no longer charged with taking the ships.[122] The Dutch ships had been within sight of the king's ships for two days and nights, but the latter had not moved to seize them.[123]

Despite Charles's initial promises, therefore, Company leaders soon found him less than sympathetic. In the immediate aftermath of the failure to take the Dutch prizes, they delivered a petition to Charles, which he "looked upon, and found long," before asking them to summarize it for him. They did, explaining that they wanted justice for Amboyna, "wherein there hath been a dilatory proceeding and nothing done." Charles promised "three times" that he would take care of the matter, folded up the petition, and put it in his pocket.[124]

Days later, at the Company's 1625 court of election, the Company seemed about to act on the threat its leaders had made to the king and Privy Council about the difficulty of continuing the trade without restitution. Without restitution or even a believable promise of it, members of the generality declared themselves less inclined to invest their money in the Company. The situation was not aided by investment returns in the 1620s that were significantly lower than they had been a decade before—the first joint stock (1613–1623) had earned an average profit of 87 percent, while the second joint stock (1617–1632) earned only an average of 12 percent.[125] The governor and committees were able to persuade these men "not to fall so suddenly upon such a resolution" to withhold their adventures. Nevertheless, what Company leaders had threatened to do so often to the king and Privy Council was happening—and not at their instigation or choice. While the leaders were able to persuade disgruntled members not to pull out entirely and to give them time to inform Charles of the state of affairs first, the general court voted "to shorten the trade until the Company be relieved by the state effectually." In other words, the trade would be run much more conservatively until the regime showed decisive support.[126]

With the strong support and inclination of the generality to abandon the trade, Morris Abbot once more presented that possibility to the Privy Council, not as a threat, but as an increasingly likely probability. He explained to the Earl of Marlborough, then lord treasurer, that the members of the generality were discouraged, because of "losses so great without hope of any reparation from the state," and especially by the news that the Dutch ships had been allowed to pass unmolested by the king's ships. Several councilors claimed to be ignorant of the fact that Dutch ships had been allowed to pass, but they were still not pleased to hear of the resolution to abandon the trade.[127] A letter from the Privy Council to Company leaders emphasized that Charles would vindicate the Company and instructed them to "rest very confident and assured that his Majesty will not only not abandon but will not slacken the care of your welfare and protection." The "danger of this present season"—presumably a reference to the ongoing outbreak of plague in London—prevented monarch and Council from taking up the matter further at that moment, but they urged the Company to proceed in the trade as usual, "notwithstanding any rumor or suspicion that may have been conceived of anything that may tend to your prejudice."[128] They wanted the court of committees to convince the generality of the Privy Council's support, though plague effectively prevented calling the generality together at the time.[129] After 29 July, no meetings took place until 4 October on account of plague.

In any case, within two weeks, the Privy Council had changed its opinion. It sent a much harsher letter directly criticizing Company leaders' handling of the Amboyna affair. The letter censured what the Council saw as "a determinate purpose in the generality of your Company to discontinue the trade." The Council chastised Company leaders for their criticism of the state and their "presuming to give law unto yourselves in what as you conceive should have been done for you and that having been omitted and neglected, by those ministers that should have done it." The councilors also found the Company's criticism presumptuous, exclaiming that "this language we are not wont to receive from any company and it ill becomes you thus to return upon the state." In short, they expected the Company to follow Charles'"express pleasure" and continue the trade.[130] Given the tenor of the Council's second letter, Company leaders found themselves caught between two competing directives: from the generality to limit the trade, and from the Privy Council to follow its orders to continue the trade. Between this awkward position and the plague outbreak, Company leaders did not immediately follow up on the issue with either group.

Once the Company began meeting again several months later, the court of committees once more turned to petitioning as a possible means to secure redress. Skinner, who had written the book on Amboyna, now had written another remonstrance against Dutch evils. After some debate, Company leaders decided to frame a new petition to the king and Privy Council stating openly that the Company would pull out of the trade if it did not receive restitution from the king and Council.[131] Company representatives delivered the petition and read it aloud. Unlike the last time they delivered a petition to Charles, when he put it in his pocket without reading it, this time the monarch and Privy Council listened to the entire petition. Possibly Charles's neglect of past petitions explained the Company representatives' attempt to have the petition read aloud in their presence in the Council chamber. The Council asked them to withdraw while it discussed the matter and to come back the next day to discuss it further. That same day, the governor received word that a richly laden Dutch ship had arrived off the coast of Ireland. Company leaders thought the news was providential and that they might "make advantage thereof." They hoped to convince Charles to seize the ship, which "is come unto us offering, as it were, herself into our hands," for reparations.[132]

The next day, back in the Privy Council, the topic of the ships that had been let go several months before came up. The councilors commented that it was too bad the ships had not been captured, but if another chance arose, the king's ships would take action. That was the opening the governor was waiting for, and he brought up the Dutch ship off the Irish coast. Clearly the king and Council had not yet learned of this ship and had very neatly, and unwittingly, led the way for the Company leaders to propose that Charles's ships take it as a reprisal. Upon hearing of the ship, "his Majesty and the lords were silent." The Council asked the Company representatives to withdraw again and began what must have been a vigorous and unplanned discussion, which led Conway, the secretary of state, to go back to his chamber several times for more papers.[133]

Put to the point—with a ship at hand, ready to be seized—Charles balked, assuring the Company that he would take care of it, but not now and not with this ship. He told the Company representatives to "be of good cheer and not to doubt of his royal protection." They responded that they would be unable to keep the generality from ending the trade when news of Charles's refusal became known. Backed against the wall, with the apparent choice between a trade cessation and the seizure of a Dutch ship Charles, "being thus importuned on every side and finding that nothing would give satisfaction, but a stay of their ships, seemed somewhat displeased, and said, will nothing content you, must you have the ships stayed this present hour?" He then revealed what Company leaders had not known: he claimed that he could not take action until the limitation specified in his "protestation" to the States General had passed, and the Company representatives, realizing they had pushed the matter as far as possible, "submitted themselves to his Majesty's pleasure and the state" and withdrew.[134]

The protestation that Charles mentioned was his reply to the Treaty of Southampton, which had been signed in September 1625 between England and the United Provinces. Negotiations for the treaty had taken place while the Company was not meeting due to plague, and thus it is unclear how much Company leaders knew of the negotiations with Francois Aerrson, the Dutch ambassador. Few documents related to Aerrsen's embassy have survived in English state papers, and it is possible that the plague outbreak had effectively hidden the negotiations until the treaty was a fait accompli. Charles had taken exception to a clause in the treaty prohibiting each nation from ordering reprisals against the other and instead demanded that some conclusion to Amboyna take place by the end of eighteen months. In short, while the Company understood this as the treaty prohibiting reprisals for eighteen months, from Charles's viewpoint, he was reserving the right of reprisals at sea, though giving the Dutch a set period in which to respond before exercising that right.[135]

Meeting with Charles a few days later, Company leaders claimed to understand and accept his explanation of the exception, but they still protested that they required the same protection from their state that the Dutch Company received from its. They argued that without similar support, they could not run a similar trade. Charles's response was to bring up a proposal first floated by James, for the monarch to become a member of the Company and thus give it his protection that way. Charles said that "if they would have him interested in their cause, this was the way." There followed an awkward refusal by the governor, couched in excuses that the Company had used to refuse similar requests by James. Their reasoning was accepted, but with the somewhat menacing comment by the lord chamberlain that the king's membership was "not pressed upon the Company but left to their consideration. Yet . . . they desire protection from his Majesty which he is content to give them, but cannot do so properly, without interesting himself in the cause as an adventurer." Abbot's risky response was that Company members would suggest that "if your Majesty can protect us [by] being an adventurer, you may be pleased to do as much without." The king left them with more assurances that he cared for them and the trade, that they should go cheerfully about their business, and that if in eighteen months no settlement had been made, then nothing would stop Charles from taking the matter into his own hands.[136] A meeting intended to reassure Company leaders had in fact given them grounds for concern.

Given what Company leaders saw—perhaps unfairly, given that Charles had actually been negotiating with the Dutch and had in fact reserved the right for future seizures of ships—as airy promises from Charles and the overwhelming likelihood that nothing would be settled for over a year, they once more turned to discuss the cessation of the trade. In the first meeting of the court of committees after the latest audience with the king, the governor summed up the situation. Company leaders had considered their situation several times, the governor said, but resolved nothing. They still hoped, however, "that the king and state had so seriously taken the East Indian trade to heart, that all differences would be removed, injuries repaired, and the trade upheld." They decided to continue the trade at least for another year.[137] At a general court meeting shortly afterward, the governor reported everything to the generality, from the ship that Charles would not allow to be seized, to the two-day meeting with the Privy Council and the promises and protestations Charles made to them. The governor put to a vote the question of whether or not to continue the trade, instructing the generality that "as many of you as upon these encouragements and promises of his Majesty will follow the trade hold up your hands." Upon those promises, the generality voted to continue the trade.[138]

Charles's official protestation to the Treaty of Southampton meant that no martial resolution could take place within eighteen months. Indeed, a letter from the Venetian ambassador at The Hague mentioned that Buckingham had released some ships in March 1626, "giving orders that no more ships should be arrested for that cause [the Amboyna affair] during the 18 months appointed for the settlement of that affair."[139] However, judicial resolution to Amboyna was still possible, and Charles hoped to persuade the Company to agree to send commissioners to settle the matter. The Company did not want to send commissioners; they preferred to receive them, assuming that a commission that met on English soil would secure more from the Dutch than would a commission that met on Dutch soil. The question of whether or not the Company would send commissioners, especially with Charles urging them to do so, was especially sensitive, as Company leaders knew that Charles could change the commission after the commissioners were appointed. The matter and how to settle it would then be out of the

Company's hands. Giving legitimacy to the commission could therefore be not only inconvenient to the Company, but also dangerous. The commissioners would nominally represent the Company and would be chosen by Company leaders, but they would not have absolute or final say as to what the commissioners' objectives would be, it "being in the power of the state to revoke any commission they should make unto him, and to give him new directions, when once they have engaged him in this service." The Company's resolution of Amboyna would be according to Charles's standards of acceptability—a concession Company leaders did not want to make.[140] The court of committees voted on the matter and decided not to send commissioners. They also seem to have realized that Charles would not act as they wished on their behalf for some time, and they resolved temporarily to stop petitioning him on the matter.[141] On that somber note, they left the matter unresolved for many months. The Company's difficulties could not be tabled, however, and by the time they could revisit Amboyna after eighteen months, the instability introduced in part by the events at Amboyna had spread and the Company had other difficulties facing it as well.

Amboyna was a problem for the Company. The events there showed the Company's vulnerability in the East Indies, where its men might be targeted, as well as its vulnerability at home, where it might not be able to count on the support of the state. Yet under different circumstances, it might have been an opportunity for the Company. If the regime had backed the Company, Amboyna could even have been mobilized to show the Company's resources in adversity, its ability to defend its men and successfully compete against its European counterparts. In the early months after news of the events at Amboyna reached England, Company leaders worked hard to make the situation an opportunity rather than a problem. They attempted to shape the news, to encourage the regime and the public to back them. Their success at cultivating public opinion, however, led the regime to quash their public actions and cast their petition into a sort of limbo. From the point of view of Company leaders and of members of the generality, it seemed increasingly unlikely that the Company's desires could be aligned with the objectives of the regime.

9

Taking Stock and Looking Forward

The Difficulties of the Late 1620s

IN APRIL 1628, the court of committees charged Thomas Mun with drafting a petition to Parliament. Mun had been a committee of the Company for years and had some experience writing works to support it, having written *A Discourse of Trade* in 1621 (see Chapter 5). He titled the product of his labor in 1628 *A Petition and Remonstrance of the Governor and Company of Merchants of London Trading to the East Indies.*[1]

A Petition and Remonstrance was an open appeal to Parliament, a fact that was explicit in the title and first page. It was treated as such in internal Company debates. The court of committees hoped that the petition, "with certain articles thereunto annexed, showing the honor and benefit accruing to his majesty and his kingdoms by the East Indian Trade," would lead Parliament to declare its support for the Company. The petition included the criticisms commonly made of the Company—the "aspersions that lie upon the Company, by which aspersions the Adventurers are much discouraged"—and the Company's explanations and answers to the criticisms.[2] In the publicly sold, printed version of the petition, Company leaders asked that if members of Parliament found the trade to be unprofitable to the commonwealth, it be ended, but otherwise that it "be SUPPORTED AND COUNTENANCED BY SOME PUBLIC DECLARATION."[3]

The petition was presented in Parliament on 7 May. Members of the court of committees took considerable care to make sure it was as perfect as they could make it. They had the petition read "publicly" in the Company several times, with Mun on hand to amend it as necessary. They entreated the deputy governor to "use his best means that the petition may be read at a full assembly," and appointed several committees to attend Parliament on the appointed day.[4]

Yet Parliament proved to be a less sympathetic audience than Company leaders had hoped. The *Commons Journal* noted only that a petition by the Company was read and referred to the committee on trade, "to proceed with as much expedition [as possible]."[5] Several parliamentary diaries, however, recorded Sir Edward Coke's strong negative reaction to the petition. In response to the petition, he announced, *"Paucorum nocuit scelarata licentia: argento mutat dum monopola piper"*—in other words, "That accursed license held by a few men is harmful; it changes pepper to silver as long as there is a monopoly."[6] The petition did not elicit the positive response Company leaders had hoped for and, though they could not know this yet, Parliament would never give its enthusiastic approval to the Company. Indeed, besides the introduction of the petition, the only other noteworthy interaction the Company had with Parliament in 1628 was when the House of Lords ordered the Company to pay Warwick £4,000 to end the matter of his seized pirate ships (see Chapter 7).

The fact that Company leaders turned to Parliament for support in 1628 was surprising, given the wariness with which they had previously considered appeals to that body. However, in that year Company leaders were unsettled. The period since 1626 had been difficult for the Company. The alliance between Company and crown had been tested and ultimately weakened after the events at Amboyna. The unraveling of the alliance began at the end of James I's reign but continued and accelerated under Charles I. In the late 1620s, the Company's ongoing failure to secure restitution for Amboyna led to a lack of willingness by members of the generality to continue investing with the Company. Without proof of support from the king, the threats the Company had been making about abandoning the trade nearly came true, as members of the generality were increasingly less inclined to turn over their money to a venture so unable to demonstrate the support of the regime. The Company's recent history also seemed full of examples of the monarch compelling the reluctant Company to act as he wished (for example, in the case of the money demanded for Hormuz), without providing anything in return. In consequence Company leaders were exploring alternate avenues of support.

These years saw the Company become increasingly alienated from the monarch. However, the failure of the 1628 appeal to Parliament reinforced the point that the Company's best support had to be the monarch. Yet it seemed to Company leaders that the monarch was increasingly unsympathetic to the needs of the Company. The king continued to make it difficult for the Company to trust him, including by encouraging a disruptive factional threat that challenged the foundation of the Company's government and organization. The importance of the prerogative to the Company meant that it could not be independent of the king. Despite the lack of resolution of the matter of Amboyna, the factional threats, and the murmurings about Parliament, all of which reinforced each other, the decade ended with Company leaders recommitting to the crown as their best and most important support.

The Ongoing Problem of Amboyna: A Turn Away from the Crown?

In October of 1626, in anticipation of the end of Charles's eighteen-month moratorium on pushing for a resolution of Amboyna, Company leaders decided that the time had come for Amboyna to be "revived by the Company to his Majesty and the state."[7] With the generality now very much in danger of abandoning the trade, the court of committees discussed whether there was "some middle way" between giving up the trade, as some Company members wanted, and pursuing it wholeheartedly, as the regime wanted. Court members considered sending one ship a year to the East Indies "until they shall understand the intention of the state whether to relieve them or not." That would "keep life in the business" and avoid giving Charles an excuse to send his own ships to keep the trade alive, but it would limit the damage the Dutch could do to Company men and goods.[8]

The court of committees once more began canvassing for support. Company leaders took action on all fronts despite the disappointments of their previous attempts before the moratorium. They soon had a petition approved and ready to be presented to the king.[9] On the Company's behalf, Sir John Wolstenholme made an impassioned speech to Buckingham, the king's favorite, about the benefits of the East Indies trade and the oppressions of the Dutch. When Buckingham asked Wolstenholme to write out the points he had made, the court of committees hastened to put together a remonstrance to that effect.[10] Buckingham claimed to be committed to the cause, though he reminded Company leaders that Charles could not act on their behalf until the eighteen months were over.[11] The leaders also began to make renewed preparations to have Skinner's book about Amboyna reprinted and a new remonstrance by Skinner printed. Company minutes had mentioned nothing about publications in over a year, but with the eighteen months drawing to a close, and with a new Dutch pamphlet circulating that justified Dutch actions at Amboyna, the Company once again considered taking public action.[12] Between king, Buckingham, and the public, the court of committees was exploring all the avenues available to them for securing support.

With Skinner's new remonstrance, the Company prepared to reenter the public arena, to reignite interest in Amboyna and stories of Dutch cruelty. Debating how best to print the message, Company leaders concluded that they ought to print the Dutch remonstrance alongside Skinner's new work: with "the objection and answer going together the truth of things may the better be understood."[13] This decision to print the two together, and the reasons they gave for the decision, demonstrated the leaders' attempt not just to publicize the affair, but to persuade people—to demonstrate the truth of the matter (the Company's version, of course) by allowing readers to judge for themselves.

Yet even as the Company's public maneuverings were gaining new life, the official response the leaders were receiving was less than wholly supportive. The king and Privy Council were strongly urging the Company to accept the offer of a new commission to the Netherlands to settle the matter of Amboyna, but the leaders were still reluctant to allow Dutch commissioners to judge the matter.[14] Soon the court of committees learned that someone had convinced the Stationers' Company to halt the publication of the Company's printed book about Amboyna, which meant that some official person with some clout had ordered the stay and presented a warrant to that effect.[15] It emerged that the printer, Nicholas Bourne, had sold a copy of the Company's book without the knowledge of Company leaders to Sir Noel Caron, the Dutch ambassador, who had caused the book to be confiscated.[16] Just as Richard Greenbury's showing of his painting about Amboyna had led it to be banned, so Bourne's sale of the book caused it to be banned—the danger of public appeals meant that, quite literally, the speaker sometimes lost control of the message. The printed version of the book that was to have been for sale never appeared. Printing was not the only way to publish a book, and the Company ordered nicely written copies of it to present to the lords of the Privy Council.[17] Nonetheless, the new Amboyna narrative never got a wider public airing: the confiscated books remained in the possession of the Stationers' Company by order of the Privy Council for over a year, and when they were ultimately released to Sir Morris Abbot at the end of July 1628, it was with the instruction to keep them safe "without the publishing of any of them."[18]

This aborted attempt to revive the events at Amboyna in print was the practical end of the Company's experiments with pamphlet wars and the politics of publicity in support of its desired restitution for Amboyna. In 1625 the Privy Council had stepped in to suppress a painting and a play that had already had too public an airing. In 1627 a Company remonstrance and account about the Dutch actions at Amboyna could not even make it out of the printer's shop. The efficacy of the Company's public manipulations had definitely ebbed. It was not the end of their experiments with the public sphere, but it was more or less the end of their ability to do so openly with regard to Amboyna.[19] Evidence suggests they attempted, unsuccessfully, to reprint Skinner's *True Relation* in 1631, and they did so successfully in 1632, but the circumstances surrounding those reprints are unclear since the volume of Company court minutes for the year is missing.[20] The aborted 1631 attempt was the third time an Amboyna-related publication was suppressed before becoming publicly available.

The Amboyna narratives and printed works had always been aimed at persuading the generality, as well as the wider public, of the need for action and the continued viability of the East Indies trade. The mounting inability of Company leaders to keep the Amboyna issue alive—and to signal publicly that they were doing so—and the apparent unwillingness of the regime to take action made arguments about the strength of the trade difficult, especially given that many general members were already daunted by recent poor returns. Amboyna and the discouragements it represented made it that much harder to go "cheerfully" about the trade, as Charles often recommended the Company to do.[21] Thus, the sense of discouragement was not due to any particular failure of the king to take action. In fact, throughout the spring and summer of 1627, the Venetian ambassador in England reported that the king and Privy Council were pushing the matter of Amboyna despite the protests of a Dutch commissioner. The regime was taking official action on Amboyna, therefore, though the ultimate conclusion it reached, against Company wishes, was that the Amboyna trial should take place in the Netherlands.[22] Company minutes, however, do not reveal any sense among the Company members that the regime was taking positive action on behalf of the Company, even after they learned of the planned trial. Instead, in mid-1627 Company leaders and members of the generality explored their worst-case scenario: the cessation of the East

Indies trade, not as a threat to compel the regime to take action, but as a sound business decision.

Company leaders officially opened up a Company-wide debate on the question of a trade cessation at the 1627 election meeting. They had already had a number of meetings specifically devoted to discussion of the state of the East Indies trade.[23] Some of the leaders expressed concerns about openly considering the issue. Thus, while some committees wanted to discuss the cessation "darkly" and to place all blame on the "Hollanders' obstinacy," others thought it best not to make the possible hiatus public yet, "holding it unfit to be debated in a public court whence it might be certified to the Hollanders."[24] However, the matter was already being debated widely, albeit unofficially, within the Company.

When Governor Abbot introduced the possible trade cessation to the generality, he did so in guarded terms but with the expectation that they already knew about it. In fact, the minutes did not record any direct mention of a cessation of trade; the matter was alluded to as a matter that Abbot did not doubt "they had already heard upon the Exchange what it is," and one that he asked them to consider even without its being "publicly revealed" to them. The governor's delicately worded suggestion that his listeners would already know what he was talking about revealed how widely the news of a possible trade cessation had already spread. Abbot suggested that some "10, 12, 15 or 20 of the chiefest and greatest adventurers of the Generality" be chosen to meet with the court of committees about the matter of the trade.[25] Ultimately, seventeen members of the generality joined with the court of committees to consider the topic. Each participant was a substantial investor in the trade, with adventures of at least £4,000.[26]

The group of selected adventurers and committees discussed the trade cessation in depth and came to some surprising conclusions. The subject of the meeting—the trade cessation—was not itself extraordinary, given that Company leaders had been threatening to cease trading for years. But the length and depth of the discussion was unusual—the minutes recording the debate took many pages—as were the frank appraisals attendees made of the Company's prospects.

The attendees laid out their reasoning about and justification for a trade cessation in detail. They presented the debate on a trade cessation as the culmination of the events of the past twenty or twenty-two months—namely, the period of the continued inability or disinclination by first James, and then Charles, to act to secure redress for Dutch crimes against the

English in the East Indies, of which the Amboyna massacre was the best known and most outrageous example. By this point, the only course of action from the regime that would give the Company the support it needed was active reprisals against the Dutch. Diplomacy and the trial would come to nothing, the attendees argued, "seeing the government of the Low Countries is so intermixed that the Bewinthebbers [the leaders of the Dutch East India Company] whensoever the business shall come to a judicial trial will be both parties and judges."[27] In other words, the overlap between the government of the Dutch East India Company and the Dutch government, which made the Dutch Company so much stronger than the English Company from the viewpoint of Company members, was so great that the two could not be separated. There was no way the Company could secure a fair trial of the perpetrators of Amboyna in the Netherlands, because all the judges would be compromised.

If diplomacy could not succeed, then the Company required reprisals at sea—yet those who attended the meeting recognized that they were unlikely to get such reprisals given the current political climate. One speaker, Sir Edwin Sandys, explained that "the difficulty rests only in this, because at present the king being engaged in foreign wars receives aid from [the Dutch], and therefore [it is] unlikely that he will pursue any such course howsoever his Majesty may do what he please."[28] Charles's continental military engagements required Dutch support, and whatever the monarch may have wished, he was in no position to force the Dutch to do anything. Additionally, Sandys pointed out the difficulty that Charles faced even if he was willing to pursue the matter with the Dutch: the government of the Netherlands was "popular," as opposed to England's monarchical government, and thus the States General could not compel the Dutch citizens as Charles could compel his subjects.[29] Given these circumstances, Sandys was convinced to support the move for a trade cessation.

Some of the discussants were uneasy with the idea that a trade cessation might be seen as a criticism of the regime (which it was). One unnamed person objected "that our own state, perhaps displeased with this resolution, will withdraw their promised assistance, and so the Company shall be forced to sit down without any satisfaction at all." A Company officer added that "it is not fit for the Company [in] any way to blame the state who will help nobly when cause shall require."[30] Both speakers, therefore, highlighted the fact that a cessation would not be simply an economic decision but could be seen as an inappropriate commentary on the state's lack of action.

However, the majority of discussants wanted it to be clear that a trade cessation was a direct response to the lack of support by the state. They were emphatic that they did not want their actions to be taken as "intermeddling with or questioning the proceedings of the state"—they were not trespassing on the *arcana imperii*, the secrets of state. Most did see the lack of action by the king as the cause of their difficulties. They would not pretend that a trade cessation was due to a lack of stock—that they did not have enough money and goods to properly run the trade—as that would reflect badly on the honor of the Company, "nor is that indeed any cause of the cessation." Rather, the cause was that "the king hath promised his protection of the Company," but "there is hitherto no redress." Knowing that the trade was so vulnerable and unsupported, no one wanted to risk their money in it. As the minutes put it, "it is not want of ability, but want of will in the adventurers."[31]

In light of this situation, the select committee decided to cease the trade. They voted on the proposal, recording the wording of the question: "As many as think it is for the honor of the state, and profit of the Company to follow the trade as now it is, notwithstanding it is so much wronged by the Netherlanders, hold up your hands, and by general erection of hands it was concluded to desist, as suiting neither with the honor of the king, nor benefit of the Company to be pursued as now it is."[32] The Company response toed a fine line: its members separated the decision to follow or cease the trade from a consideration of the proceedings of the state, yet they acted to uphold the honor of the king. They were not questioning the actions of the state, but reacting to the situation—which was that the king had promised the Company protection that he had not delivered. There may have been little practical difference between the Company's decision to withdraw from the trade because the king had not provided the promised protection and questioning the proceedings of the state, but it was a distinction the members did make.

A final note by one participant suggested that some still hoped their decision would have a positive outcome. After appointing the governor and a few others to call on various privy councilors to inform them of the Company's momentous decision—as was "necessary to be done in point of civility"—Sandys stated what others also may have been hoping. He commented that far from providing encouragement to the Dutch, news of their proceedings would "exceedingly daunt them, because by this, the business is devolved to the state, who in all likelihood will not suffer so rich a trade to be lost for want of the redress required."[33]

At first it seemed as though Sandys was right and the king would, when put to the point, take action when the trade was really at stake. When Wolstenholme informed the king of the planned trade cessation and the declining East Indies trade, he reported that Charles "seriously protested he would not lose the East India trade, and seemed to require the Company to set down their demands what they would have him to do for them."[34] This response led some committees to wonder, once again, "whether they should stir at all, or leave it wholly to the wisdom of the state." Both sides were represented in internal Company debates: "some knowing well, that court affairs move slowly without solicitation, did therefore conceive it necessary that the Company should pursue the business at court lest it die," urged the Company to lobby the Privy Council and call on its court connections. Others argued for a more conservative approach and "advised [the Company] not to stir, but leave it to the state to pursue their own course . . . that the less the Company solicit the support of the trade, by so much more the state will be quickened to right them and will carefully provide to uphold the same." Indeed, ultimately Company leaders decided that it was better for men by "private solicitation" to try to persuade the king of the Company's need, rather than that "the Company should solicit the same," an interesting comment on the possible waning of the Company's influence at court.[35]

The resolution to cease the trade was bearing the results Company leaders had wished for: in September 1627, Charles had three Dutch ships stopped at Portsmouth. Moreover, soon there were rumors that the ships carried as passengers the Amboyna judges, which made the seizure of the ships not only symbolically important as an action by the regime to secure reparations for Amboyna, but also materially important to any possible trial in England or the Netherlands about Amboyna.[36]

The Company sent a very carefully worded message to the king, thanking him while hinting that the seizure was only the first necessary step. They "in all humble manner return his Majesty their hearty thanks for this his beginning, and beseecheth this his noble resolution, whereby the ships may not be released until the business between the Company and the Dutch be brought to some good issue, for that this is the only way to accommodate these differences, and to encourage the Company to go on in the Trade."[37] In the guise of thanking the king, in other words, the Company leaders advised him on what his next steps should be. Upon receiving the message, Charles promised his continued support, "but withal expected they should now follow the trade bravely."[38] The Company should not broach the trade cessation or a reduction in ships or stock again.

Having the Dutch ships under arrest did what the Company leaders had hoped, and soon the Dutch were willing to send commissioners to England to settle the matter. Judges were also appointed for a trial to consider the events at Amboyna. Resolution on the Company's terms seemed closer than it had in years.[39] A newsletter written soon after the seizure had predicted that the Dutch would pay attention now that the ships had been seized, commenting that Charles had acted "to do himself and the English company that right and satisfaction . . . it will move a great deal of complaint and discontent on their [the Dutch] parts."[40] Certainly the Venetian ambassador in England noted the outrage and frustration of the Dutch ambassador in October at the continued holding of the Dutch ships.[41]

With Charles having finally taken action on the Company's behalf, Company leaders considered their actions with regard to the monarch very carefully. As long as the ships were in the king's possession and the matter unresolved, he had considerable leverage over them. Thus they decided not to send him any more petitions and to leave the matter "wholly to the care of the king and state," trusting that at this point Charles would not allow the ships to go without vindicating not just the Company's honor, but his own.[42] It is also possible that some or all of the committees gave Charles a large loan as a sweetener or thank-you for the seizure of the ships, though the evidence is incomplete and the loan may have been a rumor.[43] Meanwhile, the Dutch ambassador to England was putting pressure on Charles to release the ships, though without success.[44]

If the seized ships represented Charles's leverage over the Company, the little leverage the Company had still was by not promising Charles that they would continue the trade. The ships were a bargaining chip not only between England and the Netherlands, but also between Company leaders and Charles. The leaders held off on sending more petitions to Charles, but they also suspected that their only power lay in keeping their future plans unknown. While the Dutch ships remained at Portsmouth, it was in the Company's best interest to be quiet. To make known definitively that they either would or would not pursue the trade would hurt them:

> For if the state shall understand that the Company will desert the trade, it will then as was observed by another committee be a means to dull their edge in pressing the Hollanders for satisfaction and procuring an accommodation of the trade for the future, if it shall be known that the Company are resolved to continue the trade, and that they have raised or intend to raise a new stock that likewise may prove inconvenient to them,

for that hereby the king and state perceiving that the Company are able to subsist of themselves, and that they do resolve still to prosecute the trade, his Majesty may peradventure be persuaded to leave the Company to themselves and not to take them into his royal protection without which it is in vain to prosecute the trade.[45]

To commit to continuing the trade would remove the urgency of securing restitution and give an impression of strength the leaders did not feel, and to commit to abandoning the trade would remove the most pressing reason for why restitution was needed. Thus, even with the Dutch promising to send commissioners to England, the leaders decided that the only way to ensure a satisfactory conclusion was to keep their commitment to the trade unknown.

In January 1628 the leaders debated sending a laden ship east, but they decided to wait, to see "how his Majesty and the state will right the Company for the injuries done by the Dutch unto them."[46] In February, however, the Company was forced to show its hand a bit. The leaders had petitioned Charles for a license to export English gold, and Charles had made known his unhappiness with the small size of the fleet: "his majesty had seemed discontented against the Company partly because they send out so few ships this year." For his "better satisfaction," the Company drew up a list of reasons why he should be content, stating that though they were sending only two ships that year, they still planned to bring back the same amount of cargo as in the previous year.[47]

Given Charles's history with regard to restitution from the Dutch, Company leaders were not confident that he would stand by his promises to them. They continued sending occasional petitions and letters entreating help for their cause, and the Company minutes were full of updates on the status of the Dutch ships. In February 1628, for example, the leaders ordered the framing of a petition to send to Buckingham, to enlist his aid in keeping the three Dutch ships in Portsmouth, where they had now been for several months, while the Dutch ambassador and commissioners grew increasingly restive.[48] At this point, Company leaders were probably aware or at least suspected that the monarch was wavering in his support.

It was in this context, with the Dutch ships under arrest but only so long as the king held out against Dutch pressure to release them, that Company leaders decided to petition Parliament to give its support to the East Indies trade. The Company's faith in the monarch was low in early 1628, and

Parliament looked increasingly attractive as an alternative to the monarch that might prove sympathetic to the Company. Parliament was not a natural ally of the trading companies, which often came under intense scrutiny and criticism by early Stuart parliaments for being specie-sucking monopolies (among other charges). Since the privileges of trading companies generally came from royal grants and the power of the prerogative, and they dealt with foreign affairs, the crown and Privy Council were instead the companies' natural governmental connection. But by 1628, the East India Company was not the only chartered trading company to have problems with Charles. For example, a number of merchants of the Levant Company were refusing to pay increased impositions on currants, and both the Levant and East India Companies had long-running disputes with the monarch over diplomatic representation.[49] In the face of the events at Amboyna and these other disputes, Parliament began to look like a possible ally.[50] The decision of Company leaders to approach Parliament was thus a sign of just how tenuous their faith in Charles had become by 1628.

Nonetheless, before delivering their petition, Mun's *A Petition and Remonstrance*, to Parliament in spring 1628, members of the court of committees discussed whether they should run their parliamentary petition by the king and Privy Council first. They ultimately decided to do so.[51] Thus, even as the Company was planning to ask Parliament for help, with its leverage slipping again, Company leaders were checking the reaction of the king and Council first. It is possible that they hoped the petition would nudge Charles to finally end matters related to Amboyna in a way they found satisfactory. They did not get the king's and Council's impressions of the planned petition, but they did get advice from Secretary of State John Coke, Sir Dudley Digges, and the Council's lord president, the Earl of Manchester (who, incidentally, was a member of the Company). All expressed approbation, though Coke thought that the leaders might wish to wait till the "great business" of Parliament was settled.[52]

The trouble with Parliament was that it was a public forum for expressing grievances—one that everyone had access to. Thus, while the Company was appealing to Parliament because they felt unsupported by the king, some members of the generality were also going to Parliament because they were unhappy with the Company's current government. Company leaders were well aware of how evidence of internal dissatisfaction and division would hurt their claims that they were a functional and beneficial trade and weaken their carefully constructed case with both Parliament and Charles.[53]

The deputy governor, Sir Christopher Clitherow, was a member of Parliament in 1628 and introduced the petition. Company leaders could not prevent factions in the generality from approaching Parliament, and Clitherow asserted that leaving the charges by Company critics unanswered would weaken the force of the Company's petition, saying that it would be "a great disreputation to the court in general . . . if the aspersions thus openly laid upon the government of this Company shall not be publicly cleared."[54] Sandys concurred, adding that the presence of the Dutch ambassador heightened the importance of the success of the petition.

The entire experiment with Parliament was an exercise in appearances, even if Parliament did not seem inclined to show approbation of the Company. If Parliament was cold, Company leaders could still gain from the publicity, by printing Mun's *A Petition and Remonstrance* and reminding politicians and investors alike of the value of the trade. Ideally, they would have secured a show of support from Parliament, but the court of committees' actions in this case (presenting the petition to the Privy Council before presenting it to Parliament) showed that, even as Company leaders explored a possible new alliance with Parliament, they still were open to maintaining their alliance with the crown and possibly hoped that the petition would spur not Parliament but the crown and Council to make a show of support. Despite the lukewarm reception that the petition received in Parliament (including Sir Edward Coke's direct criticism of the East Indies trade), the leaders had it printed with a dedication to the House of Commons.[55] It was printed and sold by Nicholas Bourne, who received £15 and 4 shillings from the Company for it. How many copies the Company bought of the petition was not noted, but that sum would have bought a considerable number.[56]

Essentially, nothing came of the 1628 *A Petition and Remonstrance*—certainly it led to no public avowal of support for the East India Company. When the House of Lords took up Warwick's suit against the Company in June, the lords sided with Warwick. Parliament was prorogued in late June, and when it resumed in early 1629, it did not return to the Company's petition.

The Company was at low ebb in spring 1628. Though arguably in a position of some hope with regard to the events at Amboyna, Company leaders had little trust in the monarch. Their adventurers were skeptical about the soundness of continuing the trade, and the leaders were still unable to secure the strong sign of support they needed. They could not get pamphlets about Amboyna published, and while they could publish their petition to Parliament, they could not get Parliament to grant their request. Ready to explore support beyond the king and Privy Council, Company leaders were finding that the alternatives were unreliable too and might fuel faction within the Company. Parliament had not proved to be the savior they had hoped for, and although the crown might be unreliable, it might be their best hope.

Whither Next?

In mid-1628, Charles was keeping a close eye on the affairs of the East India Company. He may even have been keeping a closer eye than Company leaders realized. From the perspective of the crown, trading companies were proving themselves unreliable, unwilling to pay customs or extend loans to the king. The Levant Company was the primary offender in this regard, having refused since 1627 to pay tonnage and poundage, a type of customs assessed on import and export goods, but the East India Company was also not extending loans willingly and was pressuring Charles about Amboyna. Additionally, the Company and the Levant Company had many members in common, which made the Company guilty by association. In consequence, while Company leaders were trying to decide whether to trust the monarch again, and how deeply, the monarch was exploring ways to change the Company so he could better trust it to answer his needs. In early July 1628, he was experimenting on several fronts.

Charles's first attempt to gain greater control over the Company in 1628 was also the most straightforward: he offered to become a member of the Company. James had made a similar proposal after the initial news of the Amboyna massacre, and Charles had made the same offer shortly after becoming king in 1625. The wariness of Company leaders to admit the monarch has already been examined, as has the variety of reasons they gave for why the monarch's membership was undesirable.[57] What is noteworthy here is the timing of Charles's 1628 offer: it came in early July 1628, right before the Company's yearly election (the governor's announcement of the offer to the court of committees came literally minutes before the general election meeting), days after Parliament had been prorogued (without granting Charles any of the revenue he needed), and while Charles still held the seized Dutch ships—with Company leaders uncertain how long he would keep them.[58]

The king's offer was not helped by the fact that, just days before, he had pressed the governor for a substantial loan from Company coffers. Charles claimed that he only wanted the money (£10,000) for a few weeks to use for the relief of the besieged Huguenot stronghold of La Rochelle, France. Neither James nor Charles had been reluctant to request large loans from the Company, but in this case, Charles had already approached the corporation of London and the Levant Company and been turned down by both.[59] The East India Company likewise refused to grant his request. Company leaders were struggling to find investment enough to send even two ships to the East, and it was impossible for them to loan Charles so much money. More importantly, if Charles's request for money became known, the governor believed that the Company would never secure the additional adventures it still needed because people would worry that their money would go to fund a loan rather than the trade. Charles wanted the court of committees to present his request to the general membership at the election meeting that was taking place later that afternoon, but the court decided not to do so.[60] It is possible that the governor delayed discussing the king's request until the last possible moment—right before the election meeting began—to limit the possibility of Charles's finding a means to change the minds of the Company leaders. Thus on 2 July, before the election meeting, the court of committees had to decline both the king's offer of membership and his request for a large loan.

Charles did have a trick up his sleeve, however. He sent a messenger, Lord Dudley Carleton (formerly Sir Dudley Carleton), to the Company's election meeting on 2 July, in an effort to sway opinion among the generality. Carleton had worked for years on the behalf of Company interests as English ambassador to The Hague, and he now gave a public speech about the king's love for the Company, telling them "that such is [Charles's] love to commerce in general, and to this Company in particular," that he had "in his Princely wisdom" sent them a declaration of his "favor and good affection unto them." Carleton also hinted at things to come with regard to negotiations with the Dutch, "intimat[ing] that the Company in all likelihood would have news very shortly to their own contentment."[61] Overall, the king's message promised support and care.

Carleton's visit and the message he delivered also showed how closely the king was tracking Company affairs. The minutes explained that Charles had sent Carleton after "taking knowledge of a general court that had been held this day sennight [that is, the previous week]." They noted that Charles hoped Carleton's intervention would stop the Company from delivering a new petition, "which he understood they intended to exhibit to his majesty for his protection against the Hollanders."[62] Charles's information was not entirely correct: the general court had met the week before and discussed the need for written assurance from the king, but no firm plans for a new petition had been made.[63] However, Charles was still well informed about internal Company affairs that had never been formally shared with him.

Together with the king's request that the possibility of a loan be put to the general court and the broaching again of the admission to the Company, Carleton's happy message from the king looked much less like a simple message of support and much more manipulative. Had Charles's request for a loan been put to the generality, the king could reasonably have expected his messenger to sway at least a few members—especially with the promises of a resolution to the conflict with the Dutch. Each of these interactions seemed to support the worst fears Company members had about the overlap of crown and Company.

The court of committees delayed informing the monarch that he would not be admitted as a member of the Company. In a meeting two weeks later between the governor and a few Company representatives, the Privy Council, and the monarch about the question, the Company representatives expressed their concerns. The Privy Council assured the Company leaders that Charles had meant only to help the Company with his offer of membership. The king's offer was "done not to deceive, but thereby the better to protect the Company."[64] The matter was ostensibly dropped, though the monarch's subsequent actions raise questions about the extent to which he abandoned his hope of gaining greater control of the Company.

Charles's other schemes were even more manipulative and certainly more disruptive of Company business. Around the same time, a man with Charles's secret backing was creating disturbances within the Company and agitating for changes to the Company's organization that would benefit the monarch. This man was Thomas Smethwick.[65] In May 1628, he and several other adventurers presented a petition to the Privy Council against the court of committees.[66] Smethwick's complaints at the time included allegations that the court of committees had made fortunes from the East Indies trade by keeping information from the generality and that the trade had been woefully mismanaged; in other words, he was complaining about rampant private interest.[67] Whether this meeting with the Privy Council was how Smethwick came to Charles's notice or whether their association had already been established at that point is unclear. Certainly the timing of Smethwick's agitations was very convenient for Charles.

Smethwick was a member of the East India Company at least as early as 1624, and from 1627 to the time of his death in late 1641 or early 1642, he regularly stirred up trouble; led factions; and, from the perspective of the court of committees, generally made a nuisance of himself. He spent his career with the Company on the outs with its governing body, and at one point he was almost disenfranchised for his conduct. He also served as a committee for at least one year, which suggests that he had some support in the generality at times. Beyond his appearances in the court minutes, however, little is known of Smethwick. Certainly how and where he was drawn into court circles is unclear.[68] What is clear is that he ended up working for the regime.

By May 1628, when he petitioned the Privy Council, Smethwick had been casting aspersions on the government of the Company for months, both publicly and privately.[69] Smethwick's petition to the Privy Council seems to have gone nowhere, but weeks later, at the same 2 July election meeting where Carleton spoke, Smethwick once again came to the attention of the court of committees (and everyone else present at the annual election court), this time with an even more pointed attack on the Company's government. Despite the lack of success of his petitions within the Company and to the Privy Council in May, Smethwick had circulated a libel in England and sent copies of it into Holland. In this document, he accused the governor, deputy governor, and committees of the Company of mismanagement and demanded their removal.[70] He was employing public maneuverings similar to the ones the Company had used to stir up anti-Dutch feelings after Amboyna, only instead of trying to drum up support for the Company, he was trying to discredit it both at home and abroad.

Not only had Smethwick questioned their reputations both to their faces and in a libel, but members of the court of committees learned that he had petitioned the king to have a commission appointed to examine them, "which complaint is done secretly and behind their backs." As before, Smethwick's complaints emphasized the need to reform the government of the Company. In the governor's estimation, Smethwick's aim was "for no other end as is conceived but wholly to overthrow the trade."[71]

As debate continued, a committee brought up a separate petition that had been delivered to the king, a petition that was delivered by "some false brother" and that proposed a radical reorganization of the Company. This petition suggested a restructuring of the Company's stock so that a fifth of it would belong to the king, "as a recompense for his royal protection." The committee reminded the assembly that James had offered to be an adventurer in the Company, and that the problem with the suggestion was that its legal counsel had informed Company leaders that if the king owned part of the stock, he would own all of it: "the whole right of the Company's stock would devolve to his Majesty for there can be no partnership held with the king."[72] The committee hesitated to reveal the name of the false brother, but Smethwick stood up and identified himself as the author of this petition as well. He claimed that he had come up with the idea "by having conference with some noble men," and he was shouted down and thrown out of the election meeting, which appeared to have proceeded quietly thereafter.[73]

Smethwick's complaints and proposals varied depending on his audience. The printed libel that Company leaders had addressed early in the meeting focused on classic factional charges, like mismanagement by the court of committees and lack of transparency regarding decision making and account books. In contrast, the proposal that had been produced after discussions with men at the royal court and that had gone to court was to radically reorganize Company stock with the aim of bringing the monarch into the Company.[74]

Though a connection between Smethwick and the royal court seems clear, the exact nature of Smethwick's relationship to Charles remains ambiguous—including whether or not Smethwick had been put up to this second petition by Charles himself or other people at court. Smethwick's statement about having conferred with some noblemen suggests the latter. However, Charles sent a message to Company leaders a few days later, asking them to be lenient and "deal fairly and favorably" with Smethwick, who had intended only to aid the king. This suggested a direct tie between Smethwick and the crown. Company leaders found it difficult to comply with Charles's request as Smethwick's actions had potentially serious consequences, including negatively affecting their ability to raise new stock. A committee noted that Smethwick's actions might look to Charles like a benefit to the king in the short term, but they were not, as they hurt the trade, and that what was "by his Majesty conceived to be a service is a very great disservice, for it discourageth the adventurers."[75]

When the factionally inclined Smethwick proved unrepentant, the Company decided not to be lenient as Charles had requested. They called Smethwick before the court of committees, where he delivered another piece of writing to them. After reading it and "finding it to be very scandalous," the court of committees got him to sign and date it. After another exchange, with Company leaders chiding Smethwick, who refused to recant, the court of committees decided to go to the Privy Council, and in particular to show his libel to the lord treasurer (probably the Earl of Portland, who succeeded the Earl of Marlborough as the lord treasurer on 15 July 1628 and who I suspect was presumed to be Smethwick's patron), "under whose favor he assumes to himself protection."[76] This connection to the lord treasurer might have explained Smethwick's court connections and why Charles had written the Company on his behalf. Alternatively, given Portland's ties to the crown, his patronage of Smethwick could also have been a blind for Charles's patronage of the man.

Smethwick was a loose cannon. Even if he had a high-ranking sponsor, he was an unreliable tool. One might note, for example, that one attribute of an effective mole was to be silent about who backed him. The Company's minutes did not record the outcome of the meeting with the lord treasurer. Smethwick's attempts to reshape the Company's internal government did not end, though this was the incident in which he most loudly proclaimed that he had friends in high places. It is possible that the lack of discretion that characterized Smethwick's actions may have lost him some of those friends and led Charles to reconsider his usefulness. Certainly, unlike the factional battles of 1618–1619, Smethwick's challenges to the Company were not sustained across multiple general court meetings but were sporadic and uncoordinated. In addition, his subsequent actions drew the ire of the regime, and on at least one occasion the Privy Council forced him to make a written apology to the court of committees.[77]

Smethwick's machinations were taking place in conjunction with Charles's offer of membership in the Company, Carleton's message of support hinting at some resolution to the events at Amboyna, and Company leaders' concern about the seized Dutch ships. In short, in the middle of 1628, Charles was using a variety of means to attempt to gain some degree of mastery over the Company. One can trace the hand of the king not only in his direct requests for membership or money but also in the behind-the-scenes use of a discontented Company member whose wish to reform the Company's internal government seemed to make him well-suited to promote or suggest changes to the Company's structure that would make it more financially favorable to the monarch. Had any of these attempts succeeded, the result would have been a change in the running of the Company that would either have allowed the monarch to more easily elicit funds from it or have reshaped the structure of the Company overall and given the monarch a direct role in its government. Despite the fact that the attempts were unsuccessful, they testify to Charles's willingness to alter the Company fundamentally so that it would better suit his needs.

Despite Carleton's comment on 2 July that the Company would soon learn something to its benefit, what Company leaders learned greatly worried them. In mid-July 1628, while still dealing with Smethwick's disturbances, the leaders received troubling news about the future of the seized Dutch ships. Company agents in the Netherlands reported that rumors were circulating there that Charles and the Dutch had reached an agreement and that the ships would soon be released. The news led Governor Abbot to plan to head to court and try to meet with the king to dissuade him from releasing the ships.[78] That same day, though, he and a few others were summoned to meet with the Privy Council, where the king himself informed them that he had decided to release the ships, but "upon such conditions as is not hurtful but rather beneficial to the Company." The king and councilors gave the Company representatives a list of reasons why the ships were being released. In the face of these reasons, Abbot decided it was useless to protest, determined to "submit the same [matter] wholly to his majesty's wisdom," and hurried back to a scheduled general court that afternoon (he and the others who had attended the king were late).[79]

Following the governor to the general court was a group of courtiers chosen by Charles to explain the situation to the generality—the king was sending another direct message to the general members. The courtiers were the lord keeper of the great seal (Thomas Lord Coventry), the lord privy seal (either Sir John Coke or Sir Robert Naunton), the Duke of Buckingham, the lord steward (the Earl of Pembroke), the lord chamberlain (the Earl of Montgomery), the Earl of Suffolk, and Lord Dudley Carleton. This was an illustrious group of influential men. Though they were not adventurers in the Company, most of them had had interactions with the Company, and as noted above, Carleton had represented Company interests in the Netherlands when he was ambassador to The Hague.

The king's chosen representatives arrived en masse and delivered a message of support for the Company from the king, albeit one that clearly defended Charles's actions regarding the released Dutch ships. They reported that Charles had "a gracious care and zeal of the prosperity and welfare of this Company," and that it was for the Company's benefit that he was releasing the ships. There followed an account of how much Charles valued the Company for the good it did the kingdom as well as his customs. According to Charles's messengers, such was his care to make restitution to the Company for the events at Amboyna, that when he became king, even though he was at war with Spain, "yet did he not spare to capitulate with the Dutch for a just and honorable satisfaction." And later, even when Charles was at war with France—"engaged in a greater war"—he still had not avoided arresting the Dutch ships, which he had now had in his possession for so many months. No offers had dissuaded him from keeping the ships until justice was secured. The lords' message emphasized Charles's "constancy," demonstrated by his keeping the ships despite Dutch efforts to release them. He was willing to let the ships go now because, due to his constancy, the Dutch had finally agreed to a trial for the Amboyna judges and promised to send commissioners to England. In other words, the Dutch had promised finally to begin to deal with Amboyna. This was not the same as having the matter settled and restitution secured, but the Dutch concession gave Charles an opportunity to release the ships honorably. He claimed that he always intended to keep the ships only until the Dutch agreed to deal with the matter of Amboyna. In contrast, Company leaders had thought that he was keeping the ships until a fair resolution was reached.

In losing the ships, the Company lost its bargaining chip, and Company leaders tried to discover the parameters of the new situation. Committees asked what the king would do should the Dutch prove faithless, as they had been in the past. When someone asked what security the Company had that it would finally receive justice, the lords answered that "they have engaged the public faith of their state, which is the greatest obligation between state and state and was never done till now." The lords claimed that Charles was thus making the issue of Amboyna more of a state matter than it had been before by publicly avowing his support and commitment. Others pressed to know what the king would do if the Dutch did not provide recompense and whether, in that case, Charles would agree to seize other ships. The lords promised to "move his Majesty herein," but were careful not to suggest that such a course was in any way promised, though they thought it was reasonable and possible.[80] Thus, despite the message of support, the Company materially was no better off—and arguably worse off—than before with regard to Amboyna. One newsletter writer observed that with the release of the Dutch ships, "the East India Company are like to dissolve," which reveals how seriously some people believed that the decision affected the Company.[81]

Charles's decision to release the ships left Company leaders with a mess on their hands. Years of pushing for restitution, culminating in the arrest of three ships, had resulted only in more promises that they would get justice, with no guarantee that the king would take aggressive action to guarantee real restitution. They had the reasons why Charles had not—first the war with Spain and then the war with France—and they had his willingness to proclaim his care for the Company and to make a visible show of that care. The leaders tried to turn those things into strengths: on the same day that the "act of state" to release the ships was read at a Company general court in July, the deputy governor reminded the generality that Charles prized the Company more than any other company and had demonstrated that care by "sending down seven of his greatest lords to show his affection and care," and that there was "no doubt to be made of his Majesty's resolution in the performance of what is promised."[82] Even if this seemed unconvincing, the court of committees had no other option.

However, the court of committees also decided that on the basis of the release of the ships and a new set of promises of royal support, it could no longer hope to raise enough money to send a fleet to the East Indies in the following year. A week later, members of the court of committees prepared to go to the Privy Council and present this state of affairs to the king. Too few investors were attempting to carry the whole trade, and "the burthen of this work cannot be supported upon the shoulders of a few." They attributed the lack of investment squarely to the lack of reparation and the release of the Dutch ships with no definite promise of restitution. They wanted to make sure that the king and Privy Council knew that if the trade failed, it was despite their best efforts.[83] Later in the month, they made plans to go back to the Privy Council to update it about their fund-raising difficulties, noting that this was despite "it [being] well known to the court that his Majesty and the state have their eye upon this business." With the three Dutch ships released, Company leaders hoped the Privy Council might have some suggestion as to how it could "give life again to this action."[84] At a meeting between the president of the Council and the governor a few weeks later, Abbot said that the king needed to show real support of the Company, that it "must not be done as formerly by fair word and promises only (for that will not serve the turn) but by some real act to be manifested to the world." If no such act was forthcoming, not only would men not adventure more money, but they would pull out their investments and the Company—and the East Indies trade—would disintegrate.[85]

Company leaders were once again asking for action by the king, using almost the same threat of ending the trade that they had used years before. As it had been then, the threat was a real one. The prospects for the trade looked especially bad when the court of committees learned of a damaging rumor that was circulating: that Charles had received a large cash payment from the Dutch to release the ships. In other words, as the court of committees understood this rumor, Charles had refused to back the Company against the Dutch and had refused to support English merchants against Dutch depredations, not to preserve amity between the nations or to advance another ideological objective of the state, but for a payment or bribe.[86]

What happened next showed how tenuous the Company's connection to the Privy Council and king had become. Company leaders told the Privy Council that their agents in Amsterdam had reported that Charles had received this money. They asked whether the rumor was true. The lord president said that he had told Charles of the rumor, and that Charles had said he could use the money and would be more than willing for the Company to give it to him and thus make the rumor true—but otherwise it was only a rumor. The councilor then chastised the leaders for spreading a false and damaging rumor which reflected badly on the king and Council, and told the leaders to be "more circumspect and wary."[87]

The leaders took this comment as a break in protocol, a criticism of their doing something that they saw as part of the normal back-and-forth between the Company and Privy Council, in which the two worked together and shared information. One testy committee replied that he was sorry that the Company's "zeal and duty to the state" had caused offense, as Company leaders had often brought to the Council intelligence, sometimes unwelcome, from letters from their agents and factors and never before had such an action been complained of:

> He had many times in the like case upon letters received from his factors abroad made his repair to the lord treasurer and secretary of state then being, and imparted unto them divers passages of state, and many times things that were not welcome or pleasing unto them to hear, and yet he received always thanks at their hands and encouragement to continue his advertisements unto them, and this being a business which (as the Company conceived) concerned both his Majesty and state in honor they durst do no other than acquaint their Lordships therewith. But if his Majesty and the lords be offended at what they in their duties have done, they humbly crave pardon, and will hereafter if it be their pleasure be more sparing in this kind.[88]

This exchange clearly owed much to high tempers and perceived criticism on both sides, but at its heart was a question about the relationship between the Company and the state: whether or not the Privy Council wanted the information the Company could provide, which was useful and necessary to the state, but the cost of which was that the Privy Council had to pay more attention to the Company's concerns and interests.

This incident seemed to illustrate the ways the court of committees no longer enjoyed insider status in the regime. The facts that the court of committees' information could be so significantly different from what the Privy Council assured them, and that members of the Company could be faulted for their information, whether it was incorrect or correct, was a sign that they were on the outside—they were no longer partners in a mutually beneficial relationship. In further defense of their intelligence, one committee noted that, even if the information was wrong, the agent was only reporting the common opinion in Amsterdam. The perception there, he claimed, was that the Dutch had paid Charles a sum of money to release the Dutch Company's ships, and that the rumor was no more than was "in the mouths of almost every man upon the Exchange" in London. In the view of Company leaders, the Company served to gather information and pass on relevant news to the regime. In this case they had heard information about the state that concerned them, but in checking its veracity with the Privy Council, they had been criticized for scandal mongering. The leaders claimed that the only difference between this case and other similar cases was that this time they had heard news about their own country, and they resented being faulted for the news they had heard abroad and passed on as they had done with much other news they had heard abroad.

Of course, in some ways the Company's answer was disingenuous: this was not a neutral piece of information, something of interest only to the state. They had shared this piece of news, which touched on Company interests, to discover whether or not it was true. Yet regardless of intent, the relationships and implications involved did not change: if the king and Council wanted the benefit of the Company's information networks, they had to have some consideration for the Company's interests. Although the court of committees was appalled by the Privy Council's response to its member's question, the chastisement was in fact quite mild. Ultimately, the Privy Council did not want to lose the information the Company could and did provide them, and councilors could only tell Company leaders to be more careful with sensitive matters next time.[89]

Plans for the Amboyna trial further revealed the gulf between Company and regime. The Company had wanted the trial to be held in England. Charles had now agreed that it could be in the Netherlands, and to add insult to injury, he wanted the Company to send over its witnesses' testimony and possibly the witnesses themselves, as well as all the documentary evidence relating to Amboyna, including the "books, tables, and other writings wherein the parties executed left a dying testimony of their innocency."[90] These materials included a psalm book of one of the executed men, a bill of another, and various declarations of innocence.[91] Therefore, Charles wanted to send to the Netherlands the most emotionally charged evidence the Company possessed. The Company would keep only copies and authentications of the originals. To Company leaders, these requests to send their sensational evidence abroad for use in a trial about which they were already skeptical looked like another attempt to hamstring them. The evidence was valuable not only for the proof it provided, but also for its ability to elicit emotions—specifically horror and sympathy. To lose these items was to lose a valuable weapon in the Company's arsenal. The news from the Netherlands did not inspire confidence that sending the psalm book and other items would accomplish the objectives of Company leaders: the promised Dutch commissioners were delaying in coming to England, and the trial was delayed, supposedly because the witnesses had not been sent. The Company did eventually send several witnesses, including Ephraim Ramsey and John Powell, as well as George Forbes, who had served as a translator at Amboyna.[92] The governor was of the opinion that all of this was just window dressing, and that the Dutch never meant to condemn their actions at Amboyna.[93]

Though Company leaders did not revisit the use of printed pamphlets to sway public opinion or official action, someone in the Company did attempt to circulate papers about Amboyna at the end of 1628. Secretary of State Edward Conway wrote to Sir Robert Heath, the attorney general, about papers that were circulating—"certain printed papers that go from hand to hand"—that described the Amboyna massacre and were "set down in such a manner as may breed much disaffection between his Majesty's subjects and those of the Low Countries." With Charles now taking a direct hand in resolving the matter, such commentary was both unnecessary and improper. Conway wanted Heath to suppress all writings that did not suit the "good terms of amity and correspondence" between the two nations. "Loose papers and reports" only stirred up bad feeling between the English and the Dutch.[94]

It is impossible to say for sure what the papers were or with whom they originated (Conway did not know). Two sources are possible. One possibility is that these were copies of Forbes's deposition about Amboyna, circulated with at least the tacit approval of the court of committees. The other is that these documents owed their circulation to Smethwick and were an attempt by him to sway either the Privy Council or the court of committees.[95] Regardless of their source, if the papers were in print rather than manuscripts, they had been printed unofficially and were therefore illicit. Perhaps they were even the banned printed pamphlets that had been released to the Company in July 1628. Either because the action skirted legality or because Company leaders did not know about it, neither the papers' production nor their circulation was mentioned in the court minutes. In any case, the papers aroused official ire for their potential to foster negative public opinion about the Dutch. Even if the Company had wanted to try again to appeal to the public, it would have been unsuccessful. A resolution to the events at Amboyna may have been close, but Company leaders' control over it was less than they might have hoped or expected.

Tonnage and Poundage

The major issue roiling Parliament, crown, and the trading companies in late 1628 and early 1629 was whether the monarch's levying of tonnage and poundage was legal. The question touched on constitutional issues and mercantile matters and involved a number of merchants who were members of the Company. The Company could be expected to have a prominent role in the debate over tonnage and poundage, yet the dispute seems hardly to have registered with it. The Company ultimately did not join with the Levant Company in its refusal to pay tonnage and poundage in 1628 or 1629, even though the companies shared many members. The Company's reluctance to act on the matter was a recognition of how much it needed the support of the monarch—not Parliament.

The controversy over tonnage and poundage barely appeared in the Company's minutes. The first mention in the minutes that anyone from any company was refusing to pay tonnage and poundage did not appear until February 1629, when the Privy Council requested the use of one of the Company's warehouses to store "such goods of the merchants as are seized upon for refusing to pay the King custom." The court of committees pleaded to be excused from complying with the request, citing their "continual use" of the warehouses as the reason they could not accommodate the king.[96] The request of the Privy Council certainly suggested that the Company was not refusing to pay tonnage and poundage, as many Levant Company merchants were (in fact, some of them had been refusing since 1626). Indeed, Company ships that arrived in late 1628 seem to have paid the duties. The goods from the ships had been sold, meaning that they had been released from the custom house, and Company leaders had granted a gratuity of thirty pounds of pepper to each of three deputies at the custom house for their help in dealing with Company goods.[97]

The merchants' refusal to pay tonnage and poundage was a major issue for crown and Parliament in early 1628 and 1629. The Privy Council had begun proceedings against some Levant Company merchants in early 1627, and Parliament took up tonnage and poundage as a cause célèbre in its 1628 and 1629 sessions, treating it as a matter of the defense of liberty against monarchical overreach.[98] The Levant Company minutes for the period recorded discussions on numerous days about how to handle the demands for the payment of tonnage and poundage, and newsletters from the period recorded how Levant Company merchants were refusing to pay imposts on their merchandise.[99] Robert Brenner in particular sees the refusal to pay tonnage and poundage as a sign of the vibrancy and strength of merchant opposition in 1628 and 1629, and of the alliance between the merchant opposition and the House of Commons.[100] However, Company minutes did not record any discussions similar to those that took place in the Levant Company in 1628, and Company leaders did not suddenly find themselves friends of Parliament.

Members of the Company were almost undoubtedly sympathetic to the concerns of the Levant Company—many of the most prominent Company merchants were also Levant Company merchants, including Governor Morris Abbot, William Garway, and Nicholas Leate. As Levant Company merchants they were refusing to pay impositions—yet as East India Company merchants, they seem to have paid them. Indeed, Abbot, Garway, and Leate were among a group of Levant Company merchants who forcibly entered a locked warehouse where their seized goods were being held and liberated them in September 1628. Some thirty merchants took part in this action, and a few were later imprisoned.[101]

It is possible that the logistics of running a trade through a joint stock discouraged the type of refusal that so many Levant Company members engaged in. Individual merchants in the East India Company could not refuse to pay their portion of tonnage and poundage unless all of them did, as none of the goods belonged to particular merchants. A particularly determined Levant Company merchant could refuse to pay duties on the goods on his ships, while another might complain but still pay duties on his goods. The collective nature of the East Indies trade, however, might have made Company leaders more willing to pay for the whole, as they had fewer options for refusal without involving the entire stock and members of the generality, all of whom might not have wanted to refuse.

The first mention in the minutes of the Company's possibly delaying paying customs was in March 1629, when the court of committees debated whether to enter cloth at the custom house (so tonnage and poundage could be assessed) or to delay. This debate was not about paying customs on newly arrived goods, but about paying export customs on goods to be sent to Persia, as tonnage and poundage covered both imported and exported goods. Because members of the court of committees had heard that "a declaration will come forth within a few days from his Majesty and the state," they decided to delay. This declaration would better inform them of how and what they were to pay—in other words, "how to carry themselves in a business of so great consequence."[102] A few days later, Abbot brought the matter as a whole before the court of committees, observing that it was "high time to resolve what they will do concerning [customs]."[103] Time was short: the ships for Persia needed to be loaded and sent off quickly, or they would risk missing that year's trade.

The court of committees' debates on what course of action to take showed the members' understanding that they relied on the monarch in a way that other trading companies did not, and that the structure of their trade differed as well. In Abbot's view, the issue came down to the fact that "the Company and other merchants are not alike for many reasons." Without directly mentioning it, he thus referred to the Company's special reliance on the patent and prerogative. In particular, the Company needed the king, especially for diplomatic representation, in a way that no other company did, and to challenge the king on this matter would jeopardize any future support from him: "to contest with the king . . . in a business of this nature and at this time were no way fit considering the many occasions they have now with the king from whom the Company cannot expect any favor if herein they should show themselves refractory."[104]

In principle Company leaders might have taken a greater part in the refusal to pay tonnage and poundage in spring 1629, but in practice they could not risk waiting at that time of year. They continued to delay while waiting for word from the king, deciding "to defer the entry [of the cloth] for a day or two upon hope that within that time some alteration might happen." If no such alteration happened, however, they decided, "in respect of the present state of the Company's affairs both with relation to his Majesty and state, and also to the good of the voyage . . . there was conceived a necessity to enter and send away the said cloth speedily."[105] They were waiting, presumably in solidarity with the Levant Company's aims, but they could not continue doing so without losing a year's trade. The time demands of the Company's trade simply were different from those of the Levant Company's. Two days later, the court of committees decided not to delay the entry of the goods any longer, and this ended the Company's involvement in the customs boycott.[106] When the Privy Council approached the Company once more about lending warehouses to store impounded goods, the Company agreed and turned over two warehouses to the king's use.[107]

The years 1628 and 1629 were tumultuous ones for the Company. They were also tumultuous ones for the nation as a whole, and Company affairs intersected with national ones on numerous occasions. The issues that most touched the Company in these years had their roots in the continuing problem of Amboyna. The tense discussions with the monarch and Privy Council, the factious maneuverings of Smethwick, the failed attempt to court parliamentary support—all were shaped by the Company's attempts and failure to secure a favorable resolution to Amboyna. Even when members of the Company found themselves discussing what role, if any, they should take in the controversy over tonnage and poundage, their actions were conditioned by the Company's reliance on the prerogative and the support of the monarch that had been so clearly exposed by the events at Amboyna.

Amboyna continued to make occasional and unpredictable appearances in Company affairs after 1629. Charles lost any leverage he might have had over the Amboyna verdict when he signed treaties first with France and then with Spain in 1630. The Amboyna trial took place in the Netherlands in 1630, with an acquittal rendered in 1632.[108] With the verdict in, what Company leaders hoped to gain by reprinting Skinner's *True Relation*, as they tried unsuccessfully to do in 1631 and then did successfully in 1632, is opaque, in part because the relevant volume of court minutes is missing. Presumably they printed the pamphlet in reaction to the news of the acquittal, though they may instead (or also) have been responding to the periodic appearance of new Dutch accounts of Amboyna, one of which also appeared in 1632.[109] The issue of Amboyna attracted public attention again during the Anglo-Dutch wars of the 1650s and was officially resolved in the 1654 Treaty of Westminster. In 1665 the Company finally received financial reparations in the amount of £3,615, long after the initial participants were dead or no longer active in the trade.[110] The heyday of Amboyna for the Company was the 1620s, though, when it dominated Company discussions and meetings and colored Company dealings with the regime.

What the negotiations about Amboyna in the late 1620s highlighted was that Company leaders could not rely on the regime for the diplomatic support that they (and the members of the generality) saw as necessary for the running of the trade. Their relationship with the monarch and Privy Council was more distant than it had been, with Company leaders finding it difficult to gain access to the monarch and sometimes being chided by the monarch and councilors for their demands.

Yet their brief attempt to secure parliamentary support demonstrated that distant or no, the monarch and Council were still more sympathetic to the Company than Parliament was. By mid-1629, the Company had made peace of a sort with the king. It was not an unqualified peace: Amboyna was still not resolved, the Dutch ships had been released, and Company leaders had no immediate hope that the situation would change in their favor. But the Company paid its customs and acknowledged that its trade was not like other trades. The Company needed the support of the monarch. The years 1628 and 1629 had tried the relationship between it and the crown, but for Company leaders, the strained and more distant relationship that had developed by 1629 was still their best hope for making the trade work. The big question was whether Charles would give up on his designs to more closely control the East Indies trade.

10

Crown Manipulations of the East Indies Trade

Dismantling the Company in the 1630s

I N SPRING 1636, a fleet of four ships and a pinnace departed for the East Indies under the command of Captain John Weddell. It had been outfitted with supplies for a long voyage and the bullion and goods needed to trade in the East Indies at a cost of some £120,000, and the captain was a man with considerable experience with the East India Company, having served it on several voyages in the 1610s and 1620s. He had knowledge of the ports and sea lanes of the East Indies and knew a number of the governors and officials in those ports. In short, it was a fleet with the specialized knowledge and economic backing to make a successful trading voyage. In fact, a fleet much like it sailed every year. The problem was that this was not an East India Company voyage, but that of a crown-backed rival to the Company.

This voyage was organized and paid for by a small group of investors who have come to be known as the Courten Association. They had extensive and demonstrable support from Charles I. The Courten Association has attracted some attention as the group that spearheaded English colonization projects in Madagascar as well as privateering ventures in the Caribbean, though scholarly work on any of these topics is surprisingly thin. The group also appears briefly in accounts of the early East India Company as rivals and interlopers in the East Indies trade—though with little attention to the reasons why Charles would have been particularly interested in backing the Company's rivals in the 1630s.[1]

Yet the activities of the Courten Association indicate that it was much more than a simple, if unexpectedly well-organized, group of interlopers. The Courten Association was essentially the mirror image of the East India Company: it was granted many of the same rights and privileges, but its charter was to a small group of aristocrats and merchants with direct and close ties to Charles and the royal court. In fact, the Association was a sign of a carefully orchestrated breakdown of the alliance between crown and the Company that had characterized the latter's activities in the early 1600s. It represented Charles's attempt essentially to dismantle the Company and remake the East Indies trade via a body constructed to work not with the crown, like the Company, but for the crown.

The events of the late 1620s reaffirmed the Company's reliance on the crown, but they prompted Charles to try to gain more control over the Company and the East Indies trade. Merchant intransigence encouraged him to explore non-Company alternatives to develop the East Indies trade. Charles wanted a trade that was more obviously imperial rather than solely commercial, with fortified settlements and a greater English presence in the East Indies. Thomas Smethwick, a crown-backed adventurer within the Company, had already tried to introduce plans to reorganize the East Indies trade and funnel more profits to the king (as discussed in Chapter 9), but those plans had failed. In the 1630s, Charles threw his net wider. He sent voyages to explore new trading routes, and crown-backed rivals of the Company flouted its right to exclusive trade in the East Indies. The careful balancing act between Company, state, and empire that had functioned for over thirty years was transformed as Charles attempted to assert more oversight and control of the state's overseas activities.

Experimenting with the East Indies

Almost from the moment he became king, Charles had attempted, through a variety of means, to shape the actions of the Company leaders. His efforts ranged from direct requests for membership or money to the behind-the-scenes use of Smethwick, a discontented Company member whose wish to reform the Company's internal government seemed to make him well-suited to promoting or suggesting changes to the Company's structure that would make it more financially favorable to the monarch. The result of each of these unsuccessful attempts would have been a change in the running of the Company that would either allow the monarch to more easily elicit funds from the institution or would reshape the structure of the Company overall and provide the monarch with a direct role in its government. When changing the Company from within failed, Charles attempted to change the East Indies trade itself.

Beginning in 1630 (in other words, shortly after his failure to gain access to the Company through membership requests or Smethwick's actions) and continuing through the decade, Charles began creating and licensing groups of rivals to the Company. In 1630 Charles granted privileges to Richard Quayle, a sea captain, in several letters that instructed him to take his ship, the *Sea Horse*, and "range the seas all the world over." The letters made no exclusions or prohibitions about where Quayle could sail. In other words, they did not prohibit him from sailing to areas where the Company traded.[2] The initial letter to Quayle listed as a reason for the grant simply that he had asked for it, along with "private reasons best known unto" Charles.[3] These reasons, as stated in another letter, were Charles's attempts to target Spain without open hostilities, though his letter also instructed Quayle to target the goods and ships of rulers "not in league" with England. In fact, Quayle was not supposed to come home before he had seized goods worth £10,000, of which he and his company would keep one-third, with the rest going to Charles.[4]

This was not the first time the monarch had licensed a rival to the Company. On a few occasions, James I had granted letters to people that seemed to infringe on the Company's patent. As discussed in Chapter 6, the 1604 patent granted to Sir Edward Michelborne and 1607 license to Richard Penkevell, for example, gave those men access to parts of the East Indies that the Company could (and did) argue were encompassed in its patent. Michelborne sent at least one ship, though at the time of his death he seems to have been negotiating with the Company to turn over his patent to it. Penkevell never actually used his patent, though he took part in explorations for the northwest passage, and the Company does not seem to have taken action with regard to him. It is not clear whether that was because Company leaders did not know of the patent or judged it not to be a concern.

Those grants, which infringed on the Company's patent, were given in the infancy of the Company. The motivation behind them is unclear. It seems possible that James was using the grants of privileges as inexpensive rewards to courtiers he wished to favor, or that he was trying to spur further expansion of trade in the East Indies and did not think that the entire enterprise should be turned over to one body—certainly more than one body was granted patents to lands in the Atlantic and North America. Perhaps James did not think the Company would be so zealously protective of its privileges or so profitable that jeopardizing its success was undesirable as it was, and thus decided it was not worth antagonizing in later years. Or perhaps rewarding courtiers at the Company's expense became less politically expedient as more and more courtiers became members of the Company and thus had a stake in preserving its privileges. Regardless, after Michelborne and Penkevell, James did not grant other patents to people that infringed so clearly on the Company's grant, though he did test the boundaries of what Company leaders would accept. The 1617 grant to Sir James Cunningham, for example, was to start a Scottish East India Company. It was arguably not an infringement of the English East India Company's patent, though Company leaders saw it as such. The Company managed to quash that venture. The other obvious case of interlopers in the trade—the Earl of Warwick's piracy in the East Indies in the late 1610s—was not conducted under James's auspices, despite the support in England for Warwick. Instead, Warwick sailed with letters of marque from the Duke of Savoy. After Michelborne and Penkevell, in short, for decades the monarch did not directly license rivals to the Company.

Thus when Charles began licensing rivals to the East India Company in the 1630s, he was doing something new—or at least, something that had not been done in almost thirty years. Additionally, the grants Charles made were distinctly different from those of James to Michelborne or Penkevell. Charles gave his licensed rivals to the Company extensive state support to become viable alternatives and challengers. They were part of a concerted campaign to weaken the Company.

Quayle's 1630 expedition was, in many ways, an experiment. It involved only one ship and was answerable directly to Charles, who provided instructions for Quayle that were both involved and somewhat open-ended. The instructions directed Quayle to go to the Red Sea or elsewhere. They told him to target the Spanish or any other shipping of kingdoms and rulers not in amity with England (in other words, he could not target the shipping of friendly nations). The same letter that instructed Quayle not to come back without a cargo worth £10,000 hinted at the complications implicit in Quayle's charge: his mission was not to be made known even to the crew until they were out at sea. Once he informed them of the voyage's objectives, Quayle was supposed to make them swear an oath of allegiance to the monarch.[5] This secret mission was Charles's own, in other words.

The Company seems not to have heard of the *Sea Horse* for some time. The first mention of the ship in Company accounts was not in spring 1630, when Quayle received his letters from Charles, but in early 1632, when Company leaders in London received a December 1631 letter from the commanders of the Company's fleet. The commanders wrote that they had met a ship belonging to Charles, "immediately set out by him," and captained by Quayle. Quayle had possessed a royal commission to go to the Red Sea, "by commission under his Majesty's hand and seal." As the Company commanders could not prove that Quayle had done anything against his commission, and as the commanders were aware of the "force" of that commission, they had to let Quayle go. They immediately wrote to London to inform the leaders of a design that "cannot be pleasing." This letter was not received for several months after its December 1631 composition, and it was the first notice the leaders had that Charles had given a commission for the East Indies to someone outside the Company.[6]

A few months later, Company factors in India wrote to London to inform Company leaders that the *Sea Horse* had been targeting trading ships in the Red Sea and taken a number of prizes. The factors' biggest concern about Quayle's actions in the Red Sea was that they did not know who he was targeting, and they worried that the Company would be held liable for Quayle's actions—or rather, they knew that they would be expected to pay for the depredations of Quayle on any of the Mughal emperor's subjects.[7] The letter presented the events as dangerous and expensive: the ship was "ransacking and pillaging the traders in the Red Sea," and the factors feared not only that the Company would have to pay for someone else's crime, but also that Quayle's activities would lead to the "utter loss of your Red Sea Trade (which stood on fair terms)" and that even the Levant Company might find itself held liable in Constantinople for Quayle's actions on behalf of Charles.[8]

Ultimately the *Sea Horse* returned to England with a cargo supposedly not worth much.[9] Yet the ship's voyage was not the only such experiment conducted by Charles. The monarch challenged the Company's patent numerous times and in a variety of ways in the early 1630s. In March 1631, via Company member Sir John Wolstenholme, Charles approached the court of committees about a proposal to send a ship to discover the northwest passage. If the voyage was successful, it would end up in the Far East, perhaps at Bantam (also known as Banten), in Java, and Wolstenholme explained that Charles wanted to know if the Company would allow the ship to be loaded with pepper there. Company leaders would not agree, seeing this as an attempt to enable private trade outside their patent privileges. However, they were willing—if the ship made it that far—to send Company pepper back to England on the ship for reasonable freight charges.[10] Wolstenholme also wished the Company leaders to give advice on what types of goods the ship should carry: in the event that it made landfall in Japan, he wished to know what colors and sorts of cloth might find favor there.[11] In short, on Charles's behalf, Wolstenholme was feeling out the Company on what the ship could do abroad without causing the Company to cry infringement.

Charles had started exploring possible voyages in search of the northwest passage even before he had anyone approach the Company about such voyages. For example, in January 1630, he had approached Sir Thomas Button about a voyage to the northwest passage. Button had sailed under the aegis of Prince Henry in search of the passage (and the fate of Henry Hudson) in the early 1610s. Button's advice for Charles and Secretary of State Viscount Dorchester was to talk to Wolstenholme and Sir Dudley Digges, who had also been involved with Henry's overseas plans in the early 1610s.[12] A 1635 commission mentioned numerous voyages sent by Charles to look for the northwest passage, though Company minutes include only limited references to these voyages (unsurprisingly, none of them actually made it to the East Indies).[13]

Additionally, in early 1634 the Company's governor, Sir Morris Abbot, reported that he had heard rumors of a new Scottish East India Company that Charles meant to set up. The court of committees adopted a wait-and-see policy, letting the issue rest for months, though the court may have been mobilizing support in the interim. In mid-October, the governor reported that Secretary Sir John Coke and the lord treasurer the Earl of Portland (who had been a member of the Company since 1617) had discussed the matter and informed Charles that a Scottish company would complicate matters for and hurt the English Company. Being "informed of the inconvenience and prejudice that may redound thereby," Charles agreed to recall the patent for the Scottish Company.[14] Thus the proposed Scottish Company came to nothing, but not without causing some concern.

Lastly, in the mid-1630s, a number of people at court were enthusiastic about developing a colony on Madagascar. Technically, Madagascar was encompassed in the Company's patent, and Company ships regularly stopped at St. Augustine Bay, though their activities in Madagascar were limited. The supporters of the Madagascar colony hoped that it would serve as a means to challenge Dutch influence in the East Indies and help develop English trade. The proposals for a Madagascar colony in 1636 had a distinctly Protestant and royalist slant, as one of the prime supporters of the venture was Rupert, son of Elizabeth Stuart and Frederick of Bohemia, who saw himself in the role of conquering hero. Endymion Porter was one of the most active proponents of the colony. Other supporters included the Earl of Arundel; Sir Thomas Roe; and William Davenant, who wrote a poem about Rupert's yet-to-occur conquest of Madagascar.[15] But while enthusiasm for the venture was high in 1636 and 1637, it never got off the ground—even though Arundel revived the plan in 1639.

Even without challenging the Company's patent, some people at the royal court were challenging its monopoly on access to the East Indies. In August 1630, William Feilding, the Earl of Denbigh, received permission from Charles to travel to the East Indies. Denbigh's voyage seems to have been at his own request—he was going not as an ambassador but as a private person, and he described himself as a "volunteer," and "one that desires only to see those countries."[16] The king was not unwilling to help him, however. Charles ordered the Company to help Denbigh by transporting him and his entourage in one of its ships. Charles's letter suggested that the experience Denbigh would gain on the voyage would help him better aid the regime in future, though he did not specify how.[17] The king anticipated that Denbigh's voyage would reach as far as the Mughal empire and Persia and provided him with letters to the Persian and Mughal emperors, entreating them to welcome Denbigh to their courts. The letters explained Denbigh's purpose as arising from his "desire to be an eye witness" and to see the splendor of foreign courts, though at least one newsletter writer noted that Denbigh had gone "in ambassage."[18] Denbigh's voyage in many ways seems to have been intended as an extension farther afield of the voyages to Europe that aristocratic men increasingly took in this period and that became the basis for the Grand Tour, though he offered to do any service he could for Company leaders while he was in the East Indies.[19]

Company leaders were not enthusiastic about transporting Denbigh. They deferred taking action on Charles's letter several times, but knew they could not really refuse. They hoped at least that taking Denbigh would not prove an expensive proposition, both in terms of his transportation and the effect he might have on trade and the factors abroad.[20] Someone outside the Company hierarchy could cause complications on board ship and in the

East Indies. For example, Denbigh and Company leaders engaged in a complicated negotiation over which ship and cabins the earl could have on the voyage east. Company leaders hoped to send him in the second ship of the fleet, as the first was used by all the factors, who needed to be able to confer with the fleet's commander as necessary. Turning over the great cabin in the main ship to Denbigh would mean that it could not be used for those consultations. Denbigh cited his military service and his honor and refused to be put in the second ship. He noted that whatever ship he was in should be the one flying the flag, and he offered to vacate the great cabin when it was needed for consultations and "dispose himself in some other place of the ship until their consultations be ended." Company leaders did not like this plan but felt compelled to accede to it.[21]

While Denbigh assured the leaders that there was no ulterior motive to his trip besides increasing his own experience and education, the pointed questions the leaders asked about whether he was going as an ambassador showed exactly what they were concerned about. An ambassador could made decisions or enter into agreements that would have lasting consequences for the trade, and could do so without consulting Company factors. If Company ships were transporting Denbigh, the leaders wanted it clear that he was not one of them or representing them. Even the formal agreement between Denbigh and the Company about how large Denbigh's entourage would be, and how much Denbigh and his people would pay for their portion of regular shipboard victuals had the effect of highlighting the distinction between the two parties, which was surely part of the leaders' intent.[22] Denbigh ultimately returned in 1633 with goods from the East Indies, including at least one Indian or Persian outfit (in which he was shortly thereafter painted by Anthony Van Dyck), but he seems to have had limited effect on Company affairs.[23]

Taken as a whole, these unconnected ventures reveal that there was considerable interest from the regime in voyages to the East Indies that did not directly involve the Company. They show that numerous people at the royal court, not least the monarch, were actively engaged in planning for eastern voyages in ways that did not involve the Company, although they may have relied on the specialized knowledge and even personnel at the Company's disposal.[24] Kevin Sharpe in particular has traced the ventures spearheaded by the regime during the Personal Rule of the 1630s, the "novel" schemes aimed both to raise new monies for the crown and to better regulate trade according to the aims of the monarch. These overseas ventures were part of that experimentation, which often employed the granting of new patents: by mid-decade, Charles had granted a number of patents for a variety of industries.[25] However, Company leaders were hardly aware of those larger trends. As they saw it, these schemes represented the monarch's infringement on privileges they had held from the monarch for decades.

These experimental ventures represented tests by Charles of the bounds of the Company's control in the East Indies and of the ways he could maneuver around the Company—and to some extent, of how well the Company could still mobilize support at court. When James had tested the bounds of Company's power, it had usually been able to mobilize considerable support at court. In the 1630s, in contrast, what was noticeable was how late Company leaders learned of the ventures and how little control they had over the outcome. Despite Company protests, the ventures proceeded apace. Thus, it is in the context of a monarch already pursuing alternatives to the Company, albeit in small, one-off efforts, that one must view the Courten Association.

Courten's Venture

In 1635, Sir William Courten Sr., Endymion Porter, Thomas Kynnaston, and Samuel Bonnell entered into a partnership to pursue an East Indies trade. Their partnership has come to be known as the Courten Association, though that name is actually a misnomer—the group of adventurers had no official name, and the name is taken from the 1637 charter given to Courten and his associates, not a term they used themselves. Nonetheless, given that Company leaders saw Courten and his son, Sir William Courten Jr., as the prime movers behind the group of rival adventurers, the name is apt here. Sir William Courten Sr. was the son of an émigré Protestant clothier with extensive personal and economic ties to the Netherlands, where he had spent time in his youth.[26] By the 1630s, he had gained a massive fortune via European and Atlantic trading ventures and had cultivated ties with Charles, including via thousands of pounds of loans in the 1620s. Indeed, at Courten's death in 1636, Charles supposedly owed him some £25,000.[27] When Courten died, his son inherited and took over his role in the overseas ventures. Porter was a courtier, a groom of the bedchamber, and a long-time friend of Charles. Bonnell was a merchant and one of Courten's employees, and Kynnaston was also a merchant and part of the London mercantile community.[28] Unlike the earlier one-off voyages Charles had sent, in this case there would be a proper trading fleet. The four men financed a voyage—

Courten borrowing or supplying the lion's share of the £120,000 cost of the fleet—and secured the services of a knowledgeable captain, John Weddell.[29]

Weddell was well-suited to the venture and was no stranger to the court of committees. He had served the Company as early as 1617 as a master's mate, and soon thereafter he captained a number of Company ships. He was part of the English contingent of the combined Persian-English force that took Hormuz from the Portuguese in 1621–1622 (see Chapter 7). His involvement with the Company, in short, was of long standing.[30] He was also a man with both initiative and some willingness to skirt rules. In April 1631, for example, he appeared before the court of committees to answer charges of private trading, both trading on his own and allowing others to bring back private goods.[31] By the 1630s, in short, Weddell had proven knowledge of the East Indies, a long-standing history with the Company that involved some rule breaking (on his most recent trip he had brought back a leopard but, supposedly contrite after the charges of private trading, he offered it to the court of committees to present to the king and queen), and proven marine knowledge.[32] How and when Courten and his associates came to know Weddell is unknown, but by December 1635 he had agreed to lead their fleet, and a former Company factor, Nathaniel Mountney, had agreed to go and serve as cape merchant (that is, head merchant or factor) in the venture.

It is impossible to know to what extent Courten and his associates approached Charles or were approached by him. It is possible that the germ of the idea for the venture lay with Weddell himself, or in something he said regarding new possibilities for the East Indies trade in Goa. Perhaps Charles then put him in contact with Courten and Porter, perhaps Weddell sought out Courten and Porter, or perhaps Courten and Porter sought Weddell out after hearing something of his claims. Certainly, Weddell seems to have been telling people after he returned in 1635 that he knew of a way for the king to benefit even more from the East Indies trade, and that it involved Goa.[33] In all likelihood, Charles was well aware of the Courten-backed trip and encouraging it even before he granted letters of commission for the venture. However, all that survives of the planning for it are the several letters of commission from Charles in December 1635 that spelled out the parameters of the voyage.

Collectively, these letters of commission showed Charles shaping this enterprise according to the model of Company voyages but with more favorable terms for and closer ties to the crown (and arguably for the adventurers as well). For example, the first letter, from 6 December 1635, promised Charles's support, including a hefty personal investment in the voyage: "for assurance of our real affection to the prosperity" of the voyage, Charles pledged to invest £10,000 in the joint stock.[34] This pledge to invest in the voyage was a distinct change from the Company's long-standing policy, which had refused offers by both James and Charles to adventure in the joint stock. Charles possibly saw his part in the voyage as guaranteeing the loyalty of the adventurers, as well as providing a possible and convenient source of income.

The most interesting of the letters concerned the royal commission to Weddell for the voyage. It outlined the aims, restrictions, and privileges that would shape the voyage. Charles recognized Weddell's earlier experience with the Company and specifically mentioned his interactions with authorities in Goa and Malabar, India—places the letter specified would be the voyage's destinations—and encouraged him to enter into trade negotiations there and at other points east. The letter noted explicitly that the Company had not used the "manifold privileges" granted to them to develop a trade to those places, nor had they built fortifications abroad—with the result that Charles had not "received any annual benefit from thence (as other princes do) by reason of the said Company's neglect." The Company had pursued "their own present profit and advantage" without providing for the long-term health of the trade, he concluded. The current problems of the East Indies trade were due, quite simply, to the Company's "supreme neglect of discovery and settling of trade."[35] In short, the letters presented a vision of the Company's commercial gain taking place at the expense of national gain, which should have had a distinctly imperial component, given the mention of fortifications, that the commercial venture had neglected.

Charles's letters of commission explained that, despite the Company's shortcomings, "having maturely and seriously considered that the increase of trade and navigation is the principal means to bring honor and wealth to this our kingdom," and always looking forward to what would secure these benefits for all his subjects, he remained convinced that the East Indies trade was key. He noted that he had already backed several voyages to discover the northwest passage, "which have not been so successful as was expected," but he still had hopes of finding the passage and the promises of the Japan trade. Charles gave Weddell full authority over the three ships and assorted pinnaces of the voyage and instructed him to go to Goa, the

Malabar coast, the Chinese coast, and Japan to begin the process of developing a trade there. All of these were areas that the Company's ships had traveled to and where they had traded in the past. All were also areas where the Company did not have permanent factories or ongoing trade relationships. In short, the Company could easily argue that these areas were within the scope of its patent, and the new adventurers could easily argue that they were not infringing on areas of developed Company trade. However, the letter then listed all the other possible places Weddell's voyage might go to trade—the Cape of Good Hope, Mozambique, the Persian Gulf, Sumatra, Java, and the Philippines—many of these being places where the Company did indeed have a trading presence. The aim of the voyage was to trade, selling English goods as well as buying foreign commodities, though Charles wanted Weddell to be alert for information relating to the northwest passage.[36]

A key difference between this letter of commission and the Company's patent emerged in the instructions about what else Weddell was supposed to do abroad: namely, claim lands. Charles's letter made specific provision for Weddell to appoint a person to explore in an effort to discover the northwest passage and authorized him to give that person "order and authority to take possession of us of all such lands as they shall discover and conceive may be of advantage and honorable for us to own and hold." To spur the adventurers to claim and possess land, Charles promised them in perpetuity half of the customs revenues that came from their trade or plantations.[37] Either Charles expected the plantations to earn little money, or he was providing a large incentive to spur English empire in the East Indies. It was true that many plantations in the Americas, for example, failed or provided lackluster earnings, but it was also true that one of Charles's biggest sources of income in the 1630s was customs revenue, and signing over a half interest in perpetuity for any type of such revenue was a significant concession.

The letters provided Courten, Weddell, and their associates with additional powers that the Company did not have. One letter specified what seal this new "company" could use—"a lion passant gardant between three imperial crowns," a design that emphasized the direct connection between the Courten Association's voyage and the crown, as well as the distinctly imperial agenda of the venture.[38] The last provision the king made for the Courten Association was to provide another sign of the regime's support: he authorized the ships to fly royal colors—"the same colors commonly called the union flag, which our own ships, and none but the ships employed in our particular service ought to bear."[39] Company leaders had occasionally discussed how helpful it would be to fly the royal colors on their ships, and both James and Charles had offered the right to fly the colors as an enticement to allowing the monarch to invest in the Company. When the leaders rejected the monarch's adventure, it meant forgoing the use of the colors. That privilege was now granted to the ships of the Courten Association.

The association's voyage was not hastily put together. The letters of commission revealed carefully thought out objectives and a plan of action. As noted above, the letters drew on the model of the Company, but with key changes that both boosted the authority of the venture and tied it symbolically and financially to the crown. Charles's letters of commission made clear that he was commissioning Weddell to do what the Company had not, and to prepare for the future possibility that the "aforesaid Company should fail."[40] Essentially, the king was both planning for and planning on the Company's failure.

In January 1636, about a month after Charles had commissioned Weddell, the first rumors about the Courten venture reached the Company's court of committees. The governor and deputy informed the other members of the court about the "general report spread abroad" about Courten's proposed voyage to the East Indies.[41] They began a series of inquiries to find out more information and, they hoped, to gather support. Company leaders did not get, or apparently seek, a meeting with the king. Instead, they called on an old ally, Lord Cottington, who promised to talk to Secretary of State Sir Francis Windebank, who in turn promised to talk to Charles.[42] Given that Windebank had earlier come to an agreement with the Courten adventurers to invest a token sum of money in their voyage, how hard he would have worked on the Company's behalf is open to debate.[43] Company leaders did not know that such an arrangement had been made, however. The monarch's response to their inquiry was not reassuring. He told them not to worry but gave few particulars as to why they need not worry: "he would not have the Company to trouble themselves about the business, for though it be true that these ships are to go forth by his privity and allowance, yet not to any of those parts that may prejudice or endanger the Company." Instead, he informed them, rumor lied. The ships would indeed go to the Red Sea, but "they are to be employed upon some secret design which his Majesty at present thought not fit to reveal."[44]

A remonstrance prepared by the Company leaders shortly thereafter underscored their concerns that the proposed voyages would undermine the stability and continuity that they argued characterized their trade in the East Indies. An anonymous written response to the Company's concerns emphasized that, despite rumors, the ships would not go near the Red Sea and that Company leaders could not know what would be on the ships (that is, what kind of goods would be carried) and so should not assume it was a rival venture. Most importantly, the respondent suggested that Company leaders acted more out of jealousy than anything else: "It seems the past actions of the said Company renders them thus jealous of any preparations for discovery lest it should find some print of their stops in those parts they mention, which they would have locked up from all men's eyes but their own." The author charged that Company leaders' desire to keep their knowledge secret or restricted led them to act in a way that hindered new discoveries. In short, the respondent argued, "there is no man will undertake any discovery, if he must be obliged first to acquaint the East India or any other Company with the particulars of the design or voyage."[45]

Further information suggested to the court of committees that despite Charles's assurances, Courten's voyage was, in fact, intended for the East Indies and the Red Sea.[46] The governor and deputy went again to speak with Cottington, who again promised that he would pass the Company's concerns along to Charles. Striking, once more, was how little direct access Company leaders had to the monarch or Privy Council in these inquiries. The governor once more emphasized the possible negative consequences of Courten's voyage and stated that the Company's concern was "so they may be free from blame if any unexpected accident shall befall the Company by this occasion," and that what they wished was "only to inform the state thereof beforehand." Charles's response, delivered via Cottington, was once again that the Company leaders should trust him and "that upon the word of a king and as he is a Christian king there is nothing intended to hinder or damage the Company in their trade."[47]

The actions and debates of Company leaders over the next few days revealed their unease and anxiety, as well as their lack of knowledge about the particulars of the voyage. They did not even know what to call the rival voyage. They referred to "Sir William Courten's intended voyage" but did not seem to know who had invested in the venture beyond Courten himself. On 4 March they noted that rumors of the voyage were increasing daily, and though reports initially mentioned one ship and one pinnace, current word referred to four ships and a pinnace. In addition, it was rumored that the rival adventurers had hired a number of Company factors and seamen and bought commodities that would sell in the East Indies. In short, despite Charles's reassurance, the evidence strongly suggested an East Indies destination. This conflicting evidence caused problems within the court of committees. Some members wanted to trust Charles, with the court minutes repeating, in a distinctive font, that the king had promised "as he was a Christian king," while others argued that it was "not safe for this court to sit still."[48]

Company leaders' attempts to deliver a petition to the king revealed further strain and anxiety in their relationship to Charles. The account in the court minutes of the delivery testified to a persistent difficulty in getting the king's ear, much less in persuading him to do as the leaders wished. Four men went to Whitehall "expecting by the means and favor of my Lord Cottington and Mr. Secretary Coke to have had private access to his Majesty and then to have delivered the Company's petition concerning Sir William Courten's design and likewise upon that occasion to have enlarged by word of mouth what was not expressed in their petition." Instead, they found that "although they attended in the Privy Chamber all the morning," they could not get access to the king. The minutes charted all the places Charles went that day—to chapel, back from chapel, to dinner—while, presumably, the men simply waited for him. They seem to have stopped him on his way back from dinner, handed him the petition, and then waited for hours outside the Council chamber without seeing him again. They eventually set up a meeting with William Laud, Archbishop of Canterbury, for the next day but left without any plan to meet the king, and in their account of their meeting with the Privy Council two days later, they made no specific mention of their having spoken with the monarch.[49] Tensions were high enough that one newsletter recorded how only days later, when Company leaders went to deliver a different petition to the king, which "at last the king snatched from them," he assumed it was another protest about the Courten adventurers and was relieved to discover it was merely about the Dutch and Amboyna.[50] The efforts of Company leaders at the royal court had no effect on the proposed Courten voyage, and Weddell and the ships left England for points east sometime in early 1636.[51]

The rumors and then certain knowledge of the rival expedition inflamed already heightened tensions within the Company. The financial struggles of the Company at the time had led to a number of confrontations between members of the generality and the court of committees over access to the Company's account books and letters from the East Indies. In the wake of the news of the rivals' departure and the ongoing weak performance of the Company's trade, at the July election a member of the generality had even proposed not reelecting Abbott as governor, "in hope that by a change the Company might have better success in their affairs than of late they have had."[52] Company members had expressed concerns about incumbency on numerous occasions, but never phrased those concerns in terms like this, where change was imagined as a last resort. Though this suggestion was not well received and Abbot was reelected, the fact that it was made was one indication of how low morale and trust in the Company's future was among some members of the generality in 1636.

There was also clear evidence of how committed Charles was to the success of the Courten venture. Sir William Courten Sr. died in late May 1636. His son inherited his father's adventure (and debts). In June 1636, with William Courten Jr. trying to settle his father's estate and finding himself in great debt, the king stepped in to aid him. Charles ordered several wealthy City merchants to loan Courten Jr. money or tell Charles why not they would not do so. Some people at court suggested that the whole Courten venture be offered to the East India Company to buy out. That seems not to have happened—at least, Company court minutes record no discussion of such an offer—and within a few weeks, Courten Jr. was negotiating with Porter about how to proceed with their venture.[53]

By late October, with Weddell long departed, the Company court of committees met to discuss what to do next. They talked about how Charles's favor to the rival group would hurt their trade, especially since rumors suggested that Charles might also allow a third group into the East Indies in the next year. Company leaders decided to press Charles to confirm their patent, and if he would not do so, to pull their men and goods from the East Indies—in other words, to give up the trade.[54] Once again they were contemplating a trade cessation, but for a very different reason than they used in dealing with the events of Amboyna. In a meeting with the Privy Council, Abbot laid out the Company's situation: its trade still suffered; its investors were discouraged by news of Courten's ships; and Weddell was making for Surat, where he should not be and where he would raise commodity prices and further hurt the Company's trade. "If the king and state do desire the supportation of the East India trade they must be cherished and comforted," the governor concluded.[55]

The trouble was that Company leaders did not have much time to figure out how to deal with Courten and his adventurers. Under normal circumstances, no one would expect Weddell and Mountney to return for four or five years. Unknown to the Company, however, the rival adventurers had sent out two ships in advance of Weddell's fleet in spring 1635, with a commission from Charles "to range the seas all the world over."[56] The two ships sent were the *Roebuck* and the *Samaritan*, and the seas they ended up in were in the East Indies, though the leaders of the Company seem to have known nothing about them for a year and a half.

In late 1636, the Company received word that the *Samaritan* and the *Roebuck*, under the command of William Cobb, had seized a Surat junk in the Red Sea, resulting in the arrest of two Company factors and the seizure of Company goods in Surat.[57] The news was known in London, since at least one newsletter reported the event, including the gruesome details of the tortures the crews had supposedly unleashed on the captured men.[58] For Company leaders, the news began a sleuthing mission, as they attempted to discover more about the trip—for example, by speaking to a cooper about whether he had hooped casks for a ship called the *Samaritan* a year and a half before and who had paid him, and investigating what type of insurance policy the merchants had taken out on the ships.[59] "Our merchants are in great distraction," one observer mentioned, noting the secrecy that had shrouded the venture and how little the Company merchants knew about where the ships had been bound and what they might have done.[60]

Company leaders discovered the names of several men behind the venture and took immediate action to prosecute them. They attributed the venture to Courten Sr., Kynnaston, and Bonnell. They had Kynnaston seized and arrested, though Charles soon ordered him released. Bonnell fled to France. Company leaders began a suit against the two men in the Admiralty courts for thousands of pounds in damages.[61] Porter was also involved—in March 1635 he kept twenty-two men of the crews of the two ships from being pressed into naval service—though Company leaders did not move against him.[62] Courten Sr. was dead by this point, but Company leaders attempted to prosecute Courten Jr. as his heir.[63]

The Company leaders had a meeting with the Privy Council days later about the ships. At least sixteen councilors, in addition to the king, were present to hear Company leaders read a petition and extracts from letters from the East Indies, recounting the seizure of two ships in the Red Sea by Courten's men, the torture by Courten's men of the people aboard the ships, and the subsequent arrest of Company factors in Surat. Charles was skeptical of the activities Courten's men were alleged to have committed, noting that while he had in fact set forth some ships around that time "with his Majesty's privity," he had sent them "with no warrant or direction from his Majesty or with his consent to do any act to the prejudice of the said Company." Charles continued in his denials, saying that while he would send a letter to Surat disavowing the actions and clearing the Company of culpability if Courten's men had seized the ships, yet "his Majesty conceives it is not very clear that the said act hath been committed by Englishmen."[64] Charles would make sure that reparations were paid to the Company, but he doubted that they would be necessary. The petition the Company leaders read before the Privy Council and king seemed to anticipate Charles's skepticism, imploring the councilors to hear what they had to say and "thereupon to be intercessors to his Majesty" and convince him to act on his behalf.[65]

Courten Jr. meanwhile denied the Company's accusations that he was implicated or at fault. His father, he claimed, was in no way involved with the *Roebuck* or the *Samaritan*, and he—Courten Jr.—should not be liable for their actions abroad, nor should any ships he wished to send be stopped.[66] Charles's response to Courten Jr. mimicked the skepticism he had earlier displayed to the Company: "knowing that the petitioner's father did not set forth the two ships . . . and holding it most unjust that the petitioner should be troubled for that business," he declared that the Company could not be allowed to hold Courten responsible or "vex" him in any way.[67] Courten soon presented the petition and response to the court of committees, who did not know what to do about the mounting evidence of the Company's loss of royal support.[68]

Abbot approached Windebank, who gave the Company no encouragement at all, weakening even further the tenuous chain that connected Company leaders to the monarch in the mid-1630s. Windebank essentially told the leaders not to further involve him in their petitions and said that "there was no cause for the Company to petition his majesty."[69] Company leaders did not fully take Windebank's advice of dropping the matter entirely, though they did give up the proposal for recompense for the Surat seizures as a lost cause. The petition they presented to Charles acknowledged his decision about the *Samaritan* and *Roebuck* but requested him not to absolve Courten Jr. of his father's liability in the Weddell expedition. In other words, they hoped still to prosecute Courten Jr. if word came back that

Weddell's expedition had infringed on Company privileges. They reminded Charles that he had promised them on his honor that the Weddell expedition would not trade in any of the areas where the Company was already established.[70]

Perhaps in response to Charles's promise to send a letter to Surat, and in spite of the mounting evidence that they did not have the king's ear, sometime in early 1637 Company leaders compiled a list of letters they wanted from the king. What they requested were: letters to the Mughal emperor, the governor of Surat, and the viceroy of Goa "disavowing the late piracy"; a letter to William Methwold, the chief factor in Surat, "commending his care and pains"; and a letter to Weddell, warning him of the king's displeasure with his actions regarding the Company.[71] Company leaders were asking for explicit support from the regime for the specific people and policies they had in place in the East Indies. The official letters they requested would reaffirm their privileged place in Indian polities, but they received only one of the letters.

Charles sent a letter to Weddell, but its contents were hardly what Company leaders had hoped for. Instead of warning Weddell away from Company territory, the letter focused on Charles's disapproval of the Company's actions. Charles claimed that he would have supported the Company in securing recompense for their monetary losses via legal channels, "but when we perceived the said Company went about not so much to prove their said pretended losses, and the occasion thereof, as to fall on [that is, arrest] the person of those that set forth the said ships the *Samaritan* and *Roebuck*, which we must avow to have been sent with our privity and license," they had lost his approval. Company leaders had spread rumors that Charles had "totally declined their protection," he wrote, in an attempt to discredit Weddell's expedition. They had dispersed these rumors "underhand and in an insinuating and subtle way," and Charles was concerned lest the Company's "merchant-like dealing and rumors" reach Weddell's ears and lead him to think that Charles did not support him. Instead, Charles wrote "to assure you hereby of our constant and continued gracious favor." In fact, the Company's actions, Charles wrote, had spurred him to confirm the commission of the rivals under the great seal of England.[72] In other words, Charles's letter to Weddell asserted his commitment to the Courten adventurers, promised that the privileges they had would be formally granted by patent, while also distancing himself from the Company. The gulf between Charles's desires and those of Company leaders in the mid-1630s was vast.

Dismantling the Company

As damning as the letter from Charles to Weddell was, since it essentially disavowed the Company, was a series of five papers about the East Indies trade delivered to Charles in May 1637. They were probably composed while Charles was considering formalizing the Courten patent, and each consisted of three to four close-written pages. Based on the handwriting, they were the work of at least several authors, and each may have been written by a different author. These papers were memos exploring a variety of possible courses of actions that Charles could take with regard to the East Indies trade. They were detailed—sometimes critical of the Company, sometimes critical of the move to circumvent it—and revealed that the author or authors had a deep and sometimes personal knowledge of the East Indies trade and Company. Their topics demonstrated that the Company still had supporters at the royal court who saw it as necessary for the trade, but it was also clear that Charles, or someone close to him, was laying the intellectual groundwork for abandoning the Company and backing the rival adventurers.

The first two memos explored the possibility that the Company would either fall apart or end, and what the consequences would be for Charles should that happen. The initial paper, titled "Information and observations that the East India Company are resolved to divide and leave the Trade," gave reasons for the coming failure of the trade regardless of any actions of the monarch. This was a memo critical of the current state of affairs, opening with the declaration that "it is certain, that as it is managed, it is a trade of loss to the particular adventurers." The author suggested that Company leaders were sending out fewer ships each year, winding down the trade unobtrusively "by degrees," because they knew the king would not like such a course of action. The writer noted that there were private rumors circulating among Company leaders that this would be the last voyage. The Company would slowly pay off debts while refraining from sending new goods and funds, which the author took as "infallible proof they will dissolve," as the amount of money left after the Company's debts were paid would not be enough to run the trade.[73]

The most insurmountable reason for the coming failure of the East Indies trade, according to the author of the first memo, was the problem of unruly Company members. The author noted that the Company was divided against itself, stating that "there are, and have ever been, a malignant, popular, and mutinous party among that Company, who only reign at their general, or quarter courts, and these have ever been clamorous against the government and committees."[74] The language was notable, echoing characterizations a decade before of misbehavior in the Virginia Company at the time of its dissolution by the monarch.[75] The East India Company, the author argued, would dissolve in large measure not because of the economic difficulties it faced (though those were great) but because of these "malignant, popular, and mutinous" people, who "now seek their revenge to break the Company."[76] It would do so by dissolving the stock, with each adventurer reclaiming his share, and thus the Company's trade would be at an end. The end of that trade would mean the end of English trade in the East Indies, regardless of the presence of willing rivals. Obliquely touching on the Courten-led rivals, the author stated that "it will be found a very great difficulty to procure new undertakers, and underwriters, for so great a stock as must manage the trade of the Indies." Rivals one might find, but rivals willing to finance the entire extensive and expensive Company trade were rare. Instead, the Dutch would be the winners, effectively running all of Europe's trade with the East Indies, and dictating prices to everyone.[77] Thus, despite the author's misgivings about the style of the Company's political life, he did not seem to be advocating that the monarch take an active role in dissolving the trade.

While the first memo set up the likelihood of a dissolution of the trade, the second memo considered the effects of such a dissolution on the customs and other revenues of the kingdom. The author of "The particular loss of his Majesty in his Customs and of the kingdom in general, by consumption of stock, if the East India Company shall dissolve, and desert the Trade," was deeply concerned about the negative effects on England of abandoning the East Indies trade. The author made no reference to alternative undertakers of the trade, successful or otherwise, and instead treated the dissolution of Company as the end of England's East Indies trade. "It is," the author argued, "a very great danger to alter the course of trade, which like great rivers keep their own and natural channels . . . or find new passages to the sea." He saw the economic ramifications of the trade as complex: "if they change, all the lesser streams must also change, or be stopped, or find new passages to the sea." The author recognized that the thirty-five years of the Company's trade had seen a great realignment of trade routes into England (spices now came via the sea route and not the Mediterranean, for example). He showed exactly how the trade brought wealth into England—besides customs revenue of at least £100,000, the trade helped employ English merchants and mariners, for example. In fact, he argued, the majority of the money the Company spent directly benefited the English through shipping costs and wage payments, while only a small amount went to East Indian polities. Additionally, when English merchants reexported East Indian goods, he claimed, they were effectively turning East Indian goods into English goods, for "once brought in, and paid the customs, it is naturalized, and become an addition to the stock of the kingdom." East Indies goods became English goods, and when the East Indies trade failed, he argued, other English trades would suffer as well: the failure of one trade hurt all.[78]

Like the author of the first document, the author of this one emphasized that the Dutch (and the Portuguese, to a much lesser extent) would be the real beneficiaries of the dissolution of the Company. Dutch merchants and shipping would supply the English lack: "the Hollander in an overflowing shall reap the gain." English consumers would pay higher prices, but more important, England as a state would be weaker by having a neighbor so strengthened at its cost. The situation, the author warned, would "give us indeed true warning to take heed of the excessive increase of any neighbor both in wealth and power." In short, at stake with the East Indies trade was not only the success of some merchants, but also England's place in Europe. England could not hope to counterbalance the burgeoning Dutch and would fail to "keep him an humble, obsequious, and necessary friend" if the Company, and hence the East Indies trade, floundered.[79]

The third document turned to the question of whether private adventurers could run the trade in the absence of a company and joint stock. Though the author of this document never mentioned the Courten-led rivals by name, the title—"Objections and propositions resolved and answered that the Trade into the East Indies may be otherwise maintained, than by a Company and joint stock"—made it clear that this was an analysis of the sustainability of groups like them. The author explored two questions: whether the king would benefit by opening the trade to private adventurers, and whether piracy in the East Indies would bring more profit than trade.[80]

In response to the first question, the author concluded that a company and joint stock were necessary for the East Indies trade in a way that they simply were not for the Levant trade. He echoed many of the arguments Company leaders had frequently made. Like them, he argued that the amount of capital required and the length of the voyages necessitated a joint stock. And like them, he maintained that organizing and governing a system of factories in the East Indies was necessary for a profitable trade but required a single authority to administer them and represent them to East Indian polities. He also discussed the problem of the transition from a joint stock run by a company to private merchants. There would be several years between the dissolution of the Company and the establishment of private merchants, and in that time the Dutch would strengthen their trade at English expense and represent to East Indian authorities that the English trade was "broken," so that treaties already in place would lapse.[81]

To answer the second question, the author maintained that abandoning the trade entirely and focusing on piracy, or "trade by force," could not supply a sustainable or honorable course for the East Indies trade. Piracy, he argued, would gain wealth once but not consistently, as people in the East Indies would learn to avoid the areas that the English targeted. The author suggested that seizing ships near the Red Sea would fail to hurt Ottoman trade, but it would hurt English trade in the Levant. Piracy further east would mean that the English were targeting other Europeans, as it was Europeans who carried the trade of the spice islands. In none of these cases would piracy help the English on a long-term basis. Additionally, the author saw piracy as a morally problematic choice for the English. Honor demanded that the English avoid "taking away the goods of men lawfully possessed by the bounty of God." Resorting to piracy would give the English in the East Indies the reputation of thieves, which the author was sure the Dutch would be sure to emphasize and which would further hinder the English.[82]

The first three memos, without definitively advocating for the Company or openly discussing the Courten venture, presented the alternatives to a Company-run trade as misguided and unlikely to succeed. They were sometimes critical of the current state of the Company, but they still saw the Company-run trade—especially when properly conducted—as a bulwark against Dutch influence and necessary to England's welfare. Taken together, the first three memos evaluated the Company and the best way to run the East Indies trade. The final two memos gave two answers to an entirely different question, however: whether the regime should fix the Company or abandon it. These memos were direct and prescriptive. One memo explained how the monarch could aid the Company to help it survive and flourish. The second advocated for jettisoning the Company and supporting the Courten adventurers.

The author who wrote in support of the Company saw fixing it as a difficult venture, and one that required extensive support from the monarch. This memo did not have a real title, though it was endorsed as "Humble considerations proposed how to preserve the stock and trade into the East Indies, for his Majesty," wording that gave a sense of its aim. The author began with a comment that he had conferred directly with Company leaders about why the membership was so divided (a circumstance the first memo had noted). Perhaps because of this conference with Company leaders, his analysis of the state of the Company and its problems was comprehensive. The Company's problems had no one cause, instead having roots in events over the previous decade. The author alluded to Amboyna and Smethwick's agitation, delicately attributing some of the Company's problems to decisions Charles had made. For example, the author suggested that the monarch should "take the point concerning the regulation of commerce with the Dutch into his serious consideration, as a matter of state, and by treaty . . . so to settle a correspondence for the time to come (and if no recompense can be conveniently procured, at least an amnesty of all quarrels and pretenses past)." Elsewhere the memo gently chided the regime, noting that "the ears of the state have been always open, to hear and receive the clamors of some of [the Company's] own malignant members, who principally have occasioned all the fractions and distempers among them."[83]

The author also identified the likely possibility of licensed rivals as another cause of concern to the generality. He noted that some members of the Company were concerned about the "discountenance or want of protection in their privileges conceived, and a general loss from these causes proceeding." The author specifically noted various rival adventurers who, with the approval of the regime, had challenged the Company's patent privileges, citing "the *Samaritan* and *Roebuck* set out in the name of Mr. Porter, the fleet of Sir William Courten, and the report of a great liberty" granted to yet another contender.[84]

The biggest difficulty facing the Company was its relationship with Charles. He was both the cause of and the only real solution to the Company's problems. Company members felt that they had "a particular opinion of disfavor from his Majesty." Indeed, the writer elaborated that "some of the principal of the Company, upon whose voice many others do depend, do conceive that his majesty hath an ill opinion of their persons and endeavors, and that they stand not fair in his grace, which doth discourage them in their labors, and makes them desirous to withdraw from the occasion." They felt this coolness had been revealed in a number of ways, from Charles too readily believing critics of the Company and authorizing inquiries into the actions of Company leaders to his granting others Company privileges.[85]

The memo's author believed that only Charles could heal those relationships and vouchsafe the vitality of the Company. The author was clear about this point, saying that the remedy "is only in the power of his Majesty if he please to defend" the Company. Charles would have to meet directly with Company leaders and assure them of his desire for them to continue the trade and of his continuing favor. He would also have to stop meddling in the Company's government and support the leaders openly, so that people like Smethwick would stop challenging them—though the author of the memo expressed this opinion in softer terms: the king, he said, should "recall petty and private enquiries upon the governors and government, and be pleased to appoint a public hearing either in his own presence, or by a choice committee of his lords, of all manner of complaints against them . . . and that being by so honorable a trial and judgment cleared of all accusations" they would be "set right in the opinion of his Majesty and the world." Such a course would mean that those "clamorous persons" who falsely accused Company leaders would get whatever "censure and punishment as to the wisdom and justice of his Majesty shall seem convenient." Charles would also have to promise not to disregard the privileges granted in the Company's royal charter, like exclusive trade in the East Indies. The Company should be given "his gracious protection of their privileges" and the knowledge that "of the future his royal charter and privileges granted unto them shall not be broken." If these steps could be taken, then the Company stood a good chance of surviving and rebounding. Charles's actions would help Company leaders secure the adventures they needed, and the East Indies trade would reap the benefits.[86]

In contrast to this attempt to reconcile the king and Company, the final document of the collection argued that Charles should confirm the Courten Association's charter under the great seal. This document was not a policy analysis so much as a narrative of why Charles had approached Courten (not the other way around) and commissioned the trade. The new rival trade, in other words, was as much Charles's venture as that of Courten and his associates, according to the memo. In this narrative, the Company had refused to explore a trade in Goa, Malabar, and China—places where the king of Spain had fortifications—which had caused Charles to "send for"

Sir William Courten and "command him to undertake and open a trade." Charles had encouraged Courten by pledging £10,000 of his own money for the voyage, and on account of this encouragement Courten had spent some £120,000 in outfitting the expedition. The rival adventurers had no plan to "hinder or disturb" the East India Company but might, should the Company fail, help ensure the continuance of the trade (this was, of course, the same language used in Charles's commission to Weddell in December 1635). What the Courten voyage really needed, however, was a commission under the great seal, to prove Charles's commitment to the endeavor. Charles should ignore the Company, which for self-serving reasons, and not thinking of the good of England, sought to "hinder his Majesty from making good his royal word and promise, by staying the commission from passing under the great seal." In this narrative, the Company was almost unconnected to the regime, while the rival trade was "his Majesty's own creation" and evidence of Charles' "gracious and real intentions in this work." The author made no mention of fixing the Company, nor did he acknowledge that the Company had any value for the state. Instead, it was an obstacle to the success of Charles's East Indies venture.[87]

On the first day of June 1637, Charles granted a patent to the Courten Association.[88] The memos had laid out different interpretations of the state of the Company and the problems facing it, and the one whose argument Charles agreed with was the one that most closely resembled the convictions he already had. The narrative of the final memo had proved more persuasive or attractive than trying to solve the problems that arose out of the complicated history between the Company and Charles. Charles decided to affirm his commitment to the Company's rivals.

The patent he gave the rivals was markedly different in form from that of the Company. The first half restated the content of the letters Charles had given Weddell and included some of the criticisms of the Company that had led Charles to look favorably on its rivals—some adventurers within the Company had complained to him, and the Company had not taken advantage of all its privileges and neglected to trade in some East Indian locations. It echoed the sentiments of the final memo delivered to Charles only days before.[89]

The second half formally granted the privileges enumerated in the first half of the letter to Porter, Courten Jr. (his father had died the year before), Kynnaston, Bonnell, Weddell, and Mountney. It mentioned other adventurers and associates but did not name them. This portion of the letter used the prerogative language of letters patent, granting the rights to these men by "especial grace, certain knowledge and mere motion." The patent formally granted for five years what Charles had granted to Weddell for the 1635 voyage. It protected the adventurers from challenge by the Company and encouraged them to take and fortify lands in the East Indies while ideally finding the northwest passage that Charles was still sure existed.[90] The letter emphasized Charles's personal interest in the venture, noting that he had "contribute[d] [his] royal grace and favor to an enterprise of this nature."[91] There was a discussion of to whom any claimed lands would belong—half to the adventurers and half to the monarch—with the same division applying to any other tolls, customs, or revenues that arose from those lands.[92] No such provisions had been made in the Company's patent, which did not elaborate any right to claim lands. Also, unlike in the Company's patent, there was no discussion of the corporate structure of the body, or even if there would be a corporate body. There was no explanation of internal government or procedures, though that information had occupied so much of the Company's patent. Indeed, based on other documents from the venture, it is possible that their trade was never intended to be open to investors, but open only to themselves and their heirs.[93] Charles's chosen rivals to the Company were now official.

The Company responded with still more petitions to Charles, hoping to sway both the regime and its own general membership. In late June, for example, there was an investigatory meeting held by a group of privy councilors, courtiers, and Company leaders about the causes of the Company's troubles. The meeting also included some Company dissidents, like Smethwick. This was exactly the sort of meeting that the fourth memo had suggested was counterproductive in terms of increasing faith in the monarch by Company members, given that it included at least one man Company leaders would never have regarded as impartial. At this meeting, Company leaders argued that infringement of their charter by the Courten voyage as well as by the *Samaritan* and *Roebuck* was a cause of significant difficulties for them. They repeated that with proof of the king's favor, they could revitalize the trade, but without it, the trade would languish.[94] Company leaders begged the king to allow them to press their case against Kynnaston and Bonnell for the actions of the *Samaritan* and *Roebuck*. When they reported their actions to the general membership, their account emphasized both their actions and the fact that they were dependent on the king's inclinations, noting that the Company "must have patience, and attend his Majesty's leisure." There was little optimism in the account.[95]

Missing court minutes for the period from July 1637–July 1639 make it impossible to determine the full scope of actions by Company leaders. But surviving documents from the period testify to a sense by the leaders that the king was withholding aid from the Company, and that their situation was getting even more dire. The first shipment of pepper from the Courten venture arrived in January 1638.[96] A Company petition from the same month mentioned numerous requests leaders had made to the regime that had either gone unanswered or been deferred. That petition noted that the leaders had also recently asked Charles to renew the Company's charter, though such a renewal had not yet taken place.[97] An account from February 1638 of the state of the Company mentioned that the trade was in such a poor condition that members of the generality had called for a vote on discontinuing it when asked to subscribe enough to send out anything more than the smallest amount of goods and money. Initially, the members agreed to send the smallest amount possible to make sure that the factors abroad did not suffer. Only more promises by Company leaders that the king would really support them this time—that this time "they did not doubt, but they should reap the fruits, both of his justice and favor"—led to a majority of the generality voting to send £25,000 worth of stock instead of the bare minimum, averting imminent disaster.[98] Overall, the Company's trade was undeniably in a bad state.

The Company was able to mobilize some support, however, or was more robust than it had seemed. For instead of allowing the Company to fall apart, as its precarious state suggested it might, Charles began plans to formally combine the Company and Courten's venture. Possibly Courten's financial problems made his venture a less-robust heir to the Company's business than Charles needed. Charles appointed two men, Sir Paul Pindar and Wolstenholme, to explore how the ventures might be joined. Wolstenholme was a Company member but also part of a major customs farming syndicate, and he was active in the Virginia plantation and had helped organize Charles's northwest passage voyages. Pindar had been an ambassador for the Levant Company in the 1610s and had been involved in the same customs farm as Wolstenholme, though he had withdrawn from it in 1638. In addition, Pindar had loaned significant sums of money to Charles and was hardly uninterested in the East Indies trade—he had also loaned £36,000 to Courten Sr. in 1635 to help fund his East Indies venture. In short, Charles had appointed someone to represent each company.[99]

The opinion of Company leaders was that "for many public reasons," Courten Jr. should sell his venture to the Company. Courten responded that he was willing to consider that course, depending on the price the Company would offer. Company leaders seemed content enough to settle with Courten and his associates, until some troubling rumors came to their ears. The rumors concerned the likelihood that Charles would give other grants of privileges that would infringe on the Company's patent. Potential rivals were continuing to present themselves to Charles, promising to take on the East Indies trade when the Company failed. Settling with one rival only to have to deal with others did not appeal to the leaders.[100]

In May 1638, the Privy Council appointed a committee to consider if the structure of the East Indies trade could be changed. It had several proposals to consider, including whether the trade should be converted from a joint stock to something like the Levant trade, with a loose central government but no joint voyages; how to manage the Anglo-Dutch rivalry in the East Indies; and how Courten's venture might be merged with the Company without disadvantaging anyone.[101] Proposals for a new company suggested that one possibility being entertained was to create a second East India Company alongside the original Company, with the East Indies divided between them.[102] Some of Charles's actions in the previous months suggest that this plan was a real possibility. In March 1638, he had forbidden the Company from trading on the Malabar coast of India, where "Mr. Porter and Mr. Courten or their agents or factors have factories settled." And his letter to Weddell informing him of this essentially treated the two ventures as equals, explaining that as Charles had earlier told Weddell not to infringe on Company trade, now he was telling the Company not to infringe on Weddell's trade.[103]

This committee never ended up meeting—perhaps because, ultimately, the Courten Association did not turn out to be a success.[104] The shipment of pepper that arrived in January 1638 turned out to be the only Courten cargo that made it back to England. Weddell and Mountney should have arrived in England in 1639, but their ships were lost on the voyage home, along with a cargo supposedly worth some £150,000.[105] By the end of the year, the king and privy councilors were listening more sympathetically to Company leaders. A petition from the Company in October 1639 led to the appointing of a committee of councilors to examine the Company and suggest ways to address its problems.[106] The report the committee delivered in December 1639 to the full Privy Council, assorted Company members, and Courten Jr. was decidedly sympathetic to the Company, and was delivered with the aim of encouraging new subscriptions to the Company's stock. The committee recommended calling in Courten's patent and all similar patents, giving Courten only enough time to bring his ships back to England. It also suggested that the Company have the full benefit of law to pursue its rivals, and that Charles grant it a new charter, giving it a number of the new privileges Company leaders wished to secure. In early 1640, Lord Cottington announced to the Company the plans for the new charter.[107] Instead of planning for the dissolution of the Company, the committee recommended measures that should enable to Company to survive and even grow. The Courten Association did not last—by 1642, Courten Jr. was bankrupt.[108] The Company survived, though not unscathed, and managed to rebound over the middle decades of the seventeenth century.

The king's grant of the Courten patent in 1637 and his willingness to let the Company fail, as well as his occasional actions to hasten that failure, represented a definitive, symbolic disavowal of a merchant company that Charles had long found reluctant to follow his lead. By the end of the 1630s, the close relationship with king and Privy Council that the Company had relied on for so long had fallen apart. Company members regularly questioned the king's motivations and support, and Company leaders found themselves unable to get access to king and Council with the frequency they had in previous years. The king had shown that he preferred others to the Company, and that he would have reorganized the trade had his rivals proven successful. His great experiment with the East Indies—his turning away from the Company and hope for plantations, and the promise of greater revenues to the crown—did not succeed. Charles ultimately took steps to salvage the Company. Company leaders had learned that their "business of state" needed the king; the king was learning that the state might need their business in return.

Conclusion

F ROM ITS INCEPTION, the East India Company lay at the heart of English political life. The course of English expansion in the East Indies was the product of the unique relationship between the crown and the Company. They worked together (sometimes harmoniously and sometimes less so) to manage English expansion there. Company leaders were constantly considering the requirements of the English state, and the regime was constantly assessing and balancing Company needs against state objectives. Company activities occurred under the oversight of monarch and privy councilors, with Company and crown acting (mostly) in concert to protect the East Indies trade.

The intersection of the Company with English politics was at the most basic level a consequence of the nature of its patent and joint stock. The Company brought together hundreds of adventurers, ranging from wealthy merchants to privy councilors and from courtiers to shopkeepers, and commanded hundreds of thousands of pounds in adventures. The Company's active membership, which spanned the social spectrum; its joint stock with extensive capitalization; and its governing body that met so frequently distinguished it from other trading companies. In part because of the heterogeneous constitution of the body and the large sums of money involved, Company members struggled with questions of how power and authority should function within the institution. The patent gave the Company power to govern itself but drew the structure of its government in only the broadest of strokes. Beyond mandating a yearly election and naming a handful of officers, the patent left the Company's government to the discretion of Company members. This meant that the patent also left the rules, structure, and organization of the Company's government open to contestation by Company members.

Company members grappled with questions of how power should be apportioned, established, and maintained in the Company. People were asking these questions in a wide variety of forums in this period, from the level of the state on down. From monarch to church select vestries, those in power considered secrecy to be a normal and desired characteristic of the assertion of power. While the political language of Company government was hardly unique, the comparative detail of the Company records reveals in greater depth than is usually possible the motivations and concerns about the nature of power that fed into Stuart political culture. Within the Company, these questions surfaced on multiple occasions and involved a constellation of issues relating to access, transparency, incumbency, and representation. Secrecy and access defined power. Company leaders worked to establish and maintain their power by controlling access to information within the Company, even guarding Company secrets from the Company's own generality.

Yet even as those in power guarded secrets, those not in power challenged restricted access to information. Members of the Company's generality were often far from powerless themselves. They pushed back against decisions by Company leaders to limit access, especially as increasing numbers of adventurers were drawn from court circles in the 1610s and 1620s. They also challenged practices of Company government that encouraged incumbency, which they saw as compounding the problems of secrecy. The court of committees, primarily made up of merchants, had wanted the connections and specialized knowledge of these men, but it found their demands and suggestions about how the Company should function less desirable. Charges of the lack of transparency in the conduct of their affairs frequently dogged Company leaders, and the actions of people and groups that Company leaders labeled "factious" often sought to increase access and transparency, though with only mixed success.

Debates about the nature and function of the Company extended far beyond the confines of the general court. The Company's nature and function were of interest to audiences whose members played no part in Company general courts. Not only did newsletter writers and diplomats regularly report Company business, but other men, often with no connection to the Company, also debated it in published pamphlets. These authors opened up discussion (and criticism) of the Company to a wider public. Company policies and actions became evidence used in their proposals for alternative ways to organize England's overseas activities. For example, one author blamed the expertise and capital tied up in the East India Company for the failure of merchants to develop a herring fishing trade that he argued would enrich the commonwealth.[1] Company affairs were not solely Company affairs, and in this case they represented missed opportunities for the wider nation.

The printed attacks on the Company led Company writers themselves to enter the realm of print. Internal debates reveal how aware they were that they were venturing into an unfamiliar medium, and how unsure they felt about the utility and appropriateness of public appeal. Yet within a few years, both an acquired familiarity with public appeal and their conviction that it was useful and appropriate were readily apparent in the eagerness with which Company leaders commissioned, published, and repeatedly returned to pamphlets to make their case in response to the Dutch "massacre" at Amboyna in 1623. The scope of the early pamphlet debates involving the Company was considerably smaller—there were only a few pamphlets on each side—than would become regular in the late seventeenth century, but they were actual debates, with authors directly responding to each other and openly appealing to readers who had read the other pamphlets. Similarly, the Amboyna documents—which included books, images, and a ballad and were aimed at a variety of audiences—showed that Company leaders and others had at least recognized the possible payoff of public appeals (even if they had not mastered the form). They also became aware of some of the dangers, many of them political, of pursuing this type of appeal, as members of the regime forced the Company to abandon particular publications. This uneven experience with public appeal was, in essence, what publicity and the politics of information looked like in the early seventeenth century.

The affairs of the Company in that period intersected with those of the regime in other ways as well. Viewing politics and political engagement through the lens of a corporate body such as the Company reveals a version of the English polity in which merchants regularly appeared before the monarch and Privy Council and saw themselves as active agents in government. Company business, as Company leaders put it, "concern[ed] the state in many things," and they worked with the king and Council to do the state's business.[2] The Company existed because of the power of the royal prerogative and relied upon royal authority in an ongoing fashion for the various privileges it needed to act abroad. In practice, the interaction between regime and merchants was even more complex and intertwined. A number of privy councilors were members of the Company, and for much of the early seventeenth century, the relationship between Company, crown, and Council was strong. Company leaders saw themselves as state actors and conceived of the new trade they were developing as integral to England's prosperity. Members of the regime shared this regard for, lent their support to, and sometimes invested their money in the trade. Even episodes that demonstrated the growing distance between the Company and the regime—for instance, when Company leaders were chastised by the Privy Council for bringing unwelcome news in 1628 (discussed in Chapter 9)—revealed the frequent and easy recourse between representatives of the two bodies that Company leaders saw as normal. Indeed, the leaders' defense in that instance was to remind the Privy Council of how implicitly they considered themselves as acting as state agents at all times.[3]

The early Stuart state that the Company knew and referred to was focused on the king and Council rather than Parliament. Yet this conception of the state that Company leaders spoke of so frequently and referred to so directly has proved far slipperier for historians. Despite the claims of revisionist historians that early modern politics mostly took place outside of Parliament, and that therefore historians need to look beyond that institution, Parliament still plays an outsize role in studies of the period. In some ways this state, centered on king and Council, is a more mundane version of the English polity, with few oratorical fireworks on display, no diaries of meetings that later circulated, or any of the other accouterments of parliamentary culture that had become normal and expected by this period. Instead, this was a state where meetings and consultations, paperwork and clerks, and privy councilors and people like Company merchants held center stage, and where center stage was behind chamber doors.

The early Stuart state viewed through the lens of the Company reveals the day-to-day governance of the realm via the Privy Council and monarch, and how the prerogative worked as a political tool. There might not have been oratorical fireworks, but there were fireworks aplenty. The collaboration between regime and Company could be fraught and complicated, especially when the needs of the regime in Europe differed from the needs of the Company in the East Indies. Over the first decades of the Company's operation, Company leaders learned how to work with the regime. The cornerstone of the working relationship between the Company and the regime was in the easy access Company leaders had to the Privy Council and the monarch. Company minutes from the first two decades reveal the frequent meetings of Company representatives and privy councilors. Company leaders resorted to court, sometimes daily, as they reported to privy councilors, petitioned for actions, and provided requested follow-up information. Company leaders and representatives of the regime were not always in agreement, and negotiation between the two groups was sometimes smoothed or rewarded by generous gifts or loans of money from the Company coffers (or the private coffers of Company leaders) or by grants of privileges or promises for particular actions from the regime. All of these strategies were on display, for example, as crown and Company worked out what to do with the Scottish East India Company patent. Differences could be negotiated and favors traded as long as there were open avenues of communication between the two parties.

In the mid-1620s, the relationship between Company and crown began to change. Several events involving issues of diplomacy and state force, notably James I's demands for payment for Hormuz and the question of the initial response to Amboyna, strained the relationship between the regime and Company leaders. The Company's demands for restitution in the matter of Amboyna were particularly unwelcome to both James and Charles I. Though sympathetic to the Company's plight, neither monarch was swayed by the Company's demands for immediate military action. The attempts by Company leaders to use public appeals to influence the regime drew the ire of the king and Council as frequently as their sympathy. Amboyna placed Charles especially in a difficult position: he needed Dutch support to make his martial aims possible and could not risk antagonizing allies by pressing the Company's claims. Yet in not providing the response that Company leaders demanded, he risked alienating a wealthy and well-connected corporation—albeit one less financially powerful than in its early years.

It was not entirely a surprise that Charles found the Company difficult to work with. However, his antipathy to the Company did not spring solely from Amboyna. Since his accession, Charles had been less happy to work with the Company in the manner that James had, and his increasing reluctance led to a marked difference in how the Company engaged with the regime during his reign. Charles's actions seemed to Company leaders to weaken the Company's ability to raise money and thus were partly responsible for the shaky state of the Company at the time. From the perspective of Company leaders, the story of the late 1620s and 1630s was one of limited access. They struggled to make their requests of the regime, let alone negotiate accommodations between Company and crown. A real transformation in the Company's relationship with the regime, therefore, arose from the change in monarch.

Charles was attempting to make the Company into a form that better suited his aims and ambitions for a territorial empire. Almost from his accession he took steps to gain greater control over the Company. By the 1630s, he had abandoned that program and instead focused on creating alternatives to the East Indies trade carried out by the Company. He did not want to lose the trade, but he did not want to leave it in the hands of a merchant company (his disparagement of "merchant-like" behavior to Captain John Weddell was telling), instead backing rival ventures like that of Courten and his associates.[4] Thus by the 1630s, Charles was actively dismantling the relationship between Company and state that had developed in the first two decades of the seventeenth century. The relationship between Company and crown that characterized the early seventeenth century—with the Company recognized as a "business of state"—could no longer be assumed by the middle of the century.

As well as a deeper understanding of the prerogative as a tool of governance, studying the Company provides insights into other aspects of Stuart political culture, in particular recurring questions of the relationship between authority and public and private interest. This relationship played out both in challenges within the Company and in considerations of the place of the Company in the state. The conflict of public and private thus took place at every level of the Company's operation. The Company existed because of public authority in the form of the monarch's private will—in other words, the prerogative. It depended on the exercise of state powers such as diplomacy and military force to function. However, it was also a collection of private interests whose success was supposed to secure the public good. The patent was supposed to be the mechanism by which the private interests within the Company were fully recruited to serve the public good, yet the patent did not render the Company immune to criticism. Members of the generality at odds with the court of committees charged Company leaders with acting only in their private interests at the expense of the generality. Critics of the Company in print argued that the East Indies trade benefited only Company members at the expense of the commonwealth. When Company leaders were in accord with the monarch and Privy Council, they carried out the business of the state; yet at other times, their motives were scrutinized and found wanting, as privy councilors warned them that their interests were not the same as the regime's.

The Company as an institution embodied a tension between public and private that was common across the early modern state. State objectives were regularly carried out by private bodies endowed with state power or recruited to the aims of the state by the grant of particular powers or privileges. Yet the intermingling of public authority and private interest was also a feature that made bodies like the Company vulnerable to contemporary criticism, as opponents charged that they wrongfully gave preference to private interest over public benefit or that they were corrupt. In other words, this mixing of public and private that was necessary for the state and its agencies to function also provided an easy and attractive target for attacks. These attacks could be direct, targeting perceived corruption (indeed, the frequency of corruption charges against a number of Stuart officials in the 1620s and the fact that those charges were so readily believed testifies to this). They could also be indirect, using questions about public and private interest in particular contexts to address potentially more sensitive political questions. The pamphlet war between Company writers and authors like Robert Kayll in the 1610s and early 1620s treated debates over public and private interest in the Company as emblematic of broader issues in the Stuart polity. These included the limits of the monarch's authority, whether any individual's self-interest could secure the greater good, and the role of monopolies (and trading companies) in the commonwealth. In these pamphlets, the East India Company, more than any other venture, embodied the greater question of what benefit England's overseas activities had to the nation. Its organization and actions, in that sense, represented the possibilities and dangers of English overseas activity in the early seventeenth century.

The Company, Overseas Expansion, and Empire

The focus on the Company in such debates, along with the multiple layers of connection between Company and state uncovered in this book, point to the need to reassess underlying assumptions about how contemporaries approached and valued English expansion in the early seventeenth century. The Company's story complicates the narrative of the early English empire that historians have developed in the context of the Atlantic world. Focusing primarily on the development of England's territorial empire means that the experiences of the East Indies are generally left out or glossed over—until in the late seventeenth century, or more commonly the eighteenth century, the East Indies suddenly takes center stage. Yet this book has shown how central the Company was to the regime, court observers, and ambassadors from its founding. Even the ferocity of the Company's critics testified to the perceived importance of the East Indies. In other words, settlements and plantations in the Atlantic world constituted one side of an equation that had the growing commercial ventures of the trading companies on the other. Shoehorning East Indies commercial ventures into definitions of empire as currently understood has not been my aim: these ventures were not actively or openly imperial in that way at this time.

However, East Indies commercial ventures were deeply enmeshed with the regime. As the joining (both informal and formal) of the Muscovy and East India Companies in the matter of the Scottish East India Company illustrates, the separation of different trades and spheres of overseas activity was often notional at best. Territorial empire and commercial expansion also developed in tandem. The same people—merchants, courtiers, privy councilors, and the monarch—oversaw the expansion of trade in the East Indies and the expansion of territory in the Atlantic world. Though this book has not aimed to establish how the connections between the East Indies and the Atlantic world played out on the ground, the demonstrable connection between the Company and the state in London points strongly to the need to reassess the meaning and scope of English overseas activities in the period. Further examinations of the links between the East Indies and Atlantic world in terms of personnel and policy will be fruitful and necessary for a fuller picture of English expansion that truly engages as seriously with the East Indies as with the Atlantic world.

A view of the early modern English empire that does not make room for expanding commercial networks misses the ways merchants like Sir Morris Abbot and Sir Thomas Smith negotiated with, cajoled, threatened, and petitioned the king and Privy Council, and the ways the king and Council similarly negotiated with, cajoled, requested, and threatened Company leaders, creating the structures and function of English commercial expansion between them. It overlooks how notions of political economy developed in corporate debates and were worked out directly with the offices of the state. Even Charles's attempts to remake the East Indies trade into a more openly imperial venture demonstrates that commercial enterprise and imperial settlement inhabited conceptual spaces that were surprisingly closely related.

Historians should reassess what we look for and where we look for it when we seek empire. The tension between commerce and territoriality and between public and private, the influence of the domestic setting on overseas ventures, and the overlap of company and state—in short, what this book has argued were the fundamental features of the early East India Company—were not limited to the experience of the Company in the early seventeenth century. There were intrinsic in the experiences of every overseas venture, whether commercial, territorial, or both. They may have been transformed over time, but they never faded. The ability of each overseas venture to marshal power and economic and political resources was not equal, and the particular experiences of the Company were not necessarily representative of other enterprises. Nonetheless, the concerns and processes that shaped the Company shaped other ventures as well.

Overseas expansion was made up of multiple negotiated relationships. In the case of the Company, for example, formative relationships included those between the regime and Company leaders, Company leaders and the generality, the Company in London and its observers and critics in England, the Company in London and its factors in the East Indies, and those factors and the wider worlds of the East Indies. Every study cannot examine every relationship (indeed, this book focused on the first three noted here, though all of them made an appearance as all of them at times influenced the others), but historians must recognize each level where negotiation took place because each of them shaped in key ways the overall experience of overseas expansion. The domestic negotiations and setting have too often been undervalued, especially the ways in which there was ongoing interplay between overseas enterprise and the domestic situation.

Thus the roles of the City of London, court, monarch, Privy Council, and Parliament in overseas expansion must be reassessed as well. Empire and expansion did not happen only overseas and did not happen because of the actions of atomized companies, proprietors, merchants, and colonists. People were influenced by their political worlds and influenced them in return. Their decisions and choices were shaped by their circumstances and shaped them in return. That might mean that sometimes metropolitan politics were played out by proxy in the various settings of overseas expansion (which certainly happened at times). It also meant that the groups and institutions associated with overseas expansion were themselves often players in metropolitan politics, both constrained by and feeding into them. The story of English (and later British) empire and expansion should be hard to tell without reference to the domestic setting.

Looking Forward: The Company and the State

As this book has shown, the Company played a central role in a range of key developments in early Stuart politics. Beyond the reevaluation of the English empire that a deeper understanding of the Company prompts, studying the Company's formative years uncovers the inner workings of the early Stuart state. The development and oversight of the East Indies trade was a collaborative venture that drew upon the knowledge and resources of both Company leaders and members of the regime, including the monarch. With its internal controversies about proper governance, negotiations between Company leaders and privy councilors to balance state objectives and Company requirements, and criticisms of the use of private interest as a guiding principle to secure public benefit, the history of the Company reveals how contemporaries engaged with the most pressing political concerns of the day.

There was no operation of the Company separate from the state during the Company's formative years in the early seventeenth century. From its founding, the Company was intertwined with the state. It remains to be explored how (and the full extent to which) the state lost oversight of the overseas activities of the Company over the course of the seventeenth century. If one looks for these connections and asks these questions, it is possible that the story of English expansion and empire will be recast.

The attempted reorganization of the East Indies trade by Charles in the 1630s, for example, presents a fascinating and revealing counterfactual example. Had a civil war not intervened, who can say if Charles would not have returned to pushing an "imperialist" policy—with greater focus on territorial acquisition and a more visible and obvious royal hand in overseas ventures—once he had broken the hold of the Company on the East Indies trade? Even though there was a rapprochement between Company and regime in December 1639, there are certainly hints that Charles at minimum would have pressed the Company into a different form with different aims and possibly would have effected a more wholesale transformation, taking "state" matters out of the hands of a group of merchants (even when that group included a large number of courtiers). One can imagine a Caroline empire in which plantation became the dominant overseas mode not just in the Atlantic world but also in Madagascar, India, and Sumatra, and in which English ships sailed under royal colors instead of corporate arms.[5] It turned out that the Courten adventurers were not the best tools for implementing such changes, but perhaps another means would have effected the desired transition.

Regardless of what may have been possible from the viewpoint (or perhaps in the daydreams) of the late 1630s, Charles's imperial East Indies ambitions languished as a civil war intervened. Both merchants and monarch found themselves facing entirely different problems in the 1640s.[6] The civil war years saw the London-based Company floundering in turbulent times. The membership was split between royalists and supporters of Parliament, with the latter eventually gaining control. In 1643, for example, the Company's governor, Sir Henry Garway, was removed from office by Parliament on account of his royalist sympathies.[7] Additionally, the political uncertainty made members reluctant to invest, so Company trade faltered. By the end of the 1640s, Company ships were recruited to the war effort and had joined the side of Parliament. Thus, a fundamental realignment seemed to be have occurred, as traditional loyalties to the monarch, already stretched by the events of the 1630s, appeared to have disappeared.[8] Certainly, after Charles's execution, there was no monarch at hand to be loyal to.

Yet even in the absence of the monarch, the Company's patent and privileges remained a contested issue. Both Charles and Parliament had licensed people outside of the Company to venture to the East Indies during the 1640s. Charles needed revenue and had already shown himself willing to circumvent the Company's exclusive rights. Many members of Parliament had an ideological problem with monopolies and patents issued through the royal prerogative and thus had few qualms about licensing interlopers. Indeed, with the abolition of the monarchy and Charles's execution, with the result that no royal prerogative existed any longer, the power guaranteeing the Company's patent was at an end and the patent effectively voided. Additionally, because patents had always been granted through the prerogative, it was not clear how Parliament would go about issuing a patent, even if members were inclined to do so. The result was that by the early 1650s, Oliver Cromwell had repeatedly declined the pleas of Company leaders to renew the Company's patent, and even people within the Company were not sure what form the body should take.[9] The Company still sent ships to the East Indies, but its exclusive access to the region was at an end. Far from driving the prices of East Indian goods down (as critics had long claimed ending the monopoly would do), the increased competition without central organization created instability at several points of the trade: English competitors in the East Indies drove up prices in East Indian ports, while at times English markets were flooded with particular goods, or goods had to be reexported to European markets too cheaply to prevent such flooding. All the while Company leaders worried that the diplomatic arrangements they had negotiated in the East Indies would be rendered null by the actions of so many English competitors who, they claimed, were not always scrupulous about observing negotiated rules and norms.[10]

The trade disorganization was so great that in 1657 Cromwell gave the Company a new patent, notwithstanding concerns about the abuse of monopolies. Neither the actual patent nor copies of it have survived, though contemporary Company descriptions argued that it was little different from the 1609 patent it replaced. It did have some key alterations that we know about. It revoked several of the privileges Company leaders had secured years before, in some ways constraining the Company's use of state authority (for example, by repealing the Company's authority to use martial law) and its ability to establish bylaws. In other ways it augmented Company powers: evidence suggests it granted the power to claim and fortify land, which was a major change from the earlier patent and could greatly alter the Company's operations on the ground in the East Indies.[11] Indeed, over the coming decades, the Company made use of those new powers.

The Company's experiences in the 1640s and 1650s reflected the same concerns that had shaped the early decades of its history although they played out in different political contexts and set the stage for later changes. The role of the patent and the questions of self-government, order, and authority were all familiar from the first decades of the Company's history. Tensions between the public and private roles of the Company still lay at the heart of the venture, and competing arguments for the benefit or otherwise of the Company for the commonwealth still framed debate about it. When Company leaders were proposing new forms the Company could take, for example, one proposal was to have a Company president in the East Indies who would be "qualified with the authority and style of a public person and reside in those parts as an agent from His Highness on behalf of the nation."[12] In other words, even after the civil war, after the Company's loss of its patent, and with the trade in chaos, Company leaders still saw themselves as state agents with the capacity of benefiting the state.

The issues explored in this book, therefore, remained central to the Company's history, though Company leaders of the 1650s and 1660s operated in a vastly changed institutional world as the civil war, interregnum, and restoration reshaped the structure and function of the English state. Historians studying the Company's actions in the late seventeenth and eighteenth centuries have demonstrated that it began to act as a sovereign body in the East Indies, a "company-state" that exercised its own sovereign authority over the territories it governed.[13] The well-known story of the Company in the late eighteenth century is mainly one of attempts by Parliament to extend and exert its authority over Company activities, culminating in the mid-nineteenth century with the incorporation of the Company's empire into the British empire. In other words, the relationship of Company and state remained problematic and central to the Company's existence throughout its history.

In the early seventeenth century, the later history of the Company could not even be imagined. The fact that England's prosperity would depend on overseas ventures would have come as no surprise to Company leaders, however. They were convinced that trade would bring wealth and honor, and they worked diligently with members of the regime to bring that to pass. Far more than trade took place at Company meetings, and the Company itself represented more than the potential for profit. The East India Company's "business of state" (sometimes frustratingly for both the regime and Company leaders) commanded the action and attention of the early seventeenth-century political nation and revealed and enabled the expanding reach of the early Stuart state.

Abbreviations

Add.	Additional Manuscripts
APC	*Acts of the Privy Council, 1542–1631,* eds. J. R. Dasent et al., 45 vols. (London: H. M. Stationery Office, 1890–1964).
BL	The British Library
CCM	*Calendar of the Court Minutes etc. of the East India Company, 1635–1659,* ed. Ethel Bruce Sainsbury, 5 vols. (Oxford: Clarendon Press of Oxford University Press, 1907–1916).
CO	Colonial Office Records
Commons Journal	*Journal of the House of Commons, Vol. 1, 1547–1629* (London: H. M. Stationery Office, 1802).
Court and Times of Charles I	Thomas Birch, *The Court and Times of Charles the First* (London: Henry Colburn, 1849).
CSPC East Indies	*Calendar of State Papers, Colonial Series, East Indies, China and Japan, 1513–1634,* ed. W. Noel Sainsbury, 5 vols. (London: H. M. Stationery Office, 1864–1892).
CSPD	*Calendar of State Papers, Domestic (James I and Charles I),* eds. Mary Anne Everett Green, John Bruce, William Douglas Hamilton and Sophia Crawford Lomas, 27 vols. (London: H. M. Stationery Office, 1856–1893).
CSPV	*Calendar of State Papers and manuscripts, relating to English affairs, existing in the archives and collections*

of Venice, 1592–1639, eds. Horatio F. Brown and Allen B. Hinds, Vols. 9–24 (London: H. M. Stationery Office, 1864–1947).

Dawn of British Trade Henry Stevens, ed., *The Dawn of British Trade to the East Indies as Recorded in the Court Minutes of the East India Company, 1599–1603* (London: Henry Stevens and Son, 1886).

Foedera Thomas Rymer, ed., *Foedera, conventions, literae, et cujuscunque generis acta publica, inter reges Angliae, et alios quosuis imperatores . . .* 20 vols. (London, 1704–1735).

GC General court

IOR India Office Records

Letters of John Chamberlain John Chamberlain, *The Letters of John Chamberlain,* ed. Norman McClure, 2 vols. (Philadelphia: American Philosophical Society, 1939).

Letters Received *Letters Received by the East India Company from Its Servants in the East,* ed. Frederick Charles Danvers and Sir William Foster, 6 vols. (London: S. Low Marston, 1986).

Lords Journal *Journal of the House of Lords, volume 3, 1620–1628* (London: H. M. Stationery Office, 1767–1830).

ODNB *Oxford Dictionary of National Biography* (Oxford: Oxford University Press, 2004).

PROB Prerogative Court of Canterbury, probate wills

Proceedings in Parliament, 1626 William Bidwell, Maija Jansson, and Mary Frear Keeler, eds, *Proceedings in Parliament, 1626,* 4 vols. (New Haven, CT: Yale University Press, 1991).

Proceedings in Parliament, 1628 William Bidwell, Maija Jansson Cole, and Mary Frear Keeler, eds, *Proceedings in Parliament, 1628,* 6 vols. (New Haven, CT: Yale University Press, 1977).

TNA The National Archives

Notes

Introduction

1. TNA SP 14/90/54, f. 97r.
2. Ibid. There was a strain of contemporary thought in which the monarch's compelling his subjects to pay him money could be considered a type of prerogative taxation. See David Harris Sacks, "The Paradox of Taxation: Fiscal Crises, Parliament, and Liberty in England, 1450–1640," in *Fiscal Crises, Liberty, and Representative Government, 1450–1789*, ed. Philip T. Hoffman and Kathryn Norberg (Stanford, CA: Stanford University Press, 1994), 54–56; Francis Wormuth, *The Royal Prerogative 1603–1649: A Study in English Political and Constitutional Ideas* (Ithaca, NY: Cornell University Press, 1939), 69–82.
3. TNA SP 14/90/54, f. 97r–98r. The fine that the author mentioned was assessed on some new members as the cost of freedom of the Company. See Chapter 3 for more information.
4. The scheme likely came to nothing. Minutes from later years make no mention of payments or loans to the monarch such as those outlined in the memo. It is possible that the king could have compelled a loan from Company leaders on the strength of the proposals outlined in the memo, but no evidence of a loan in relation to this memo has survived.
5. Thomas Mun, *A Discourse of Trade, From England unto the East Indies: Answering to Diverse Objections which are Usually Made Against the Same. By T. M.* (London, 1621), 1 (italics in the original); TNA SP 84/85/212 (Bell to Carleton: 22 August 1618).
6. BL IOR B/9, 16 July 1624; TNA SP 14/170/20 ([Conway] to the East India Company: 19 July 1624).
7. There are few studies of the early East India Company, though interest in it is increasing. Philip Lawson's survey of the Company, which covers the early

period only briefly, is one basic reference work on the history of the Company, along with K. N. Chaudhuri's invaluable study of the Company's economic history. See Philip Lawson, *East India Company: A History* (London: Longman, 1993); K. N. Chaudhuri, *The English East India Company: The Study of an Early Joint-Stock Company, 1600–1640* (London: F. Cass, 1965). On the early history of the Company in the East Indies, see William Foster, *England's Quest of Eastern Trade* (London: A. & C. Black Ltd., 1933); Kenneth R. Andrews, *Trade, Plunder, and Settlement: Maritime Enterprise and the Genesis of the British Empire, 1480–1630* (Cambridge: Cambridge University Press, 1984); John Keay, *The Honorable Company: A History of the English East India Company* (London: HarperCollins, 1993). Some of the best accounts of the early history of the Company can be found in the prefaces and introductions to the wonderful calendars that describe the East Indies. See *CSPC East Indies 1513–1616*; *CSPC East Indies 1617–1621*; *CSPC East Indies 1622–1624*; *CSPC East Indies 1625–1629*; *CSPC East Indies 1630–1634*; *CCM 1635–1639*.

Generally when not explicitly studying the Company, historians have omitted the East India Company from their consideration. The exceptions include Robert Ashton, who studied the relationship between the crown and London's merchant communities in the early seventeenth century; Theodore K. Rabb, who studied investment by the gentry in the overseas trades; and Robert Brenner, who studied the political allegiances of merchant groups in the decades leading up to the English Civil War, with a focus on which merchant groups sided with Parliament and which with the crown in the 1640s, and why. See Robert Ashton, *The Crown and the Money Market, 1603–1640* (Oxford: Clarendon Press of Oxford University Press, 1960), and *The City and the Court, 1603–1643* (Cambridge: Cambridge University Press, 1979); Robert Brenner, *Merchants and Revolution: Commercial Change, Political Conflict and London's Overseas Traders, 1550–1653* (Princeton, NJ: Princeton University Press, 1993); Theodore K. Rabb, *Enterprise and Empire: Merchant and Gentry Investment in the Expansion of England, 1575–1630* (Cambridge, MA: Harvard University Press, 1967). All three historians were focused on "merchant" topics.

Few historians examining topics not obviously mercantile have referred to the East India Company except in passing. For the Company in the late seventeenth century, see Philip J. Stern, *The Company-State: Corporate Sovereignty and the Early Modern Foundations of the British Empire in India* (Oxford: Oxford University Press, 2011). Stern observes the same lack of study of the late seventeenth-century East India Company in "'A Politie of Civill & Military Power': Political Thought and the Late Seventeenth-Century Foundations of the East India Company," *Journal of British Studies* 47, no. 2 (2008): 253–283. Lastly, Andrew Ruoss has just completed a dissertation that examines the Company alongside the Dutch East India Company in the mid- to late seventeenth century. See Andrew Ruoss, "Competitive

Collaboration: The Dutch and English East India Companies and the Forging of Global Corporate Political Economy (1650–1700)" (PhD diss., Duke University, 2017).

8. Imperial historians have rarely been more than moderately interested in the very early days of the Company, ignoring the period when the Company was a bit player in the East Indies in favor of the period when it was a major political and economic player in the East—namely, the eighteenth and nineteenth centuries. Simply put, the early history of the Company does not provide a good illustration of the path to empire as commonly understood—in aim and scope, the early decades of the Company's activities in the East Indies were resolutely humble, with no guarantee that force or fortification were in the Company's future—which might explain why the early history has been so neglected. The official story of the Company tends to pick up in the early or middle parts of the eighteenth century (when the Company was already an established presence in the East Indies and London), though how that presence was established is not easy to explain. One of the few articles to try to trace how ideas toward overseas activity changed in the pre-Plassey period is Ian Bruce Watson, "Fortifications and the 'Idea' of Force in Early English East India Company Relations with India," *Past and Present* 88, no. 1 (1980): 70–87.

9. Recent work on institutional culture has emphasized the way institutions created and underscored identities. See Anne Goldgar and Robert I. Frost, eds., *Institutional Culture in Early Modern Society* (Leiden, the Netherlands: Brill, 2004).

10. The Company's government resembled the governments of livery companies with some key differences. Most livery companies had courts of assistants, headed by a master and several wardens. These were analogous to the Company's governor, deputy governor, treasurer, and court of committees. Besides the differences in names of offices, the biggest differences were that in almost no livery companies were the master, wardens, or assistants chosen by the full body of the membership, as they were in the East India Company; and that the Company had no shadow government for its yeomanry, whereas most livery companies did. This was a key variation, which spoke to the different ways that participation and membership were conceptualized in the Company. For more on the governments of livery companies, see Ian Archer, *The Pursuit of Stability: Social Relations in Elizabethan London* (Cambridge: Cambridge University Press, 1991), 101–4; Steve Rappaport, *Worlds within Worlds: The Structures of Life in Sixteenth-Century London* (Cambridge: Cambridge University Press, 1989), 218 and 250–52; Sylvia Thrupp, *A Short History of the Worshipful Company of Bakers of London* (Croydon, UK: Galleon Press, 1933), 83–85.

11. Catherine Patterson, *Urban Patronage in Early Modern England: Corporate Boroughs, the Landed Elite, and the Crown, 1580–1640* (Stanford, CA: Stanford University Press, 1999), 18. The Corporation of London was also an outlier, and its aldermen had significant financial resources at their disposal.

12. Unlike the livery companies, where nearly all members shared the experience of apprenticeship in their craft, the members of the East India Company came from varied backgrounds. Many of the merchant members of the East India Company had ties to other London bodies, from livery companies to other trading companies, but Company members of higher social status were unlikely to have ties to livery companies. The Virginia Company was the other trading company with a large membership that also included significant numbers of both merchants and gentry. Rabb has calculated that over 44 percent of the Virginia Company's more than 1,000 members were gentry. See Rabb, *Enterprise and Empire*, 30.

13. John Appleby, "War, Politics, and Colonization, 1558–1625," in *The Origins of Empire*, ed. Nicholas Canny, vol. 1 of *The Oxford History of the British Empire* (Oxford: Oxford University Press, 1998), 57.

14. Chaudhuri, *The English East India Company*, 91.

15. The separate voyages of the Company's first year were also centralized joint ventures.

16. For more on the Levant Company, see Mortimer Epstein, *The Early History of the Levant Company* (London: Routledge and Sons: 1908); Alfred Cecil Wood, *A History of the Levant Company* ([London]: Oxford University Press, 1935). An examination of the Levant Company's experiences in the Levant can be found in James Mather, *Pashas: Traders and Travelers in the Islamic World* (New Haven, CT: Yale University Press, 2009).

17. A "committee" in Company parlance was an elected official. "Twenty-four committees" meant twenty-four elected officials, not twenty-four groups of individuals.

18. Nothing remotely like the archives of the East India Company for this period exists for the other English companies. For example, for the period 1600–1640, nineteen volumes of court minutes, most running 300–600 pages, survive for the East India Company, in addition to volumes of correspondence from the factors in the East Indies. By contrast, two volumes, not nearly as detailed, survive for the Levant Company before 1640; the archives of the Russia Company were lost to fire in the late seventeenth century; and the Eastland company archives were lost as well. The Virginia Company minutes have survived in part, though no minutes before 1619 are extant. The crown revoked that company's patent in 1624, after which the structure of the enterprise and its records changed.

It is not just compared to trading companies that the East India Company's archival richness is notable. No livery company, town, or parish archive is as detailed. The archives of the corporation of London, though many volumes of different types of meeting have survived, do not preserve the types of debate and detail that the Company's archives do. Even English state papers have few equivalent examples. For example, the surviving records of the Privy Council, the *Acts of the Privy Council*, record only the *acts* of the Privy Council, not the *debates* of the Privy Council.

A discussion that did not lead to a decision, or debate that took place over several days, effectively does not exist according to the *Acts of the Privy Council.*

19. Trading companies provided arenas for political involvement not only in the early seventeenth century. Mark Freeman, Robin Pearson, and James Taylor have recently examined political activity in corporations in the eighteenth and nineteenth centuries. See Mark Freeman, Robin Pearson, and James Taylor, *Shareholder Democracies? Corporate Governance in Britain and Ireland before 1850* (Chicago: University of Chicago Press, 2011).

20. I suspect that similar claims could be made about how merchants in some of the other long-distance trading companies understood their roles in the state, especially given how many merchants in the East India Company were also active in other such companies. The Muscovy, Levant, and Virginia Companies in particular had many members in common with the East India Company. However, without some unexpected archival discovery, such an examination of the other companies is impossible.

21. Michael Braddick, *State Formation in Early Modern England, c. 1550–1700* (Cambridge: Cambridge University Press, 2000), 20.

22. Steve Hindle, *The State and Social Change in Early Modern England, c. 1550–1700* (Basingstoke, UK: Macmillan, 2000); Braddick, *State Formation in Early Modern England.*

23. Braddick, *State Formation in Early Modern England,* 91.

24. Mark Goldie, "The Unacknowledged Republic: Officeholding in Early Modern England," in *Politics of the Excluded, c. 1500–1850,* ed. Tim Harris (New York: Palgrave, 2001), 159–162.

25. Braddick, *State Formation in Early Modern England,* 427; Hindle, *The State and Social Change,* 1–2. To be clear, this "state" was not the modern bureaucratic state.

26. Hindle, *The State and Social Change,* 17 and 20.

27. A few works have looked at merchants in the early seventeenth century, but their authors were primarily concerned with explaining how and why merchant allegiances developed in the Civil War. See Valerie Pearl, *London and the Outbreak of the Puritan Revolution: City Government and National Politics, 1625–43* ([London]: Oxford University Press, 1961); Ashton, *The City and the Court, 1603–1643*; Brenner, *Merchants and Revolution.*

28. The work of Conrad Russell is a good example of this tendency. While he openly acknowledged that Parliament was an occasional event and that most political engagement took place outside it, his work still primarily concerned Parliament. His masterful *Parliaments and English Politics, 1621–1629* (Oxford: Clarendon Press of Oxford University Press, 1979) is a fundamental work on the changing political climate of the 1620s, but it is focused exclusively on what happened in the parliaments of the 1620s. Chris Kyle's recent study paints a rich picture of early Stuart political culture, including contemporary expectations about the performance and consumption of politics, and in

many ways turns the parliamentary focus on its head—while still focusing on Parliament. See Chis Kyle, *Theater of State: Parliament and Political Culture in Early Stuart England* (Stanford, CA: Stanford University Press, 2012). Other recent work is beginning to widen the lens, looking beyond Parliament. For example, see Noah Millstone, *Manuscript Circulation and the Invention of Politics in Early Stuart England* (Cambridge: Cambridge University Press, 2016).

29. For example, the Tudor and Stuart navy was, in large part, made up of merchant ships that were pressed into public service in times of war. In acknowledgment of this possible public use of private ships, merchants or others building ships could apply for a subsidy to support the building costs. The subsidy was a certain number of shillings per ton, and while far from paying for the ship, the payment of the subsidy recognized the connection between public use and private means. The bounty was one crown per ton in 1616, for example, and gained the Company that year some 2,946 crowns for building three ships. See *CSPC East Indies 1513–1616*, no. 1142.

30. David Harris Sacks, "Private Profit and Public Good: The Problem of the State in Elizabethan Theory and Practice," in *Law, Literature, and the Settlement of Regimes*, ed. Gordon J. Schochet (Washington: Folger Institute, 1990), 121–142. Sacks limits his examination to the Elizabethan period, but his comments are also applicable to the early Stuart period.

31. This central feature of the early modern state was not limited to England. The mixing of public and private characterized the endeavors of many early modern states around the world, though Niels Steensgaard argues that linking incorporation to the mixing of public and private was a particularly English development. See Niels Steensgaard, "Companies as a Specific Institution in the History of European Expansion," in *Companies and Trade: Essays on Overseas Trading Companies during the* Ancien Régime, ed. Leonard Blussé and Femme Gaastra (Leiden, the Netherlands: Leiden University Press, 1981), 247–48.

32. Steensgaard sees this "dual nature of the companies, partaking in both public and private rights," as the distinctive characteristic of the early modern trading company. See ibid., 247. On the other hand, Phil Withington has argued that historians have too long overlooked the associational and social elements of corporations, observing that "to focus simply on 'the state' or 'private interest' elides the mode of social organization—that is voluntary and purposeful associations of 'free men'—through which government and profit were to be achieved." See Phil Withington, *Society in Early Modern England: The Vernacular Origins of Some Powerful Ideas* (Cambridge: Polity Press, 2010), 205.

33. BL IOR B/6, 20 March 1618.

34. *Letters of John Chamberlain*, 1:488 (to Carleton: 25 November 1613) and 2:388 (to Carleton: 14 July 1621); *Court and Times of Charles I*, 1:406. For another

example of critical commentary, see TNA SP 14/103/46 (Pory to Carleton: 25 October 1618).

35. Richard Cust noted a similar flexibility in the meaning of the "public" in humanist commentaries about politics in the same period. See Richard Cust, "The 'Public Man' in Late Tudor and Early Stuart England," in *The Politics of the Public Sphere in Early Modern England*, ed. Peter Lake and Steven Pincus (New York: Manchester University Press, 2007), 117 and 121.

36. Disentangling public and private benefit was a problem at all levels of the state in the early modern period. It was common knowledge and expectation that private benefit came from public office, even as charges of corruption and misuse of public office gained traction in the period and were used to bring down several influential officials in the 1620s. See, for example, Lawrence Stone, "The Fruits of Office: The Case of Robert Cecil, First Earl of Salisbury," in *Essays in the Economic and Social History of Tudor and Stuart England*, ed. F. J. Fisher (Cambridge: Cambridge University Press, 1961), 89–116; Linda Levy Peck, *Court Patronage and Corruption in Early Stuart England* (London: Unwin Hyman, 1990); John Barcroft, "Carleton and Buckingham: The Quest for Office," in *Early Stuart Studies: Essays in Honor of David H. Wilson*, ed. Howard S. Reinmuth (Minneapolis: University of Minnesota, 1970), 122–136.

37. It is not only in relation to the Company that prerogative as a tool of governance has been understudied. The pull of Parliament as a focus for political history has meant that the prerogative and the Privy Council have received far too little attention, despite the fact that they were responsible for much of the day-to-day governance of the realm. A very small amount of scholarship has examined the issue, though these types of questions and analysis promise to widen our understanding of how people understood the state, and how involved the state—meaning the Council—might be in their lives. See, for example Victor Morgan, "Whose Prerogative in Late Sixteenth and Early Seventeenth Century England?," *Journal of Legal History* 5, no. 3 (1984):39–64; Catherine Patterson, "*Quo Warranto* and Borough Corporations in Early Stuart England: Royal Prerogative and Local Privileges in the Central Courts," *English Historical Review* 120, no. 488 (2005): 878–906.

38. David Armitage, *Ideological Origins of the British Empire* (Cambridge: Cambridge University Press, 2000); Anthony Pagden, *Lords of All the World* (New Haven, CT: Yale University Press, 1998); Ken MacMillan, *Sovereignty and Possession in the English New World* (Cambridge: Cambridge University Press, 2009) and *The Atlantic Imperial Constitution: Center and Periphery in the English Atlantic World* (Basingstoke: Palgrave Macmillan, 2011).

39. See, for example, Lauren Benton, *Search for Sovereignty: Law and Geography in European Empires, 1400–1900* (Cambridge: Cambridge University Press, 2009); Lauren Benton and Richard Ross, eds., *Legal Pluralism and*

Empires, 1500–1850 (New York: New York University Press, 2013); Eliga Gould, "Entangled Histories, Entangled Worlds: The English-Speaking Atlantic as a Spanish Periphery," *American History Review* 112, no. 3 (2007): 764–86.

40. William Pettigrew suggests a new category of "corporate constitutionalism" as a way to address the limitations of existing interpretive frameworks and focus attention on the unique peculiarities of structure and function of the trading companies. He highlights the opportunities for challenging conventional narratives that studies of corporations allow. I am sympathetic to his aims, and certainly some of the concerns he raises are central to my own work. However, I worry that isolating trading corporations from the state and other types of corporations can also obscure the contingent history of each institution that I argue is key to understanding the East India Company, at least. See William Pettigrew, "Corporate Constitutionalism and the Dialogue between the Global and Local in Seventeenth-Century English History," *Itinerario* 39, no. 3 (2016):487–501.

41. Alison Games, *Web of Empire: English Cosmopolitans in an Age of Expansion* (Oxford: Oxford University Press, 2008). The merchants and gentry who invested in one overseas trade often invested in multiple such trades. Some scholars have recently pointed out the extent to which people cycled through employment in different companies and voyages to different places. John Smith, famous for his activity in Jamestown, had earlier experience in the Levant, for example. See Karen Ordahl Kupperman, *The Jamestown Project* (Cambridge, MA: Harvard University Press, 2007), 43–72. Some historians have begun to challenge the boundaries of the Atlantic world. See, for example, Alison Games, Philip J. Stern, Paul W. Mapp, and Peter A. Coclanis, "Forum: Beyond the Atlantic," *William and Mary Quarterly*, 3rd ser., 63, no. 4 (2006): 675–742.

42. Braddick, *State Formation in Early Modern England*, 379–420, and "The English Government, War, Trade, and Settlement, 1625–1688," in *Origins of Empire: British Overseas Enterprise to the Close of the Seventeenth Century*, ed. Nicholas Canny (Oxford: Oxford University Press, 1998), 286–308.

43. Depending on the definitions of "non-Western" and "sustained" being used, the activities of the Levant Company or the Muscovy Company might also lay claim to being the first. One should note that the Levant, Muscovy, and the East Indies are none of them in the Atlantic world, and like the East India Company, neither the Levant Company nor the Muscovy Company plays a significant role in studies of the origins of empire.

44. See Chapter 10.

45. Philip Stern, *The Company-State: Corporate Sovereignty and the Early Modern Foundations of the British Empire in India* (Oxford: Oxford University Press, 2011).

1. The Patent and the Formation of the Company

1. Wool and cloth goods made of wool accounted for 75–90 percent of English exports in the early seventeenth century. See Barry Supple, *Commercial Crisis and Change in England, 1600–1642* (Cambridge: Cambridge University Press, 1959), 6.

2. These companies were joined by a number of other chartered companies that secured the rights to exclusive trade with specific European nations, such as the Spanish Company that operated briefly in the early 1600s. See Pauline Croft, *The Spanish Company* (London: London Record Society, 1973).

3. BL Lansdowne MS 100, f. 142r and 145–46r ("A discovery of lands beyond the equinoctial," 1573).

4. Zelia Nuttall, trans. and ed., *New Light on Drake: A Collection of Documents Relating to His Voyage of Circumnavigation, 1577–1580* (London: printed for the Hakluyt Society, 1914), 390. The equinoctial line referred to in both patents mentioned here was essentially the equator, and thus "lands beyond the equinoctial" might encompass any number of specific places.

5. A few royal patents that granted one or more of these powers survive from earlier in the century, but after the 1555 Muscovy Company patent, prospective adventurers seeking patents wanted all three powers. Henry VIII's 1530 grant to merchants trading to Andalusia, for example, granted self-government but did not directly mention incorporation, though it referred to the "fellowship" of the merchants. See Cecil Carr, ed., *Select Charters of Trading Companies, A.D. 1530–1707* (London: Bernard Quaritch, 1913) 1–3. One should note that there were many patents granted in the sixteenth and seventeenth centuries to individuals that did not include grants of incorporation or provisions for institutional self-government. My remarks are specific to trading companies. Ken MacMillan has written insightfully and convincingly about the shared legal language found in patents granted for exploration and possession of lands in the Americas. His account also describes the formal steps involved in securing a patent. See Ken MacMillan, *Sovereignty and Possession in the English New World* (Cambridge: Cambridge University Press, 2009), 79–120.

6. Hubert Hall, *Studies in English Official Historical Documents* (Cambridge: Cambridge University Press, 1908), 235–48; Hubert Hall, ed., *Formula Book of English Historical Documents* (Cambridge: Cambridge University Press, 1908), 1:53–60; MacMillan, *Sovereignty and Possession*, 89–94. MacMillan has demonstrated the shared powers granted by letters patent that enabled and encouraged colonization in the Americas. Whether to individuals or corporations, the New World patents granted the power to claim land. Not all patents for overseas ventures granted this power. Indeed, the patents I discuss here were unified by a number of shared powers, but not that of colonial possession.

7. The grants of exclusive access limited only English access. Dutch traders could, and did, bring nutmeg, for example, to England without contravening an English letter patent.

8. Carr, ed., *Select Charters of Trading Companies*, xiii and 1–3; George Cawston and A. H. Keane, *The Early Chartered Companies* (London: Edward Arnold, 1896), 249–54.

9. See, for example, the 1600 patent of the Levant Company (in Carr, ed., *Select Charters of Trading Companies*, 31–32) or the Muscovy Company patent (in Richard Hakluyt, *Principal Navigations, Voyages and Discoveries of the English Nation, Made by Sea or over Land, to the Most Remote and Farthest Distant Quarters of the Earth at any Time Within the Compass of these 1500 Years* (London: George Bishop and Ralph Newberie, deputies to Christopher Barker, 1589), 305.

10. See William Sheppard, *Of Corporations, Fraternities and Guilds: Or, a Discourse, Wherein the Learning of the Law Touching Bodies Politic Is Unfolded, Showing the Use and Necessity of That Invention, the Antiquity, Various Kinds, Order and Government of the Same* (London: Printed for H. Twyford, T. Dring, and J. Place, 1659); for Coke's report on Sutton's Hospital, see *The English Reports* (Abingdon, UK: Professional Books Ltd., 1986), 77:962–75.

11. Hakluyt, *Principal Navigations*, 305; Carr, ed., *Select Charters of Trading Companies*, 32–33 and 54–55.

12. Francis Newton Thorpe, ed., *Federal and State Constitutions, Colonial Charters, and Other Organic Laws of the States, Territories, and Colonies Now or Heretofore Forming the United States of America* (Washington: Government Printing Office, 1909), 7:3783–802 (the 1606 and 1609 patents for the Virginia Company are both included here).

13. BL Lansdowne MS 100, f. 142r and 145–46r.

14. Quoted in Thorpe, *Federal and State Constitutions*, 7:3796.

15. Quoted in Hakluyt, *Principal Navigations*, 305–6.

16. Harold G. Fox, *Monopolies and Patents: A Study of the History and Future of the Patent Monopoly* (Toronto: University of Toronto Press, 1947), 57; William Hyde Price, *English Patents of Monopoly* (New York: Houghton, Mifflin and Company, 1906), 7. The 1555 Muscovy Company patent can be found in Hakluyt, *Principal Navigations*, 304–9.

17. The number comes from a 1601 list drawn up by Salisbury, printed in Price, *English Patents of Monopoly*, appendix D, 148–49.

18. David Harris Sacks, "Private Profit and Public Good: The Problem of the State in Elizabethan Theory and Practice," in *Law, Literature, and the Settlement of Regimes*, ed. Gordon J. Schochet (Washington: Folger Institute, 1990), 125. See also David Harris Sacks, "The Countervailing of Benefits: Monopoly, Liberty, and Benevolence in Elizabethan England," in *The Tudor Monarchy*, ed. John Guy (London: Arnold, 1997), 144. For an examination of William Cecil's acceptance of monopolies as a means of

spurring the economic development of the commonwealth, see Felicity Heal and Clive Holmes, "The Economic Patronage of William Cecil," in *Patronage, Culture and Power: The Early Cecils*, ed. Pauline Croft, (New Haven, CT: Yale University Press, 2002), 199–229. The expansion of the state through the licensing of local officials in the name of the state is a process identified by both Braddick and Hindle, See Michael Braddick, *State Formation in Early Modern England, c. 1550–1700* (Cambridge: Cambridge University Press, 2000); Steve Hindle, *The State and Social Change in Early Modern England, c. 1550–1700* (Basingstoke, UK: Macmillan, 2000). Patents of monopoly constitute a rich topic that has attracted little recent scholarly attention. See Fox, *Monopolies and Patents*; E. Wyndham Hulme, "The History of the Patent System under the Prerogative and at Common Law," *Law Quarterly Review* 12 (1896): 141–54; E. Wyndham Hulme, "The History of the Patent System under the Prerogative and at Common Law," *Law Quarterly Review* 13 (1897): 313–18, and E. Wyndham Hulme, "The History of the Patent System under the Prerogative and at Common Law," *Law Quarterly Review* 16 (1900): 44–56; and Price, *English Patents of Monopoly*.

19. Quoted in Sir Simonds D'Ewes, *Journals of All the Parliaments during the Reign of Queen Elizabeth: Both of the House of Lords and the House of Commons* (London, 1682), 547. We run into a problem of terminology here. "Monopoly" is often used by scholars as a descriptive term for a limited trade, while contemporaries often used it pejoratively, with implications of an unfairly limited trade. What scholars refer to as monopolies, contemporaries could sometimes also have referred to as a patent, privilege, a project, and governed trade.

20. Bacon's speech, delivered on 20 November 1601, is quoted in Price, *English Patents of Monopoly*, appendix H, 154.

21. Quoted in Fox, *Monopolies and Patents*, 113.

22. In 1603 James had issued a proclamation against monopolies, but he granted many patents during his reign—including ones that critics considered monopoly grants. The extent of the royal prerogative was a major question for James and his parliaments, and many of James's speeches to Parliament were defenses of his interpretation and use of prerogative powers. See, for example, his speeches to Parliament on 9 November 1605, 31 March 1607, and 21 March 1610. King James VI and I, *Political Writings*, ed. Johann P. Sommerville (Cambridge: Cambridge University Press, 1994), 147–203.

23. William Noy, *Reports and Cases, Taken in the Time of Queen Elizabeth, King James, and King Charles* (London: Printed by F. L. for Matthew Walbancke, 1656), 182.

24. George Birdwood and William Foster, eds., *Register of Letters etc., of the Governor and Company of Merchants of London Trading into the East Indies, 1600–1619* (London: Bernard Quaritch, 1893), 163–89; *Charters Granted to the East India Company, from 1601, Also the Treaties and Grants, Made with, or*

Obtained from, the Princes and Powers in India, from the Year 1756 to 1772 ([London] [1773]), 27–53. For more on the Courten Association, see Chapter 10.

25. Thorpe, *Federal and State Constitutions*, 7:3783–89. A patent granted by Henry VIII in 1530 to merchants trading to Andalusia also gave and granted, but the language of special grace, willing, and motion by the monarch was absent. See Carr, ed., *Select Charters of Trading Companies*, 1–3.

26. This language was part of the formula for charters and letters patent that appeared as early as the reign of Edward IV. See Hall, *Studies in English Official Historical Documents*, 237. Ken MacMillan suggests that English monarchs were consciously echoing the language of the papal bull *Inter caetera* (he cites a 1583 document that made exactly that claim), but the formulation had antecedents in earlier centuries. It is possible that the phrasing had new resonance in light of *Inter caetera*. See MacMillan, *Sovereignty and Possession*, 106–7.

27. Carr, ed., *Select Charters of Trading Companies*, 1–3; Hakluyt, *Principal Navigations*, 304. The Andalusia patent is interesting in that it granted self-government but made no mention of exclusive privileges or special reliance on the prerogative.

28. All of these patents can be found in Carr, ed., *Select Charters of Trading Companies*. The language is found throughout the patents from the middle of the sixteenth century on. It persisted after the Restoration, though one interesting difference between the early and late seventeenth century patents was the preponderance of the word "royal" in the title of the trading companies newly chartered in the late seventeenth century. MacMillan notes that the language of prerogative power was part of the formula of letters patent by the end of the sixteenth century. See MacMillan, *Sovereignty and Possession*, 79–80.

29. John Bruce, *Annals of the Honorable East-India Company, from Their Establishment by the Charter of Queen Elizabeth, 1600, to the Union of the London and English East-India Companies, 1707–8* (London: Black, Parry, and Kingsbury, 1810), 1:109–10; Nandini Das, "Elizabeth and India," in *The Foreign Relations of Elizabeth I*, ed. Charles Beem (New York: Palgrave, 2011), 202–4.

30. *Dawn of British Trade*, 8. This volume is a printed version of the Company's first volume of court minutes, covering 1599–1603.

31. Ibid., 1–5.

32. MacMillan, *Sovereignty and Possession*, 80–82.

33. *Dawn of British Trade*, 8–9. Nandini Das highlighted the role of Richard Hakluyt in aiding the merchants and providing them with information about the East Indies. See Das, "Elizabeth and India," 211–12.

34. *Dawn of British Trade*, 9.

35. *Dawn of British Trade*, 11. The maneuverings towards a peace treaty are discussed in Wallace T. MacCaffrey, *Elizabeth I: War and Politics, 1588–1603* (Princeton, NJ: Princeton University Press, 1992), 220–32.

36. TNA CO 77/1/17 ("Certain reasons why the English merchants may trade into the East Indies": [1600]). The Huntington Library holds another copy of the memo. This copy has some key differences in wording from that in the National Archives: it presents a slightly less aggressive justification of the English right to trade in the East Indies. The reason for this difference is not known. See Huntington Library, MS EL 2360.

37. TNA CO 77/1/17 ("Certain reasons why the English merchants may trade into the East Indies": [1600]). Hakluyt produced a translation of Hugo Grotius's *Mare Liberum* (or *Free Sea*) sometime between 1609 and 1616. Though Grotius is the writer most associated with the concept of the *Mare Liberum*, he was not the first person to explore it as a justification for traffic into the East Indies despite Spanish or Portuguese claims. Grotius wrote *Mare Liberum* in 1604 and published it anonymously in 1609. See Hugo Grotius, *The Free Sea*, ed. David Armitage (Indianapolis, IN: Liberty Fund, 2004).

38. TNA CO 77/1/18 (Greville's report on "Certain reasons why the English merchants may trade into the East Indies": [1600]).

39. Hatfield House Archives, Cecil Papers 83/22 (petition of the merchants trading to the East Indies to the lords of the Privy Council: [1600]).

40. Hatfield House, Cecil Papers 142/172 (commission to James Lancaster: 24 January 1601).

41. Both Elizabeth's 1600 patent and James's 1609 patent specifically called for the Company to have these elected positions. Both documents can be found in *Charters Granted to the East India Company*.

42. *Charters Granted to the East India Company*, 7.

43. *Charters Granted to the East India Company*, 7–10.

44. *Charters Granted to the East India Company*, 15–17.

45. *Dawn of British Trade*, 189.

46. TNA CO 77/1/21 (minutes from the lordships to the merchants trading into the East Indies: October 1601).

47. Ibid.

48. Ibid.

49. *Dawn of British Trade*, 185.

50. Ibid., 196.

51. Ibid., 207.

52. The concerns by Company leaders that the needs of Anglo-Spanish diplomatic relations would require the termination of the English trade did not end in 1600. A Company petition in 1604, delivered while English and Spanish commissioners were negotiating the Treaty of London, emphasized both the good for the nation and the great expense to which the Company had been to establish the East Indies trade. Company leaders hoped the Privy Council would protect them and not agree to any prohibitions on English trade in the East Indies. See Hatfield House, Cecil Papers 190/12 (merchants trading to the East Indies to the lords commissioners for the treaty with Spain: [1604]).

53. *Dawn of British Trade*, 61–62. The threat and promise was repeated a few months later. See ibid., 110.
54. Ibid., 164–65.
55. BL IOR B / 9, 28 March 1625.

2. Constituting Authority: The Court of Committees and the Generality

1. BL IOR B / 6, 23 July 1619. For more on the 1619 accord, see Chapter 8.
2. A growing body of works has examined corporate citizenship and its consequences, though more investigation remains to be done. See Mark Goldie, "The Unacknowledged Republic: Officeholding in Early Modern England," in *Politics of the Excluded, c. 1500–1850*, ed. Tim Harris (New York: Palgrave, 2001), 153–194; Paul Halliday, *Dismembering the Body Politic: Partisan Politics in England's Towns, 1650–1730* (Cambridge: Cambridge University Press, 1998); William Pettigrew, "Corporate Constitutionalism and the Dialogue between the Global and Local in Seventeenth-Century English History," *Itinerario* 39, no. 3 (2016): 487–501; Phil Withington, *The Politics of Commonwealth: Citizens and Freemen in Early Modern England* (Cambridge: Cambridge University Press, 2005) and *Society in Early Modern England: The Vernacular Origins of Some Powerful Ideas* (Cambridge, MA: Polity Press, 2010). Drawing on Jürgen Habermas's theory of the "bourgeois public sphere," Withington has defined this type of corporate political activity as constituting the "civic public sphere" and argued it that both prefigured and helped shape its "bourgeois" counterpart. See Phil Withington, "Public Discourse, Corporate Citizenship, and State Formation in Early Modern England," *American Historical Review* 112, no. 4 (2007), 1018. Elements of corporate identity are evident even far outside of towns and cities. See, for example, Steve Hindle, "Hierarchy and Community in the Elizabethan Parish: The Swallowfield Articles of 1596," *Historical Journal* 42, no. 3 (1999): 835–51.
3. Withington has recently argued that ideas of society and company, which were often evident in corporate bodies, were instrumental in the growth of state power both in England and its colonies. See Withington, *Society in Early Modern England*, 204–5.
4. Some of these contestations are examined in Chapter 4.
5. East India Company, *Laws or Standing Orders of the East India Company* ([London?], 1621). The full description of the *Laws or Standing Orders* was given on the third page and was laid out on the page as an expansion of the title: they were the "Laws or Standing Orders Made and Ordained by the Governor and Company of Merchants of London Trading to the East Indies, For the Better Governing of the Affairs and Actions of the Said Company here in England Residing, Anno Dom. 1621." A table at the beginning of the pamphlet listed different headings within the work, most of which were

different jobs and offices within the Company. Most of the offices named in the *Laws or Standing Orders* were not named in the patent that prescribed the Company's government, and many of these positions were not held by people elected annually and seem to have been appointments. They might be thought of as Company employees rather than Company officials, and different from the elected leaders. These were not positions that required their occupants to be members of the Company or gave them any say in the Company's central government: most of the holders of these almost sixty offices and positions—ranging from a clerk of the stores, a beadle, and a secretary to ship stewards, gunners, and carpenters—would not have been able to vote for the elected officials.

6. *Charters Granted to the East India Company, from 1601, Also the Treaties and Grants, Made with, or Obtained from, the Princes and Powers in India, from the Year 1756 to 1772* ([London] [1773]), 13–14.

7. East India Company, *Laws or Standing Orders*, 4–5 and 9–11.

8. Ibid., 2.

9. Ibid., 2–3 and 10.

10. The passive usages here reproduce the style of language in the court minutes. The fine was twelve pence for missing a meeting. See, for example, BL IOR B/3, 4 July 1609, GC, or BL IOR B/5, 5 July 1614.

11. See, for example, BL IOR B/5, 13 July 1614.

12. East India Company, *Laws or Standing Orders*, 6–7.

13. The mandated meetings were for the yearly election and when the ships arrived from the East Indies. The *Laws or Standing Orders* also mentioned that a yearly meeting of the generality could be ordered for the purpose of reading the *Laws or Standing Orders*, if deemed necessary.

14. BL IOR B/3, September, November, and December 1609.

15. The minutes of the general court at which the 1623 election took place mentioned that according to a former order, six committees would change each year. See BL IOR B/8, 2 July 1623, GC. In 1621, however, exactly how many committees should be changed was still being debated. See BL IOR B/7, 4 July 1621, GC.

16. Sir Thomas Smith served as governor in 1600–1601, 1607–14, and 1614–21 (and probably for some of the intervening years, though missing court minutes make the holder of the office unknown at times). Sir William Halliday (or Holliday) served from 1621 until he died in office in 1624. Sir Morris Abbot served as deputy governor from 1615 to 1624 and as governor from 1624 to 1638. Sir Christopher Clitherow was deputy governor from 1624 to 1635, then governor from 1638 to 1642. A few others held the offices for one- or two-year stints, but the men mentioned above held office for long periods of time.

17. For more details, see Basil Morgan, "Sir Thomas Smyth [Smith]," *ODNB*; Andrew Thrush, "Sir Morris Abbot," *ODNB*.

18. BL IOR B/5, 5 July 1615, GC.

19. The years for which comparisons with the year before are possible were 1608–1609, 1615, 1619, 1623–1628, and 1633–1635. I did not include men chosen to be special committees, as happened on rare occasions, since those people were chosen to consider specific issues and were not part of the twenty-four committees named in the patent.

20. The rule for removing at least six committees was in place for the 1623 election.

21. For example, between 1601 and 1635, Henry Garway served as a committee seventeen times; Jeoffrey Kirby and Thomas Mun sixteen times; Thomas Stiles fifteen times; Anthony Abdy, Robert Bell, and Nicholas Crispe thirteen times; Hugh Hammersley and Richard Venn twelve times; and Humphrey Brown, Alderman James Cambell, Job Harby, Nicholas Leat, and Thomas Westrow ten times.

22. BL IOR B/13, 2 March 1629, GC.

23. BL IOR B/17, 6 February 1635, GC.

24. Theodore Rabb counted 1,318 names associated with the Company before 1630 but acknowledged that that number is likely to be an underestimate. See Theodore K. Rabb, *Enterprise and Empire: Merchant and Gentry Investment in the Expansion of England, 1575–1630* (Cambridge, MA: Harvard University Press, 1967), 149–50. William Scott and K. N. Chaudhuri have been able to reconstruct the overall amounts of capital each joint stock was able to raise, but they made no attempt to determine the number of members. See K. N. Chaudhuri, *The English East India Company: The Study of an Early Joint-Stock Company, 1600–1640* (London: F. Cass, 1965), 207–23; William Scott, *Constitution and Finance of English, Scottish and Irish Joint-Stock Companies to 1720* (Cambridge: Cambridge University Press, 1910), 2:95–115.

25. What was unusual about that particular vote is that it was a vote conducted by ballot box. One candidate received fifty-four balls and the other forty-two. See BL IOR B/18, 3 July 1635, GC. No note was made of abstentions, if any occurred.

26. *Laws and Standing Orders*, 12.

27. Ibid., 12–13 and 65.

28. BL IOR B/10, 1 July 1625.

29. *Laws and Standing Orders*, 12.

30. BL IOR B/15, 29 November 1632. The responsibilities set out for the secretary in the *Laws and Standing Orders* included "tak[ing] note" of Company affairs and "faithfully and truly" setting them down in a "fair book for that purpose," *Laws and Standing Orders*, 12.

31. Joseph Ward, *Metropolitan Communities: Trade Guilds, Identity, and Change in Early Modern London* (Stanford, CA: Stanford University Press, 1997), 86–87.

32. Edward Raymond Turner, *The Privy Council of England in the Seventeenth and Eighteenth Centuries 1603–1784* (Baltimore, MD: Johns Hopkins

University Press, 1927), 1:121–23; Michael Barraclough Pulman, *The Elizabe-than Privy Council in the 1570s* (Berkeley: University of California Press, 1971), 159–60.

33. See, for example, *Dawn of British Trade*, 203 and 222; BL IOR B/12, 28 November 1627. There are many more examples.

34. For examples of the court of committees referring to "the nation," see BL IOR B/5, 10 August 1614 and 12 September 1615.

35. Paul Griffiths, "Secrecy and Authority in Late Sixteenth- and Seventeenth-Century London," *Historical Journal* 40, no. 4 (1997): 926–27. For Elizabeth and James on the mysteries of state, see, for example, Elizabeth's message to Parliament in 1571, in *Proceedings in the Parliaments of Elizabeth I*, ed. Terence Hartley (Leicester, MA: Leicester University Press, 1995), 1:199, and James I's speech in Star Chamber, 20 June 1616, in King James VI and I, *Political Writings*, ed. Johann P. Sommerville (Cambridge: Cambridge University Press, 1994), 212–13. See also David Coast, *News and Rumor in Jacobean England: Information, Court Politics and Diplomacy, 1618–25* (Manchester, UK: Manchester University Press, 2014), 48–81.

36. See, for example, Griffiths, "Secrecy and Authority," 925–951; Janelle Jenstad, "Public Glory, Private Gilt: The Goldsmiths' Company and the Spectacle of Punishment," in *Institutional Culture in Early Modern Society*, ed. Anne Goldgar and Robert I. Frost (Leiden, the Netherlands: Brill, 2004), 207–8; Turner, *The Privy Council of England in the Seventeenth and Eighteenth Centuries*, vol. 1; Ward, *Metropolitan Communities*, 87.

37. BL IOR B/5, 11 July 1615. This rule was codified in East India Company, *Laws or Standing Orders*, 2.

38. BL IOR B/15, 10 December 1632.

39. Privy councilors also wrestled on numerous occasions with the question of how secret matters became public. See Turner, *The Privy Council of England in the Seventeenth and Eighteenth Centuries*, 1:118–20.

40. East India Company, *Laws or Standing Orders*, 51–53.

41. BL IOR B/5, 13 January 1614. The amount of information management (particularly document management) that Company men had to undertake in the East Indies was impressive. Miles Ogborn has examined the early uses of writing and particular types of documents that Company representatives carried with them in the East Indies, as well as how the documents were solicited, composed, and used. See Miles Ogborn, *Indian Ink: Script and Print in the Making of the English East India Company* (Chicago: University of Chicago Press, 2007), 33–46.

42. See, for example, BL IOR B/5, 13 January and 11 and 12 July 1614.

43. Ibid., 16 July 1614.

44. See, for example, Griffiths, "Secrecy and Authority," 925–951; Randolph Head, "Knowing Like a State: The Transformation of Political Knowledge in Swiss Archives, 1450–1770," *Journal of Modern History* 75, no. 4 (2003): 745–782.

45. The literature on this topic is extensive and varied. For a few examples of the range of what historians have examined with regard to the topic, see Christopher Bayly, *Empire and Information: Intelligence Gathering and Social Communication in India, 1780–1870* (Cambridge: Cambridge University Press, 2000); Markus Friedrich, "Archives as Networks: The Geography of Record-Keeping in the Society of Jesus (1540–1773)," *Archival Science* 10 (2010): 285–98; Betty Joseph, *Reading the East India Company, 1720–1840: Colonial Currencies of Gender* (Chicago: University of Chicago Press, 2004); Ogborn, *Indian Ink*; Angel Rama, *The Lettered City* (Durham, NC: Duke University Press, 1996).

46. BL IOR B/5, 30 August 1615.

47. BL IOR B/7, 26 June 1622.

48. Ibid., 26 September 1621.

49. Ibid. Also see Head, "Knowing Like a State"; Jerry Brotton, *Trading Territories: Mapping the Early Modern World* (London: Reaktion Books, 1997). Both authors examine control of information—in Randolph Head's case, regarding city archives, and in Jerry Brotton's case, regarding control of maps and knowledge of trade.

50. BL IOR B/14, 11 February 1631, GC.

51. BL IOR B/15, 29 November 1632. The committee who wanted to loosen restrictions on access was Thomas Smethwick. That request was consistent with his attitudes about the Company's affairs, though it was a minority position. For more on Smethwick, see Chapters 4 and 9.

52. BL IOR B/15, 17 April 1633.

53. BL IOR B/5, 17 June 1614.

54. Ibid., 4 July 1614.

55. Private trade, as a topic in the history of the East India Company, has a long and venerable tradition, though again, most studies do not treat the early seventeenth century, and private trade in the eighteenth century generally referred to individual trade in the East Indies for private profit, rather than illicit importation of goods to England. See, for example, Holden Furber and Rosane Rocher, eds., *Private Fortunes and Company Profits in the India Trade in the Eighteenth Century* (Aldershot, UK: Variorum, 1997); Peter James Marshall, *East Indian Fortunes: The British in Bengal in the Eighteenth Century* (Oxford: Clarendon Press of Oxford University Press, 1976).

56. Smuggling goods secretly could take place without letters, of course. In 1631, the court of committees learned that the purser's mate, steward, and cooper of the newly arrived *Exchange* had gone into the ship's hold late at night, allegedly to liberate their private trade goods. See BL IOR B/14, 5 January 1631.

57. BL IOR B/5, 30 September 1614.

58. Ibid., 7 October 1614

59. Ibid., 5 May 1615.

60. Ibid., 7 October 1614.

61. Ibid., 15 November 1614.
62. Ibid., 14 August 1614.
63. BL IOR B/7, 18 March 1622.
64. BL IOR B/1, 29 March 1602.
65. The two main agents the Company employed in the Netherlands in the early seventeenth century were Robert Barlow and Edward Misselden. The name of the Dutch East India Company (technically the United Dutch East India Company, as it was an amalgamation of several earlier merchant groups) in Dutch was the Verenigde Oost-Indische Compangnie.
66. BL IOR B/5, 2 and 13 January 1614.
67. Ibid., 15 and 17 January 1614.
68. Ibid., 13 January 1614.
69. Ibid., 19 April 1614.
70. L. Grenade, *Les Singularitéz* [*sic*] *de Londres*, trans. Gill Healey and Ann Saunders, in *The Royal Exchange*, ed. Ann Saunders (Leeds, UK: London Topographical Society, 1997), 48–49. See also Ann Saunders, "The Organization of the Exchange," in *The Royal Exchange*, ed. Ann Saunders, 85–98.
71. The best contemporary image of the Royal Exchange is a 1644 image by Wenceslas Hollar. There is also an image of it by Franz Hogenberg from 1569. Aaron Kitch names some of the plays in which the Exchange appeared. See Aaron Kitch, *Political Economy and the States of Literature in Early Modern England* (Farnham, UK: Ashgate, 2009), 3–4.
72. BL IOR B/5, 15 September 1615.
73. BL IOR B/5, 27 September 1614.
74. BL IOR B/16, 10 January 1634.
75. BL IOR B/6, 3 February 1618.
76. BL IOR B/8, 22 October 1623.
77. Ibid.
78. Ibid.
79. BL IOR B/5, 10 January 1615. It is possible that the burned works, brought by Captain Saris from Japan, were household paintings—an artistic genre whose conventions, including frank depictions of sexual intercourse, might have seemed obscene to European eyes.
80. TNA SP 14/75/28 (Chamberlain to Carleton: 25 November 1613).
81. BL IOR B/7, 15 February 1622.
82. BL IOR B/14, 26 November 1630, GC.
83. Ibid., 31 December 1630.
84. BL IOR B/5, 8 September 1615.
85. Ibid, GC. The order that allowed the committees' actions was dated 27 October 1610. Pamphlets critical of the Company that had appeared in 1614 and 1615 might have partially explained their feeling of being embattled.
86. Ibid.
87. Ibid., 3 October 1615.
88. Ibid., 6 October 1615.

3. Wooing Adventurers: Membership and Useful Men

1. TNA SP 84/85/212 (Bell to Carleton: 22 August 1618). Robert Bell was one of the London merchants who founded the East India Company and a significant investor in it and other companies.
2. BL IOR B / 6, 3 July 1618, GC. This was a controversial suggestion, with a variety of reasons for and against it. See Chapter 4.
3. Ibid., 2 July 1619.
4. For a work invaluable for tracing gentry investment in the overseas trading companies, see Theodore K. Rabb, *Enterprise and Empire: Merchant and Gentry Investment in the Expansion of England, 1575–1630* (Cambridge, MA: Harvard University Press, 1967), especially 128. Robert Brenner notes that the Company relied on both the City elite and a number of supporters at court. See Robert Brenner, *Merchants and Revolution: Commercial Change, Political Conflict and London's Overseas Traders, 1550–1653* (Princeton, NJ: Princeton University Press, 1993), 89 and 199–203.
5. See Robert Ashton, *The City and the Court, 1603–1643* (Cambridge: Cambridge University Press, 1979), 83–156. At points, Brenner also shares this view. See especially Brenner, *Merchants and Revolution*, 199–239.
6. According to K. N. Chaudhuri, the average profit on the early separate voyages through 1612 was a whopping 155 percent, and from 1613 to 1623 (the period of the first joint stock) it was a still enormous 87 percent—but from 1617 to 1632 (the second joint stock) it was a slim 12 percent. See K. N. Chaudhuri, *The English East India Company: The Study of an Early Joint-Stock Company, 1600–1640* (London: F. Cass, 1965), 22.
7. Theodore Rabb examined gentry investment in all companies, but most scholarly attention on the subject has focused on the Virginia Company. For example, Andrew Fitzmaurice has emphasized the use and appeal of the rhetoric of commonwealth creation found in the sermons and pamphlets publicizing the Virginia Company. Rabb, *Enterprise and Empire*; Andrew Fitzmaurice, "Classical Rhetoric and the Promotion of the New World," *Journal of the History of Ideas* 58, no. 2 (1997): 221–43, "The Civic Solution to the Crisis of English Colonization, 1609–1625," *Historical Journal* 42, no. 1 (1999): 25–51, and *Humanism and America: An Intellectual History of English Colonization, 1500–1625* (Cambridge: Cambridge University Press, 2003). See also Louis B. Wright, *Religion and Empire: The Alliance between Piety and Commerce in English Expansion, 1558–1625* (Chapel Hill: University of North Carolina Press, 1943).
8. The most successful merchants could be knighted in recognition of their commercial accomplishment or other services to the king and common-wealth (the services sometimes included significant financial gifts or loans). These prized knighthoods did not automatically turn their holders into landed gentry. Although some merchants did buy estates in the country, others remained in London and seem not to have changed their primary

social identity from merchants. This is a reminder that the presence of "Sir" in front of a name does not guarantee a particular background. Nonetheless, it is also worth remembering that many elite merchants had ties to the gentry regardless of title. The eldest son of a gentry family might inherit land (and a title), while younger sons might go into trade.

9. Thomas Stuart Willan, *The Muscovy Merchants of 1555* (repr., Clifton, NJ: Augustus M. Kelley, 1973), 10–11.

10. Francis Newton Thorpe, ed., *Federal and State Constitutions, Colonial Charters, and Other Organic Laws of the States, Territories, and Colonies Now or Heretofore Forming the United States of America* (Washington: Government Printing Office, 1909), 7: 3783; Wesley Frank Craven, *The Virginia Company of London, 1606–1624* (Charlottesville: University of Virginia Press, 1957), 3.

11. Rabb, *Enterprise and Empire.*

12. Ibid., 30–31 and 47–48. Rabb notes that the Eastland, French, New Merchant Adventurer, Senegal, Levant, Muscovy, Spanish, and Venice Companies restricted the roles of nonmerchant members.

13. William Cavendish, whose name appeared on the original patent, became Baron Cavendish of Hardwick in 1605 and Earl of Devonshire in 1618. In the seventeenth century he was involved in a number of overseas ventures, especially in the Americas.

14. Certainly by the mid-eighteenth century, there was a lively trade in Company shares, with people buying and selling shares quickly and easily. See H. V. Bowen, *The Business of Empire: The East India Company and Imperial Britain, 1756–1833* (Cambridge: Cambridge University Press, 2006), 84–117.

15. BL IOR B/7, 4 July 1621, GC.

16. This policy was formalized by November 1617, when a transfer was contested on grounds of fraud. One man had paid cash for an adventure, while another claimed he held a mortgage on it. See BL IOR B/6, 11 November 1617.

17. *Charters Granted to the East India Company* ([London] [1773]), 9.

18. East India Company, *The Laws or Standing Orders of the East India Company* ([London?], 1621), 71–72. These three methods reflected procedures for gaining the freedom of the city used in the livery companies. Freedom through apprenticeship, patrimony, and redemption (purchase) were all possible in the livery companies. See Steve Rappaport, *Worlds within Worlds: The Structures of Life in Sixteenth-Century London* (Cambridge: Cambridge University Press, 1989), 23–24. East India Company leaders could also reduce the amount of the fine according to their inclinations, and sometimes they required £40 instead of £50, for example. The specific fines for membership were set by October 1615. See BL IOR B/5, 31 October 1615.

19. For example, Charles Edmondes was admitted by patrimony, despite the fact that his father, Sir Thomas Edmondes, had been admitted gratis. See BL IOR B/11, 20 April 1627.

20. BL IOR B/3, 30 May 1609. Though it is possible that other aristocrats were granted freedom in the years before 1609 and the relevant records have not

survived, the language describing the 1609 admittance suggested that this was a new development. Most of the men granted membership had prior or subsequent connections to English overseas expansion.

21. BL IOR B/3, 5 September 1609 and 9 January 1610. The court minutes continued occasionally to refer to the 1609 order when Company leaders gave someone his freedom gratis. See, for example, BL IOR/13, 27 February 1629.

22. The important caveat here remains that the court minutes are incomplete for the full period. The numbers I have provided reflect information in the surviving minutes. It is always possible that the information in missing records would change the numbers significantly.

23. The gentry who paid fines often seemed to be based outside of London. For example, William Wignall was admitted in 1615 for a fine of £20. The minutes listed him as a "gentleman of the county of [blank]." The omission suggests a certain lack of interest in his personal situation. See BL IOR B/5, 28 April 1615. John Machell, a gentleman of Wendover, Buckinghamshire, was admitted in 1617 in return for a fine of £50. See BL IOR B/6, 14 November 1617. Sir Gregory Norton was admitted by fine in 1629. See BL IOR B/13, 30 January 1629. However, similar men were still sometimes admitted gratis, as Thomas Hobbs, esquire, "of Tooting in the county of Surrey" was. See BL IOR B/6, 31 March 1618.

24. BL IOR B/5, 11 and 18 July 1615.

25. BL IOR B/3, 4 July and 27 October 1609.

26. For similar feasts in the Haberdashers' Company, see Ian Archer, *The History of the Haberdashers' Company* (Chichester, UK: Phillimore, 1991), 126–32.

27. BL IOR B/3, 23 August 1609. He worked specifically with alienations cases, and thus might prove helpful with cases involving contested corporate rights.

28. BL IOR B/5, 8 February 1614.

29. BL IOR B/3, 9 January 1610.

30. BL IOR B/5, 19 March 1614.

31. Ibid., 31 March 1614.

32. Ibid., 10 November 1615.

33. BL IOR B/5, 4 July 1614.

34. Ibid., 27 September 1614.

35. Ibid., 14 November 1617.

36. Ibid., 30 December 1617. His admission was on 2 January 1618, but the notice was appended at the end of the court minutes for 30 December 1617 and thus is found in the 30 December entry.

37. Ibid., 27 October 1618.

38. BL IOR B/5, 5 July 1614.

39. BL IOR B/6, 12 May 1619.

40. Ibid., 12 December 1617.

41. Ibid., 28 May 1619.

42. BL IOR B/5, 4 August 1614. Given Sandys's altercations with the Company's court of committees in the next decade, his promise was possibly a bit optimistic.

43. The date of Sandys's freedom is unknown. It likely took place in one of the periods for which the court minutes are missing. Regardless, he was definitely active in the Company by 1614.

44. BL IOR B/6, 23 January 1618.

45. Ibid., 27 February 1618.

46. Ibid., 17 March 1618. For more on the Scottish patent, see Chapter 6.

47. BL IOR B/5, 5 July 1614. Paget's involvement in the Virginia Company as an adventurer and hence his interest in overseas ventures may have helped convince Company leaders to do as he requested.

48. Ibid., 12 November 1614.

49. BL IOR B/6, 9 January 1618; ibid., 23 September 1617, GC; ibid., 25 June 1618.

50. Ibid., 14 November 1617 and 10 April 1618.

51. Ibid., 30 June 1618.

52. Ibid., 27 February 1618.

53. Ibid., 25 November 1617.

54. Ibid., 5 December 1617.

55. Ibid.

56. Ibid., 24 February 1618.

57. Many aspects of corporate life had a performative element to them. In the Goldsmiths' Company, for example, punishments were conducted publicly within the company. Substandard goods could be broken down in company meetings for the body of members to watch. See Janelle Jenstad, "Public Glory, Private Gilt: The Goldsmiths' Company and the Spectacle of Punishment," in *Institutional Culture in Early Modern Society*, ed. Anne Goldgar and Robert I. Frost (Leiden, the Netherlands: Brill, 2004), 209–10.

58. BL IOR B/6, 16 December 1617.

59. Ibid., 23 December 1617. Finch sat in several parliaments, was the recorder of London from 1621, and in 1626 was Speaker of the House of Commons.

60. Ibid., 30 June 1618.

61. Ibid., 30 July 1619.

62. Francis Bacon, *The Works of Francis Bacon, Baron of Verulam, Viscount St. Alban, Lord High Chancellor of England* (London: printed for A. Millar, 1740]), 1:10. The quotation comes from "On the True Greatness of the Kingdom of Britain." This essay was not published during Bacon's lifetime, though an earlier version was published in 1612. For more on the versions of the essay, see Francis Bacon, *History of the Reign of King Henry VII and Selected Works*, ed. Brian Vickers (Cambridge: Cambridge University Press, 1998), 248n.

63. BL IOR B/9, 28 July 1624. There were at least three offers by James and Charles to become adventurers in the East India Company, from James in

1624 and from Charles in 1625 and 1628. A more detailed exploration of the consequences of the events at Amboyna appears in Chapters 8 and 9.

64. The court minutes referred to this legal advice on several occasions during Charles's reign but always dated it to James's reign. See BL IOR B/10, 9 November 1625; BL IOR B/13, 2 July 1628.

65. BL IOR B/9, 28 July 1624.

66. Ibid.

67. BL IOR B/10, 9 November 1625. It is not clear when and how Charles lost his freedom of the Company, since he had it as a prince. Given the negotiations about his admittance as monarch, however, it seems certain that he did.

68. Ibid., 9 November 1625. The court of committees reiterated this reasoning when they met two days later. Ibid., 11 November 1625.

69. BL IOR B/13, 2 and 16 July 1628, GC.

70. BL IOR B/9, 6 August 1624; TNA SP 14/182/62 (Minutes of proceedings of the Privy Council, 7 August, 1624); BL IOR B/10, 9 November 1625; BL IOR B/13, 16 July 1628, GC.

71. BL IOR B/9, 16 July 1624.

72. Ibid., 28 July 1624.

73. BL IOR B/5, 17 October 1615.

74. Ibid., 3 January 1615.

75. Ibid., 15 September 1615.

76. BL IOR B/6, 28 November 1617.

77. East India Company, *Laws or Standing Orders*, 63.

78. TNA SP 14/75/53 (Chamberlain to Carleton: 30 December 1613).

79. TNA SP 14/77/4 (Gosson to Somerset: 3 April 1614).

80. BL IOR B/7, 26 November 1621.

81. Ibid., 3 December 1621.

82. Ibid., 4 January 1622.

83. BL IOR B/14, 23 December 1630.

84. BL IOR B/8, 2 January 1624.

85. Carleton's various attempts to secure office and court favor have attracted some attention. He and Sir Henry Wotton both sought the provostship of Eton; Wotton eventually received it. Carleton's gift to Buckingham of an expensive carved chimneypiece has been used to illustrate the corrupt practices of office seeking in early Stuart England, as well as to argue that the giving and receiving of gifts was simply one of the mechanisms by which the early Stuart political system functioned. See John Barcroft, "Carleton and Buckingham: The Quest for Office," in *Early Stuart Studies: Essays in Honor of David H. Wilson*, ed. Howard S. Reinmuth (Minneapolis: University of Minnesota, 1970), 122–136; Robert Hill and Roger Lockyer, "'Carleton and Buckingham: The Quest for Office' Revisited," *History* 88, no. 289 (2003): 17–31; Linda Levy Peck, *Court Patronage and Corruption in Early Stuart England* (London: Unwin Hyman, 1990); Logan Pearsall Smith, *The*

Life and Letters of Sir Henry Wotton (Oxford: Clarendon Press of Oxford University Press, 1907).

86. TNA SP 84/91/132 (Carleton to Chamberlain: 10 August 1619).

87. *Letters of John Chamberlain*, 2:261 (to Carleton: 23 August 1619).

88. Ibid., 2:265 (to Carleton: 2 October 1619).

89. Ibid., 2:271 (Chamberlain to Carleton: 13 November 1619).

90. TNA SP 14/111/30 (Edmondes to [Carleton]: 18 November 1619).

91. TNA SP 84/93/118r (Carleton to Chamberlain: 30 November 1619).

92. TNA SP 84/94/5r (Carleton to Chamberlain: 1 January 1620).

93. TNA SP 84/94/96r (Digges to Carleton: 28 January 1620).

94. TNA SP 84/95/3r (Carleton to Chamberlain: 5 March 1620).

95. *Letters of John Chamberlain*, 2:326 (to Carleton: 4 November 1620).

96. BL IOR B/8, 24 September 1623.

97. One classic work on the topic is Lawrence Stone, "The Fruits of Office: The Case of Robert Cecil, First Earl of Salisbury," in *Essays in the Economic and Social History of Tudor and Stuart* England, ed. F. J. Fisher (Cambridge: Cambridge University Press, 1961), 89–116.

98. For more on the ways that the requirements of England's overseas trade put new demands on traditional tools of statecraft, like diplomacy, see Rupali Mishra, "Diplomacy at the Edge: Split Interests in the Roe Embassy to the Mughal Court," *Journal of British Studies* 53 (January 2014): 1–24.

99. BL IOR B/5, 28 June 1615.

100. Ibid., 1 October 1614. For more on the New Exchange, see Peck, *Court Patronage and Corruption*, 155–56.

101. BL IOR B/6, 9 January 1618. A writ of *Ne Exeat Regnum* prevented someone from leaving the kingdom legally.

102. Ibid.

103. Ibid., 20 January 1618.

104. BL IOR B/5, 20 June 1614.

105. TNA SP 14/95/3 (Brent to [Carleton]: 2 January 1618).

106. BL IOR B/6, 7 January 1620.

107. BL IOR B/5, 3 February 1615; BL IOR B/6, 20 November 1618; BL IOR B/9, 6 April 1625.

108. BL IOR B/10, 13 May 1625..

109. Ibid.

110. Ibid., 27 April 1625. Company leaders debated sending a petition to this effect to the lord admiral but decided against it when they discovered that all carpenters and workmen, not only Company men, had been impressed into naval service.

111. BL IOR B/11, 8 September 1626. The minutes are unclear about whether the forty additional workmen were previously impressed Company workers or new workers who would be impressed to serve the Company.

112. Ibid., 24 January 1627. The provision of one other commodity in particular showed the complex balancing between the requirements of different state

interests: saltpeter. Since the production of gunpowder was a royal monopoly, the Company's production of it sometimes resulted in complaints from the regime, and how much they could import or export was a matter of state interest. David Cressy's recent study of saltpeter illuminates the complicated role of the substance, though further study of the Company's saltpeter and gunpowder production would be welcome. See David Cressy, *Saltpeter: The Mother of Gunpowder* (Oxford: Oxford University Press, 2013), 133–35.

4. Division within the Company: The Problem of Faction and Representation

1. BL IOR B/6, 2 July 1619, GC.
2. Nothing in the court minutes suggests that Company leaders knew of the box ahead of time or were instrumental in its creation.
3. Amazingly, Holloway's ballot box has survived. Since 1676 it has been in the possession of the Saddlers' Company, which still uses it for its yearly elections. It is unclear what happened to the box after the 1619 East India Company's election and before it entered the Saddlers' Company's possession. Many thanks to the Saddlers' Company, which was kind enough to allow me to examine the ballot box in person, and to Sue Hurley, archivist of the Saddlers' Company, who met with me.
4. At least as early as 1621 Company leaders used the ballot box for counting votes at a meeting of the court of committees. See BL IOR B/7, 1 August 1621. There is no way to know if Holloway's ballot box was actually used for Company business or if Company leaders secured their own ballot box.
5. People of the time imagined faction as a political ill, which led multiple groups to claim to speak for what should have been a single institution. For a view on faction in corporate towns, see Paul Halliday, *Dismembering the Body Politic: Partisan Politics in England's Towns, 1650–1730* (Cambridge: Cambridge University Press, 1998), 3–4.
6. "Shopkeepers" is a term used in the Company's records. Though the records do not give a formal definition of this group, they do distinguish shopkeepers from merchants. That identification might have reflected differences in the scale of wealth and operations, or between engaging or not engaging in the selling of goods to the public. Regardless, one should note that since the minimum adventure was £100, no member of the Company was poor.
7. A number of the London livery companies had occasional instances of conflict or tension between their governing bodies, which often included many merchants, and the yeomanry, most of whose members were craftsmen. A common criticism was that the leadership of a livery company did not reflect the interests of the wider membership. In some ways, these tensions within other livery companies were analogous to what happened in the East India Company—with some members of the generality arguing that the

court of committees did not represent their interests—but in other key ways, the similarities were only superficial. The distinction between the court of committees and the generality of the Company did not reflect the social and economic distinction between merchants and craftsmen, nor were the Company's election procedures as restrictive of those of most livery companies—in which the following year's leaders were chosen by only a small, elite segment of the body. See for example, Ian Archer, *The Pursuit of Stability: Social Relations in Elizabethan London* (Cambridge: Cambridge University Press, 1991), 101–04; Steve Rappaport, *Worlds within Worlds: The Structures of Life in Sixteenth-Century London* (Cambridge: Cambridge University Press, 1989), 218 and 250–52; Sylvia Thrupp, *A Short History of the Worshipful Company of Bakers of London* (Croydon, UK: Galleon Press, 1933), 83–85.

8. BL IOR B/6, 18 June 1619.
9. Ibid.
10. Paul Halliday notes that in corporate town elections, division was considered a departure from normal, and when it occurred, people expected that it should be concluded with the election. See Halliday, *Dismembering the Body Politic*, 3–5. Mark Kishlansky argues that prior to 1640, election to Parliament was a selection rather than an election, with consensus greatly prized. He highlights the fact that people gave voice, rather than voted. See Mark A. Kishlansky, *Parliamentary Selection: Social and Political Choice in Early Modern England* (Cambridge: Cambridge University Press, 1986), 10–12.
11. The 1621 *Laws or Standing Orders* allowed for voting to take place via a ballot box or by erection of hands, though no votes using the ballot box had been recorded before 1619. See East India Company, *Laws or Standing Orders of the East India Company* ([London?], 1621), 11.
12. BL IOR B/6, 25 June 1619.
13. Ibid. The East India Company at that point regularly met at Sir Thomas Smith's house in Philpot Lane. The Muscovy Company and Virginia Company also held meetings there.
14. Ibid., 2 July 1619. The negotiations with the Dutch were the discussions that led to the 1619 treaty.
15. *Dawn of British Trade*, 28; BL IOR B/1, 3 October 1600.
16. BL IOR B/6, 2 July 1619.
17. Ibid.
18. Ibid.
19. Ibid., GC.
20. Ibid.
21. Ibid.
22. Ibid.
23. Ibid.
24. Ibid.
25. Ibid.
26. Ibid.

27. Ibid.
28. These committees at large do not seem to have been appointed every year. In fact in most years, only the expected twenty-four committees appear in the election minutes.
29. Digges had gone in part on the Company's behalf as ambassador to Russia the year before (see Chapter 6). Russell was involved with nearly every trading company, including the Virginia Company and the Levant Company in addition to the East India Company. Merrick was involved with the East India Company, the Virginia Company, and other companies. Smith was also involved with the Virginia Company. Suckling was involved only with the East India Company. See Theodore K. Rabb, *Enterprise and Empire: Merchant and Gentry Investment in the Expansion of England, 1575–1630* (Cambridge, MA: Harvard University Press, 1967), 34, 369, 379, and 385.
30. TNA SP 14/119/11 (Marshe to Nicholas: 8 January 1621).
31. Theodore K. Rabb, *Jacobean Gentleman: Sir Edwin Sandys, 1561–1629* (Princeton, NJ: Princeton University Press, 1998) 339–44.
32. BL IOR B/6, 3 July 1618, GC.
33. Ibid.
34. *Letters of John Chamberlain*, 2:251 (Chamberlain to Carleton: 15 July 1619).
35. TNA SP 84/91/46v (Locke to Carleton: 17 July 1619); TNA SP 94/23/215 and 215v (Cottington to Naunton: 17 July 1619).
36. *Letters of John Chamberlain*, 2:311–12 (to Carleton: 8 July 1620).
37. The standard work on the subject is still Craven, *Dissolution of the Virginia Company: The Failure of a Colonial Experiment* (Gloucester, MA: Peter Smith, 1964).
38. See James F. Larkin and Paul L. Hughes, eds., *Stuart Royal Proclamations* (Oxford: Clarendon Press of Oxford University Press, 1973), 2:27–29, "A proclamation for settling the plantation of Virginia."
39. Membership data for the Virginia Company are from Rabb, *Enterprise and Empire*.
40. Wesley Craven discusses but does not emphasize the factional division in the Virginia Company. See Craven, *Dissolution of the Virginia Company*, 109–47 and 305–10. The Virginia Company court minutes that detail the election of April 1619 are far less revealing than East India Company court minutes detailing courts of election, though they do present the change in leadership. See Susan Myra Kingsbury, ed., *The Records of the Virginia Company of London* (Washington, DC: Government Printing Office, 1906), 1:211–14.
41. BL IOR B/7, 4 July 1621. According to the minutes, Smith had requested that he not be reelected for reasons of health. It is possible to read the change of government as a referendum on Smith, but I do not think it was. He had been pleading ill health for years and was about sixty-three at this time. He died only a few years later in 1625.

42. *Letters of John Chamberlain*, 2:388 (to Carleton: 14 July 1621).
43. BL IOR B/8, 2 July 1623. The court minutes that would have discussed the election of 1622 have not survived.
44. BL IOR B/6, 2 July 1619, GC.
45. TNA SP 84/94/96r (Digges to Carleton: 28 January 1620).
46. BL IOR B/6, 4 February 1620, GC. The minutes of this general court included many parentheticals that I have reproduced here because they were so consistently and frequently used, though they seem to have been used for elaborations that were not usually marked off with parentheses.
47. Ibid.
48. Ibid.
49. Ibid. The Mr. Cotton involved here might be the same Mr. Cotton who was chosen as a special committee in 1627, though it is difficult to confirm that definitively. In 1620, nobody by that name held a special position in the Company's government, so the two Cottons might be the same person.
50. Ibid., 14 April 1620, GC.
51. Ibid.
52. Ibid. Questions of proper representation sometimes emerged in livery companies as well. For example, when the Grocers' Company first used a ballot box in 1622, they had to repeat the vote when more ballots were counted than there were people voting. The lord mayor and senior warden had each voted twice, assuming that their importance meant they got two votes. The company eventually decided to follow the principle of one man, one vote. See Joseph Ward, *Metropolitan Communities: Trade Guilds, Identity, and Change in Early Modern London* (Stanford, CA: Stanford University Press, 1997), 92–93.
53. BL IOR B/6, 14 April 1620, GC.
54. BL IOR B/12, 28 April 1628. A William Bonham had been elected a committee in 1607 and 1608 and had been nominated in 1614. It is possible that the William Bonham who presented the petition in 1628 was not the same person but was his son or other relative and thus had never been a committee, but further clarity is not possible. Polstead was nominated numerous times in the period 1621–1634 and seems to have been a committee in 1622.
55. Ibid., 28 April 1628.
56. Ibid., 20 May 1628, GC.
57. Ibid. Smethwick is discussed in greater detail in Chapters 9 and 10.
58. Ibid.
59. BL IOR B/13, 6 March 1629.
60. Ibid., 2 March 1629, GC.
61. Ibid., 6 March 1629.
62. Ibid., 8 May 1629, GC.
63. BL IOR B/14, 11 February 1631, GC.
64. Ibid., 29 June 1631, GC.

65. TNA CO 77/4/99 (copy of minutes of a general court: 11 May 1631) and CO 77/4/103 (East India Company to Coke: [October?] 1632). The date on the copy of the minutes is given as 1631, but that seems to be an error, and should say 1632. Internal details of the document are consistent with those given in the letter to Sir John Coke, which definitely describes events in 1632.

66. TNA CO 77/4/103 (East India Company to Coke: [October?] 1632). It is hard to assess what disorders the speakers were referring to, or to trace much about the compilation of the *Laws or Standing Orders*. The minutes for the period from 14 April 1620 to 4 July 1621 are missing. The month of publication of the *Laws or Standing Orders* is unknown, but the minutes for the second half of 1621 do not mention it—which suggests that the year of meetings that led to the publication took place between 14 April 1620 and 4 July 1621.

67. Unusually, the minutes of the general quarter court did not list the committees present. Instead, beyond the governor, deputy governor, and treasurer, it named ten men as attending, along with "divers others." The ten were Lord Saye and Sele, Lord Brook, Lord Lovelace, Sir Francis Crane, Sir Dudley Digges, Sir Robert Crane, Sir Edward Wardour, Sir John Wolstenholme, Alderman Henry Garway, and Alderman Anthony Abdy. It is possible these were the members of the select committees who were at the meeting. If that is the case, then the group included some men who had previously been supportive, and some who had been critical, of the court of committees. TNA CO 77/4/99 (copy of minutes of a general court: 11 May 1631).

68. TNA CO 77/4/103 (East India Company to Coke: [October?] 1632).

69. TNA CO 77/4/99 (copy of minutes of a general court: 11 May 1631).

70. Ibid.

71. Ibid.

72. Ibid.

73. Ibid.

74. Ibid.

75. Ibid.

76. Ibid.

77. Ibid.

78. TNA CO 77/4/103 (East India Company to Coke: [October?] 1632).

79. Ibid.

80. BL IOR B/15, 13 March 1633.

81. Ibid., 5 July 1633, GC.

82. CO 77/4/103 (East India Company to Coke: [October?] 1632).

83. See Chapters 9 and 10.

84. BL IOR B/15, 17 April 1633.

85. BL IOR B/16, 22 November 1633.

86. BL IOR B/17, 3 October 1634, GC; 21 November 1634, GC; and 24 December 1634.

87. Ibid., 6 February 1635.

88. BL IOR B/18, 13 November 1635.

5. Merchants, Trading Companies, and Public Appeal

1. Robert Kayll, *The Trade's Increase* (London: printed by Nicholas Okes, 1615), 32.
2. Ibid., 53–55.
3. TNA CO 77/4/99 (copy of minutes of a general court: 11 May 1631).
4. Michael Oppenheim, "The Royal Navy under James I," *English Historical Review* 7, no. 27 (1892): 484; Reginald Godfrey Marsden, "English Ships in the Reign of James I," *Transactions of the Royal Historical Society* 19 (1905): 333.
5. BL IOR B/3, 27 October 1609.
6. Ibid. Given that the Company at this time was just nine years old, the idea of an ancient silk with the Company's arms is particularly intriguing.
7. Ibid., 29 December 1609.
8. TNA SP 14/50/92.
9. Richard Barbour, *Before Orientalism: London's Theatre of the East, 1576–1626* (Cambridge: Cambridge University Press, 2003), 88–89; Aaron Kitch, *Political Economy and the States of Literature in Early Modern England* (Farnham, UK: Ashgate, 2009), 156–58 and 176–78.
10. Oppenheim, "Royal Navy under James I," 484.
11. TNA SP 14/77/36 (Chamberlain to Carleton: 9 June 1614).
12. Though the Company showed no doubt as to his authorship, it must have been an open secret, for he published it anonymously. The only indication of authorship were the suggestive initials I. R. at the end of the dedication, perhaps meant to imply that the monarch (I.R. being the initials for King James in Latin) did—or should—approve of the author's words.
13. BL IOR B/5, 16 February 1615.
14. Ibid., 22 February 1615.
15. As the various pamphlets connected to the Company constitute one of the most visible and best documented cases of a body experimenting with public appeal and the public sphere, the pamphlets have received some scholarly attention in recent years. Miles Ogborn's excellent book on printing and writing in the East India Company examined various types of writing used in the Company in the seventeenth century. One of the strongest chapters of the work considers the pamphlets investigated in this chapter as part of the Company's early experiments with the public sphere. See Miles Ogborn, *Indian Ink: Script and Print in the Making of the English East India Company* (Chicago: University of Chicago Press, 2007), 104–56. Anthony Milton has also considered the Company as a body engaged in the public sphere in the early seventeenth century, tracing its attempts to use works on Amboyna (see Chapter 8) to sway public opinion and the regime. See Anthony Milton, "Marketing a Massacre: Amboyna, the East India Company and the Public Sphere in Early Stuart England," in *The Politics of the Public Sphere in Early Modern England*, ed. Peter Lake and Steven Pincus (Manchester, UK: Manchester University Press, 2007), 168–90.

16. BL IOR B/5, 29 March 1615.
17. Ibid.
18. *APC 1615–1616*, 99 and 107–8.
19. Sir Dudley Digges, *The Defense of Trade. In a Letter to Sir Thomas Smith Knight, Governor of the East-India Company, &C. From One of That Society*, 2nd ed. (London: William Stansby for John Barnes, 1615).
20. There are several extant copies of *The Trade's Increase*, and while none of them specify that they are second editions, the pamphlet appears to have been reset at some point. See, for example, the copy in the Huntington Library collection and the copy in the Harvard University Library's collection, both of which are available in Early English Books Online (https://eebo.chadwyck .com/home). It is certainly possible that these differences are simply the normal variations between texts so common in printed material of the period. See Adrian John, *The Nature of the Book: Print and Knowledge in the Making* (Chicago: University of Chicago Press, 1998). For references to *The Trade's Increase* in library collections, see Folger Shakespeare Library MS L. d. 776 (inventory of Nathaniel Bacon's books, c. 1623); W. O. Hassall, ed., *A Catalogue of the Library of Sir Edward Coke* (New Haven, CT: Yale University Press, 1950), 81. The modern cataloguer of Coke's library has provided an incorrect English Short Title Catalogue (http://estc.bl.uk) number for *The Trade's Increase*, but given that the rest of the information on the pamphlet is correct, I assume that this is a cataloguer error of the number. *The Trade's Increase* was also listed among the books of Sir Roger Townshend's library. See Robert J. Fehrenbach and Elisabeth S. Leedham-Green, eds., *Private Libraries in Renaissance England: A Collection and Catalogue of Tudor and Early Stuart Book-Lists* (Binghamton, NY: Medieval and Renaissance Texts & Studies, 1991), 1:134.
21. This episode did not involve an early version of Jürgen Habermas's public sphere. Indeed, attempts to revise the date of its beginning seem beside the point. Instead, the most useful aspect of applying the concept of the public sphere to this period has been its drawing attention to the ways people thought about the role of the public and attempted public appeals, even in cases where those appeals may have had limited effect. A number of works using the language of the public sphere and popular appeal have appeared in recent years and have helped transform the study of early modern political culture. Most of them take as given that the Habermasian public sphere was not present in the sixteenth or early seventeenth century, but that the analytical tools and categories developed to study it are useful when applied to the earlier period. See, for example, the essays (and particularly the introduction) published in Peter Lake and Steve Pincus, eds., *The Politics of the Public Sphere in Early Modern England* (Manchester, UK: Manchester University Press, 2007).
22. Kayll, *The Trade's Increase*; E. S., *Britain's Busse, or a Computation as well of the charge of a Buss of Herring Fishing Ship. As Also of the Gain and profit thereby*

(London: William Iaggard for Nicholas Bourne, 1615); Tobias Gentleman, *England's Way to Win Wealth, and to Employ Ships and Mariners: Or, a Plain Description What Great Profit It Will Bring Unto the Commonwealth of England, by the Erecting, Building, and Adventuring of Busses, to Sea, a Fishing: With a True Relation of the Inestimable Wealth that is Yearly Taken out of his Majesties' Seas, by the Great Numbers of Busses, Pinks, and Line-Bearers, Etc.* (London, 1614). The *ODNB* gives some information on Tobias Gentleman. He lived in Yarmouth and seems to have had some cartographic skills, as he made a map of the town in 1611. See *ODNB*. The English Short Title Catalogue (http://estc.bl.uk) identifies E. S. as Edward Sharpe. No more information about him can be found under either name, however.

23. See Kitch, *Political Economy and the States of Literature*, 80–84.

24. See William Welwod, "Of the Community and Propriety of the Seas," in *The Free Sea*, ed. David Armitage (Indianapolis, IN: Liberty Fund, 2004), 65. David Armitage notes that the only response to the *Mare Liberum* that Grotius answered was Welwod's. See David Armitage, introduction to *The Free Sea*, xviii.

25. E. S., *Britain's Busse*, A2v.

26. Gentleman, *England's Way to Win Wealth*, 38–39 and 45.

27. E. S., *Britain's Busse*, Ev and E2r.

28. Kayll, *The Trade's Increase*, 15–20.

29. Gentleman, *England's Way to Win Wealth*, 9.

30. E. S., *Britain's Busse*, Fv.

31. Ibid., F2r–v.

32. Kayll, *The Trade's Increase*, 4–5, 14–15, and 18.

33. Ibid., 1, 20, 26–30, and 38.

34. Ibid., 51–53.

35. Ibid.

36. Ibid., 53.

37. Ibid., 53–55.

38. Ibid., 55–56.

39. He was one of the committees at large chosen in 1619 and served as an ambassador to Muscovy in 1618 in unusual circumstances, described in Chapter 6. Suffice it to say here that his ties to the Company seem to have been instrumental in his appointment to the embassy.

40. The description of Digges as "one of that society" is quoted from the title page of Digges, *The Defense of Trade*.

41. Ibid. 1–2 and 49–50.

42. Ibid., 4.

43. The metaphor of merchants as bees and the state as the hive was not new when Digges used it, nor was he the last to employ it; Thomas Hobbes used the same example in *Leviathan*, and Bernard Mandeville's *Fable of the Bees* openly referred to it as well.

44. Digges, *The Defense of Trade*, 2–3.
45. Ibid., 2 and 16–18.
46. Ibid., 19–27.
47. Ibid., 32–33.
48. Ibid., 32. The punctuation of the original is confusing, but the sentence breaks are preserved here.
49. Ibid.
50. Ibid.
51. Even more than for his work as a Company leader, Mun is remembered today for the works he wrote on economics, especially his posthumous *England's Treasure by Foreign Trade*. In 1620 he also served on a royal commission that investigated the trade depression in England.
52. East India Company, *The Petition and Remonstrance of the Governor and Company of Merchants of London Trading to the East Indies* (London: printed for Nicholas Bourne, 1628), 7–8; Thomas Mun, *A Discourse of Trade from England Unto the East Indies: Answering to Diverse Objections Which Are Usually Made Against the Same*, 2nd ed. (London: printed by Nicholas Okes for John Pyper, 1621), 50. *The Petition and Remonstrance* was published as a Company work, so Mun's name did not appear officially on it, but he was the author.
53. East India Company, *The Petition and Remonstrance*, 14–15. Mun's reference to adventurers who did not understand this profit-loss relationship was an acknowledgment of the turmoil in the Company in 1628 about the direction of the East Indies trade. See Mun, *A Discourse of Trade*, 9.
54. Mun, *A Discourse of Trade*, 7–9.
55. Ibid., 5–6.
56. Ibid., 6–7.
57. Ibid., 7. For further information on the silk projects, see BL Add. MS 5496 f. 48; Linda Levy Peck, *Consuming Splendor: Society and Culture in Seventeenth-Century England* (Cambridge: Cambridge University Press, 2005), 73–111.
58. East India Company, *The Petition and Remonstrance*, 8.
59. Ibid.
60. See, for example, Gentleman, *England's Way to Win Wealth*, 1–2; Edward Misselden, *Free Trade: Or, the Means to Make Trade Flourish. Wherein, the Causes of the Decay of Trade in This Kingdome, Are Discovered, Etc.* (London: printed by John Legatt for Simon Waterson, 1622), 27; Mun, *A Discourse of Trade*, 3; Gerard Malynes, *The Maintenance of Free Trade, According to the Three Essential Parts of Traffic; . . . Or, an Answer to a Treatise of Free Trade Lately Published, Etc.* (London, 1622), 58–59.
61. East India Company, *The Petition and Remonstrance*, 11–13 and 30–31. Mun explained how more money could be created by melting down plate, for example, but only trade would increase the amount of wealth available.
62. Ibid., 14–17 and 34.

63. Part of the reason why Digges did not respond directly to Kayll's critique of trading companies was no doubt because the section of Kayll's pamphlet that he excerpted did not include the passages about these companies.

64. Misselden, *Free Trade.*

65. Misselden was not the only author to appear before the Company, printed work in hand. For other examples of authors currying favor with the Company via printed pamphlets, see Chapter 8.

66. BL IOR B/7, 1 and 31 August 1621; BL IOR B/8, 21 October and 4 November 1623. See also Andrea Finkelstein, *Harmony and Balance: An Intellectual History of Seventeenth-Century English Economic Thought* (Ann Arbor: University of Michigan Press, 2000), 54–55.

67. Misselden, *Free Trade*, 53–54.

68. Ibid., 53–55, 57, 73, and 84–85.

69. Interestingly, these ideas also accorded with a strain of republican thought that drew on Aristotelian ideas of justice. Thus, Misselden echoed the conviction that the proper end of freedom was an arrangement "that accords with nature," instead of the arrangement that provides the same opportunities to everyone, and he directly referred to Aristotle in places as well. See Eric Nelson, *The Greek Tradition in Republican Thought* (Cambridge: Cambridge University Press, 2004), 14–15.

70. Misselden, *Free Trade*, 60–61.

71. Ibid., 61–63.

72. Ibid., 64–66.

73. Ibid., 66–67.

74. Ibid., 68 and 87–90.

75. Ibid., 74–78.

76. Ibid., 78–82 and 84. Misselden's pamphlet was not his last and was not unanswered, but at this point the terms of the debate shifted away from the direct consideration of the East India Company and the role of government in trade. A merchant named Gerard Malynes answered Misselden in 1622 with *The Maintenance of Free Trade.* Misselden responded in 1623. See Edward Misselden, *The Circle of Commerce. Or the Balance of Trade, in Defense of Free Trade: Opposed to Malynes Little Fish and His Great Whale, and Poised against Them in the Scale. Wherein Also, Exchanges in General Are Considered, by E. M[isselden]. Merchant* (London: Printed by John Dawson for Nicholas Bourne, 1623). Malynes responded to that work in the same year. See Gerard Maylnes, *Center of the Circle of Commerce, Or, a Refutation of a Treatise, entitled The Circle of Commerce, or the Balance of Trade, lately published by E.M.* (London, printed by William Jones for Nicholas Bourne, 1623). Malynes's central concern was currency exchange rates, and though he also had concerns about the East India Company, they were not central to his works.

6. The Changing Patent: Negotiating Privileges between Company and Regime

1. Isaac Le Maire has received little scholarly attention in English, though his colorful life would reward further attention. He was an early and heavy investor in various Dutch ventures to the East Indies, including the Dutch East India Company (VOC), in which he was the largest shareholder at the time of its founding. Disagreements between him and the other members of the VOC led him to explore alternative pathways to the East Indies. See Donald Lach and Edwin J. Van Kley, *Asia in the Making of Europe* (Chicago: University of Chicago Press, 1993), 3:446–48; John Norman Leonard Baker, *A History of Geographical Discovery and Exploration* (London: G. G. Harrap and Co, 1931), 149–50.

2. BL IOR B/6, 14 April 1618 and 15 April 1618, GC.

3. Ibid., 17 April 1618.

4. The legal mechanism used to recall and revoke a patent by the monarch was called *quo warranto* (meaning, by what warrant). This was a prerogative writ used to call in patents and charters, including town charters, and in 1624, it was the writ used to call in the Virginia Company's patent. *Quo warranto* was not used against the East India Company, though given its use against other corporations, this was always a possibility. For information on the crown's use of *quo warranto* to revoke town charters and regrant them in the late seventeenth century, see Paul Halliday, *Dismembering the Body Politic: Partisan Politics in England's Towns, 1650–1730* (Cambridge: Cambridge University Press, 1998). Halliday also provides an insightful overview of late seventeenth-century corporations and charters. See ibid., 29–55. Unfortunately for my purposes, the sources that provide much of his information were compiled several decades after the end date of the period studied here.

5. I have generally used "patent" in preference to "charter," following the contemporary usage of the Company itself. Originally patents and charters were different types of royal grants, but by the sixteenth century those differences had eroded.

6. BL IOR B/5, 27 September 1614.

7. TNA SP 14/141, f.86r (grant to the East India Company: 14 December 1615).

8. TNA SP 14/141, f. 105 r–v (grant to the East India Company: 11 July 1616).

9. Hatfield House Archives, Cecil Papers 142/172 (commission to James Lancaster: 24 January 1601).

10. BL IOR B/5, 9 September 1614.

11. Ibid.

12. From grants like this, one can trace the beginning of what Philip Stern has called the "company-state." The Company had only limited control over its factors in the East Indies—indeed, one of its diplomatic goals in the Mughal empire in this period was to secure extraterritoriality—but a continuous grant of martial authority over its mariners, soldiers, and factors was arguably

necessary for the mostly autonomous Company outposts, factories, and settlements that were in place by the end of the seventeenth century. There was no straight trajectory from martial law to company-state, but grants like this allow one to see how conceptions of autonomy might evolve. For the development of the company-state as a sovereign polity in the late seventeenth century, see Philip J. Stern, *The Company-State: Corporate Sovereignty and the Early Modern Foundations of the British Empire in India* (Oxford: Oxford University Press, 2011).

13. BL IOR B/5, 15 November 1614.

14. Ibid., 4 October 1614.

15. The letters were form letters, with blanks for the agent's name to be filled in as necessary. They acknowledged royal support but were not royal appointments. For an analysis of the uses of these letters, see Miles Ogborn, *Indian Ink: Script and Print in the Making of the English East India Company* (Chicago: University of Chicago Press, 2007), 27–66.

16. BL IOR B/5, 4 October 1614.

17. Ibid., 14 October and 2 November 1614. See also Rupali Mishra, "Diplomacy at the Edge: Split Interests in the Roe Embassy to the Mughal Court," *Journal of British Studies* 53 (January 2014): 1–24.

18. BL IOR B/5, 4 October 1614.

19. Ibid., 2 November 1614.

20. TNA SP 14/78/61 (Chamberlain to Carleton: 24 November 1614).

21. The challenges continued well beyond the pamphlet debates of the 1610s and 1620s. The best-known challenge to the Company's patent was *East India Company v. Sandys*, a 1684 case known as the great case of monopolies. See Stern, *Company-State*, 46–58; Steven C. A. Pincus, "A Revolution in Political Economy," in *The Age of Projects*, ed. Maximillian E. Novak (Toronto: University of Toronto, 2008), 122–25.

22. The patent was printed in *Foedera*, 16:582. Beyond the patent and a very few mentions of Michelborne in Company minutes, little documentation of his venture survives.

23. *Dawn of British Trade*, 178. It is possible that Company leaders were happy to have an excuse to lose Michelborne, who was an associate of the Earl of Essex and had been arrested for possible involvement with his rebellion. Michelborne escaped with a fine and ultimately found favor with James, who made him a gentleman pensioner and granted him the East Indies patent. See Kenneth R. Andrews, *Trade, Plunder, and Settlement: Maritime Enterprise and the Genesis of the British Empire, 1480–1630* (Cambridge: Cambridge University Press, 1984), 278; Sir William Foster, *England's Quest for Eastern Trade* (London: A. and C. Black, 1933), 149; "Michelborne, Sir Edward," *ODNB*, 2004. William Scott saw the Michelborne episode as the counterpart of parliamentary critiques of the Company in 1604. See William Scott, *Constitution and Finance of English, Scottish and Irish Joint-Stock Companies to 1720* (Cambridge: Cambridge University Press, 1910), 2:98–99.

24. BL IOR B/3, 11 July 1607 and 26 January and 19 and 23 February 1608. It is unclear whether the East Indians were employees or enslaved. The Company considered hiring them for their knowledge of the East Indies. Michelborne noted that they should not be sent back to their own country, presumably because they would run away; he noted that one had already run away in England, and Michelborne had a warrant to capture him.

25. BL IOR B/3, 27 July 1609.

26. Penkevell was never active in the East Indies, though he did play a role in Prince Henry's court and was involved in Henry Hudson's ventures to the New World. See "Richard Penkevell," in *The History of Parliament: The House of Commons, 1558–1603*, ed. P. W. Hasler (London: H. M. Stationery Office, 1981); *CSPC East Indies 1513–1616*, 146.

27. Scott, *Constitution and Finance of English, Scottish and Irish Joint-Stock Companies to 1720*, 2:100. The grant to Penkevell is printed in *Foedera*, 16:660–63.

28. There was also a grant in 1612 to Sir Henry Thynne of the power to use martial law on the voyage to Persia. See *CSPC East Indies 1513–1616*, 236.

29. Ostensibly, Thynne's ship was sailing for France. Company leaders argued to the lord admiral that Thynne intended to secure a commission for the East Indies from the French king and that this was unbecoming to an English subject. Given the privileges that James had granted Thynne in 1612, at least the king had known that the object of the voyage was Persia, not France. See BL IOR B/5, 2 November 1614.

30. Ibid., 15 November 1614.

31. Ibid., 2 December 1614.

32. Ibid., 27 January 1614.

33. Ibid., 11 February 1615.

34. Ibid., 1 July 1614.

35. Ibid., 3 March 1614

36. Ibid., 11 February 1615.

37. Ibid., 29 March 1615.

38. Ibid., 14 March 1614; *APC 1613–1614*, 378–79. Ultimately, the recalcitrant investor, a Mr. Newman, was released after submitting a petition to the Council, which ordered him to submit to the governor and the Company, "acknowledging his faults and craving pardon for the same." See BL IOR B/5, 19 March 1614. He made a "strange submission" to the governor, acknowledging that he was wrong to question the authority of the clerk of the Council, but not his faults to the Company. Smith explained the situation to the clerk, who promised to get Newman to submit an apology in writing. See ibid., 22 March 1614.

39. For more on the idea of Great Britain, see Keith M. Brown, *Kingdom or Province? Scotland and the Regal Union, 1603–1715* (Basingstoke, UK: Macmillan, 1992), 86–111; Andrew D. Nicholls, *The Jacobean Union: A Reconsideration of British Civil Policies under the Early Stuarts* (Westport, CT: Greenwood Press,

1999); Sarah Waurechen, "Imagined Polities, Failed Dreams, and the Beginnings of an Unacknowledged Britain: English Responses to James VI and I's Vision of Perfect Union," *Journal of British Studies* 52, no. 3 (July 2013): 575–96; David Harris Willson, "King James I and Anglo-Scottish Unity," in *Conflict in Stuart England: Essays in Honor of Wallace Notestein*, ed. William Appleton Aiken and Basil Duke Henning (New York: New York University Press, 1960), 41–55; Jenny Wormald, "'A Union of Hearts and Minds'? The Making of the Union between Scotland and England, 1603," in "Forms of Union: the British and Spanish Monarchies in the Seventeenth and Eighteenth Centuries," special issue, *International Journal on Basque Studies* 5 (2009): 109–24. Though Scottish nobles had a significant presence among James's gentlemen of the bedchamber, other administrative structures of the two kingdoms remained separate. James and Charles I both appointed Scottish courtiers to the English Privy Council, so Scottish influence in England was not entirely circumscribed. See Brown, *Kingdom or Province?*, 21–23; Neil Cuddy, "The Revival of the Entourage: the Bedchamber of James I, 1603–1625," in *The English Court from the Wars of the Roses to the Civil War*, ed. David Starkey (London: Longman, 1987), 173–225, and "Anglo-Scottish Union and the Court of James I, 1603–1625," *Transactions of the Royal Historical Society*, 5th ser., 39 (1989), 107–24.

40. Nor was the Darian Company the last Scottish company aimed at the East Indies trade. For an examination of the consequences of the 1707 Act of Union on the possibilities of a Scottish East India Company, see Andrew Mackillop, "A Union for Empire? Scotland, the English East India Company and the British Union," *Scottish Historical Review* 87, suppl. (2008), 116–34.

41. BL IOR B/6, 18 November 1617. Sir James Cunningham was related to James Cunningham, the seventh Earl of Glencairn, who was one of James' privy councilors. The southeast passage referred to the sea route to the East Indies via the Cape of Good Hope—that is, the route used by the English East India Company. The Company leaders' information was late: Cunningham's patent was given in May 1617.

42. Ibid.

43. George Birdwood and William Foster, eds., *Register of Letters etc., of the Governor and Company of Merchants of London Trading into the East Indies, 1600–1619* (London: Bernard Quaritch, 1893), 490–91.

44. *Letters of John Chamberlain*, 2:134–35 (to Carleton: 31 January 1618). Elizabeth's charter to the Company specified that the privileges she gave were for the merchants and their "successors," with no mention made of heirs. George Birdwood and William Foster, eds., *Register of Letters*, 168 and 75.

45. *Letters of John Chamberlain*, 2:134–35 (to Carleton: 31 January 1618).

46. BL IOR B/6, 3 February 1618.

47. There is no mention in the *APC* of Sir James Cunningham and his patent in late January or early February 1618, but given that the *APC* mainly contains

letters and records of orders from the Privy Council and not minutes of all that passed at the Council table, such an omission may not be surprising. According to the Company's minutes, after all, the lords of the Council had discussed the matter but had not yet taken action.

48. The *APC* and Company court minutes record different dates for the meeting (15 and 10 March, respectively). The meeting described in both accounts appears to be the same, despite the discrepancy in the dates.

49. BL IOR B/6, 20 March 1618.

50. Ibid., 10 March 1618.

51. Ibid., 17 March 1618.

52. *APC 1618–1619*, 71.

53. Ibid.

54. BL IOR B/6, 10 March 1618.

55. *APC 1618–1619*, 71.

56. Ibid., 77 and 204.

57. Ibid., 205.

58. *Letters of John Chamberlain*, 2:150 (to Carleton, 16 March 1618).

59. BL IOR B/6, 20 March 1618.

60. Ibid.

61. Ibid., 26 March 1618.

62. Ibid., 27 March 1618.

63. Ibid., 20 March 1618; Scott, *Constitution and Finance of Joint-Stock Companies to 1720*, 2:55–56. The joint ventures, which focused on the whaling trade, were unprofitable, and the joint stock was wound up in two years instead of the projected eight. Details about the short-lived merger between the two companies are murky. See J. T. Kotilaine, *Russia's Foreign Trade and Economic Expansion in the Seventeenth Century* (Leiden, the Netherlands: Brill, 2005), 100; Maria Salomon Arel, "The Muscovy Company in the First Half of the Seventeenth Century: Trade and Position in the Russian State—A Reassessment," (PhD diss., Yale University, 1995), 48–51.

64. TNA SP 91/2/58 ("Reasons to Induce his Majesty to the Loan of Money": [1618]); *APC 1618–1619*, 151–53.

65. *APC 1618–1619*, 151–52 and 154.

66. *Letters of John Chamberlain*, 2:154 (to Carleton: 1 April 1618).

67. TNA SP 14/157/9 (Lovelace to Carleton: 6 April 1618).

68. TNA SP 15/42/69 (petition to the lords of the Privy Council). The account was undated but probably from 1620 or 1621.

69. *Foedera*, 17:257.

70. Digges received a warrant to go as ambassador on 28 May 1618. See *APC 1618–1619*, 151.

71. TNA SP 14/157/9 (Lovelace to Carleton: 6 April 1618).

72. BL IOR B/6, 10 April 1618.

73. *APC 1618–1619*, 151–54. Thomas Kiffin suggests that the Company had picked Digges for the embassy, but that by that time Digges had established himself

as a client of the Marquess of Buckingham, and that the Buckingham connection was more important to his being named ambassador. See Thomas Kiffin, "Sir Dudley Digges: A Study in Early Stuart Politics" (PhD diss., New York University, 1972), 98–99.

74. TNA CO 77/1/64, 64i (Privy Council to Smith and Muscovy Company: 9 July 1618). The letter can also be found in *APC 1618–1619*, 204–5. The letter was addressed to Smith and the Muscovy Company, but the partial merger of the two companies included their joint responsibility to compensate Cunningham.

75. BL IOR B/6, 14 July 1618.

76. Ibid., 17 July 1618.

77. Ibid., 21 July 1618.

78. TNA CO 77/1/66–66i (answer of the united companies of Muscovy and East India merchants to a letter to Smith: 8 August 1618).

79. BL IOR B/6, 11 December 1618.

80. Ibid., 14 December 1618.

81. Nicholls, *The Jacobean Union*, 168–70; Robert Ashton, *The City and the Court, 1603–1643* (Cambridge: Cambridge University Press, 1979), 103.

82. Ashton, *The City and the Court*, 103.

83. BL IOR 6, 22 December 1618.

84. Ibid.

85. *Letters of John Chamberlain*, 2:172 (to Carleton, 14 October 1618). *Animus revertendi* is a Latin phrase meaning "with intention to return" and is a type of property law ownership often applied to livestock or pets. Thus, for example, a claimed animal wandering off its owner's land still belongs to its owner.

    Kiffin explored the reasons for the fiasco of the embassy, which included the ongoing war and personal sickness. Digges never met with the tsar, instead entrusting the money to his kinsman and personal secretary, Thomas Finch. See Kiffin, "Sir Dudley Digges," 104–8.

86. BL IOR B/6, 20 October 1618.

87. TNA SP 14/103/46 (Pory to Carleton: 25 October 1618).

88. BL IOR B/6, 6 November 1618.

89. Ibid., 24 November 1618.

7. "What His Men Have Done Abroad": Martial Engagements and the Company

1. Samuel Rawson Gardiner, ed., *Notes of the Debates in the House of Lords, Officially Taken by Henry Elsing, Clerk of the Parliaments*, A.D. *1624 and 1626* ([Westminster, UK]: Camden Society, 1879), 14; Robert E. Ruigh, *The Parliament of 1624: Politics and Foreign Policy* (Cambridge, MA: Harvard University Press, 1971), 185–86.

2. BL IOR B/8, 24, 28 April 1624.

3. *Proceedings in Parliament, 1626,* 1:420–22.

4. See, for example Kenneth R. Andrews, *Trade, Plunder, and Settlement: Maritime Enterprise and the Genesis of the British Empire, 1480–1630* (Cambridge: Cambridge University Press, 1984 and *Elizabethan Privateering: English Privateering During the Spanish War, 1585–1603* (Cambridge: Cambridge University Press, 1964); David Delison Hebb, *Piracy and the English Government, 1616–1642* (Aldershot, UK: Scolar Press, 1994). David Hebb's study examines policy toward piracy in the early Stuart period, with a focus on the Barbary pirates.

5. *Charters Granted to the East India Company, from 1601, Also the Treaties and Grants, Made with, or Obtained from, the Princes and Powers in India, from the Year 1756 to 1772* ([London] [1773]), 20–21.

6. Ibid., 45. Elizabeth's charter had limited the grant to fifteen years.

7. Ibid., 47.

8. BL IOR B/5, 27 January and 3 and 9 March 1614.

9. The conflict between the Company and the Earl of Warwick (Sir Robert Rich's title from 1619) has received little scholarly attention. Mark Hanna explores Warwick's role in Atlantic world piracy, which included sailing under letters of marque from the Duke of Savoy in the West Indies as well, but makes no mention of the East Indies part of the story. See Mark G. Hanna, *Pirate Nests and the Rise of the British Empire, 1570–1740* (Chapel Hill, NC: University of North Carolina Press, 2015), 67–78. In his study of Warwick and the Earl of Holland (Warwick's younger brother), John Beatty notes it only in passing. See John Louis Beatty, *Warwick and Holland: Being the Lives of Robert and Henry Rich* (Denver, CO: Alan Swallow, 1965), 81–82.

10. *Letters Received,* 6:161 and 174–75. Factors' letters at other times had explained how custom in the Ottoman empire and India allowed an alien community as a whole to be held responsible for the debts of individual members of that community.

11. A letter written in the East Indies in November 1617 would not reach the court of committees in London until spring 1618.

12. BL IOR B/6, 24 February 1618.

13. Wesley Frank Craven noted the presence in 1616 of an agent from the Duke of Savoy in England and the interactions between Rich and the agent. Wesley Frank Craven, "The Earl of Warwick, a Speculator in Piracy," *Hispanic American Historical Review* 10 (1930):461.

14. John Appleby, "War, Politics, and Colonization, 1558–1625," in *The Origins of Empire,* ed. Nicholas Canny, vol. 1 of *The Oxford History of the British Empire* (Oxford: Oxford University Press, 1998), 73–74; Andrews, *Trade, Plunder, and Settlement,* 302 and 313; Robert Brenner, *Merchants and Revolution: Commercial Change, Political Conflict and London's Overseas Traders, 1550–1653* (Princeton, NJ: Princeton University Press, 1993), 156. For more on the relationship of piracy to the growth of empire in the Atlantic world, and

particularly Warwick's role, see Mark G. Hanna, *Pirate Nests and the Rise of the British Empire*, 67–78. For more information on Warwick and the Caribbean Somers Island Colony, see Karen Ordahl Kupperman, *Providence Island 1630–1641: The Other Puritan Colony* (New York: Cambridge University Press, 1993); Beatty, *Warwick and Holland*.

15. BL IOR B/6, 27 February 1618. Given that at the same time Rich and Sir Edwin Sandys were challenging Sir Thomas Smith's leadership of the Virginia Company, leaders of the East India Company may have felt especially threatened by Rich's attempts to discover damaging material about them. See Wesley Frank Craven, *Dissolution of the Virginia Company: The Failure of a Colonial Experiment* (Gloucester, MA: Peter Smith, 1964), 82–85; Brenner, *Merchants and Revolution*, 100.

16. BL IOR B/6, 17 July 1618.

17. Ibid., 23 October 1618.

18. TNA SP 14/103/46 (Pory to Carleton: 25 October 1618).

19. BL IOR B/6, 27 October 1618. The Guinea and Binney patent was awarded later in 1618. See Andrews, *Trade, Plunder, and Settlement*, 113. Neither Buckingham nor Company leaders seemed to find the distance of the west coast of Africa from the Red Sea (and hence how difficult one might find it to use the former as a base to harass ships in the latter) worthy of comment.

20. TNA SP 14/105/3 (Smithe to Carleton: 7 January 1619).

21. BL IOR B/6, 22 January 1619.

22. Ibid.

23. Sir Thomas Roe, *Embassy of Sir Thomas Roe to India, 1615–19, as Narrated in His Journal and Correspondence*, new and rev. ed., ed. Sir William Foster (London: Oxford University Press, 1926), 390–91.

24. TNA SP 14/105/67 (Wynne to Carleton: 28 January 1619).

25. TNA SP 14/105/104 (Wynne to Carleton: 14 February 1619).

26. TNA SP 14/105/118 (Abbot to Roe: 19 February 1619).

27. BL IOR B/6, 23 February 1619.

28. Ibid., 26 February 1619.

29. Ibid., 17 May 1619.

30. Ibid., 15 November 1619.

31. Ibid., 19 November 1619.

32. Ibid. (emphasis in the original).

33. Ibid., 6 December 1619.

34. Ibid., 8 and 10 December 1619.

35. Ibid., 10 December 1619.

36. Ibid., 13 December 1619.

37. Ibid.

38. One other case involving these legal questions occurred in the mid-1610s, when the *Pearl* (not a Company ship) claimed a prize from a Portuguese ship in the East. The Company tried to assert a claim to that cargo, through the

logic that their patent granted them sole right to sell East Indies goods in England, regardless of provenance. The regime claimed the goods. The difference between Warwick's venture and that of the *Pearl* was that Warwick did not take from the Portuguese, but rather targeted Mughal ships—which the Company argued greatly threatened its trade. For one study of the *Pearl*, see Calvin F. Senning, "Piracy, Politics, and Plunder under James I: The Voyage of the *Pearl* and Its Aftermath, 1611–1615," *Huntington Library Quarterly* 46 (1983): 187–222.

39. BL IOR B/6, 17 December 1619.
40. Ibid., 17 January 1620.
41. Ibid., 31 January 1620.
42. Ibid., 31 January and 7 and 21 February 1620.
43. Ibid., 15 March 1620. The original wording of the quotation is awkward: "his Lordship desireth to have a meeting with the Company, being willing to make a peaceable end with them, and not to urge them to go unto the king any more."
44. Ibid., 17 March 1620.
45. Ibid.
46. Ibid., 28 and 31 March 1620. Each side chose two arbitrators, with Warwick proposing Sir William Harvey and Sir Ferdinando Gorges, and the Company proposing Digges and Alderman William Halliday. When Warwick pressed for an umpire, chosen by James, the Company leaders demurred, suggesting that no umpire was needed. If Warwick pressed for an umpire, however, they proposed Lord Chief Justice Henry Hobart, "against whom there can be no just exceptions taken." They did not mention that Hobart was a member of the Company.
47. BL IOR B/9, 14 February 1625.
48. Warwick may have been influenced by Lady Dale's parliamentary suit the year before. She had been seeking £10,000 that she claimed was due her as Sir Thomas Dale's widow for goods he had seized in the East Indies as a Company commander before he died. Company leaders had denied that the money was owed to her. In 1624 she petitioned Parliament to take up her case against the Company, though Company leaders managed to avoid a final judgment on the case by parliamentary committee. There is no good treatment of this case.
49. BL IOR B/9, 16 February 1625.
50. See below, on Hormuz.
51. BL IOR B/9, 4 March 1625.
52. In 1627, Warwick approached the Company for either a "friendly end" or their answers to his claims, so he would know which legal approach to take. Members of the court of committees were willing to concede that they held some money that was due Warwick and noted that as he was engaged in setting out a fleet for the West Indies, he might be more willing to settle than he had been before. See BL IOR B/11, 28 February 1627.

53. Indeed, Conrad Russell cited Warwick as one of the prototypical well-connected members of the House of Lords, close but not too close to court and to whom a number of representatives in the House of Commons owed their nominations. See Conrad Russell, *Parliaments and English Politics, 1621–1629* (Oxford: Clarendon Press of Oxford University Press, 1979), 15–17 and 79.

54. BL IOR B/12, 18 June 1628.

55. Ibid.

56. Ibid.

57. Russell, *Parliaments and English Politics*, 322–89.

58. Additionally, the 1628 parliament in other respects was very sympathetic to merchant concerns, especially when those concerns pitted merchants against the regime. The tonnage and poundage crisis was, essentially, an aligning of merchants with Parliament against the regime. See Chapter 9.

59. BL IOR B/12, 25 June 1628, mixed court meeting; 27 June and 2 July 1628. The accounts of this negotiation from the *Lords Journal* and parliamentary diaries are not nearly as complete as the Company's account: the fullest account notes only that Warwick presented a petition and that after negotiation, the Company agreed to pay £4,000. See *Proceedings in Parliament, 1628*, 5:705.

60. Hormuz, as a both a strategic and cultural center, has attracted some recent scholarly attention. See, for example, Dejanirah Couto and Rui Loureiro, *Revisiting Hormuz: Portuguese Interactions in the Persian Gulf Region in the Early Modern Period* (Wiesbaden, Germany: Harrassowitz Verlag, 2008). See also Niels Steensgaard, *The Asian Trade Revolution of the Seventeenth Century: The East India Companies and the Decline of the Caravan Trade* (Chicago: University of Chicago, 1974).

61. TNA SP 94/25, f. 46v (Aston to Digby: 23 March 1622).

62. For an example, see BL IOR E/3/5 (Connock to East India Company: 2 April 1617).

63. TNA CO 77/2/1 (copy of the articles of Hormuz: 11 January 1622). Many of the English records relating to the fall of Hormuz can also be found in Samuel Rawson Gardiner, ed., *Documents Illustrating the Impeachment of the Duke of Buckingham in 1626* ([Westminster]: printed for the Camden Society, 1889).

64. TNA SP 99/24/140. The secretaryship of state was, at the time, being split between Sir George Calvert, Sir Edward Conway, and Sir Robert Naunton, and each was responsible for different areas. The Venetian ambassador at Constantinople had received news from Aleppo about Hormuz a month earlier. See *CSPV 1621–23*, 376.

65. TNA SP 94/25 f. 336r (extract of a letter written from Madrid: 19 December 1622). The Venetian ambassador in England noted that in September news had reached the Company that Hormuz was taken. See *CSPV 1621–23*, 466.

66. TNA SP 94/25 f. 339r (Bristol to Calvert: 20/30 December 1622).
67. *CSPV 1621–23*, 545.
68. TNA SP 99/24/140 (Wotton to Calvert: 22 August 1622).
69. *Letters of John Chamberlain*, 2:468 (to Carleton: 21 December 1622). A letter from the Venetian ambassador also noted the complaints of the Spanish ambassador. See *CSPV 1621–23*, 519. The Spanish ambassador at the time was Don Carlos Coloma.
70. TNA SP 94/26/6 (Bristol to Calvert: 12/22 January 1623).
71. TNA SP 94/26/4 (extract of a letter from Madrid, likely Bristol to Calvert: 12/22 January 1623).
72. TNA SP 14/147/88 ([Conway] to Calvert: 30 June 1623).
73. TNA SP 14/148/5 (Calvert to [Conway]: 1 July 1623).
74. The letter is the first surviving official letter to the Company about Hormuz. The court minutes from mid-1622 to mid-1623 have not survived, but they probably discussed the Hormuz business.
75. BL IOR B/8, 4 July 1623.
76. Ibid., 9 July 1623.
77. Ibid., 23 July 1623.
78. Ibid.
79. TNA CO 77/2/83, 198r (notes from the Privy Council on Hormuz: 23 July 1624). This set of notes covered the period from 23 July 1623 to 23 June 1624 and appears to be similar to the Company's minutes, but from the Privy Council's perspective. They are much more complete than what was recorded in the Privy Council register, and indeed the meetings recorded in the notes do not appear in *APC*.
80. Months earlier, the Venetian ambassador had opined that the Company was not a willing participant in the action but had been forced to take part by the Persians. See *CSPV 1621–23*, 519.
81. BL IOR B/8, 25 July 1623.
82. *CSPV 1623–25*, 95; TNA SP 14/149/48 (Chamberlain to Carleton: 26 July 1623).
83. TNA SP 14/149/97 ([Conway] to Fotherley: 30 July 1623 and TNA SP 14/149/99 (Conway to the governor of the East India Company: 30 July 1623).
84. BL IOR B/8, 6 August 1623.
85. Ibid., 1 August 1623.
86. TNA SP 14/151/5 (Calvert to [Conway]: 18 August 1623).
87. TNA SP 94/27/189r (complaint of the Spanish ambassadors: 18/28 August 1623).
88. TNA SP 14/151/38 ([Conway] to Calvert: 22 August 1623).
89. TNA SP 94/27/211 ([Conway] to the Spanish ambassadors: 22 August 1623).
90. See Thomas Cogswell, *The Blessed Revolution: English Politics and the Coming of War, 1621–1624* (Cambridge: Cambridge University Press, 1989), 6–53. See also Glyn Redworth, *The Prince and the Infanta: The Cultural Politics of the*

Spanish Match (New Haven, CT: Yale University Press, 2003); Robert Cross, "Pretense and Perception in the Spanish Match, or History in a Fake Beard," *Journal of Interdisciplinary History* 37, no. 4 (2007): 563–83.The Venetian ambassador's take on the diplomatic difficulties between the Spanish and English was that the English seizure of Portuguese goods benefited the Spanish. It could compensate for the proposed dowry for the Spanish match, but it forced James to anger either the Spanish or his merchants. See *CSPV 1623–25*, 95. It should be noted, however, that no mention of restitution to the Spanish occurred after this point, which suggests that once the Spanish match was no longer a possibility, James was far less concerned about appeasing the Spanish ambassador.

91. TNA CO 77/2/85 ("Propositions Concerning the Profits to be Raised to his Majesty from the Island of Hormuz": [1623?]).

92. See Edward Stanley Roscoe, *A History of the English Prize Court* (London: Lloyd's, 1924), 11–14 and 26–27. Edward Stanley Roscoe noted in particular a case in 1625–1626 in which the regime confiscated and used prize money without following Admiralty court procedure, to Marten's dismay.

93. Gardiner, *Documents Illustrating the Impeachment of the Duke of Buckingham*, 73–82. The examinations began on 11 December 1623 and continued until 9 January 1624.

94. Later accounts suggested that Buckingham had learned of the fall of Hormuz in October, and that his interest in ways Hormuz might benefit him dated to that time as well. See *Proceedings in Parliament, 1626*, 1:421.

95. TNA CO 77/3/2 f. 4r-v (report of [Coke] to Buckingham about Hormuz: 20 January 1624). Michael Young suggests that Coke was behind the scheme to ask for £10,000. See Michael. B. Young, *Servility and Service: The Life and Work of Sir John Coke* (Woodbridge, UK: published by Boydell for the Royal Historical Society, 1986), 129.

96. TNA CO 77/3/2 f. 4v (report of [Coke] to Buckingham about Hormuz: 20 January 1624).

97. BL IOR B/8, 3 February 1624.

98. Ibid., 13 February 1624. Coke was the representative. He was identified in a set of notes on the Hormuz affair made by a Privy Council secretary.

99. *Dawn of British Trade*, 246–47.

100. For a description of the *Ascension*'s voyage and the sea engagement with the Portuguese, see Clements R. Markham, *The Voyage of Sir James Lancaster, Kt., to the East Indies* (London: printed for the Hakluyt Society, 1877).

101. BL IOR B/8, 18 February 1624.

102. Ibid.

103. Ibid.

104. Ibid., 27 February 1624. Company records often referred to "the Portugal" rather than the Portugese.

105. Ibid. The "line" mentioned was shorthand for the lines of amity, referring to a specified area within which the Peace of Cateau-Cambrésis held sway.

The lines were not documented in the treaty itself, as no full agreement could be reached among the English, French, and Spanish, and seem to have been verbally agreed upon. Exactly which parallel of latitude and line of meridian demarcated the lines was also unclear. Garrett Mattingly could not find an English reference to the "line" before 1630, though the Hormuz negotiations discussed here provide earlier references. He argued that in the English context, the line referred to was the Tropic of Cancer, with no specified meridian. See Garrett Mattingly, "No Peace beyond What Line?" *Transactions of the Royal Historical Society*, 5th ser., 13 (1963):145–46 and 161.

106. Gardiner, *Notes of the Debates in the House of Lords*, 14; David R. Ransome, ed., "The Parliamentary Papers of Nicholas Ferrar, 1624," in David R. Ransome, Mike J. Braddick, Mark Greengrass, and J. T. Cliffe, *Seventeenth-Century Political and Financial Papers* (London: Cambridge University Press, 1996), 43. See also Ruigh, *The Parliament of 1624*, 185–86.

107. Parliament diaries record debates beginning on 24 February that identified the East India Company's exportation of silver as a cause of the decay of trade in the kingdom. See *Proceedings in Parliament, 1624*, forthcoming. My thanks to the History of Parliament Trust for generously making its typescripts available to me before publication of the work. For more on the investigation of monopolies by the House of Commons in 1624, see Elizabeth Read Foster, "The Procedure of the House of Commons against Patents and Monopolies, 1621–1624," in *Conflict in Stuart England: Essays in Honor of Wallace Notestein*, ed. William Appleton Aiken and Basil Duke Henning New York: New York University Press, 1960), 59–85.

108. Nicholas Ferrar's parliamentary diary noted that Sir Edward Seymour, who put forward the stay, contended that the Company fleet included 1,500 mariners, "which was too great a number to spare considering the great want that was of them." Abbot disputed the number and argued that the East Indies ventures also added to the monarch's honor. See Ransome, ed., "The Parliamentary Papers of Nicholas Ferrar," 43.

109. BL IOR B/8, 5 March 1624.

110. Ibid., 8 March 1624. Abbot also noted that Martin Bond, a member of Parliament for London, "did but whisper a few words to a gentleman next him" and was chastised. Abbot used the incident as proof of the "heat" in Parliament against the Company. Though Abbot did not clarify this point, the gentleman that Bond whispered to was Bateman. Parliamentary diaries for 6 March corroborate the incident involving Bond's chastisement for whispering. See *Proceedings in Parliament, 1624*, forthcoming. See also Andrew Thrush, "Martin Bond," in *The History of Parliament: The House of Commons 1604–1629*, Andrew Thrush and John P. Ferris, eds., 6 vols. (Cambridge: Cambridge University Press, 2010).

111. BL IOR B/8, 8 March 1624. Mun had been present at both the parliamentary debates and the meetings of the court of committees, exclaiming at one

point that he "doubted not to satisfy the parliament that the strength, the stock, the trade, and the treasure of the kingdom are all greatly augmented by the East India trade." See ibid. There is no definitive dating for Mun's writing of *England's Treasure by Foreign Trade*, which was not published until 1664. Scholars have dated it to the 1620s, but the wording of Mun's exclamation echoes so closely the title of his *England's Treasure by Foreign Trade* that it is possible that this parliamentary debate was the spur for the composition. See Barry Supple, *Commercial Crisis and Change in England, 1600–1642* (Cambridge: Cambridge University Press, 1959), 211–18.

112. BL IOR B/8, 8 March 1624. The "original" referred to in the minutes has not survived.

113. Notes on the proceedings in the Admiralty court, which include the examinations and cross-examinations, have survived. See Gardiner, *Documents Illustrating the Impeachment of the Duke of Buckingham*, 90–111.

114. Ibid., 94.

115. Ibid., 112. The order came on 16 March 1624.

116. TNA CO 77/2/83 198v–199v (notes from the Privy Council on Hormuz: 18 March 1624).

117. Ibid.

118. Ibid., 199v.

119. BL IOR B/8, 2 and 7 April 1624.

120. Ibid., 24 and 28 April 1624. The Venetian ambassador shortly related that Buckingham used his proceeds to provision naval ships for war. See *CSPV 1623–25*, 325. The payment to James did not take place immediately—in June 1624 the court of committees was still arranging for it. See BL IOR B/8, 25 June 1624. In July, James's representatives were complaining that £2,000 had yet to be paid. See BL IOR B/9, 9 July 1624. The final payment seems to have taken place shortly after 15 July 1624, the date of the last chiding reminder from James—in this case via Conway. See TNA CO 77/3/23 ([Conway] to the East India Company: 15 July 1624).

121. BL IOR B/10, 27 February 1626.

122. Ibid., 20 March 1626.

123. Ibid., 22 March 1626. The court of committees held back the unregistered minutes, which would have included fuller accounts of Company debates. The surviving minutes are the registered ones, and only occasional hints appear of what the Company censored from the full minutes. According to one such hint, the unregistered minutes included "many private passages between his late majesty, the Duke of Buckingham, and the Company." See BL IOR B/10, 22 March 1626.

124. *Proceedings in Parliament, 1626*, 3:18–9.

125. Ibid., 3:29–30.

126. Ibid., 1:420–21.

127. Ibid., 1:422–24.

8. The Dutch East India Company and Amboyna:
Crisis and Response in the Company

1. This complicated episode has received little scholarly attention, though that is changing. For English-language works, see D. K. Bassett, "The 'Amboyna Massacre' of 1623," *Journal of Southeast Asian History* 1 (1960): 1–19; Adam Clulow, "Unjust, Cruel, and Barbarous Proceedings: Japanese Mercenaries and the Amboyna Incident of 1623," *Itinerario* 31, no. 1 (2007): 15–34; Alison Games, "Violence on the Fringes: The Virginia (1622) and Amboyna (1623) Massacres," *History* 99, no. 336 (2014): 505–29. Both Alison Games and Adam Clulow are working on book projects that examine the events at Amboyna. Clulow's larger project is called *The Murderous Conspiracy at Amboina: Fear and Panic in the Dutch Empire*. Games's work is called *The Invention of the Amboyna Massacre* and examines the event and its long history in British culture.

2. Simon Adams has argued that one of the main tensions that shaped early Stuart foreign policy was the question of religious allegiance—specifically, to what extent England's religious ties should determine its foreign policy. Another was the financial tension between crown and subject. See Simon Adams, "Spain or the Netherlands? The Dilemmas of Early Stuart Foreign Policy," in *Before the English Civil War: Essays on Early Stuart Politics and Government*, ed. Howard Tomlinson (London: Macmillan, 1983), 79–101. Joyce Appleby has demonstrated how frequently English writers used "the Dutch" as a benchmark comparison and the model to be emulated in economic writings. See Joyce Oldham Appleby, *Economic Thought and Ideology in Seventeenth-Century England* (Princeton, NJ: Princeton University Press, 1978), 73–98. Marvin Breslow has examined how puritan writers characterized the Dutch and attempted to neutralize Anglo-Dutch conflict. See Marvin Breslow, *A Mirror of England: English Puritan Views of Foreign Nations, 1618–1640* (Cambridge, MA: Harvard University Press, 1970), 74–99. For a general interpretation of English borrowing from the Dutch, see Lisa Jardine, *Going Dutch: How England Plundered Holland's Glory* (London: Harper Press, 2008).

3. The Dutch East India Company was chartered in 1602. However, it was not the first Dutch East Indies venture. In the previous decade, eight companies representing various merchants and regions of the Netherlands had sent ships to the East Indies. The unification of those companies resulted in the formation of the Dutch East India Company (whose full name was the Verenigde Oost-Indische Compagnie, meaning the United East India Company). For an overview of Dutch activities in the East Indies, see C. R. Boxer, *Dutch Seaborne Empire, 1600–1800* (New York: Knopf, 1965); Jonathan I. Israel, *Dutch Primacy in World Trade, 1585–1740* (Oxford: Clarendon Press of Oxford University Press, 1989); Geoffrey Vaughan Scammell, *The First Imperial Age: European Overseas Expansion c. 1400–1715* (London: Unwin Hyman, 1989).

4. *Dawn of British Trade*, 112–13.

English attitudes to the Dutch were complicated and not limited to the East Indies ventures. Elizabeth I had loaned the Dutch men and money to aid them in their revolt against the Habsburg empire. Military campaigns gave way to a stalemate between the United Provinces and Spain in the early years of James's reign and ultimately led to the Twelve-Year Truce, which began in 1609. England still held several Dutch towns, known as the cautionary towns, which had been given in return for English aid against Spain. Dutch leaders knew they would need English aid once the treaty lapsed. This position of English power was complicated by England's economic dependence on the Low Countries. England's largest export commodity, wool (and goods made of wool), depended on cloth workers in the Low Countries for finishing. Many English merchants and aristocrats lamented the fact that the United Provinces reaped such large economic benefits from English wool that could go instead to English workers. In the 1610s, Alderman William Cockayne spearheaded a project to develop England's cloth industry so that English workers would dye and finish English cloth, rather than sending it to the Low Countries. However, this plan did not work well and was a significant cause of an English economic depression in the early 1620s. See Astrid Friis, *Alderman Cockayne's Project and the Cloth Trade: The Commercial Policy of England in Its Main Aspects, 1603–1625* (Copenhagen, Denmark: Levin and Munsgaard, 1927); Barry Supple, *Commercial Crisis and Change in England, 1600–1642* (Cambridge: Cambridge University Press, 1959), 33–72. See also Wallace T. MacCaffrey, *Elizabeth I: War and Politics, 1588–1603* (Princeton, NJ: Princeton University Press, 1992), 295–98.

5. *CSPC East Indies 1513–1616*, 434.

6. TNA CO 77/1/34 (petition of the East India Company merchants to Salisbury: November 1611).

7. TNA SP 84/68/231v (Winwood to Salisbury: 31 January 1612).

8. Indeed, the State Papers, Holland, at the National Archives are peppered with East India Company matters alongside the military and religious matters that are generally better known to historians of the period. I cannot show each example, but for a representative one, see TNA SP 84/68/229r (Winwood to Salisbury: 31 January 1612). The letter begins with "upon the charge of your lordship's letters written in the behalf of the East Indian merchants, the 22th of this month I had audience in the assembly of the States General."

9. Holden Furber, *Rival Empires of Trade in the Orient, 1600–1800* (Minneapolis: University of Minnesota Press, 1976), 38.

10. G. N. Clark and Jonkheer W. J. M. Van Eysinga, *Colonial Conferences between England and the Netherlands in 1613 and 1615* (Leiden, the Netherlands: Brill, 1951), 2:25 and 65; Furber, *Rival Empires of Trade*, 33. G. N. Clark and Jonkheer Van Eysinga cite comments by both Jan Pieterzoon Coen and Hugo Grotius to this effect. The "simple trade" observation referred to in the

text was made by Grotius. Another difference was that the Company paid dividends to investors in its first decade, while the Dutch Company chose to reinvest its gains in the trade, paying for and expanding its fortifications in the East Indies. This absence of realized gains to investors led members of the English East India Company to comment on the expense and lack of returns to Dutch East India Company investors despite its greater wealth and led Dutch merchants to express frustration at their company's trade. See Femme Gaastra, "War, Competition and Collaboration: Relations between the English and Dutch East India Companies in the Seventeenth and Eighteenth Centuries," in *The Worlds of the East India Company*, ed. H. V. Bowen, Margarette Lincoln, and Nigel Rigby (Woodbridge, UK: Boydell, 2002), 50–51; Furber, *Rival Empires of Trade*, 35.

11. BL IOR B/5, 3 January 1615; TNA SP 84/71/101 (Edmondes to Winwood: 4 April 1615). The observation from the Company minutes was not denying that the Company also received state support; instead, it referred to the provision in the patent that the monarch could revoke the Company's privileges with three years' notice. For an overview of the government and organization of the Dutch East India Company, see, for example, Femme Gaastra, "The Organization of the VOC," trans. Rosemary Robson-McKillop, in *The Archives of the Dutch East India Company (VOC) and the Local Institutions in Batavia (Jakarta)*, ed. G. L. Balk, F. van Dijk, and D. J. Kortlang (Leiden, the Netherlands: Brill, 2007), 13–27.

12. Clark and Van Eysinga, *Colonial Conferences*, 2:33 and 35.

13. Furber, *Rival Empires of Trade*, 42–43.

14. TNA SP 84/68/252v (Winwood to Salisbury: 10 March 1612).

15. TNA SP 84/69/28v-29r (Winwood to the king: 13 March 1613); TNA CO 77/1/38 (Minutes of a negotiation with Holland for securing and improving the trade and navigation in the East Indies: 23 March to 20 April 1613). The two main issues were the East Indies trade and fishing near Greenland. To support their rights to trade in the East Indies, the Company cited the anonymous *Free Sea* to various people—including Hugo Grotius, without knowing he was its author. To support their claim to the Greenland fishing, the Dutch cited it back to the English. See Hugo Grotius, *The Free Sea*, ed. David Armitage (Indianapolis, IN: Liberty Fund, 2004).

16. BL IOR B/5, 8 February and 4 August 1614.

17. BL IOR B/5, 3, 6, and 13 December 1614; *Letters of John Chamberlain*, 1:563 (to Carleton: 15 December 1614).

18. BL IOR B/5, 4 July 1615.

19. TNA CO 77/1/48, f. 92r (reasons from the East India merchants about the impossibility of joining with the Dutch: [July 1615]). I am not making any comment on the actual martial or peaceful nature of English activity in the East Indies, merely reporting how the Company's leaders characterized the two nations' trades at this point. The Dutch Company's charter made the connection between trade and war explicit. See, for example, Pepijn

Brandon, *War, Capital, and the Dutch State (1588–1795)* (Leiden, the Netherlands: Brill, 2015), 52–55.

20. BL IOR B/6, 9 January 1618.

21. *Letters of John Chamberlain*, 2:166 (to Carleton: 13 August 1618). For an account of the relations between the English and the Dutch in the East in 1618, see Clark and Van Eysinga, *Colonial Conferences*, 2:127–28.

22. TNA SP 84/85/212 (Bell to Carleton: 22 August 1618).

23. *CSPC East Indies 1617–1621*, 422 and 425; TNA SP 84/86/89 (Naunton to Carleton: 24 September 1618).

24. *CSPC East Indies 1617–1621*, 468; TNA SP 84/87/6r (Naunton to Carleton: 3 November 1618).

25. BL IOR B/6, 2 October 1618.

26. TNA SP 84/88/3, 2 January 1619 (Naunton to Carleton: 2 January 1619); TNA SP 84/88 / 7 (Naunton to Carleton: 3 January 1619). The fact that the Twelve-Year Truce between Spain and the United Provinces was set to expire in 1621 might have made the Dutch more willing to negotiate in 1619 than they had been in 1613. Certainly, the Venetian ambassador to England observed in 1618 that a treaty between the English and the Dutch would prove a hindrance to the Spanish. See *CSPV 1617–1619*, 263 and 574.

27. Copies of the negotiations survived in an unlikely place—namely, in the Company's Java factory records. Presumably copies were sent there for reference, and the factors at Java were especially good at squirreling documents away. See BL IOR G/21/2A, 5r-51r (documents related to the controversies between the English and Dutch East India Companies). For meetings at Smith's house, see BL IOR G/21/2A, 46v (8 July 1619 meeting).

28. *CSPV 1617–1619*, 548–49, 555, 557, and 574.

29. *Letters of John Chamberlain*, 2:239 (to Carleton: 31 May 1619).

30. Ibid., 2:243–44 (to Carleton: 5 June 1619). Donato's account, in contrast, suggested some sympathy with Dutch arguments that the English had achieved rather more than they deserved in this case. See *CSPV 1617–1619*, 548.

31. TNA SP 14/109/91 (Edmondes to Carleton: 12 June 1619).

32. Clark and Van Eysinga, *Colonial Conference*, 2:132. Sir Clement Edmondes immediately sent a copy of the terms of the treaty to Carleton. See TNA SP 84/90/122 (Edmondes to Carleton: 28 May 1619). The outline of the terms appeared in a report from the Venetian ambassador in late June 1619. See *CSPV 1617–1619*, 563. Not everyone on both sides was pleased with the settlement. Jan Pieterszoon Coen was scathing in his opinion of it, characterizing the accord as a great gift to the Company at the expense of the Dutch Company. The English, he claimed, "could not pretend [to own] a single grain of sand of the Moluccas, Ambon or the Banda islands." The accord would force him now to "embrace the serpent." Quoted in Gaastra, "War, Competition and Collaboration," 52.

33. BL IOR B/6, 2 July 1619, GC.

34. Anthony Milton's article on the Amboyna massacre alludes to this aspect of the Company leaders' actions but does not examine them in depth, as his concern is tracing the extent of and evaluating the effectiveness of the Company's attempts to harness a nascent public sphere. See Anthony Milton, "Marketing a Massacre: Amboyna, the East India Company and the Public Sphere in Early Stuart England," in *The Politics of the Public Sphere in Early Modern England*, ed. Peter Lake and Steven Pincus (Manchester, UK: Manchester University Press, 2007), 185.

35. Thomas Cogswell, *The Blessed Revolution: English Politics and the Coming of War, 1621–1624* (Cambridge: Cambridge University Press, 1989), 13, 83–96, 234–38, 255–56, and 274; Simon L. Adams, "Foreign Policy and the Parliaments of 1621 and 1624," in *Faction and Parliament*, ed. Kevin Sharpe (Oxford: Clarendon Press of Oxford University Press, 1978), 140–45.

36. TNA SP 84/117/235v (Carleton to Conway: 28 May 1624); BL IOR B/8, 31 May 1624. Just a few weeks earlier, the Venetian ambassador in England had written that the Dutch were on "good terms with the English merchants over the East India trade." See *CSPV 1623–1625*, 23 February 1624, 221.

37. BL IOR B/8, 31 May 1624.

38. Ibid. The president was the head factor, or chief merchant, in Bantam. The council was the rest of the factors in Bantam. Collectively, they had responsibility for the Company's southeast Asian trade. There was another president and council at Surat, with responsibility for the trade in India and the Persian Gulf.

39. Ibid.

40. Cogswell, *The Blessed Revolution*, 254–56.

41. Ibid., 274–75.

42. *CSPV 1623–1625*, 343.

43. BL IOR B/8, 31 May 1624.

44. Brill was one of the three towns in the Netherlands that were garrisoned by England and served as a warning to Spain.

45. BL IOR B/8, 16 June 1624.

46. Whether at the Company's suggestion or not, several relatives of the Amboyna victims began to petition the king for restitution. The petition of one man, father to one of the victims, asked James to make the Dutch pay him his son's estate, lost along with his life in Amboyna. These petitions highlighted that it was not only the Company who felt that it was James' and not the Company's power and right that would secure restitution. TNA SP 14/165/73 (Petition of Thomas Johnson, haberdasher, to the king: June [?]).

47. BL IOR B/8, 19 June 1624.

48. Ibid., 23 June 1624.

49. *Letters of John Chamberlain*, 2:562–63 (to Carleton: 5 June 1624).

50. TNA SP 14/168/40 (Nethersole to Carleton: 25 June 1624). The writer, Sir Francis Nethersole, was the secretary to Elizabeth of Bohemia and firmly in

the Protestant camp, and thus he may have been including himself in this group of Dutch "friends."

51. TNA SP 14/168/48 (Carleton to Carleton: 26 June 1624).

52. *CSPV 1623–1625*, 359.

53. BL IOR B/9, 2 July 1624, GC.

54. BL IOR B / 9, 9 July 1624, GC. This account is presumably the one that survives in a manuscript copy in TNA CO 77/3/21. Its full title was "A true relation of the late cruel and barbarous tortures and execution done upon the English at Amboyna in the East Indies, by the Netherlands there," while it was endorsed (labeled for recordkeeping) as "The Discourse of the Execution of the English at Amboyna." The first printed pamphlet about Amboyna, from later in 1624, was essentially a printed version of this manuscript, with a few small changes of wording—though other documents were also included in the printed version, such as a translation of a Dutch account of the incident. Company leaders sent a copy of the manuscript on 10 July to Carleton at The Hague. See TNA SP 84/118/157. Their letter to Carleton noted that they were sending it to him even before they gave it to the king, and that they had held off forwarding any account of Amboyna to anyone until they could investigate and take evidence from factors under oath.

55. A "friend" from London wrote Robert Barlow, the Company's agent in Amsterdam, that the Amboyna account would soon come out in print. Barlow had already received the news by 19 July, which would mean that the information was sent to him from London around this time. See TNA SP 84/118/224 (Barlow to Carleton: 19 July 1624).

56. BL IOR B/9, 9 July 1624, GC.

57. Ibid., 9 July 1624.

58. Ibid., 12 July 1624; TNA CO 77/3/20 (Petition of the East India Company to the king, 10 July 1624) and TNA CO 77/3/21 (A True Relation of the late cruel and barbarous tortures and execution done upon the English at Amboyna in the East Indies, by the Netherlanders there).

59. TNA SP 14/169/41 (Locke to Carleton: 11 July 1624) and TNA SP 14/169/50 (Conway to Buckingham: 12 July 1624).

60. BL IOR B/9, 16 July 1624. James's offer of membership and the Company's reactions were examined in Chapter 3.

61. TNA SP 14/170/20 ([Conway] to the East India Company: 19 July 1624).

62. In contrast, Milton asserts that the Company leaders' focus on nobles and court elites shows their incomplete use of the public sphere—they did not locate political agency outside of court circles, he argues. See Milton, "Marketing a Massacre," 183–84.

63. BL IOR B/9, 22 July 1624, mixed court.

64. *Letters of John Chamberlain*, 2:569–70 (Chamberlain to Carleton: 24 July 1624). Given that Chamberlain was not a privy councilor and had no reason to be present at this meeting, the fact that he characterized the reaction in this way

suggests that this was the characterization of the event and effect that became public.

65. BL IOR B/9, 22 July 1624, mixed court.

66. Ibid., 11 August 1624. This pamphlet was probably the Dutch pamphlet dated July 1624 that was reprinted in the 1624 Company pamphlet. At some point in 1624, it was published in an English translation. A letter from Barlow in September noted that the English books were published at Flushing. It is possible he was referring to the English translation of the Dutch work. See TNA SP 84/120/88 (Barlow to Carleton: 16 September 1624).

67. BL IOR B/9, 18 August 1624.

68. Ibid. 20 August 1624.

69. Ibid., 27 August 1624, GC. Part of James's hesitation may have been due to his still waiting for an answer about whether he could join the Company.

70. *Letters of John Chamberlain*, 2:580 (Chamberlain to Carleton: 4 September 1624).

71. *CSPC East Indies 1622–1624*, 591.

72. BL IOR B/9, 18 September 1624.

73. Ibid.

74. Ibid., 20 September 1624.

75. Ibid.

76. Ibid.

77. Ibid., 29 September 1624.

78. TNA SP 14/173/12 (Locke to Carleton: 4 October 1624).

79. BL IOR B/9, 1 October 1624. The letter can be found in *APC 1623–1625*, 331–32.

80. BL IOR B/9, 8 October 1624.

81. Ibid., 15 October 1624.

82. *CSPV 1623–1625*, 409.

83. Ibid., 416; 423; and 429. Carleton had been in close communication with Barlow about the anonymous Dutch account of the events at Amboyna and his ultimately successful attempts to get it banned. See TNA SP 84/119/22 (Barlow to Carleton: 5 August 1624); TNA SP 84/119/60 (Carleton to Barlow: 8/18 August 1624); and TNA SP 84/119/85 (Barlow to Carleton: 10 August 1624).

84. *CSPV 1623–25*, 441.

85. Ibid., 455; 469; 477; 480; 493; and 508.

86. BL IOR B/9, 6 October 1624. When the court of committees spoke of breaking the press, I suspect they meant ensuring the typeset was broken up, rather than the press itself should be broken.

87. Ibid., 8 October 1624. The court of committees was indignant to learn, two months later, that someone from the Dutch Company was buying up the Dutch translations, "with a hope to suppress them that way." See ibid., 29 December 1624. The Dutch translation was called *Een waer verhael vande onlancksche ongerechte, wreede, ende onmenschelycke procedure teghen de Enghel-*

sche tot Amboyna in Oost-Indien, door de Nederlandlanders [sic] *aldaer ghemaeckt op een versierde pretentie van een conspiratie vande selue Enghelschen* (London: [J. Beale], 1624).

88. BL IOR B/9, 13 October 1624.

89. Ibid., 29 October 1624. It is unclear if Company leaders were sending Carleton copies of the book in English or Dutch. It seems likely that it was the English version, given that they apparently sent Barlow copies of this version. He wrote Carleton that he had distributed his copies but wished that the work would be translated into Dutch, which suggests that Company leaders sent him the English version, and perhaps that the planned Dutch copies took longer to produce than the English ones. Barlow noted that the recipient of one of his copies was Burgomeister De Vry. Exactly who the Company intended Carleton to give the books to is unclear—fellow ambassadors, to influential Dutch people, or a combination of the two. See TNA SP 84/121/127 (Barlow to Carleton: 26 November 1624).

90. John Skinner, *A True Relation of the Unjust, Cruel, and Barbarous Proceedings against the English at Amboyna in the East-Indies, by the Netherlandish Governor and Council there. Also the Copy of a Pamphlet, set forth First in Dutch and then in English, by Some Netherlander, Falsely Entitled, A True Declaration of the News that came out of the East-Indies, with the Pinnace called the* Hare, *which arrived at Texel in June, 1624, Together with an Answer to the Same Pamphlet. By the English East India Company. Published by Authority* (London: printed by H. Lownes for Nathaniel Newberry, 1624). Numerous copies of the 1624 edition survive, which also suggests the wide circulation of the pamphlet. Most surviving copies with red ink seem to have "Amboyna" in red, as well as "governor" and "council." Few existing copies have "unjust," "cruel," and "barbarous" in red. One example with the most words in red ink is a copy in the British Library (General Reference Collection G.4212). My thanks to Alison Games for comparing title page data with me.

91. Milton, "Marketing a Massacre," 175.

92. Skinner, *A True Relation*, A1r—A4v.

93. Ibid. See also Cogswell, *The Blessed Revolution*, 85–92 and 309. Thomas Cogswell's study examines the formation of the patriot coalition and the brief period in 1624 when the coalition's aims enjoyed broad support. Unfortunately for the coalition, by late 1624, support for the war was fading.

94. *News out of East India of the Cruel and Bloody Usage of Our English Merchants and Others at Amboyna, by the Netherlandish Governor and Council There. To the Tune of Braggendary* (London: printed for F. Coules, dwelling at the upper end of the Old Bailey, 1624).

95. Ibid.

96. It is possible that the ballad was commissioned by F. Coules, printer or bookseller, whose name appeared on the title page. It is also possible that it was commissioned by someone else, and simply printed by and/or sold by Coules.

97. BL IOR B/9, 17 November 1624.

98. Ibid., 14 November 1624.

99. Ibid., 6 December 1624. Several months later, the Venetian ambassador in the Netherlands noted that a recently arrived Dutch ship had run a "gauntlet of three English men-of-war," adding that "perhaps the English intended reprisals over this Amboyna affair." See *CSPV 1625–1626*, 68–69.

100. BL IOR B/9, 10 December 1624.

101. Ibid., 10 and 12 January 1625. This epistle does not seem to be the one Skinner wrote for the 1624 pamphlet, as Purchas brought it to the court of committees first and altered it at the members' request.

102. Ibid., 24 and 26 January 1625. The minutes gave no names but mentioned the printer in one entry and the bookbinder in another. It is possible these were the same person, or that two separate people refused to work on the epistle.

103. John Skinner, *A True Relation of the Unjust, Cruel, and Barbarous Proceedings against the English at Amboyna in the East-Indies, by the Hollanders there residing. As it hath been lately delivered to the Kings most Excellent Majesty* ([Saint-Omer]: printed [at the English College Press], 1624). The English Short Title Catalogue lists this printed account as ESTC S100312. This version of *A True Relation* lists no place of publication, contains no illustrations, and is missing the "by Authority" on the title page that the Company's version included. The publisher's letter is unique to this edition, though the rest of Skinner's narrative is reproduced in it.

104. BL IOR B/9, 7 February 1625. Archbishop Abbot's support for the Company in this case reflected the way that even if official support had flagged for the Company to publicize the events at Amboyna, specific people within the regime with ties to the Company—the archbishop's brother was Governor Morris Abbot—might still promote the Company's interests.

105. Ibid., 16 February 1625.

106. Ibid., 18 February 1625.

107. Robert Wilkinson, *The Stripping of Joseph, or The cruelty of Brethren to a Brother. In a Sermon before his Majesty at Whitehall, by Robert Wilkinson, Doctor in Divinity, Chaplain in Ordinary to his Majesty, and late Pastor of Saint Olaves in Southwarke. With a Consolatory Epistle, to the English-East-India Company, for their unsufferable wrongs sustained in Amboyna, by the Dutch there. Published and presented unto them, by Thomas. Myriell, Pastor of Saint Stephens in Walbrooke* (London: printed by W. S. for Henry Holland and George Gibbs, 1625), 1, 5–6, 12, 16, 20, and 51.

108. BL IOR B/9, 18 February 1625.

109. TNA SP 14/184/22 (Locke to Carleton: 21 February 1625,).

110. Ibid.

111. BL IOR B/9, 21 February 1625. Shrovetide ended with the beginning of Lent. There were riots on at least twenty-four of the Shrovetides between 1606 and 1641, mostly by London apprentices taking aim at supposed "bawdy

houses." See Andy Wood, *Riot, Rebellion, and Popular Politics in Early Modern England* (Houndmills, UK: Palgrave, 2002), 119.

112. *Letters of John Chamberlain*, 2:602 (Chamberlain to Carleton: 26 February 1625). *Chi ha tempo ha vita* means "who has time has life."

113. Ibid. The *APC* makes no mention of these events, so whether the book was called in for examination or to be censured or prohibited is unclear.

114. BL IOR B/9, 28 February 1625.

115. Ibid., 8 April 1625. Greenbury did at least one further portrait for the Company, of Ambassador Niqd Ali Beg from Persia, which can be seen today in the Asian and African Studies Reading Room of the British Library in London.

116. Ibid., 21 March 1625.

117. TNA SP 14/185/125 (Wilbraham to [the Duke of Buckingham]: March 1625).

118. BL IOR B/9, 30 March 1625.

119. Ibid., 4 April 1625.

120. TNA CO 77/3/72 (The East India Company's directions for stay of the Holland ships outward bound: [8 April 1625]).

121. BL IOR B/10, 25 May 1625.

122. Ibid., 22 June 1625.

123. Ibid., 1 July 1625, GC. Venetian accounts of the same event confirmed that the English had not taken Dutch ships, though they also reported that the English ships had given chase, and the Dutch were trying to hide any frustration over the matter. See *CSPV 1625–1626*, 68–69 and 73.

124. BL IOR B/10, 25 June 1625.

125. K. N. Chaudhuri, *The English East India Company: The Study of an Early Joint-Stock Company, 1600–1640* (London: F. Cass, 1965), 22.

126. BL IOR B/10, 1 July 1625, GC.

127. Ibid., 15 July 1625.

128. *APC 1625–1626*, 122. This letter was from 20 July 1625.

129. BL IOR B/10, 23 July 1625.

130. *APC 1625–1626*, 125–26. This letter was from 4 August 1625.

131. BL IOR B/10, 25 October 1625; TNA SP 16/89/75 ("Brief Extract of Divers Wrongs which the English East India Company Have Lately Sustained by the Dutch in the East Indies") and TNA SP 16/89/74 ("Complaint and Declaration" of the Governor, Deputy and Committees of the East India Company to the king: ([October 1625]). Though neither petition lists an official author, the "Brief Extract" seems to be by Skinner.

132. BL IOR B/10, 2 November 1625.

133. Ibid.

134. Ibid.

135. Ibid., 4 November 1625; Anton Poot, *Crucial Years in Anglo-Dutch Relations (1625–1642): The Political and Diplomatic Contacts* (Hilversum, the Netherlands: Verloren, 2013), 32–34. The eighteen months would be over in early 1627.

136. BL IOR B/10, 9 November 1625. Charles's letter to the Dutch taking exception to the reprisals clause in the Treaty of Southampton had noted that if no resolution had been reached by the expiration of the eighteen months, "we shall be free to seek our revenge for the lives and property of our subjects, whether it be by a letter of reprisal or by means of our forces that we seek justice for the injuries and losses that they have suffered in Amboyna . . . notwithstanding any general or particular non-observance clauses contained in and counter to the said treaty." Quoted in Poot, *Crucial Years in Anglo-Dutch Relations*, 34.

137. BL IOR B/10, 11 November 1625.

138. Ibid., 30 November 1625.

139. *CSPV 1625–1626*, 122. It is not clear what these ships are. They may not have actually been related to Amboyna at all, given that they did not appear in the Company's accounts, regardless of how the Venetian ambassador understood them.

140. BL IOR B/10, 25 January 1626.

141. Ibid., 3 February 1626. Milton suggests that the Company kept making "constant" demands to Charles about Amboyna during the treaty's duration. See Milton, "Marketing a Massacre," 181. The examples he cites, however, show the Company repeatedly tabling discussions of Amboyna rather than going to the king again, or responding to Dutch overtures sent to them through official channels rather than petitioning the king of their own accord. See, for example, BL IOR B/10, 21 April 1626; BL IOR B/11, 4 October 1626.

9. Taking Stock and Looking Forward: The Difficulties of the Late 1620s

1. Thomas Mun, *A Discourse of Trade from England Unto the East Indies: Answering to Diverse Objections Which Are Usually Made Against the Same*, 2nd ed. (London: printed by Nicholas Okes for John Pyper, 1621); East India Company, *The Petition and Remonstrance of the Governor and Company of Merchants of London Trading to the East Indies* (London: printed for Nicholas Bourne, 1628). *The Petition and Remonstrance* was published as a Company work, so Mun's name did not appear officially on it, but he was the author.

2. BL IOR B/12, 18 April 1628. For more about the place of *The Petition and Remonstrance* as part of an ongoing print debate on the East Indies trade in the 1610s and 1620s, see Chapter 5.

3. East India Company, *The Petition and Remonstrance*, A2v.

4. BL IOR B/12, 28 April 1628.

5. *Commons Journal*, 7 May 1628.

6. *Proceedings in Parliament, 1628*, 3:308 and 310.

7. BL IOR B/11, 4 October 1626. A letter a few weeks earlier from the Venetian ambassador Alvise Contarini, now posted in England, mentioned that the

eighteen months was about to lapse and the discussion about Amboyna would shortly be restarted. See *CSPV 1625–1626*, 528.

8. BL IOR B/11, 6 October 1626.
9. Ibid., 17 November 1626.
10. Ibid., 2 January 1627.
11. Ibid., 12 January 1627.
12. Ibid., 22 January 1627. The remonstrance by Skinner may have been the one put together to present to Buckingham earlier in that month. This seems possible given the close dates and the fact that the same description was used for both in the Company's minutes.
13. Ibid., 29 January 1627.
14. Ibid., 21 March 1627.
15. Ibid., 6 April 1627.
16. Ibid., 22 June 1627. Bourne claimed that he had not provided a copy of the book to Caron, but the Company still refused to pay him the £10 he wanted for printing the book.
17. Ibid., 23 April 1627.
18. *APC 1628–1629*, 61.
19. Accounts taken from the deposition of George Forbes, who had acted as an interpreter at Amboyna, circulated unofficially after 1628. They were never printed, but the Company paid Forbes a pension for years afterward. Karen Chancey, "The Amboyna Massacre in English Politics, 1624–1632," *Albion* 30 (1998), 596. They also sent Forbes with their two surviving Amboyna witnesses, Ephraim Ramsay and John Powell, to the Netherlands to attend any trial, paying him 10 shillings a week for six months for his troubles. See BL IOR B/14, 12 November 1630.
20. An undated petition from Daniel Buckocke, likely from 1631, concerned his role in upholding a warrant suppressing the publication of a book about Amboyna. See TNA SP 16/105/34. The warrant was granted on 7 September 1631 and lifted on 31 October 1631. See *CSPC East Indies 1630–1634*, no. 252. The missing volume of Company court minutes covered the period July 1631–July 1632.
21. BL IOR B/11, 23 May 1627.
22. *CSPV 1626–1628*, 154; 9 April 1627, 178; 19 April 1627, 190; 2 May 1627, 207; 2 June 1627, 240; and, 318.
23. See, for example, BL IOR B/11, 23 May 1627.
24. Ibid., 4 July 1627.
25. BL IOR B/12, 4 July 1627, GC.
26. The list of people who attended this meeting reads like a who's who of the great City investors—including Abbot, Sir Christopher Clitherow, Sir Edwin Sandys, Alderman James Campbell, Robert Bateman, Anthony Abdy, Thomas Mun, Robert Bell, William Cockayne, and Nicholas Crisp. See ibid., 20 July 1627.
27. Ibid.

28. Ibid. Sandys was one of only two participants in the debate who were identified by name in the minutes, instead of simply by the more anonymous "another said" or "some said." The other was Governor Abbot.

29. It should be noted that this use of "popular" was one of only a very few uses of the word in the Company's minutes. Even with respect to factional conflict in the Company, "popular" as a descriptive term, with its negative connotations, did not frequently appear.

30. BL IOR B/12, 20 July 1627.

31. Ibid. Within the Company, "stock" could mean the sum the adventures subscribed, or how much money they had. "Stock" could also mean the goods that made up the trade, from what they loaded on their ships to send to the East Indies, to what returned onboard ship from the East Indies. Both meanings of the word were being used at different times in the debates within the Company.

32. Ibid.

33. Ibid.

34. Ibid., 5 September 1627.

35. Ibid.

36. Ibid., 10 October 1627. Secretary of State Edward Conway had taken a hand in the seizure of the ships. See TNA CO 77/4/36, (Conway to the Admiral and Commanders of the Dutch East India Company ships in Meadhole, near Cowes: 19 September 1627), and TNA CO 77/4/37, 21 September 1627 (memorandum by Conway: 21 September 1627).

37. BL IOR B/12, 22 September 1627.

38. Ibid., 26 September 1627.

39. Ibid., 12 November 1627. The judges were appointed in September 1627.

40. *Court and Times of Charles I*, 1:269.

41. *CSPV 1626–1628*, 407 and 420.

42. BL IOR B/12, 12 November 1627.

43. Both Robert Brenner and Anthony Milton state that the Company gave Charles a loan of £30,000 in December 1627. Brenner attributes no particular political motivation to the loan—presenting the loan as merely a matter of the Company's once more coming to the aid of a cash-poor monarch—but Milton argues that the loan was an implicit thank-you for Charles's seizure of the Dutch ships. The trouble with either interpretation is that it is not certain that the loan actually took place. There is no mention of it in the Company minutes. Milton does not cite his source, though I presume he found the reference in Brenner, and Brenner's source is a letter by Joseph Mead, a Cambridge scholar. Mead's letter simply stated that the East India Company or merchants had lent the money sometime previously. It seems unlikely that the Company would loan such a large amount with no mention of it in the court minutes, as previous loans to the monarch were mentioned. Additionally, the minutes from 21 September 1627 mentioned that the Company's current debt stood at £220,000.

What is more likely—if Mead's information was not incorrect, which is also possible—is that the loan was made privately by some of the Company's merchants, and thus it was not an official loan from the Company. A letter from Alvise Contarini, the Venetian ambassador in England, from November 2, 1627 does mention that Company merchants had "given or lent" Charles an unspecified sum of money "to facilitate their designs." The letter certainly suggests that some transfer of money took place, or was at the very least suspected, though the loan could have still been personal and hence unofficial. The two pieces of evidence in the Company minutes that may (or may not) support the idea that some Company members gave a monetary gift to the monarch are from the meetings on 28 and 30 November. On those two days, a secret matter was discussed with the committees following a visit with the king. No details were recorded about the contents of the discussion or any decisions made. The secret matter might have been a loan to the king, or it might have been something else. Given that Company accounts were audited and made open to the members of the generality on a regular basis, it is difficult to imagine the committees hiding a loan of £30,000. However, a private loan from the committees could have been discussed and, because it did not require Company monies, would not have been recorded. The dates line up with Mead's dates, but not with Contarini's—which reinforces the view that rumors of a loan were circulating at the end of 1627. See BL IOR B/12, 21 September and 28 and 30 November 1627. See also *CSPV 1626–1628*, 448. Mead's letter to Sir Martin Stuteville of 15 December 1627 is included in *Court and Times of Charles I*, 1:304; Robert Brenner, *Merchants and Revolution: Commercial Change, Political Conflict and London's Overseas Traders, 1550–1653* (Princeton, NJ: Princeton University Press, 1993), 228; and Anthony Milton, "Marketing a Massacre: Amboyna, the East India Company and the Public Sphere in Early Stuart England," in *The Politics of the Public Sphere in Early Modern England*, ed. Peter Lake and Steven Pincus (Manchester, UK: Manchester University Press, 2007), 182.

44. *CSPV 1626–1628*, 407, 420, 424, 445, and 448.
45. BL IOR B/12, 19 November 1627.
46. Ibid.2, 15 January 1628.
47. Ibid., 1 February 1628. Secretary of State John Coke required the Company to certify the list. The list is TNA CO 77/4/43.
48. BL IOR B/12, 15 February 1628; TNA CO 77/4/45, 46. The Dutch ambassador in England was putting considerable pressure on the monarch to release the seized ships in early February, which may have been what prompted the petition to Buckingham. See *CPSV 1626–1628*, 583.
49. For more on the disputes that the Levant and East India Companies had with Charles, see Rupali Mishra, "Merchants, Commerce, and the State: The East India Company in Early Stuart England" (PhD diss., Princeton University, 2010), chapter 7.

50. While 1624 had marked a high point in Charles's relationship with Parliament, it quickly soured once he became king. See Richard Cust, *Charles I: A Political Life* (New York: Longman, 2005), 44–61; Michael B. Young, "Charles I and the Erosion of Trust, 1625–1628," *Albion* 22, no. 2 (1999), 217–35.

51. BL IOR B/12, 18 April 1628.

52. Ibid., 21 April 1628.

53. Ibid., 20 May 1628, GC.

54. Ibid.

55. East India Company, *The Petition and Remonstrance*.

56. BL IOR B/12, 2 July 1628.

57. For some of the reasons, see BL IOR B/9, 16 and 28 July 1624; BL IOR B/10, 9 and 11 November 1625.

58. BL IOR B/13, 2 July 1628 and 2 July 1628, GC. The matter was first mentioned on 2 July, and the court of committees considered it at greater length on 16 July.

59. Brenner, *Merchants and Revolution*, 230–31; Robert Ashton, *The City and the Court, 1603–1643* (Cambridge: Cambridge University Press, 1979), 128.

60. BL IOR B/13, 2 July 1628.

61. Ibid., 2 July 1628, GC. He had been made a baron in May, and on 25 July, Carleton was elevated further, and created Viscount Dorchester.

62. Ibid.

63. BL IOR B/12, 25 June 1628, GC.

64. BL IOR B/13, 16 July 1628, GC.

65. Smethwick's actions in the context of wider factional problems within the Company were examined in Chapter 4.

66. This petition does not seem to have survived, and there is no mention of Smethwick in *APC* in 1628. However, the petition is mentioned in the court minutes. See BL B/12, 26 May 1628.

67. The complaints presented to the Privy Council likely echoed those presented by Smethwick to the Company a few days earlier. See BL IOR B/12, 20 May 1628.

68. Smethwick appeared in the minutes in late 1624 and was active in the Company through the 1630s. He is mentioned in Brenner, *Merchants and Revolution*, 346; Ashton, *The City and the Court*, 127–29; Kenneth R. Andrews, *Trade, Plunder, and Settlement: Maritime Enterprise and the Genesis of the British Empire, 1480–1630* (Cambridge: Cambridge University Press, 1984), 279; and William Scott, *Constitution and Finance of English, Scottish and Irish Joint-Stock Companies to 1720* (Cambridge: Cambridge University Press, 1910), 2:109–10. Robert Ashton recognized that Smethwick was in the Company's court with Charles's support. Ashton says he agreed with Sir William and K. N. Chaudhuri that the discord was about different interests: merchants who had long-term vision and interests were in conflict with more marginal figures who advocated policies that would

bring short-term profit but might hurt long-term prospects. See K. N. Chaudhuri, *The English East India Company: The Study of an Early Joint-Stock Company, 1600–1640* (London: F. Cass, 1965), 58–59 and Sir William Foster's introduction to *CCM 1635–1639*, vii–x. Brenner noted that the House of Commons decided to consider a petition against the Company by Smethwick in spring 1641. He died in 1641 or 1642. See Brenner, *Merchants and Revolution*, 346. A note in a debate in 1628 mentioned that he had been a Company factor in the East Indies previously. See BL IOR B/12, 20 May 1628, GC. A Thomas Smethwick, yeoman of London, died in 1647, but nothing about his will suggested a large estate or any East Indies connections, and given the discrepancy in dates, the will was likely that of an entirely different Thomas Smethwick. See TNA PROB 11/199/477.

69. BL IOR B/12, 26 May 1628.
70. BL IOR B/13, 2 July 1628, GC. Libels were a term for controversial and usually anonymous works that targeted a topic or person for criticism. Libels could be prose or poetry.
71. Ibid.
72. Ibid.
73. Ibid.
74. Ibid.
75. Ibid., 9 July 1628.
76. Ibid., 18 July 1628.
77. *APC 1628–1629*, 322 and 354; BL IOR B/13, 30 February 1629, GC. Smethwick continued to challenge the leaders of the Company through the 1630s, and in 1641 he petitioned Parliament to investigate the Company, doubtless because his court patrons had abandoned him long before.
78. BL IOR B/13, 16 July 1628.
79. Ibid., 16 July 1628, GC. Dutch legal representatives had been putting pressure on Charles and had delivered a list of reasons for the release of the ships in early June 1628. See Anton Poot, *Crucial Years in Anglo-Dutch Relations (1625–1642):The Political and Diplomatic Contacts* (Hilversum, the Netherlands: Verloren, 2013), 74–75.
80. BL IOR B/13, 16 July 1628, GC.
81. *Court and Times of Charles I*, 1:379.
82. BL IOR B/13, 30 July 1628, GC.
83. Ibid., 8 August 1628.
84. Ibid., 20 August 1628.
85. Ibid., 12 September 1628.
86. Ibid., 1 October 1628.
87. Ibid.
88. Ibid. The court of committees' information was late. A letter from 7 August from Alvise Contarini, the Venetian ambassador in London, noted the rumor that the Dutch had given Charles £10,000 to release the ships but also

noted that there was as yet no confirmation of the rumor. See *CSPV 1628–1629*, 214.

89. BL IOR B/13, 1 October 1628.

90. TNA CO 77/4/52 (memorial for a letter to be written from Conway: [2 September 1628]), and TNA CO 77/4/52 (Charles to the Dutch ambassador: 2 September, 1628?).

91. BL IOR B/13, 1 October 1628.

92. Ramsey had offered to go to the Netherlands in May 1627. See BL IOR B/11, 11 May 1627. The Company paid him, Powell, and Forbes 10 shillings a week for their troubles while attending the trial. See BL IOR B/14, 27 October and 12 November 1630.

93. BL IOR B/13, 26 November 1628.

94. TNA SP 16/122/2 (Conway to Heath: 2 December 1628).

95. Smethwick was quite happy to challenge Company leaders in print, as he did in early 1629 during disputes within the Company about how to close the second joint stock. In February 1629, as Company members discussed these policy decisions, Smethwick published a broadside titled *A motion to the East India Company by Thomas Smethwick (an Adventurer with them) upon the reasons following* (London, 19 February 1629).

96. BL IOR B/13, 16 February 1629. The request can be found in *APC 1628–1629*, 331.

97. BL IOR B/13, 19 December 1628. The Company also held courts of sales in December and in the early months of 1629, which suggests that its goods from the recently arrived ships had been released from the custom house—in other words, that they had paid customs. It is possible that they were selling old goods and had left the new ones in the custom house, but given that no official decisions not to pay were recorded in the minutes, this seems less likely.

98. Brenner, *Merchants and Revolution*, 228–33; Linda Popofsky, "The Crisis over Tonnage and Poundage in Parliament in 1629," *Past and Present* 126 (1990): 53.

99. For examples of consideration in the Levant Company, see TNA SP 105/148, 195v. One such newsletter that described the refusal to pay can be found in *Court and Times of Charles I*, 1:433–34. The letter is from John Pory to Joseph Mead, 21 November, 1628.

100. Brenner, *Merchants and Revolution*, 228–29 and 234.

101. Brenner, *Merchants and Revolution*, 228–33; Popofsky, "The Crisis over Tonnage and Poundage," 59–60. Brenner rightfully uses this incident to assert that tensions between the companies and the crown had reached new heights by the end of the 1620s, yet because of his commitment to the concept of cooperation between the Levant and East India Companies, he does not fully grapple with why the two companies differed in whether or not they continued to pay customs, and what that difference revealed.

102. BL IOR B/13, 11 March 1629.

103. Ibid., 13 March 1629.

104. Ibid.
105. Ibid., 16 March 1629. It is possible this was a contentious decision, as a note in the minutes from the next meeting mentioned that the balloting box had been used for the vote, and the balloting box was generally reserved for controversial decisions.
106. Ibid., 18 March 1629.
107. Ibid., 4 April 1629; *APC 1628–1629*, 390. The merchants who refused to pay customs continued to refuse even after Parliament ended its session, though by late 1629 most merchants had begun trading again. See Brenner, *Merchants and Revolution*, 236–37.
108. Anton Poot has argued that Charles had attempted in 1629 to sway Anglo-Dutch negotiations that included concessions for Amboyna too heavily in favor of the Company, and that Dutch representatives would have had to agree due to Dutch dependence on English aid. Needless to say, this was not the Company's view of the matter. See Poot, *Crucial Years in Anglo-Dutch Relations*, 85, 91, and 105–6.
109. The new Dutch account of the events at Amboyna was Nederlandsche Oost-Indische Companie, *A Remonstrance of the directors of the Netherlands East India Company presented to the Lords States General of the United Provinces, in defense of the said Company, touching the bloody proceedings against the English Merchants, executed at Amboyna. Together, with the acts of the process, against the said English. And the reply of the English East India Company, to the said remonstrance and defense. Published by authority* (London: John Dawson, for the [Dutch] East India Company, 1632).
110. Chancey, "The Amboyna Massacre in English Politics," 597.

10. Crown Manipulations of the East Indies Trade: Dismantling the Company in the 1630s

1. The Courten Association is known as the Assada Adventurers in some accounts, and Courten is sometimes written Courteen. See Holden Furber, *Rival Empires of Trade in the Orient, 1600–1800* (Minneapolis: University of Minnesota Press, 1976), 69–70; Alison Games, *Web of Empire: English Cosmopolitans in an Age of Expansion* (Oxford: Oxford University Press, 2008), 181–82; William Scott, *Constitution and Finance of English, Scottish and Irish Joint-Stock Companies to 1720* (Cambridge: Cambridge University Press, 1910), 2: 112–16. Robert Brenner discusses them with a variety of other "East India interlopers." See Robert Brenner, *Merchants and Revolution: Commercial Change, Political Conflict and London's Overseas Traders, 1550–1653* (Princeton, NJ: Princeton University Press, 1993), 170–76.
2. TNA SP 16/163/12 (Charles to all Christian people: 19 March 1630); TNA SP 16/163/15 (Directions and Instructions to Quayle: March 1630).
3. TNA SP 16/163/12 (Charles to all Christian people: 19 March 1630).

4. TNA SP 16/163/15 (Directions and Instructions to Quayle: March 1630).

5. Ibid. The directions specified that Quayle should tell his men only when the ship had passed twenty leagues west of the southern islands (possibly the isles of Scilly).

6. BL IOR E/3/13, no. 1407 (Slade, Wills, Roberts, Pym and Minors, commanders of the *Mary*, *Exchange*, and *Speedwell*, to the East India Company: 9 December 1631). The commanders noted that Quayle's crew members were sick and many had died, commenting, "God send all no better success that come out on such designs." Interestingly, in January 1632, the factors at Surat sent letters with Quayle to the Company leaders in London, though the letters did not arrive with any great speed. One letter, for example, was endorsed as received from Quayle's ship in July 1634, almost a year after Quayle returned to England. See BL IOR E/3/13, no. 1416 (Surat president Hopkinson and council to the agent and council in Persia: 24 January 1632), and BL IOR E/3/13, no. 1417 (Surat president Hopkinson and council to the commanders of an expected fleet from England: 24 January 1632).

7. BL IOR E/3/14, no. 1431 (Skibbow and Bangham to the East India Company: 8 May 1632). This idea of national liability was standard in the Mughal and Ottoman Empires.

8. Ibid.

9. A year later, in 1633, when the *Sea Horse* neared England on its return voyage, the lords of the admiralty ordered men on the southwest coast of England to keep watch for the ship and secure her, to make sure the goods on board were not brought to shore illicitly. Interestingly, the orders mentioned that the ship had ventured into the Caribbean, specifically to Nevis and Saint Kitts, though the Company's information on the ship had placed her in the East Indies. See TNA SP 16/228/67 (Lords of the Admiralty to Bagg: 5 July 1633). I am not sure if this was misinformation or if Quayle had indeed ranged that far. Certainly he could have in the time available. By the end of the month, the *Sea Horse* was in port at Plymouth, and the admiralty lords ordered an investigation into its actions abroad, including what it had seized. See TNA SP 16/228/72a (Lords of the Admiralty to Maur and Bagg: 31 July 1633). At the end of the summer, the news was that the cargo on the *Sea Horse* was not worth much. See TNA SP 16/246/21 (Smyth to Nicholas: 10 September 1633).

10. BL IOR B/14, 30 March 1631. Company leaders agreed to send a letter informing their factors at Bantam about this on 15 April 1631. See ibid., 15 April 1631.

11. Ibid. April 1631.

12. TNA SP 16/161/10 and 11 (Button to Dorchester: 16 February 1630). For Button's activities in the Hudson Bay, see Kenneth R. Andrews, *Trade, Plunder, and Settlement: Maritime Enterprise and the Genesis of the British Empire, 1480–1630* (Cambridge: Cambridge University Press, 1984), 349–50.

13. *CSPD 1631–1633*, 319; TNA SP 16/215/97 (Petition of Captain Luke Fox to the Lords of the Admiralty: 28 April 1632); TNA SP 16/215/293 (Grant to Sir John Wolstenholme: 24 March 1632); TNA CO 77/4b/9 (Commission to Captain Weddel, and Nathaniel Mountney for a Voyage to the East Indies: 12 December 1625). Wolstenholme partially funded the voyage for the northwest passage on the appropriately named ship, the *Charles*. He was granted the ship itself in 1632 in return for his loan, which was still owed to him at that point. The *Charles* seems to have left England in spring 1631 and returned in late November of the same year. See TNA SP 16/203/82, 121r. Trinity House, which managed lighthouses on the coasts, had put at least £1,320 and a few shillings and pence into the voyage as well. TNA SP 16/203/24, 95r.

14. BL IOR B/16, 14 February 1634; BL IOR B/17, 15 October 1634.

15. See Games, *Web of Empire*, 185–87; *CSPC East Indies 1635–1639*, xxiii.

16. Warwick County Record Office CR 2017/C1/2 (Denbigh to son, 28 September [1630]); BL IOR B/14, 15 October 1630.

17. TNA SP 16/172/63 (Charles to East India Company: 15 August 1630).

18. TNA CO/77/4/80 (Charles to Shah of Persia: 15 August 1630); *Court and Times of Charles I*, 2:97.

19. BL IOR B/14, 15 October 1630; Games, *Web of Empire*, 17–46.

20. BL IOR B/14, 3 and 17 September 1630.

21. Ibid., 24 September 1630 and 1 and 15 October 1630.

22. Ibid., 17 December 1630. Denbigh returned in 1633 and seems to have fallen from the Company's attention. He was rumored in 1635 to be in consideration for the post of ambassador to Constantinople, though the Levant Company were not in favor of the appointment.

23. Denbigh returned to England on the *Sea Horse* instead of on a Company ship, and he seems to have brought back a number of goods for his personal use. See James Knowles, "'The Faction of the Flesh': Orientalism and the Caroline Masque," in *The 1630s: Interdisciplinary Essays on Culture and Politics in the Caroline Era*, ed. Ian Atherton and Julie Sanders (Manchester, UK: Manchester University Press, 2006), 118, note 43. For more on the Van Dyke portrait of Denbigh, see ibid., 115–18.

24. The East Indies formed the imaginative setting for some cultural productions at the Caroline court, such as the 1635 court masque by William Davenant, *The Temple of Love*. Knowles, "The Faction of the Flesh," 111–13.

25. However, Sharpe also notes that these projects were hardly without criticism. See Kevin Sharpe, *Personal Rule of Charles I* (New Haven, CT: Yale University Press, 1992), 120–23 and 257–58.

26. Furber, *Rival Empires of Trade*, 69; John C. Appleby, "Sir William Courten," *ODNB*, 2004. A very sympathetic and brief account of Courten (including the debt that plagued his estate for decades) can be found in Thomas Carew, *Hinc illae lacrimae, or, An epitome of the life and death of Sir William Courteen and Sir Paul Pindar* (London [1681]), 17–18.

27. Appleby, "Sir William Courten." Robert Ashton notes that Courten had lent £18,500 to James in 1613 and 1614 and £16,500 to Charles in the late 1620s, while Appleby mentions the £25,000 sum. See Robert Ashton, *The Crown and the Money Market, 1603–1640* (Oxford: Clarendon Press of Oxford University Press, 1960), 21–22.

28. Courten's will called Bonnell his servant and granted him £350 plus an annuity of £50 while Bonnell served Courten's son. The annuity was in addition to whatever salary the son paid Bonnell. Porter was also remembered in the will, receiving a ring. See TNA PROB 11/171/294, 207v, 208r. Kynnaston also received a ring in the will. See Brenner, *Merchants and Revolution*, 170; TNA PROB 11/171/294, 208v.

29. A few other men invested in the voyage by way of loaning Courten money, though they were not mentioned in the partnership. These included Sir Paul Pindar, who loaned Courten £36,000. Also see Robert Ashton, "Sir Paul Pindar," *DNB*, 2004. A brief and sympathetic account of Pindar's life can be found in Thomas Carew, *Hinc illae lacrimae*, 20–21.

30. For details, see J. K. Laughton, "John Weddell," *DNB*, 2004. Sir William Courten Sr. left Weddell a ring valued at £3 in his will. See TNA PROB 11/171/294, 208v.

31. BL IOR B/14, 18 April 1631.

32. Ibid., 29 April 1631.

33. Sir William Monson reported to Secretary of State Sir Francis Windebank that Weddell spoke of his interactions with the viceroy of Goa and thought Charles might benefit from opportunities he had learned of. See TNA SP 16/295/3 (Monson to Windebank: 1 August 1635). Sir William Foster thought that Weddell and Mountney had sought out Porter, who would have introduced him to Kynnaston and Bonnell, and that with Charles' blessing, Courten became interested. See *CCM 1635–1639*, xvi.

34. TNA CO 77/6/7 (Charles' undertaking to join in the adventure to the Indies: 6 December 1635). A later letter from Edward Nicholas to Porter suggests that the king's adventure may have been only on credit. Windebank seems to have adventured £1,000 on similar terms. He did not pay in the money but would benefit as though he had when the voyage returned, "as if he had brought and laid down the said thousand pounds in ready money." See TNA CO 77/6/8 (Porter, Courten, Kynnaston, and Bonnell to Windebank: 7 December 1635) and TNA CO 77/6/19 (Nicholas to Porter: 30 July 1636).

35. TNA CO 77/6/9 (Royal commission to Captain Weddell and Nathaniel Mountney for a voyage to the East Indies: 12 December 1635).

36. Ibid.

37. Ibid.

38. Ibid.

39. Ibid.

40. Ibid.

41. BL IOR B/18, 15 January 1636.

42. Ibid.
43. TNA CO 77/6/8 (Undertaking to allow a share of profits to Windebank: 7 December 1635).
44. Ibid.
45. TNA CO 77/6/16 (Remonstrance of the East India Company to Charles: January 1636).
46. BL IOR B/18, 17 February 1636.
47. Ibid.
48. Ibid., 4 March 1636.
49. Ibid., 9 and 11 March 1636.
50. *Court and Times of Charles I*, 2:237 (Rossingham to Puckering: 30 March 1636).
51. Letters from late summer refer to Weddell's progress in the East Indies. See TNA CO 77/6/20 (Kynnaston and Bonnell to Nicholas, 10 August 1636).
52. BL IOR B/18, 1 July 1636.
53. Charles targeted the customs farmers for the loan. They were some of the wealthiest merchants of London, responsible for collecting England's customs revenues and able to keep everything beyond a yearly sum that they had pledged to the king. TNA CO 77/6/18, (to the farmers of the customs: 10 June 1636); TNA CO 77/6/19 (Nicholas to Porter: 30 July 1636); TNA CO 77/6/20 (Kynnaston and Bonnell to Nicholas: 10 August 1626).
54. BL IOR B/18, 7 October 1636.
55. Ibid., 9 December 1636.
56. TNA SP 16/289/86a (Deed of covenant of Endymion Porter with Thomas Kynnaston and Samuel Bonnell; Porter: 31 May 1635). Porter, Kynnaston and Bonnell were the official backers of the 1635 voyage. The deed mentioned that Charles had commissioned the voyage on 27 February 1635. The commission does not seem to have survived, which is unfortunate because it would have shed more light on this voyage—about which little is known. The deed did not mention Courten Sr., but Company leaders seemed to harbor no doubts about his involvement.
57. BL IOR B/18, 20 and 23 December 1636; *CSPC East Indies 1635–1639*, xxii.
58. *Court and Times of Charles I*, 2:261–62 (Rossingham to Puckering: 4 January 1637).
59. BL IOR B/18, 20 December 1636.
60. *Court and Times of Charles I*, 2:262 (Rossingham to Puckering: 4 January 1637). All insurance policies were supposed to be registered in the Office of Assurances in the Royal Exchange, where others could then examine them. See Trevor Sibbett, "Early Insurance and the Royal Exchange," in *The Royal Exchange*, ed. Ann Saunders (Leeds, UK: London Topographical Society, 1997), 78.
61. BL IOR B/18, 13 January 1637; TNA SP 77/6/26 and 27; *CSPC East Indies 1635–1639*, xxi; *Court and Times of Charles I*, 2:268–69 and 273 (Rossingham to Puckering: 17 January 1637 and 1 February 1637).

62. Gervas Huxley, *Endymion Porter: The Life of a Courtier, 1587–1649* (London: Chatto and Windus, 1959), 206–7. One observer noted that many suspected Porter of involvement, but so far no suit had charged him. Additionally, he noted that Porter was trying to get Charles to show leniency. See *Court and Times of Charles I*, 2:268–9 (Rossingham to Puckering: 17 January 1637).

63. At least one newsletter writer also believed that Courten Sr. was involved, though he mentioned that it was unclear whether Courten Jr. as executor was liable for his father's actions. See *Court and Times of Charles I*, 2:262 and 268–69 (Rossingham to Puckering: 4 January 1637 and 17 January 1637).

64. BL IOR B/18, 3 January 1637; TNA CO 77/6/25 (at the court of Hampton Court: 6 January 1637).

65. TNA CO 77/6/28, January 1637. A letter from Edward Rossingham to Sir Thomas Puckering recorded a very similar account of the meeting. See *Court and Times of Charles I*, 2:265.

66. TNA SP 16/323 f. 35v (Humble petition of the Governor and Company of merchants of London trading to the East Indies: 7 February 1637).

67. Ibid., f. 36r (Petition of William Courten to the king: 7 February 1637).

68. BL IOR B/18, 27 February 1637. Charles did eventually decide to allow the Company to proceed against Bonnell and Kynnaston for the actions of the *Samaritan* and the *Roebuck*. See ibid., 28 June 1637.

69. Ibid., 8 March 1637.

70. TNA CO 77/6/34 (Petition of the East India Company: March 1637).

71. TNA CO 77/6/29, January or February 1637.

72. TNA CO 77/6/35, (Charles to Captain Weddell: 14 March 1637).

73. TNA CO 77/6/39, f. 113r ("Information and observations that the East India Company are resolved to divide and leave the Trade": May 1637).

74. Ibid., f. 113r—v.

75. A proclamation by Charles about the colony of Virginia noted that the Virginia Company had failed in part because of the "multitude" of "votes and voices" in the "popular" government of the company. See James F. Larkin and Paul L. Hughes, eds., *Stuart Royal Proclamations* (Oxford: Clarendon Press of Oxford University Press, 1973), 2:27–29. Historians of early Virginia have long known about these charges, though few have connected those issues to the political vocabulary of early Stuart England. See, for example, Richard Cust, "'Patriots' and 'Popular' Spirits: Narratives of Conflict in Early Stuart Politics," in *The English Revolution c. 1590–1720: Politics, Religion and Communities*, ed. Nicholas Tyacke (Manchester, UK: Manchester University Press, 2013), 43–61.

76. TNA CO 77/6/39, f. 113v ("Information and observations that the East India Company are resolved to divide and leave the Trade": May 1637).This observation was especially ironic given that one of the loudest of those clamoring at Company meetings was Smethwick, who had been backed by the regime in the late 1620s.

77. Ibid., f. 113r-v.

78. TNA CO 77/6/40, f. 117r–18v ("The particular loss of his Majesty in his customs and of the kingdom in general, by consumption of stock, if the East India Company shall dissolve and desert the Trade": May 1637).
79. Ibid., 118r.
80. TNA CO 77/6/41, f. 121r–22r ("Objections and propositions resolved and answered that the trade into the East Indies may be otherwise maintained, than by a company and joint stock": May 1637). This is the first line of the memo, which has no official title.
81. Ibid., f. 121r–122r.
82. Ibid., f. 122r–v.
83. TNA CO 77/6/42, f. 126r and 127r ("Upon private conference with some of the principals of the East India Company": May 1637).
84. Ibid., f. 126r–v.
85. Ibid., f. 126r.
86. Ibid., 126r–27v, May 1637.
87. TNA CO 77/6/43, 128r–29r ("Reasons to move his Majesty to be graciously pleased to confirm under the Great Seal the commission passed to Captain Weddell": May 1637).
88. The patent was printed as "A special Grant for the settling of a Trade at Goa and other Parts of the East Indies" in *Foedera*, 20:146–56.
89. Ibid., 20:146–51.
90. Ibid., 20:151–53 and 156.
91. Ibid., 20:153.
92. Ibid., 20:152.
93. The adventurers agreed to divide the proceeds of the voyage, minus the king's share, as follows: one-quarter to Porter, one-sixteenth to Bonnell, one-sixteenth to Kynnaston, proportional amounts to Weddell and Mountey based on their adventures, and the rest to Courten. The agreement between Porter, Courten Jr., Bonnell, and Kynnaston divided the proceeds of the voyage, minus the king's share. See TNA CO 77/6/21 and 22 (Draft articles of agreement between Endymion Porter, William Courten, executor to Sir William Courten and assignee of Samuel Bonnell, and Thomas Kynnaston).
94. TNA CO 77/6/46 (Answer of the EIC to a declaration exhibited to his Majesty and referred by him to Sir Abraham Dawes and others: 28 June 1637).
95. TNA CO 77/6/47 (Petition of the EIC to Charles: June or July 1637); BL IOR B/18, 28 June 1637.
96. The *Planter* arrived in January 1638. See TNA CO 77/6/50 (Pennington to the Lords of the Admiralty: 19 January 1628).
97. TNA CO 77/6/51i (Petition from the EIC to the king: January 1638).
98. TNA CO 77/6/52, (Narrative of what has been done since the king's last answer to the EIC: February 1638).
99. Ibid. See also Ashton, *The Crown and the Money Market*, 96; Robert Ashton, "Sir Paul Pindar," *DNB*, 2004.

100. TNA CO 77/6/52 (Narrative of what has been done since the king's last answer to the EIC: February 1638).

101. TNA CO 77/6/56 (Order of his Majesty in Council: 25 May 1638).

102. TNA CO 77/6/57 (Summary of Proposals for a new East India Company: June 1638).

103. TNA CO 77/6/54 (Windebank to the Governor of the Company: 15 March 1638); TNA SP 16/385/72 (Charles to Captain John Weddell: 14 March 1638).

104. See *CCM 1635–1639*, xxv–xxvi.

105. Furber, *Rival Empires of Trade*, 70.

106. *CSPC East Indies 1635–1639*, 336.

107. TNA CO 77/6/71 (Order in Council: 10 December 1639); *CCM 1640–1643*, v–vi.

108. Into the 1680s, heirs of Courten were hoping to have some of the revenues of lands they claimed Courten held, including in Barbados, restored to them. They also hoped to have the Dutch pay reparations for seizing several ships that had belonged to the Courten Association. See Carew, *Hinc illae lacrimae*, 22.

Conclusion

1. Robert Kayll, *The Trade's Increase* (London: printed by Nicholas Okes, 1615).

2. BL IOR B/6, 19 May 1618.

3. BL IOR B/13, 1 October 1628.

4. TNA CO 77/6/35, (Charles to Captain Weddell: 14 March 1637).

5. Colonization in Madagascar was actively pursued in the 1630s and 1640s. See Alison Games, *Web of Empire: English Cosmopolitans in an Age of Expansion* (Oxford: Oxford University Press, 2008), 181–217.

6. This account of the Company's experiences in the 1640s and 1650s is mostly drawn from the introductions in the *CCM* for the 1640s and 1650s.

7. *CCM 1640–1643*, xxv.

8. Philip Lawson, *East India Company: A History* (London: Longman, 1993), 38.

9. Proposals for different forms of government of the Company were raised at various times. For example, one proposal was to make the East Indies trade regulated, like the Levant Company, while another wanted the court of committees to have only fifteen members and a rotating president. See *CCM 1650–1654*, xii–xiii.

10. Company leaders made requests for the patent's renewal both to Cromwell and the council of state directly, as well as through intermediaries. See *CCM 1655–1659*, ix and xii–xiii.

11. Ibid., xiii–xvii.

12. *CCM 1650–1654*, xxiii.

13. The one element of the company-state in the late seventeenth century that Philip Stern did not explore was the relationship of the Company and the English state and the domestic context for the Company's exercise of power in the East Indies. See Philip J. Stern, *The Company-State: Corporate Sovereignty and the Early Modern Foundations of the British Empire in India* (Oxford: Oxford University Press, 2011).

Manuscript and Archival Sources

BRITISH LIBRARY, LONDON

Asia, Pacific & Africa Collections (formerly Oriental and India Office Collections)

India Office Records (IOR)

B/1, Court Book 1, September 1599 to August 1603
B/3, Court Book 2, December 1606 to January 1611
B/5, Court Book 3, December 1613 to November 1615
B/6, Court Book 4, September 1617 to April 1620
B/7, Court Book 5, July 1621 to July 1622
B/8, Court Book 6, July 1623 to June 1624
B/9, Court Book 7, July 1624 to April 1625
B/10, Court Book 8, April 1625 to June 1626
B/11, Court Book 9, July 1626 to July 1627
B/12, Court Book 10, July 1627 to July 1628
B/13, Court Book 11, July 1628 to July 1629
B/14, Court Book 12, July 1630 to July 1631
B/15, Court Book 13, July 1632 to July 1633
B/16, Court Book 14, July 1633 to June 1634
B/17, Court Book 15, July 1634 to July 1635
B/18, Court Book 16, July 1635 to July 1637
E/3/5 and 13–14, Original Correspondence
G/21/2A, Java factory records

Manuscript Room

Additional MS.
Lansdowne MS.

FOLGER SHAKESPEARE LIBRARY, WASHINGTON, DC

MS L. d. 776.

HATFIELD HOUSE ARCHIVES

Cecil Papers 83/22
Cecil Papers 142/172
Cecil Papers 190/12

HUNTINGTON LIBRARY, SAN MARINO, CA

MS EL 2360

NATIONAL ARCHIVES (FORMERLY PUBLIC RECORD OFFICE), KEW

Colonial Office Records

CO 77/1–6, East Indies

Probate Records

PROB 11

State Papers Domestic

SP 14, Jacobean
SP 15, Edward VI–James I: Addenda
SP 16, Caroline

State Papers Foreign

SP 84/67–121, Holland, diplomatic correspondence
SP 91/2, Russia, list from the Muscovy merchants
SP 94/23–27, Spain, diplomatic correspondence
SP 99 / 24, Venice, diplomatic correspondence
SP 105/148, Levant Company general court minutes

WARWICK COUNTY RECORD OFFICE, WARWICK

CR 2017/C1, Feilding family papers.

Sources Printed before 1800

Carew, Thomas. *Hinc illae lacrimae, or, An epitome of the life and death of Sir William Courteen and Sir Paul Pindar.* London [1681].

Charters Granted to the East India Company, from 1601, Also the Treaties and Grants, Made with, or Obtained from, the Princes and Powers in India, from the Year 1756 to 1772. [London] [1773].

Bacon, Francis. *The Works of Francis Bacon, Baron of Verulam, Viscount St. Alban, Lord High Chancellor of England.* 4 vols. London: printed for A. Millar, 1740.

D'Ewes, Sir Simonds. *Journals of All the Parliaments during the Reign of Queen Elizabeth Both of the House of Lords and the House of Commons.* London, 1682.

Digges, Dudley Sir. *The Defense of Trade. In a Letter to Sir Thomas Smith Knight, Governor of the East-India Company, &C. From One of That Society.* 2nd ed. London: William Stansby for John Barnes, 1615.

East India Company. *The Laws or Standing Orders of the East India Company.* [London?], 1621.

———. *The Petition and Remonstrance of the Governor and Company of Merchants of London Trading to the East Indies Exhibited to the Honorable the House of Commons Assembled in Parliament Anno 1628.* London: printed for Nicholas Bourne, 1628.

Een waer verhael vande onlancksche ongerechte, wreede, ende onmenschelycke procedure teghen de Enghelsche tot Amboyna in Oost-Indien, door de Nederlandlanders [sic] *aldaer ghemaeckt op een versierde pretentie van een conspiratie vande selue Enghelschen.* London: [J. Beale], 1624.

E. S. *Britain's Busse, or a Computation as well of the charge of a Buss of Herring Fishing Ship. As Also of the Gain and profit thereby.* London: William Iaggard for Nicholas Bourne, 1615.

Gentleman, Tobias. *England's Way to Win Wealth, and to Employ Ships and Mariners: Or, a Plain Description What Great Profit It Will Bring Unto the Commonwealth of England, by the Erecting, Building, and Adventuring of Busses, to Sea, a Fishing: With a True Relation of the Inestimable Wealth that is Yearly Taken out of his Majesties' Seas, by the Great Number of Busses, Pinks, and Line-Bearers, Etc.* London, 1614.

Hakluyt, Richard. *Principal Navigations, Voyages and Discoveries of the English Nation, Made by Sea or over Land, to the Most Remote and Farthest Distant Quarters of the Earth at any Time Within the Compass of these 1500 Years.* London: George Bishop and Ralph Newberie, deputies to Christopher Barker, 1589.

Kayll, Robert. *The Trade's Increase.* London: printed by Nicholas Okes, 1615.

Malynes, Gerard. *The Maintenance of Free Trade, According to the Three Essential Parts of Traffic; . . . Or, an Answer to a Treatise of Free Trade Lately Published, Etc.* London, 1622.

———. *Center of the Circle of Commerce, Or, a Refutation of a Treatise, entitled The Circle of Commerce, or the Balance of Trade, lately published by E.M.* London, printed by William Jones for Nicholas Bourne, 1623.

Misselden, Edward. *Free Trade: Or, the Means to Make Trade Flourish. Wherein, the Causes of the Decay of Trade in This Kingdome, Are Discovered, Etc.* London: printed by John Legatt for Simon Waterson, 1622.

———. *The Circle of Commerce. Or the Balance of Trade, in Defense of Free Trade: Opposed to Malynes Little Fish and His Great Whale, and Poised against Them in the Scale. Wherein Also, Exchanges in General Are Considered, by E. M[isselden]. Merchant.* London: Printed by John Dawson for Nicholas Bourne, 1623.

Mun, Thomas. *A Discourse of Trade from England Unto the East Indies: Answering to Diverse Objections Which Are Usually Made Against the Same. By. T. M.* 2nd ed. London: printed by Nicholas Okes for John Pyper, 1621.

Nederlandsche Oost-Indische Companie. *A Remonstrance of the directors of the Netherlands East India Company presented to the Lords States General of the United Provinces, in defense of the said Company, touching the bloody proceedings against the English Merchants, executed at Amboyna. Together, with the acts of the process, against the said English. And the reply of the English East India Company, to the said remonstrance and defense. Published by authority.* London: John Dawson, for the [Dutch] East India Company, 1632.

News out of East India of the Cruel and Bloody Usage of Our English Merchants and Others at Amboyna, by the Netherlandish Governor and Council There. To the Tune of Braggendary. London: printed for F. Coules, dwelling at the upper end of the Old-Baily, 1624.

Noy, William. *Reports and Cases, Taken in the Time of Queen Elizabeth, King James, and King Charles.* London: Printed by F. L. for Matthew Walbancke, 1656.

Sheppard, William. *Of Corporations, Fraternities and Guilds: Or, a Discourse, Wherein the Learning of the Law Touching Bodies Politic Is Unfolded, Showing the Use and Necessity of That Invention, the Antiquity, Various Kinds, Order and Government of the Same.* London: Printed for H. Twyford, T. Dring, and J. Place, 1659.

Skinner, John. *A True Relation of the Unjust, Cruel, and Barbarous Proceedings against the English at Amboyna in the East-Indies, by the Hollanders there residing. As it hath been lately delivered to the Kings most Excellent Majesty.* [Saint-Omer]: printed [at the English College Press], 1624.

———. *A True Relation of the Unjust, Cruel, and Barbarous Proceedings against the English at Amboyna in the East-Indies, by the Netherlandish Governor and Council There. Also the Copy of a Pamphlet, Set Forth First in Dutch and then in English, by Some Netherlander, Falsely Entitled, A True Declaration of the News That Came out of the East-Indies, with the Pinnace Called the* Hare, *Which Arrived at Texel in June, 1624, Together with an Answer to the Same Pamphlet. By the English East India Company. Published by Authority.* London: printed by H. Lownes for Nathanael Newberry, 1624.

Smethwick, Thomas. *A Motion to the East India Company by Thomas Smethwick (an Adventurer with them) upon the reasons following.* London: 19 February 1629.

Wilkinson, Robert. *The Stripping of Joseph, or The cruelty of Brethren to a Brother. In a Sermon before his Majesty at Whitehall, by Robert Wilkinson, Doctor in Divinity, Chaplain in Ordinary to his Majesty, and late Pastor of Saint Olaves in Southwarke. With a Consolatory Epistle, to the English-East-India Company, for their unsufferable wrongs sustained in Amboyna, by the Dutch there. Published and presented unto them, by Thomas Myriell, Pastor of Saint Stephens in Walbrooke.* London: printed by W. S. for Henry Holland and George Gibbs, 1625.

Acknowledgments

This book is the result of years of work, and I have accrued many debts in the process. I am very grateful to the kind staff members of the various archives and libraries I have worked in, including the British Library, the UK National Archives, the Huntington Library, the Folger Shakespeare Library, the London Metropolitan Archives, the Warwick County Record Office, Cambridge University Library, and Firestone Library at Princeton University (staff members in the microfilm room in particular deserve my thanks). The interlibrary loan staff members at Auburn University tracked down some truly obscure books and articles for me. I would also like to thank Sue Hurley, the archivist of the Saddlers' Company, who allowed me to examine in person the fascinating ballot box in its possession. Lastly, any historian of the seventeenth-century East India Company owes a considerable debt to Noel Sainsbury, Ethel Sainsbury, and Sir William Foster for the detailed calendars that form the starting point for working with Company archives.

The willingness of people to do a kind and generous thing for an unknown academic emailing them unexpectedly never fails to amaze me. I would like particularly to thank Natasha de Chroustchoff and Dr. Robert Wynn Jones (of https://lostcityoflondon.co.uk), who responded graciously, quickly, and helpfully to my requests for information about pictures they had taken years before. The lovely picture of a seventeenth-century ceiling boss from St. Matthias Community Center with the East India Company's seal graces the cover of this book courtesy of Dr. Robert Wynn Jones. Many thanks!

My research has been supported over the years by funding from the Folger Shakespeare Library, the Huntington Library, the Jacob K. Javits Fellowship, the

U.S. Department of Education, Princeton University, and Vanderbilt University. Auburn has provided travel and research support for numerous trips to London, and I would like to thank in particular my former department chair, Charles Israel, for helping me arrange time away from Auburn when the Huntington Library offered me a year-long fellowship. The year at the Huntington allowed me the time and space to think that is so important and in such short supply when writing a book. The book is the richer for that year. The beautiful gardens in particular helped me think through knotty problems, and I am grateful for the supportive and vibrant research community there and the companionship and scholarship of my cohort of fellows. A summer at the Folger made me equally envious of my colleagues in the Washington, D.C., metropolitan area, and access to its collection came at a critical point in the writing process for me.

I have presented portions of this book at Auburn University, the Institute for Historical Research, the Huntington Library, the North American Conference on British Studies, Princeton University, Vanderbilt University, and Yale University. I have also presented ideas from the book at conferences at Duke University and North Carolina Central University, the University of Heidelberg, and Yale University. The book has benefited from the comments and questions I received on those occasions.

There are many people I would like to thank who have listened to, read, and discussed with me the ideas explored in this book: Alastair Bellany, Carolyn Biltoft, Michael Braddick, Bill Bulman, Adam Clulow, David Como, Tom Cogswell (who has been unfailingly supportive of my project since he served on my dissertation committee), Brian Cowan, David Cressy, Carolyn Day, Freddy Dominguez, Lori Ann Ferrell, Alison Games, Anthony Grafton, Matt Growhoski, Paul Halliday, Paul Hammer (who shared information with me about Sir Thomas Smith's connection to the Essex rebellion), Cynthia Herrup, Steve Hindle (whose stewardship of the research program at the Huntington is wonderful), Brendan Kane, the late Mark Kishlansky, Chris Kyle, Noah Millstone, Anthony Milton, Jason Peacey, William Pettigrew, Steve Pincus, Nick Popper, Renée Raphael, Andrew Ruoss, Nigel Smith, Isaac Stephens, Philip Stern, Antoinette Sutto, Vanessa Wilkie, Keith Wrightson, and others whose names I may have neglected to mention but who I hope will forgive me for the omission! I would like to particularly mention Alison Games, whose own work on Amboyna challenged me to rethink the categories I was using and who spent an hour at the Washington, D.C., Marriott comparing title pages of different *True Relations* with me. To Paul Halliday, who shepherded me into the profession as an undergraduate and has remained a friend and mentor to me ever since, thank you.

A few people read the entire manuscript from start to finish, and I owe them a special debt of gratitude: Peter Lake, Ralph Kingston, and two anonymous readers for Harvard University Press offered generous and insightful comments and gently pointed out where I could and should do more. I can only hope they are pleased with the result. Certainly all errors are mine alone.

I would also like to thank everyone who helped shepherd this book into its current shape. I cannot imagine a better publisher to work with than Harvard University Press. Thanks especially to my editor, Andrew Kinney, who has been generous and kind, and a supporter of this project for a long time. I am grateful for all his work on my behalf.

My greatest intellectual debt is to Peter Lake. He has always been unfailingly generous with his time and expertise, and I know this book would be much poorer without his insights. I am in awe of his ability to see to the heart of an issue and to understand, sometimes better than I myself did, what I was trying to say. He and Sandy Solomon showed me what academic conviviality is like, and I thank both of them for all their support and friendship.

I landed at Auburn as a newly minted PhD, and my gracious colleagues welcomed me with open arms. I would like to recognize a few in particular. Donna Bohanan, Kathryn Braund, Mike Kozuh, and Ken Noe have given me sound advice and friendship, and I cannot imagine Auburn without them. Kelly Kennington started at Auburn at the same time I did and has been a close friend ever since. She has been generous with her time, insights, and advice.

My family has lived with this book for a long time. I must thank Asha, Raj, and Sonu Mishra, whose willingness to support me in an endeavor that has seemed to them both too long and needlessly complicated is much appreciated. They have been proud and supportive even when I am sure they wondered how I fell into this career. I owe more to them than I can say, and I can offer in return only a very inadequate "thank you." My husband's family, especially Frances Kingston, has lived with the book for a shorter time but also deserve thanks.

Lastly, let me note that one of the unforeseen (and best) consequences of coming to Auburn was meeting Ralph Kingston. Our daughter, Sarala, was born halfway through the writing of this book, and my life is the richer for having a young child to remind me on occasion that "work talk is silly." Ralph's love and support have meant the world to me, and certainly more than I can say here. This book is for him.

Index